NEW STUDIES IN ARCH

The evolution of the Polynesian chiefdoms

NEW STUDIES IN ARCHAEOLOGY

Series editors

Colin Renfrew, *University of Cambridge*
Jeremy Sabloff, *University of Pittsburgh*

Frontispiece. The Tahitian fleet assembled at Opare‘e, as seen during Captain James Cook's second voyage, 1774. (Lithograph based on original oil by W. Hodges: *photo courtesy Bishop Museum.*)

The evolution of the
Polynesian chiefdoms

PATRICK VINTON KIRCH

CAMBRIDGE
UNIVERSITY PRESS

Published by the Press Syndicate of the University of Cambridge
The Pitt Building, Trumpington Street, Cambridge CB2 1RP
40 West 20th Street, New York, NY 10011, USA
10 Stamford Road, Oakleigh, Melbourne 3166, Australia

First published 1984
First paperback edition 1989
Reprinted 1990, 1996

Printed in Great Britain at the University Press, Cambridge

Library of Congress catalogue card number: 84–3249

British Library Cataloguing in Publication Data
Kirch, Patrick Vinton
The evolution of the Polynesian chiefdoms. –
(New studies in archaeology)
1. Polynesia – Social conditions
I. Title   II. Series
996   HN930.7.A8

ISBN 0 521 27316 1

WD

CONTENTS

PREFACE

There are probably few areas in the world where the potential for studying the growth and development of complex, stratified social and political systems is as great as among the islands of Polynesia. In part, the analytical advantages of Polynesia are due to the often-cited 'laboratory-like' conditions that isolated islands naturally provide. Equally important is the wealth of ethnohistorical and ethnographic materials pertaining to Polynesian societies as they existed and functioned at the time of initial European contact, and the decades following such contact. The continuity from prehistory to ethnohistory allows for a more extensive and precise use of historical documents and ethnographic data in the interpretation of archaeological materials than is the case with the study of prehistoric chiefdoms in many other parts of the world.

Until quite recently, however, Polynesia was an archaeological backwater, so that discussions of social and political change in the region (such as the work of Sahlins [1958] and Goldman [1970]) were based almost exclusively on synchronic ethnographic and ethnohistorical evidence. Fortunately, the increasing pace of archaeological investigation throughout Polynesia over the past two to three decades has now provided a firm foundation for diachronic studies. We should not ignore the older ethnographic corpus, however, for, by using these data in conjunction with the temporal framework provided by archaeology, we are finally in a position to speak meaningfully about processes of change in the Polynesian islands.

My objective in this book is to dissect the several major processes that underlie the transformation of the various Polynesian societies from their common ancestor. To accomplish this, I have structured the volume into three parts. In the first, I marshal a range of evidence to reconstruct the broad outlines of Ancestral Polynesian Society, from which the various contact-period societies descended. In Part II, I dissect in analytical fashion the major processes which led to technological, environmental, demographic, social, and political change. My approach is comparative, using various data-rich case studies to exemplify general trends or processes common to many, if not all, islands. Finally, in Part III I consider three case studies (Tonga, Hawai'i, and Easter Island), and outline in diachronic fashion the transformation of these societies from their ancestral forms. Similar studies could have been made of other island groups, such as the Marquesas or New Zealand, but limitations of space prevented this. In any event, it is not my aim to provide definitive statements on the evolution of particular societies, but rather to use these case studies to exemplify processes of change in Polynesia.

This exploration into the Polynesian past mirrors a kind of personal research odyssey through several island groups over more than fifteen years. Since the book is, in part, an attempt to draw together the varied strands of my research, and since I draw heavily upon this research in my case studies, a few comments may be relevant. My interest in the development of socio-political complexity in Polynesia was first awakened during a study of the Halawa Valley, Moloka'i, carried out in 1969–70. Applying an ecological, settlement pattern approach, my colleagues and I attempted in Halawa to unravel some of the complex linkages between environment, population, subsistence (particularly irrigation), and social organization in a windward Hawaiian valley. Soon after, in 1971, the opportunity arose to carry out archaeological work in one of the most remote, isolated, and traditional of Polynesian communities, the tiny outlier of Anuta in the south-eastern Solomon Islands. The experience of excavating a deeply stratified site spanning three millennia of south-western Pacific prehistory was combined in Anuta with the privilege of participating in a vibrant, functioning Polynesian society, where no European missionaries, no traders or trade stores, indeed very little at all of Western influence had yet altered the daily pulse of life. The Anutan experience established a certain direction to my research, for, once having experienced archaeology in the midst of a traditional Polynesian community in which the possibilities for 'ethnoarchaeology' were ubiquitous, it was difficult to imagine doing anything else.

In 1974, pursuing developing interests in ecology, intensive agriculture, and cultural adaptation, I spent half a year in the West Polynesian islands of Futuna and 'Uvea, excavating a variety of sites but also conducting ethno-ecological studies of irrigation and other aspects of local ethnobotany. Though Futuna and 'Uvea are not so remote as Anuta, enough remains intact of their indigenous subsistence economies and socio-political organizations to make studies in this area quite productive.

The Futuna–'Uvea work was conducted on a veritable shoe-string budget under somewhat trying field conditions, leaving me with the desire to return again to West Polynesia to pursue further the study of cultural adaptation to island ecosystems. With the support of the Bishop Museum, plans were laid for a second phase of extended work in Futuna. As political developments would have it, the fieldwork site had to be changed at the last minute, and in 1976 some seven months were spent on seldom-visited Niuatoputapu, one of the outlying Tongan islands. With some background in the related Futunan language, a working fluency in Tongan came quickly, and our studies of traditional agriculture and fishing immersed us in the economic and social fabric of the island. The archaeology, as well, proved to be rich and fascinating, and the geomorphic evidence of environmental change striking. The long months on Niuatoputapu were a period during which my ideas on Polynesian cultural evolution began to take definite form.

There was little time for reflection on the Tongan results after my return to Honolulu at the end of 1976, however, since within three months I left again for an extended stay on anthropologically famous Tikopia, as part of the second phase of the South-east Solomons Culture History Programme. In 1977 with Doug Yen, and alone in 1978, I spent more than eight months on Tikopia, which remains not greatly changed from what Firth described in 1929: a self-contained, traditional community of fiercely independent Polynesians, its local polity dominated by four hereditary chiefs. The archaeology of Tikopia proved rewarding beyond expectations, but the constant stimulus of life in a vibrant Polynesian society was even more compelling, if not always beneficial to the archaeological work. It was in Tikopia that the outline for this book was conceived, partly as a mental diversion during weekend sojourns through the betel and breadfruit orchards to the summit of Tumuaki, yielding views of the crater lake and the sacred district of Uta. To have been set down in Tikopia, with the vast ethnography of Sir Raymond Firth as a guide, and the opportunity to explore a continuity of three thousand years of cultural change revealed in a panoply of rich sites, was an intellectual stimulus which, I fear, I may never again enjoy.

The outline of this book was actually drafted during 1978 in Tikopia, though serious writing did not begin until 1980. A précis of my ideas on Polynesian cultural evolution was published in 1980 ('Polynesian prehistory: cultural adaptation in island ecosystems', *American Scientist* 1980), originally attracting the editors of Cambridge University Press, and resulting in an offer to publish the extended work in their series. During the nearly three years that the book has been in progress, additional stimulus has been provided by the initiation of a major ethnohistorical and archaeological project in the Anahulu Valley, O'ahu, in conjunction with Marshall Sahlins. This experience has shaped some of my views on the significance of structures of social reproduction in the evolution of Polynesian chiefdoms.

A work that pulls together the varied strands of more than a decade of experiences, thoughts, and research efforts obviously owes much to a great many people, yet only a few can be singled out here for special thanks. Roger Green made possible my early work in the Halawa Valley, and has been a constant source of inspiration and a gentle mentor. Doug Yen not only encouraged my initial efforts, but provided the wonderful opportunity to join him in Anuta. Our subsequent collaborations, particularly in Tikopia, have been especially rewarding. For whatever insights I may hope to have provided on Oceanic ecology and production systems, Doug can take a healthy share of the credit (though, surely, no blame for any pitfalls). Yosihiko Sinoto has over many years provided not only the full institutional support of the Bishop Museum, but openly given of his deep knowledge of East Polynesian prehistory. In more recent years, my collaboration with Marshall Sahlins has influenced my approach to prehistory, tempering a long-standing commitment to ecology with the perspective of a strongly cultural orientation.

I would be remiss not to acknowledge the long-standing support of the National Science Foundation, which through a series of grants (SS-40294, BNS 76-04782, BNS 76-17672, BNS 82-05621) enabled my extensive fieldwork in the south-western Pacific and Hawai'i.

For specific assistance in the preparation of this volume I gratefully thank: Tom Dye for his exhaustive review of the entire draft; Matthew Spriggs for giving the final draft a critical reading; Debra Connelly-Kirch, Patrick McCoy, and Carl Christensen for reading one or more draft chapters; Eric Komori for his splendid drafting; Peter Gilpin for photographic work; and Patience Bacon for typing most of the final draft. For their courtesy in providing illustrations, or for granting permission to use copyright materials, I thank Roger Green, Thor Heyerdahl, Yosihiko Sinoto, Matt McGlone, Tim Bayliss-Smith, Marshall Weisler, and the Bishop Museum Photo Archives. And finally, my greatest debt of thanks to my wife, Debra Connelly-Kirch, for her patience and constant urging that I 'get on with it'.

P.V.K.

1
Introduction

The first European explorers to pierce the sea barriers to Polynesia wondered at the vast distribution of the Polynesian 'Nation' – from Easter Island to New Zealand, thence to Hawai'i, enclosing a watery triangle of 20 million square miles. Since Europeans had themselves only recently 'discovered' the Pacific Ocean, the idea that mere savages (however noble) had navigated a great ocean and colonized its remotest isles was astonishing. While at Easter Island in 1774 Captain James Cook wrote that 'it is extraordinary that the same Nation should have spread themselves over all the isles in this vast Ocean from New Zealand to this island which is almost a fourth part of the circumference of the Globe' (Beaglehole 1969:354). Despite their astonishment, the explorers could not miss the clear similarities in material culture, customs of behaviour, and in speech, which all bespoke a common origin for the Polynesians. As Lieutenant King of the *Resolution* astutely observed: 'The same language . . . hardly requires any other proof of those who speak it being the same people, and originating from the same country' (Beaglehole 1967:1392).

Ever since Cook's and King's observations, generations of scholars have puzzled at whence, when, and how these Oceanic 'Vikings of the sunrise' penetrated and colonized the vast Pacific. Sunken continents, multiple migration waves from both west and east, bizarre racial theories – all were invoked to explain the so-called 'problem of Polynesian origins'. A compelling explanation has emerged only in the past few decades, largely due to the advent of intensive sub-surface archaeology in the Pacific Islands. Bolstered by ancillary studies in historical linguistics, comparative ethnography, ethnobotany, and physical anthropology, archaeology has resolved the 'problem of Polynesian origins' thus: the Polynesians *became* Polynesians within their oceanic realm, their varied cultures the product of millennia of local evolution in island environments. Polynesian prehistory unfolds as an exceptional instance of evolution and diversification.

Having achieved this modern perspective on Polynesia's myriad cultural and social variations as the product of differentiation and

1

transformation from a common ancestor, a whole new array of analytical problems confronts the anthropologist and prehistorian. What particular conditions or processes propelled Polynesian societies along sometimes divergent, yet oft-times convergent evolutionary or developmental pathways? How is it that elaborate, hierarchical, and at times oppressive political systems emerged in some islands while others appear to have maintained relatively egalitarian polities? How did varying environmental constraints affect particular pathways of technological and social change? Such are the questions that continually tease the student of Polynesian ethnography and prehistory, and that have inspired the present work.

At this point I must advise the reader as to what I mean (and, as importantly, do *not* mean) by *evolution*, a term the use of which carries a certain risk that one will be pigeon-holed with some particular school of anthropology. In this book, I intend the term to apply simply to technological and social change in the most general sense. Although we are not here concerned with biological evolution, Darwin's classic phrase, 'descent with modification', is probably closest to a definition of evolution in the present context. Certainly, I wish to avoid any prejudice of association with particular theories of mechanisms for cultural or social evolution. I have my own biases, as the reader will discover, but it is upon the evidence for social and technological change in Polynesia that I want to focus, not upon some narrow theoretical argument. The reader should also be forewarned that although I use the term 'chiefdom' to characterize the socio-political organization of Polynesian societies at the contact-era endpoints, this does not mean that I regard them as exemplars of some evolutionary 'stage', or that I subscribe to the 'neo-evolutionary' schemes popular in American anthropology during the 1960s and 70s (e.g., Service 1967; Fried 1967). Indeed, for reasons given in detail below, I believe that a stadial or stagal approach to evolution in Polynesia is something of a 'dead horse', entirely inadequate as an explanatory framework.

Polynesia is as exemplary a setting for such a study of technological and social evolution as we may hope to find. It has been fashionable to speak of Polynesia as a cultural 'laboratory' (Suggs 1961:194; Sahlins 1963; Kirk and Epling 1972; Clark and Terrell 1978; Kirch 1980a; Friedman 1981:275) and the metaphor may well be appropriate, for the region offers nearly unique possibilities for analytical control (Goodenough 1957). Islands and island societies by their very nature provide microcosms for the study of ecological and evolutionary processes. As Loren Eiseley put it, islands are apt to open doorways to the unexpected. The fifty ethnographically known societies that comprise Polynesia were all demonstrably derived from a single ancestral society. Each society presents an ecological and evolutionary isolate which together can be likened to a set of historical, cultural 'experiments', in which the founding ancestor was identical, but where certain variables – ecological, demographic, technologic, and so on – differed from case to case. Sahlins (1958:ix) invoked a biological analogy when he stated that the Polynesian societies 'are members of a single cultural genus that has filled in and adapted to a variety of local habitats'. The analogy is appropriate, and just as studies of island biology from the time of Darwin and Wallace have contributed enormously to an understanding of organic evolution, so island anthropology promises to open doorways regarding the nature of social and technological evolution.

Various aspects of analytical control are inherent in Polynesia. Not only does the region represent a spectrum of societies derived from a common ancestor, but isolation between many islands effectively reduces the thorny problem of diffusion and cultural contact following initial colonization (Goodenough 1957). More, the Polynesian islands contrast remarkably in their ecological settings, offering a multi-dimensional spectrum of environmental challenges to which the founding populations variously responded. With climates ranging from tropical to temperate (indeed, sub-antarctic in the Chatham Islands), and with topography encompassing atolls, high islands, and near-continents, the ecological variability within Polynesia may be greater than that exhibited within any other culture area of the world. One additional aspect of control lies in the diverse population sizes of Polynesian societies at European contact, ranging from a few hundred to several hundred thousand persons. Population densities ranged from truly sparse (c. 0.02 persons/km^2 in southern New Zealand [Anderson 1980a:12]) to among the densest known for horticultural societies worldwide (432 persons/km^2 in Anuta [Yen 1973b]). Surely here are tantalizing data for testing the role of population growth and 'pressure' in relation to technological and social change .

To paraphrase G.E. Hutchinson, each Polynesian archipelago and island was an ecological theatre, wherein was enacted its own evolutionary play. To make sense of Polynesia's variability, we must ascertain the consistent and meaningful similarities, as well as any significant anomalies, in the developmental sequences represented by each island. Building on that framework, our ultimate aim is to isolate underlying mechanisms and processes of change or evolution. Clearly this goal extends beyond the geographic confines of Polynesia, and is relevant to the wider issue of social transformation, without regard to particular time or place.

Polynesian societies are of wide anthropological interest for another reason, owing to their socio-political structures. Chiefdoms, as an intermediate level of socio-political organization bridging the acephalous society with more complex state societies, hold a special fascination for anthropologists. Polynesian societies not only exemplify the 'typical' chiefdom, they display the limits of variation in organizational structure and complexity of such societies. Within Polynesia we find societies in which chiefs were inseparably linked as kinsmen to commoners, where redistribution was minimal, and production almost entirely a household matter. On the other hand were elaborate chiefdoms such as Hawai'i, where the chiefly class claimed descent independent from commoners, ranked themselves internally into seven or eight grades, practised sibling marriage to maintain those grades, mobilized corvée labour and organized production on a grand scale, and most notably, alienated land from ownership by commoners. These latter Polynesian chiefdoms, which 'approached the formative levels of the old fertile crescent civilizations', have been said to lie at a critical interface between the chiefdom and state (Sahlins 1963; Fried 1967; Service 1975).

Polynesia offers an opportunity to address the development and elaboration of chiefdom socio-political organization, both from the perspective of comparative ethnography and through the evidence of archaeology. What was it that led some Polynesian societies in the direction of increasingly complex, stratified polities, while others remained relatively simple? How did this trend towards increased organizational complexity correlate with population growth, agricultural intensification, or level of inter-group conflict? Since the Polynesian spectrum of socio-political variability represents evolutionary divergence from a shared ancestor, the aspects of analytical control cited above should also permit the isolation of some of the processes that helped to mould each Polynesian chiefdom throughout the course of its historical development.

This task is not entirely novel, and several classic works of anthropology have addressed themselves to a nearly identical theme (of which the most widely read is probably Sahlins [1958]). However, whereas analysis of *synchronic* ethnographic materials characterized earlier comparative studies of Polynesian chiefdoms, we can employ now a large body of archaeological data with direct, *diachronic* relevance to the problems of Polynesian evolution. Alan Howard (1972:822) presaged the role of archaeology in a general synthesis of Polynesian society when he wrote that the ethnographic theorists had provided prehistorians 'with a richer set of competing possibilities concerning social change around which to orient their [archaeological] efforts, and if they do their job well we may yet accumulate sufficient data to produce compelling reconstructions'. Three decades of intensive work in Polynesian archaeology have now brought us to a point where the data, if not totally satisfying, are at least sufficiently rich to demand an attempt at synthesis that ranges beyond mere description. Archaeology, after all, is privileged by the nature of its data to address problems of technological and social change most directly. Polynesian archaeology must avail itself of the region's analytical opportunities, and inherit the challenge left by the comparative ethnographers.

Methods, aims, and objectives

Fundamentally, this book is a study of the internal differentiation of Polynesian societies. Since these were non-literate societies, it is a study in *prehistory*, but by no means restricted to the use of strictly *archaeological* data or methods. Precisely because Polynesia as a region consists of a series of discrete, but historically related societies – all derived from a common ancestor – and because there was direct historical continuity between the 'ethnographic present' and the prehistoric past, we are in an excellent position to draw upon ethnohistoric, ethnographic, and linguistic data, as well as upon strictly archaeological evidence in an attempt to understand the region's prehistory. The Polynesian ethnographic baseline does not provide mere analogies for the interpretation of archaeological data; it illuminates directly the *endpoints* of indigenous developmental sequences.

The method of this study can be clearly described with reference to a simple model of Polynesian differentiation (Fig. 1). In the diagram, the variety of island societies witnessed at European contact is represented by their ethnographic endpoints (shaded circles, e.g., X_4, Y_3). Each of these societies was the product of an internal sequence of development from the same historical ancestor, which I term Ancestral Polynesian Society (APS). Over time, the differentiation of Ancestral Polynesian Society resulted from colonization of a range of new and environmentally contrastive islands, and from subsequent internal change, generally in isolation. In some cases, contact between island societies (as in the case of W_3 and X_3 in the diagram) may have resulted in later cultural or linguistic borrowing (diffusion) which occurred after initial colonization and differentiation and can further confuse the picture. Despite these caveats, the use of lexical and ethnographic evidence does permit a fuller reconstruction of the ancestral baseline from which the differentiation of Polynesian societies proceeded, than that which archaeology alone can provide.

In and of themselves, however, ethnographic and linguistic methods cannot inform us of the particular *sequences of development* of island societies: they simply illuminate the point of origin (Ancestral Polynesian Society) and the endpoints of indigenous change. To get at sequences of change requires properly diachronic data. Thus, as prehistorians interested fundamentally in sequences of change – and in the processes underlying change – we must rely primarily on archaeological data, the material remains from which technological and social change may be inferred. Only such archaeological data can fill in the record of change from Ancestral Polynesian Society to the diversity of endpoints that were met by the eighteenth-century European explorers.

In our quest to understand the processes that underlay and initiated change and differentiation among Polynesian societies, there is yet another body of data with potential relevance. This is the corpus of indigenous oral traditions, of which Goldman writes, 'at the very least they represent a Polynesian viewpoint on their own history, and in this important respect they reveal local historiography' (1970:xii). Each Polynesian society possessed its own body of traditions, especially of the political events surrounding the ruling elites, and these traditions are invariably tied to genealogies that provide a relative temporal

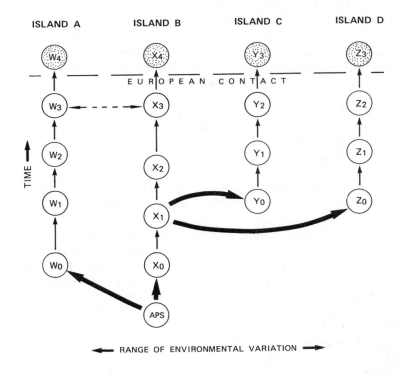

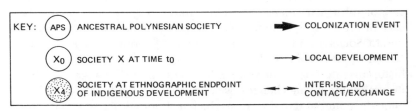

1. The differentiation of Polynesian societies from a common ancestral society (see text for discussion).

framework. There has been a cyclical debate among Polynesian scholars as to whether such traditions and genealogical records accurately reflect 'real' historical events (Suggs 1960b; E. Leach 1962; Firth 1961; Hooper 1981). My own view, based primarily on close analysis of traditional materials from Tonga, Tikopia, and Hawai'i, is that the traditions pertaining to the last few hundred years of the developmental sequences (the past several generations prior to European intrusion), do indeed represent actual events and affairs of real people, although some distortion of fact, as well as use of metaphor and allegory are obviously problems to be dealt with (cf. Vansina 1965). The Tikopia case clearly shows remarkable correspondence between indigenous oral traditions and archaeological evidence (Kirch and Yen 1982:363–8). What really matters, however, is not whether such oral traditions are literally 'true' in any Western sense of history or prehistory, but that they offer an alternative view of historical *process* and frequently illuminate the motives or inducements to change. They allow us to perceive change as the results of conscious actions on the part of knowledgeable members of society, and not merely as the precipitate of vaguely defined interaction between 'system variables' (cf. Giddens 1981:18). In short, they offer an indigenous perspective which at times may help in the analysis of our own ethnographic and archaeological formulations.

Using these several sources of data pertaining to Polynesian prehistory, each of them serving to supplement and cross-check the others, the specific objectives of this study are three-fold. First, I attempt a reconstruction of the common baseline, Ancestral Polynesian Society. Sahlins (1976:23) has said that 'history begins with a culture already there', and, as Friedman pointed out, evolutionary models begin 'with an . . . "original" structure in order to generate subsequent structures with the consequence that the initial form must remain temporarily unexplained' (1979:32). For Polynesia this baseline is Ancestral Polynesian Society, and Chapters 2 and 3 are devoted to a reconstruction of this society as it flourished in the West Polynesian archipelagos some thousand years before Christ. By combining forces with historical linguistics and comparative ethnography, archaeology can achieve a reasonably detailed outline of this ancestral baseline. The reader must understand that my primary aim is to analyse what happened to this ancestral society as its members were dispersed to the isolated islands of Polynesia, to adapt to, interact with, and modify a range of local conditions. We shall not, however, be concerned with the origins of technological and social patterns already in existence some three millennia ago. The ultimate origins of Ancestral Polynesian Society are another story that we must leave aside for now, a story that eventually must lead us back in space to island south-east Asia, and in time perhaps to the end of the Pleistocene.

My second objective, which forms the central and major portion of this volume, is an analysis of the dominant processes that resulted in the internal differentiation of Polynesian societies. Rather than treat the development of the Polynesian chiefdoms geographically, on an island-by-island basis, or chronologically, I have chosen to arrange my analysis and argument around the several major processes which appear to have dominated Polynesian developmental pathways. Thus, after an initial review of the region's ecological diversity and constraints and the reconstruction of Ancestral Polynesian Society, I turn to a consideration of the reassortment of technological and social systems, and adaptation to new conditions that inevitably accompanied the colonization of new landfalls. Successive chapters each treat other significant processes, namely population growth, environmental change, development and intensification of production, and competition and conflict. In each case I try to show how technological and social patterns already developed in Ancestral Polynesian Society were a dynamic part of the process of change.

The third and final objective is to examine three particular sequences of development, three case studies, and to compare and contrast their unique yet similar pathways of change. For this purpose, I have chosen Tonga, Hawai'i, and Easter Island, and the diachronic analysis of their sequences is the theme of the final third of the volume. In their often radical departure from Ancestral Polynesian Society, these three cases reveal the historical limits to structural transformation within the Polynesian chiefdoms.

In relation to these objectives, I would like to offer a brief comment on the idea of *explanation* in prehistory, borrowing some of the insights of a foremost student of evolution, Ernst Mayr (1961). This book is not so much an argument in favour of a particular explanation, as an attempt to specify some of the various causes, both proximate and ultimate, that lay behind Polynesian technological and social change, and to explore the often complex interrelations amongst these causes. I do not believe that any single paradigm will ever parsimoniously and sufficiently 'explain' the transformation of the Polynesian chiefdoms. What we can hope to achieve is a reasonably clear understanding of the major proximate causes for particular, observed changes in the archaeological record, and the major ultimate causes responsible for channelling evolution in certain general directions. Such an achievement is reward enough, and perhaps of more lasting value than trendy explanations tied to some particular theory of culture or society current at the moment.

Approaches to prehistoric change in Polynesia

Speculation regarding Polynesian origins and prehistory began with the eighteenth-century explorers and continued unabated throughout the nineteenth century (see Howard 1967 for a thorough review), but serious anthropological studies of the region began only about sixty years ago. The year 1920 saw 'the problem of Polynesian origins' proclaimed a major scientific issue (Gregory 1921), with the B.P. Bishop Museum initiating an exhaustive ethnographic and archaeological field survey eventually requiring two decades to complete. Among the young anthropologists enlisted in this programme was E.S.C. Handy, whose subsequent publications typify the strongly diffusionist view of Polynesian cultural origins and development, a view that held sway for several decades.

Handy's theoretical perspective was actually anticipated, in tenor if not substance, by the formulations of earlier scholars such as J. Macmillian Brown, who explained the 'strangely varied web' of Polynesian cultures as the result of 'a singularly advanced barbaric woof crossing a palaeolithic warp' (Brown 1907:xxx). In consort with the Boasian anti-evolutionism of the times, Handy maintained that variability in Polynesian societies was to be explained – not as the result of processes of cultural change and divergence within a local ecological setting – but as an amalgam of traits imported by successive movements of colonizing or conquering populations. Based upon field studies in the Society Islands, Handy (1930a; 1930b) proposed a 'two strata' theory of origins, in which the multitude of traits comprising Tahitian society was divided into those of an 'old Tahitian' or *manahune* population, and those of a later, conquering *arii* people. Such blatant diffusionist schemes appear naive in retrospect, yet it is well to consider that Handy's viewpoint not only dominated Polynesian studies for nearly two decades, echoes of it linger on in some modern formulations.

Piddington (1939), in a concluding essay to Williamson's classic works on Central Polynesia, attacked at length the 'two strata' theory of Polynesian origins. Piddington rightly criticized the lack of rigour in Handy's diffusionist approach: 'using a pair of compasses, and, taking a Polynesian institution as the centre, drawing gradually increasing concentric circles upon the map until the circumference of one of them passes through the venue of some extraneous institution bearing a superficial resemblance to its putative Polynesian offspring' (1939:341). Piddington convincingly argued that Polynesian cultural variation could readily have resulted from local developmental processes, 'that there was never more than one cultural "migration" into the area, and that the variations to be found there are due to spontaneous development from a single original culture' (1939:337). His argument freed Polynesian studies from the shackles of diffusionist logic, and opened the way for modern conceptions of prehistoric change.

In two papers published contemporaneously with Piddington's critique, Burrows (1939a, b) advocated a parallel notion of internal process in the differentiation of Polynesian cultures. Based upon a detailed trait analysis, Burrows (1939a) proposed a four-fold partitioning of the region (into Western, Intermediate, Central, and Marginal sub-groups). Cultural differentiation, Burrows argued, had been due to *in situ* historical process, not diffusion from outside Polynesia. Burrows (1939b) likewise examined variability in social organization, specifically addressing the presence within Polynesia of two kinds of social units: kinship-based groups ('breed'), and those organized on territorial principles ('border'). Although diffusion was not entirely ruled out, Burrows rightly stressed 'the role of purely local dynamic factors' in giving each region 'a pattern in some respects unique' (1939b:18). Among these dynamic factors he mentioned intermarriage, adoption, and migration, and 'perhaps most powerful of all – warfare arising from rivalry over land or ambition for enhanced status' (1939b:21).

In addition to stressing social factors, Burrows was aware of the potential role of environmental constraint and diversity in moulding characteristic aspects of each society. Burrows's seldom-cited comparison (1938) of Futuna and 'Uvea in Western Polynesia (both of which he had studied during Bishop Museum's ethnographic survey) dealt with the significant influence of topography and local ecology on social development and differentiation. Some of Burrows's conclusions appear naive or deterministic in the light of a contemporary ecological perspective, but his attempt was seminal, foreshadowing later innovations, including Sahlins's concept of 'differentiation by adaptation' (1958).

By the 1940s the anthropological consensus on Polynesian cultural diversity had shifted from a *Kulturkreise* mentality to an emphasis on the role of internal processes. Peter Buck's work (e.g., 1944), laying out a grand synthesis of Polynesian 'culture stages', exemplified this viewpoint. The role of diffusion was not entirely abrogated, however, for Buck – who held that the original Polynesian ancestors had entered the region via the Micronesian atolls – believed that crop plants and domestic animals were added to the Polynesian cultural repertoire after initial colonization. It is significant, however, that Buck used the term 'evolution', albeit a unilineal evolution synonymous with 'progress'. For instance, in discussing the geographic movement from atolls to high islands, Buck wrote that: 'The Society Islands provided an abundance of basaltic rock, thus the shell age Polynesians had the raw material with which to rise again into the stone age' (1944:474).

Under the influence of Leslie White, Julian Steward, and others, cultural evolution had become fashionable in American anthropology by the late 1940s and early 1950s. One of their students, Marshall Sahlins, saw in Polynesia the inherent advantages for a controlled study of what Steward had termed 'multi-lineal evolution'. In a justly famous though much criticized monograph, Sahlins (1958; see also 1957) advanced the thesis that 'Polynesian cultural differentiation was produced by process of adaptation under varying technological and environmental conditions. A single culture has filled in and adapted to a variety of ecological niches' (1957:291). Sahlins reviewed the forms of Polynesian social organization, and argued that two basic structural types, 'descent-line systems' and 'ramage systems' were each the result of adaptation to particular ecological conditions, compaction of resources in the former case, and dispersed resources in the latter. In contrast to high islands, the unique constraints of atolls favoured 'a multiplicity of socio-economic groups formed on different principles and connected with production and distribution of different goods or on different scales' (1957:296). In all cases, stratification was to be accounted for *vis-à-vis* its role in spurring production and in organizing the distribution of strategic goods.

Unfortunately, the logical clarity of Sahlins's argument was flawed by ethnographic and ecological inconsistencies. J.D. Freeman (1961, 1964) refuted the attribution of descent-line systems to Samoa, demonstrating instead the existence of ramage organization. Finney (1966) invoked Tahitian ecological data to reject Sahlins's contention that high islands were characterized by widely distributed resources. Instead, the valley-centred, wedge-shaped Tahitian territorial units each contained all necessary resources, and thus could be effectively exploited by a minimal ramage. Despite such criticisms, Sahlins's work had a tremendous impact, and not only within the field of Polynesian studies (see, for example, Flannery and Coe 1968; Sanders and Price 1968; Peebles and Kus 1977). As Howard (1972:822) suggests, the lasting contribution of Sahlins's monograph was to force anthropologists to 'focus our lenses on the relationship between ecological features, modes of production, distribution and consumption, and social institutions'.

Whereas Sahlins saw Polynesian societies building upon an ecological foundation, Irving Goldman (1955, 1970) presented an opposite, though complementary perspective, that these societies were moulded by 'status rivalry' inherent in their aristocratic political structures. Goldman's arguments also suffered criticism on the basis of inattention to ethnographic detail, logical tautology, and other grounds (Hawthorne and Belshaw 1957; Howard 1972), and his thesis received neither the acclaim nor notoriety of Sahlins's. Nevertheless, as Howard (1972:822) asserts, Goldman made a substantial contribution in stressing the distinction between the 'cultural concerns of high chiefs and persons of lower rank. . . . the former were primarily concerned with matters of honor, power, and prestige, while the latter were preoccupied with the pragmatics of making a living'. The ecological perspective of Sahlins and the structural orientation of Goldman together contribute elements for a more sophisticated and compelling theory of Polynesian evolution.

Those uninitiated in the history of Polynesian anthropology may wonder that in a review of theories of prehistoric change no reference has as yet been made to archaeology. Not until the 1950s did archaeology begin to play a leading role in considerations of Polynesian origins and cultural differentiation, having 'come of age' only within the past two decades. Although limited excavations had been conducted in New Zealand (even as early as the 1870s), up until 1950 Polynesian archaeology was largely confined to surface surveys of the more impressive architectural sites, and to descriptive analyses of stone tools such as adzes. Archaeology was held to offer little more than ancillary, corroborative data to historical ethnography. Even the forward-looking Piddington, while admitting grudgingly that archaeological methods were 'valid' in Polynesia, questioned whether the 'systematic exhumation of pre-European Polynesian artifacts is a profitable and urgent task for science today' (1939:335).

The serendipitous results of a university class in archaeological field techniques, conducted at Kuli'ou'ou Rockshelter, O'ahu by K.P. Emory in the spring of 1950, shattered the dogma that Polynesian archaeology was historical ethnography's poor relation. Not only did the Kuli'ou'ou deposits yield an unanticipated range and abundance of prehistoric artifacts, but a radiocarbon age determination for charcoal from the shelter's lowest level (the first ^{14}C date for the Pacific Islands, 946 ± 180 BP) pushed the initial settlement date of Hawai'i beyond expectations. At the same time Gifford's (1951) excavations in Fiji, at the western gateway to Polynesia, and Spoehr's (1957) work in the Marianas on the Asiatic fringe of Oceania, began to hint at the lengthy time depth of human settlement in the Pacific, and at the extent of local cultural development revealed by archaeological sequences. Amongst Polynesianists, a furore of intellectual excitement was generated by the realization that archaeology could indeed provide a direct means of studying prehistoric change in Oceania.

Since Emory's pioneering excavation, thirty years of increasingly intensive archaeological work has revealed the prehistoric sequences of almost every major Polynesian archipelago. Whereas scholarly consensus of the late 1940s held that most of Polynesia had been settled for no more than 1,000 years (e.g., Emory 1946), it is now evident that a time-scale in excess of three millennia is the case, at least in the western archipelagos. Ample time had therefore elapsed for significant local development. Furthermore, the archaeological evidence conclusively demonstrated a single, common origin for all Polynesian societies, and this ancestor was shown to have affinities with eastern Melanesian materials (Green 1968). Finally, even in the shorter sequences of East Polynesia, archaeological data were indicative of substantial and significant change from the time of initial colonization to European contact – in technology, settlement pattern, subsistence systems, demographic patterns, and so forth. *In situ* prehistoric change was at last empirically demonstrated, rather than a matter of speculative reconstruction based solely upon synchronic comparisons.

A consequence of its pioneering status, Polynesian archaeology has focussed until recently upon descriptive, culture–historical endeavours. Basic archaeological sequences of all major archipelagos have been worked out in some detail, as attested in three recent regional syntheses (Bellwood 1978a, 1979; Jennings 1979). From this wealth of archaeological data, one may abstract several broad and widespread trends characteristic of many (if not all) local developmental sequences. A brief catalogue of these trends should aid in orienting the reader to the main outlines of Polynesian prehistory, and to the central problems addressed in this book.

Dominant trends in Polynesian prehistory

Given that all Polynesian chiefdoms were derived from the same ancestral stock, and that the challenges of island life (despite differences of scale and local constraint) tend to be similar in kind if not degree, it is reasonable to suppose that the evolutionary processes operating on Polynesian societies were parallel in many island groups. A comparison of the dominant trends in the sequences of the well-investigated islands (Samoa, Tonga, Marquesas, Hawai'i, Easter, Societies, and New Zealand) does, in fact, reveal remarkable consistency. I list here some nine trends, each of which will be the focus of considerable analysis and discussion in later chapters.

1. With colonizing populations relatively small in numbers, population growth in the centuries following initial settlement was a fundamental trend in all Polynesian societies. Such growth was evidently rapid in many cases, for substantial population densities had built up in nearly all island groups by the time of European contact. In Chapter 5 I examine in full the proposition that population growth was a significant force (though not a 'prime mover') in the evolution of the Polynesian chiefdoms.

2. Extensive modification of island ecosystems by the colonizing populations was a continuing process, frequently resulting in reduced biotic diversity, and in creation and maintenance of artificial vegetation communities. In many cases, the modification of landscapes, including significant erosion, can only be classed as degradation. At the same time, environmental transformation may in some cases have led to the creation of micro-environments favourable to particular economic activities, such as irrigation.

3. Sequences of agricultural development in Polynesia reflect, as a general trend, increasing intensification. Such intensification can be measured archaeologically in terms of the scale and complexity of agronomic infrastructure and facilities, such as irrigation ditches and

pondfields, walled garden plots, or dryfield systems. These developments are presumed to have been accompanied by the usual indices of
intensification: increased labour per unit area, and decreased fallow
periods. In certain islands, such as the Marquesas and Society groups,
intensification took an alternative route to that of field cropping,
namely arboriculture. The trend of intensification may in fact be said to
apply to *productive systems* as a whole, and is reflected in such developments as Hawaiian fishpond aquaculture. Chapter 7 will explore these
evolutionary pathways and their relationship to demographic and
socio-political change.

4. A corollary of agricultural intensification is increased economic
specialization over time. This trend is particularly evident in those
societies that displayed the greatest degree of social stratification at
European contact. In Hawai'i, for example, there is evidence for considerable specialization in agriculture, adze production, canoe manufacture, fishing, and other activities. The ethnohistoric records for
Tonga and the Societies indicate similar specialization.

5. Increased emphasis upon storage facilities for farinaceous staples
is a trend characterizing certain tropical chiefdoms, as well as that of
New Zealand. Hawai'i, in this regard, is an exception which proves
especially enlightening as to the relationship between storage and
chiefly power, a topic pursued further in Chapter 10.

6. The prehistoric sequences of several Polynesian archipelagos
reflect changes over time in settlement pattern distribution, from
nucleated hamlets in the early, colonization phase to dispersed
household units later in time. This appears to be the case in Tonga,
Samoa, the Societies, Marquesas, and Hawai'i. It does not necessarily
hold for New Zealand or Rapa, exceptions which again illuminate certain relations between settlement, socio-political organization, and
resource use.

7. In all of the Polynesian chiefdoms, there is a dominant trend in the
development of specialized, ceremonial or public architecture, even
though different functional categories are emphasized in different
island groups. In Tonga, for example, architectural elaboration
centred upon the tombs of apotheosized chiefs. In Hawai'i, Easter
Island, and the Societies, a focus upon increased scale and complexity
of temple architecture is evident, whereas in the Marquesas emphasis
was placed upon massive tribal dancing and feasting centres.

8. The development of militarism is another dominant trend in
Polynesian cultural evolution, for which there appear to be no significant exceptions. Archaeologically, the trend is evidenced in increased
construction over time of a range of earthwork or stone fortifications,
the terraced hill forts of Rapa and the *pa* of New Zealand representing
apogees of technological development. Militarism and the socio-
political competition it reflects are truly fundamental trends to be
accounted for in any model of evolution in Polynesia.

9. Finally, there was the trend toward increased stratification and differentiation in social status and rank, which was uneven throughout the region, and led to a range of societal complexity at the time of European contact. This trend was most significant in Tonga, the Societies, and Hawai'i, in which the hierarchical differentiation of society reached new heights. It is, however, also reflected to a lesser degree in other Polynesian groups.

The nine major trends summarized above constitute a catalogue of sorts for the technological and social changes that transformed Ancestral Polynesian Society into the chiefdoms witnessed at European contact. Such a catalogue or inventory is a necessary starting-point for understanding evolution in Polynesia. To move beyond description and achieve some understanding of the processes of change leading to these trends is the primary aim of the analyses to follow.

We are not engaged in some kind of trick photography, which would produce a fuzzy conventional image, deceptively generalized; what we are looking for are characteristics held in common, which will make whatever is original stand out by contrast.

Marc Bloch (1966:xxiv)

2

Polynesian societies and ecosystems

Descendants of a common ancestor, all Polynesian societies share certain basic features – for example – in subsistence and technology, social organization, land tenure, and religion. The delineation of these commonalities provides one baseline from which we may reconstruct Ancestral Polynesian Society and assess the varied transformations undergone by particular societies. This baseline, moreover, would be incomplete without some consideration of the environmental variability inherent in the spectrum of Polynesian island ecosystems. This chapter develops such a baseline, with an ecological overview of the region's natural diversity, and with an ethnographic review of the material and social bases of Polynesian life.

The island ecosystems

In large measure, the Polynesian evolutionary drama reflects the region's great ecological variability. The islands range in size and form from atolls and diminutive volcanic specks less than 1 km², to near-continental New Zealand, while the climatic continuum spans tropical, sub-tropical, temperate, and (this may come as a surprise to some), sub-antarctic zones. Island ecosystems vary as well in other physical and biotic characteristics – their isolation, elevation, age, geological structures, local weather patterns, natural resources, soils, and susceptibility to natural disasters. As a consequence, Polynesian islands provided contrastive milieux for the development and growth of new societies, each created by the fission of colonizing parties from ancestral homes, each responding anew to the unique opportunities and constraints offered by a new landfall. The Lapita-pottery makers who first colonized the tropical western archipelagos of Samoa and Tonga about 1500 BC, and who would become the 'first Polynesians', could scarcely have imagined the environmental extremes that their descendants would discover, explore, and successfully adapt to. Probably

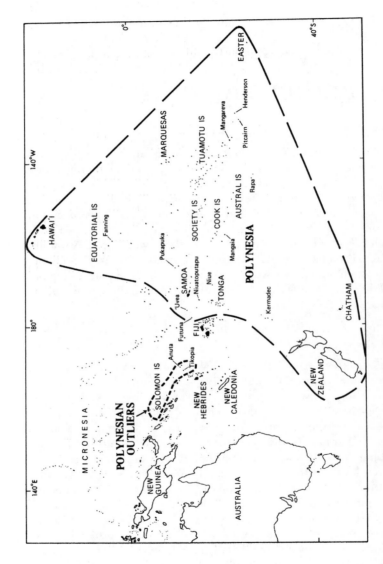

2. The Oceanic region, showing the Polynesian Triangle, the Polynesian Outliers, and the major islands and archipelagos discussed in the text.

Table 1. *Principal islands and archipelagos of Polynesia*

Island or group	Type and number of islands		Area (km²)	Estimated population*
West Polynesia				
Tonga	Raised coral; atoll; high	160	647	40,000
Samoa	High	10	3,134	80,000
Futuna	High	2	65	2,000
'Uvea	High	1	59	4,000
Niue	Raised coral	1	259	4,500
Tokelau	Atoll	4	6	1,200
East Polynesia				
Cook Is.	High; atolls	15	240	15,000
Society Is.	High; atolls	11	1,536	45,000
Marquesas Is.	High	10	1,057	35,000
Hawaiian Is.	High	10	16,692	200,000
Equatorial Is.	Raised coral; atoll	5	702	n.o.**
New Zealand	'Continental'	2	501,776	115,000
Chatham Is.	High	2	713	2,000
Kermadecs	High	1	29	n.o.
Tuamotu Is.	Atolls	76	790	7,000
Austral Is.	High	5	132	5,000
Mangareva	High; atolls	8	15	4,000
Pitcairn	High	1	5	n.o.
Easter	High	1	160	7,000
Henderson	Raised coral	1	30	n.o.
Outliers (Total 18)				
Anuta	High	1	0.4	150
Tikopia	High	1	4.6	1,250
Bellona	Raised coral	1	20	450
Nukuoro	Atoll	1	1.7	150

*Estimate at time of initial European contact.
**n.o. = not occupied at European contact, but with archaeological evidence of former Polynesian inhabitants.

nowhere else in the world has a single cultural group radiated over such a broad ecological spectrum.

Some thirty-eight major archipelagos and islands are inhabited by Polynesian peoples (Fig. 2). The majority of these lie within the Polynesian Triangle, whose apices are formed by New Zealand, Hawai'i, and Easter Island. To the west, eighteen Polynesian 'Outliers' (Bayard 1976) lie in a wide arc along the fringe of Melanesia. Together, more than 344 individual islands were, at one or another time, colonized by Polynesians (Table 1).

Despite their diversity, island ecosystems share several intrinsic properties, with far-reaching implications for their inhabitants including man. Fosberg(1963a:5–6), introducing a symposium on man's place in the island ecosystem, enumerated several of these properties. Basic to insularity are *isolation* and *limited size*, with major consequences for both genetic and cultural evolution. Acting as barrier and filter, the isolation of islands accounts for much of the uniqueness of island life. Once past the hazards of overseas transport or dispersal, a colonizing propagule was likely to find on islands an environment free of predators and competing species, with adaptive radiation a frequent occurrence. In the Hawaiian Islands, for instance, some 2,000 endemic higher plants evolved from as few as 275 ancestral immigrant stocks (Zimmerman 1948). Limitation in island size has as well the effect of restricting available resources and micro-environments, and for certain groups of biota the size of an island will therefore index its organic diversity (MacArthur and Wilson 1967).

Isolation and size are, of course, relative. In parts of tropical Polynesia, some archipelagos form inter-visible chains with islands only a few kilometres apart. Other Polynesian islands are among the most isolated landfalls on earth; Hawai'i lies 3,862 km from its closest Polynesian neighbour, the Marquesas, and 3,800 km from the west coast of North America. Despite the developed seafaring and navigating abilities of Polynesian peoples, isolation was a major factor influencing technological and social evolution. The developmental pathway of the Tongan political system, for instance, was heavily influenced by the proximity of Fiji and Samoa, and by the relative ease of maintaining exchange systems of chiefly spouses and prestige goods between those archipelagos.

Island size exhibits even greater variability than degree of isolation. The miniature 'high' island of Anuta, one of the Polynesian Outliers, is a scant 40 hectares in area, and supports a permanent population of about 160 persons (Yen and Gordon 1973). This is perhaps the smallest permanently inhabited Polynesian island, although many of the atolls have comparably restricted land areas. At the opposite extreme are the two near-continental islands of New Zealand, with a combined land surface of 501,776 km², more than all the other Polynesian archipelagos put together. Clearly, the constraints imposed on a human population by circumscribed island resources vary tremendously, and must be assessed case by case.

Among other characteristics of island ecosystems of direct relevance to the study of Polynesia is the 'extreme vulnerability' of insular ecosystems once isolation is broken down, and the 'tendency toward rapid increase in entropy when change has set in' (Fosberg 1963a:5). Though never completely stable, prior to man's advent the older island ecosystems had achieved some form of relative stability or effective equilibrium. The arrival of human populations, along with their intentional and unintentioned biotic introductions, invariably upset this dynamic equilibrium, often with dramatic and sometimes deleterious consequences.

Except for New Zealand – a pre-Mesozoic continental remnant contrasting in every aspect with the rest of Polynesia – the islands are volcanic in origin, constructed of successive flows of basalt and andesite lavas, and of pyroclastic ash, cinder, and tuff. As a result, the range of isotropic rocks available for stone tool production was restricted to fine-grained basalts, vesicular lavas, and volcanic glasses (on *makatea* islands and atolls, of course, no volcanic stone was available.) Erosion, submergence, and emergence of these igneous masses produced islands of three classic types: (1) high islands with volcanic soils; (2) low islands or atolls; and (3) raised coral or *makatea* islands (Thomas 1963).

High volcanic islands, such as the Society and Hawaiian archipelagos, offered the least constraint and greatest opportunities for colonizing human populations. Sufficiently elevated to orographically induce precipitation, high islands tend to have permanent drainages (at least on windward sides), developed and fertile soils, and are thoroughly vegetated. Because of rainfall differences, windward–leeward contrasts are often considerable on high islands, and pose different environmental challenges to human populations. The marine environments of high islands vary greatly, ranging from the rock-bound coasts of the Marquesas (Chubb 1930), through islands like Rarotonga where a fringing reef forms a narrow integument around the island (Marshall 1930), to the encircling barrier reefs and lagoons of the Society group, or of 'Uvea (Fig. 3).

Atolls and raised coral (*makatea*) islands are actually coral caps on igneous cores. The greatest limitation of these is fresh water, although the largest atoll islets support a thin sub-surface aquifer (the Ghyben–Herzberg lens) floating on salt water, and many *makatea* islands have seeps or springs. Both lack permanent watercourses, and their floras are impoverished in comparison to the high islands. The larger and older raised coral islands do have thick, fertile soils capable of sustaining intensive agriculture (e.g., Tongatapu, enriched with volcanic ash fall). The terrestrial impoverishment of atolls, however, is offset by the high organic productivity of atoll reefs and lagoons (Wiens 1962; Salvat 1970, 1972), the structure and complexity of which have been likened by Marston Bates to that of the tropical rainforest. This great marine productivity in large measure sustained human existence through the Tuamotu and other atoll habitats of Polynesia.

Some islands combine the classic volcanic–*makatea*–atoll forms in various permutations. Mangaia, for instance, consists of a volcanic core with a rim of raised coral reef (Marshall 1930). The island of Niuatoputapu in the Tongan archipelago exhibits a central volcanic ridge surrounded by an uplifted plain of coral reef and detritus, a windward fringing reef, and a leeward coast and lagoon protected by a barrier reef with offshore islets in typical atoll configuration (Fig. 4).

Cross-cutting the variability of Polynesian landforms is the climatic spectrum. Most islands are tropical, with fairly uniform and equable temperatures between about 70–80°F, and a mean annual range of 1–9°F (Freeman 1951:12). Some islands, such as Easter and the Australs, are sub-tropical, and in the higher elevations on Hawai'i and Maui Islands, true alpine conditions exist. New Zealand is temperate, and in the Foveaux Straits region of South Island, as well as in the Chatham Islands east of New Zealand, sub-antarctic conditions prevail (Sutton 1980). Looking upon the vestiges of Archaic East Polynesian settlement in the Chathams, lashed by the 'roaring forties', one can only marvel at the adaptive propensities underlying the shift from tropical horti-culturalists to sub-antarctic hunters.

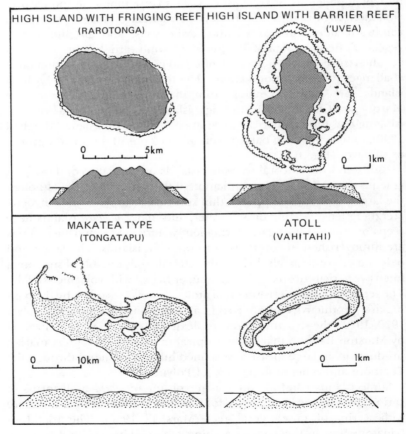

3. The major types of Oceanic islands. Dark screening represents volcanic land mass; light stipple represents coral reef or reefal limestone (adapted from Thomas 1963).

The Polynesian biota derives largely from Asia, particularly tropical South-east Asia, and as a general rule there is increasing biotic impoverishment as one moves from west to east through Oceania. Among the consequences of this depauperate biota for colonizing Polynesians was the near-total absence of food plants and of most edible land mammals or reptiles. The wild relatives of all the Oceanic crop plants do not occur eastwards of the Solomon Islands, and cultigens had to be purposely introduced throughout Polynesia. On certain of the more isolated islands, such as the Hawaiian group, adaptive radiation produced extreme endemism in the local flora. The first Polynesian settlers to Hawai'i were confronted with a 99 per cent endemic flora, the potential properties and uses of some 2,000 previously unencountered species having to be discovered through trial and error. New Zealand presented an equally challenging organic environment.

This is not to imply that the islands were totally lacking in vegetal resources, for most of the high, and even *makatea*-type islands were well forested at the time of initial human colonization. A range of soft and hard woods provided timber for construction and for firewood, and experimentation with native species led to their adaptation for dyes, medicines, and other household uses. In the process of pioneering new environments, the Polynesians frequently transferred their ethnobiological categories, or folk classifications, to the new biota. For instance, the Proto-Polynesian term for ironwood, **toa*, was transferred

4. The island of Niuatoputapu in Tonga displays a central volcanic ridge surrounded by an apron of uplifted coral reef. Note the broad lagoon, and the volcanic cone of Tafahi in the distance.

to an endemic hardwood (*Acacia koa*) in Hawai'i, where the true iron-wood was absent.

The terrestrial fauna of Polynesia was on the whole impoverished. Abundant endemic insects and land molluscs were of little direct consequence to humans. In the western islands several species of fruit bat (*Pteropus* spp.) were regularly taken for food. The only major, non-marine source of wild animal protein, however, was that of the native land birds and migratory seabirds (Mayr 1945). Several species of seabirds, such as the frigates (*Fregata* spp.). shearwaters, and the dark-rumped petrel (Procellariidae), were prized for their succulent flesh. Native land birds were taken either for their flesh, as with the Pacific pigeon (*Ducula pacifica*), and the purple swamp hen (*Porphyrio porphyrio*), or for their brilliant feathers, as with the Fijian parrots (*Vini* sp .,*Phigys* sp.) and the Hawaiian honeycreepers (Drepaniididae). In New Zealand, some thirteen species of flightless *moa* birds (Dinornithiformes) provided a terrestrial resource unparalleled elsewhere in Polynesia.

The sea provided the dominant source of protein in Polynesian diets. Littoral and inshore habitats yielded a variety of seaweeds, molluscs, holothurians, sea urchins, octopus, squid, crustaceans, and small fish, while the deeper reefs, benthic, and pelagic zones produced larger fish, rays, sharks, turtles, and cetaceans. Diversity and productivity in the marine components of island ecosystems vary considerably. For the most part, the central, tropical islands support extensive barrier reef and lagoon ecosystems with high organic productivity. Many of the sub-tropical islands have much less extensive reef development, and a less diverse marine fauna. Easter Island, lacking a fringing reef and isolated in the east Pacific, has only 140 species of fish, compared with about 450 species in Hawai'i, and more than 1,000 species in Fiji.

Polynesia is clearly an ecologically varied region, each island imposing environmental constraints and opportunities in some respects different from those of any other. The above examples demonstrate the constraints imposed by resource limitation, climatic factors, island size, geological composition, and so forth. Equally significant are a range of natural perturbations, or 'environmental hazards' (Vayda and McCay 1975). The most pervasive of these hazards in Polynesia are drought, cyclone, volcanic eruptions, and tsunami. Even larger, well-forested high islands are subject to periodic drought, sometimes of severe proportions. In the Marquesas, for example, drought is a major and recurrent phenomenon with considerable impact on the course of prehistoric cultural development (Adamson 1936; Suggs 1961). Tropical cyclones usually devastate an island's agricultural base, and constitute a major threat in the western archipelagos of Tonga and Samoa (Visher 1925). Volcanic eruptions and tsunami are more limited in their occurrence, but may have had dramatic effects upon local populations. Polynesian adaptive response to recurrent environmental perturbations, including forms of technological buffering, will be considered in Chapter 6.

The dynamic nature of Polynesian man–land relationships has become increasingly evident in the course of recent archaeological investigations. As Fosberg (1963a, b) observed, islands are fragile and vulnerable, and we are just now beginning to realize the extent to which prehistoric populations modified island ecosystems. The introduction of exotic biota, extensive burning and clearance of native vegetation, exploitation of marine and terrestrial fauna, erosion, siltation – all of these processes transformed insular landscapes. Adaptation of Polynesian societies to their island world is thus not a simple problem of technological adjustment to a set of stable environmental conditions. Environmental constraints confronting a colonizing population in any island were in most cases quite different from those which faced a descendant population generations later. The environmental constraints at the time of European contact were in many respects the *product* of human actions. Nor was the modification of island landscapes necessarily fortuitous; part of the success of Polynesian colonizing strategies must be attributed to their conscious and purposeful rearrangement of island environments. Indeed, the modification, manipulation, and all too frequently, the degradation of island ecosystems is a dominant theme of Polynesian prehistory.

Cultural and linguistic subgroups

One may distinguish within Polynesia several major cultural subgroups, the delineation and relationships of which provide important clues for the Polynesian prehistorian. The basic cultural distinction separates *West* and *East* Polynesian groups. West Polynesia incorporates the major archipelagos of Tonga and Samoa, along with the isolated islands of Futuna, 'Uvea, and Niue; the Ellice and Tokelau groups are sometimes included as well. In a major comparative study, E.G. Burrows (1939a) pointed to various uniquely shared traits – in material culture, kinship terms, ceremonial behaviour, food, and so forth – which distinguished West Polynesian societies from all others. As it turns out, the West Polynesian archipelagos were also the first to be colonized, and thus constitute the original Polynesian 'hearth' or homeland, from whence the rest of the Triangle was settled (see Chapter 3).

East Polynesia is something of a misnomer, since one of its major members, New Zealand, is geographically among the most westerly of Polynesian islands. The term East Polynesia, however, is thoroughly ingrained in the regional literature. Included in this major subgroup are the Hawaiian, Society, Marquesas, Cook, Tuamotu, Austral, and Mangarevan archipelagos, as well as Easter Island. Again, these

societies all share certain features or traits in common which distinguish them from the Western societies. Burrows (1939a) and Buck
(1944) further divided East Polynesia into Central and Marginal subgroups, the former comprising the Society, Tuamotu, Austral, and
Cook Island chains. These archipelagos, relatively less isolated than the
Marginal groups, have had considerable inter-island contact, probably
accounting for certain shared similarities in language, material culture,
and socio-political organization.

The Outliers constitute a third primary subgroup, distributed along
the eastern fringe of Melanesia. Neglected until recently by ethnologists,
linguists, and archaeologists, these societies remain lacunae in our
knowledge of Polynesian prehistory. Early opinions on Outlier culture-
history ranged from Capell's view that these societies represented remnant or relict populations left behind in the course of easterly
migrations, to the theory that they are recently derived from West
Polynesia by a process of drift voyaging. Archaeological excavations on
Anuta, Tikopia, Bellona, Nukuoro, and Taumako (Kirch and Rosendahl
1973; 1976; Kirch and Yen 1982; Poulsen 1972; B.F. Leach personal
communication), conducted within the past decade, have revealed
occupation sequences spanning three millennia, sometimes with possible hiati or cultural replacements. Evidently, many Outliers have a
lengthy and complex settlement history, and a great deal of intensive
archaeological work must be carried out before this complexity can
be unravelled.

Emory (1946) and Elbert (1953) were among the first to syste-
matically study the interrelations and subgrouping of the Polynesian
languages. Later work by Pawley (1966), Green (1966), and others has
resulted in a clear outline of the historical relationships amongst the
Polynesian languages. The widely accepted genetic subgrouping of the
Polynesian languages is diagrammed in Figure 5 (after Green 1966 and
R. Clark 1979), and constitutes a model for the primary settlement of
Polynesia, latent with implications for prehistorians.

To a significant degree, the linguistic subgrouping mirrors the
cultural subdivisions recognized by comparative ethnologists. The
linguistic unity of East Polynesia, for example, supports the delineation
of that major subgroup on ethnologic criteria. On the other hand, the
linguistic schema cross-cuts the cultural classification in certain
regions. A first-order linguistic division between Tongic and Nuclear
Polynesian languages occurs within West Polynesia. This not only reinforces the archaeological interpretation of West Polynesia as the area
of original and most lengthy settlement, but suggests that many of the
shared traits that are used to define the western subgroup resulted from
continued contact and borrowing between the Samoan and Tongan
archipelagos. The Outlier languages are most closely allied to the non-
Tongic languages of West Polynesia, that is, Samoan, Futunan, 'Uvean,
and Ellicean.

The cultural and linguistic subgrouping of Polynesian societies and languages furnishes an important basis for the reconstruction of Ancestral Polynesian Society to be developed in Chapter 3. The method of *lexical reconstruction* (Dyen and Aberle 1974) can be applied to sets of cognate terms from several Polynesian languages to determine the proto-term and its semantic value in the Proto-Polynesian language. Clearly, a knowledge of subgrouping is essential for this process. For example, since reflexes of the term for chief appear in both the Tongic and Nuclear Polynesian branches (Tongan *'eiki*, Futunan *aliki*, Hawaiian *ali'i*), one may be confident that the term for chief (**'ariki*) was present in Proto-Polynesian, and more importantly, that a concept of chiefship existed in Ancestral Polynesian Society. The same method may also be applied to ethnographic data on social organization, religion, land tenure, and so forth. If a particular social institution is present in all, or a large number of Polynesian societies, then it was most likely present in the ancestral society from which these derived. (If, however, the institution is restricted to the societies of one particular branch, such as East Polynesia, then we are justified only in reconstructing the proto-form for the immediate ancestor of that branch, e.g., Archaic East Polynesian.) With both lexical reconstruction and comparative ethnographic analysis one must also carefully consider the alternative possibilities, that borrowing (diffusion) or independent invention (innovation) were responsible for the observed similarities. Certainly, amongst geographically close islands (such as Tonga and Samoa) such borrowing is

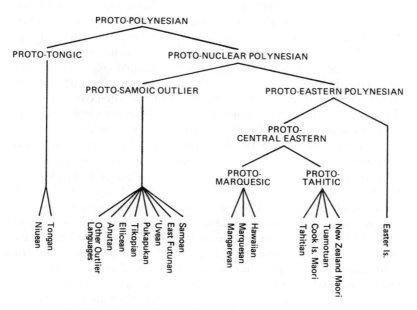

5. The subgrouping of the Polynesian languages, and their putative sequence of divergence from Proto-Polynesian.

more likely. Cautiously applied, however, these methods provide a powerful tool for the reconstruction of the ancestral society from which all of the ethnographically known Polynesian groups descended.

In the following pages, I review some of the common features shared by most Polynesian societies, and point out some of the variations which arose following dispersal and colonization of the varied island groups. This overview thus provides a necessary ethnographic baseline for the reconstruction of Ancestral Polynesian Society, the subject of Chapter 3.

The material basis of Polynesian societies

Despite some regional diversity, Polynesian societies were all predicated upon highly similar material bases. 'Neolithic' in the classic sense, Polynesians developed lithic technology to such peaks as the statues of Easter Island and the greenstone adzes and ornaments of the Maori. Subsistence was based on an advanced horticulture, intensified in some island societies into proper field agriculture, either irrigation or dryfield rotation. (The absence of cultivation in southern New Zealand, and in the Chathams, where environmental conditions were severely limiting, are exceptions that prove the rule.) Husbandry of pigs, dogs, and fowl, hunting, gathering of wild plant foods, and significant exploitation of the sea rounded out the indigenous production systems. A domestic mode of production (Sahlins 1972) based on an intricate kinship logic dictated the production, distribution, exchange, and consumption of food and material goods. At the same time, however, Polynesian chiefdoms were aristocratic societies. The structural principles of the chieftainship – genealogical rank, primogeniture, *mana*, and *tapu* – permeated the societal fabric, organizing production and mobilizing labour in ways that counteracted the centripetal tendencies of the elemental domestic units. A continual dialectic between a 'domestic' and a 'political' economy constitutes a dominant theme running throughout the evolution of Polynesian societies.

Polynesian agricultural tools were simple and limited in number, yet effective and well suited to the tasks at hand. Stone adzes and fire served as the major instruments for forest clearance, while planting poles and digging sticks were the gardener's main tools. Long-handled, fruit-plucking poles, carrying poles, and a variety of baskets aided in harvesting. The material culture associated with fishing and marine exploitation was more complex, and reflects considerable ingenuity. One-piece fishhooks for angling were made from wood, bone, shell, and stone in a wide range of sizes, and used in a variety of ways, along shorelines, with and without poles, from canoes, while swimming, and so on. Trolling lures of pearl shell were quite effective in landing the larger, prized pelagic fish such as bonito. In many islands, some form of benthic lure was used to capture octopus. Nets were manufactured in a wide range of forms, from dip and scoop nets used by women foraging on reef flats at low tide, to long-handled flying fish nets, to community-owned seines up to several hundred feet long. Other sorts of nets, traps, weirs, sweeps, floats, spears and so on are well described in the literature on Polynesian material culture (e.g., Buck 1930, 1944).

Other areas of Polynesian material culture were reasonably well developed and reflect successful adaptation to the constraints of Oceanic environments. Primary manufacturing tools included the ubiquitous adzes and chisels (generally of fine-grained basalt or andesite), files and abraders of coral, pumice, or scoriaceous lava, drill points of stone and shell, bone awls, and flake tools of obsidian or fine-grained basalt. A wide range of culinary implements served to convert crops to cooked food, including wooden and stone food pounders, bowls, basins, scrapers, graters, and storage containers, as well as serving bowls and platters. The manufacture of barkcloth from a variety of plant sources (especially paper mulberry, but also breadfruit, *Pipturus* and other species), and the plaiting of mats and other woven items, was well developed. Various strengths and types of cordage were similarly produced. Nor was Polynesian material culture restricted to utilitarian items. Darts, pitching disks and other gaming devices were widespread, as were drums, dance paddles, nose flutes, and other musical instruments. In the esoteric and ritual sphere, Polynesian religious images in stone, wood, ivory, wicker-and-feather, and so on are renowned worldwide.

Not all Polynesian societies possessed the same degree of elaborate and diverse material culture, nor did all attain equal levels of artistic expression. Among many societies – particularly those of the atolls and smaller, more isolated high islands – production of material goods was a largely domestic matter. Goods tended to be utilitarian in design, with certain items, especially *Pandanus* mats, playing a vital role in kinship-based exchanges. Among the larger archipelagos, with more complex and highly stratified chieftainships, a degree of craft specialization developed. In protohistoric Tonga, for instance, there were hereditary classes of canoe builders, navigators, stonemasons (who constructed the chiefly tombs), and tattooing experts (Martin 1818). The brilliant specimens of Polynesian art that grace museum cases – feathered cloaks and head-dresses, inlaid feather and sennit wands, temple images – were prerogatives and symbols of rank, produced by specialists who were supported by and for the chiefly classes.

The lives of all Polynesians, including the most sacred of chiefs, rotated around one central theme – the production, distribution, and consumption of food, of which starch staples were the essence. A concern with food permeated Polynesian life at all levels of the social ladder, and in all social dimensions (Bell 1931). The role of food among the

Tikopia of Outlier Polynesia, described so well by Raymond Firth, was approximated by all Polynesian groups:

Food serves as a most important material manifestation of social relationship, and through it kinship ties, political loyalty, indemnity for wrong, and the canons of hospitality are expressed. It also provides a basis for the initiation of other social relations, such as bond-friendship, or pupil and teacher in the acquisition of traditional lore. Again, the major foodstuffs rest in totemic alignment with the major social groups; ritual appeals are made to the gods and the ancestors who are regarded as the sources of food. All such situations are expressed in a body of linguistic material, rich in metaphors and circumlocutions (1939:38).

This overriding concern with food formed a critical linkage between the material conditions of production – environment, technology, and demography – on the one hand, and the social relations that directed production and distribution on the other. It is a linkage of vital concern in our analysis of technological and social change in Polynesia.

Polynesian classifications of food, and the cultural values associated with various categories, are further clues to the structuring of production and consumption. The most elemental food category, that which minimally constitutes a meal, is the starch staple, product of agricultural labour. The Anutans classify food (*kai*) into several categories of which the most basic is the marked term *kai tao*, 'baked food', usually taro, yam, or breadfruit. Two further categories of *kai* are *ngaruenga*, starch 'puddings', sweetened with coconut cream, and *kanope*, animal flesh (fish, seabirds, chicken, etc.). These are considered supplementary to *kai tao*, and a prerequisite for the entertainment of honoured guests, or for ritual purposes. This Anutan division of food is paradigmatic of Polynesian subsistence in general: a balance between the cultivation of the dominant and fundamental starch staple, and the procurement of the less abundant, but socially and ritually valued, specialities and animal flesh.

Five groups of staple-starch-producing cultigens dominated Polynesian agriculture: aroids, yams, breadfruit, bananas, and (in East Polynesia) the sweet potato. Various cropping combinations were emphasized in each island setting, depending upon several historical factors including environment and the inevitable reassortment of agricultural systems upon initial transfer (these are matters which will be taken up in detail in Chapter 7). The indigenous systems of cultivation – associations of crop plants, tools, and particular micro-environments with discrete patterns of agricultural behaviour – were of two elemental types: extensive and intensive. What appears as a dichotomy of systems, however, in reality describes the extremes of a continuum. At the extensive endpoint was shifting cultivation in the characteristic Malayo-Oceanic pattern (Spencer 1966), where swidden garden plots are cleared, fired, cropped, and fallowed in a second-growth rotational cycle. On the other hand, intensive cultivation often required the modification of hydrologic, topographic, and edaphic conditions so as to favour certain cultigens, with the creation and main- tenance of a permanent infrastructure, such as irrigated pondfields.

Animal husbandry, terrestrial hunting, and marine exploitation comprised the extra-agricultural component of Polynesian subsis- tence. A triad of domestic animals – pigs, dogs, and the jungle fowl – was transported and introduced to most island groups upon initial colonization. Production of these animals was intimately linked with the cultivation systems. Excepting New Zealand (where the endemic *moa* provided abundant game), hunting was an underdeveloped aspect of Polynesian economies, although birds were regularly taken, and in the case of remote and protein-deficient Easter Island became socially and ritually significant. As in all island societies the sea provided the major daily source of protein, and the structure and complexity of indigenous folk classifications of fish and other marine life (Titcomb 1952; Dye, in press) reflect an intense familiarity with the ocean, built up over millennia.

In sum, Polynesian subsistence was dominated by horticulture and fishing, successfully promulgated by means of a developed 'neolithic' technology. To understand the integration of this subsistence pattern into the larger societal fabric we must turn to a consideration of social groups, and of the political and ritual orders that validated the extant social relations of production.

Organizational principles of Polynesian societies
Social groups and land

As is typical with chiefdoms, the organizational basis of Polynesian societies was the conical clan, an extensive group descended from a common ancestor, ranked and segmented along genealogical lines (Kirchoff 1955; Sahlins 1968). Patrilineal in ideological basis, distinc- tions amongst clan members were made on the basis of genealogical distance from the founding ancestor. Typically, the senior male in direct line of patrilineal succession from the group ancestor claims the position of highest rank in the conical clan. The pyramidal political geometry of Polynesia underlies the significant advances in political evolution made by various societies within the region (Sahlins 1963).

A proclivity to segmentation or ramification characterizes the conical clan. On islands, after initial settlement by founding groups, popu- lation growth led to fissioning of local subgroups, or *ramages* (Firth 1936; Earle 1978:10). The head of each ramage was its senior male, and the head of the original senior ramage remained as chief of the conical clan. Each local ramage was ranked in relation to the senior ramage, just as members of each ramage were ranked internally. This pattern of segmentation, and the resulting social structure, is diagrammed in Figure 6A.

The ramification or branching of the conical clan also corresponds with a characteristic territorial division, as shown in Figure 6B. As local

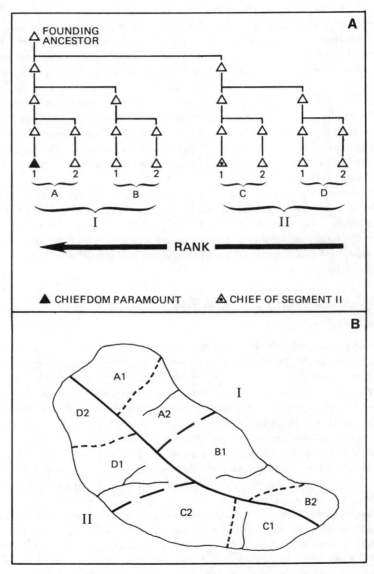

6. A. Diagrammatic model of the conical clan. B. Geographical distribution of clan segments on a hypothetical island.

groups fission, they expand to occupy new territory, so that a typical high island came to be divided in radial fashion, with each local group occupying a pie-shaped slice running from the island's core out to the reef. Such a territorial pattern has fundamental ecological implications since (in theory, at least) the territorial units lie transversely across the environmental grain of the land. That is, since island micro-environments are in general concentrically arrayed, each local group's radial segment includes all major resources: forested uplands, agricultural land, coastal plains, and marine resources. Of course, local variations in topography and distribution of particular resources (e.g., isotropic stone) dictate that such an ideal pattern is never fully realized. Nevertheless, these territorial groups, such as the Futunan *kainga*, the Rarotongan *tapere*, and the Hawaiian *ahupua'a* do tend toward economic self-sufficiency (Finney 1966). This tendency toward economic independence of local ramages is one of the centripetal forces of Polynesian society which were in opposition to those of the greater political economy.

Polynesian descent groups are not strictly unilineal, even though they have a patrilineal bias. As Firth (1957) and others (e.g., Goodenough 1955; Davenport 1959) recognized, Polynesian descent groups or ramages are, with few exceptions, *ambilateral*, that is, affili-ation may be through either male or female links. Such affiliation is, however, heavily conditioned by residence. As Firth notes, 'Residence by itself does not give title to descent-group membership, but land rights established by descent-group membership tend to remain operational only through residence' (1957:7). In fact, as Goodenough (1955) astutely observed, the ambilateral nature of Polynesian descent groups is a highly flexible adaptive strategy in situations of land short-age, such as pertain on Oceanic islands.

The classic Polynesian ramage organization may be illustrated briefly with the case of Futuna (Burrows 1936; Panoff 1970; Kirch 1975). This high island incorporates two territorial districts, each the province of a major conical clan with its paramount chief. Within each clan are a series of ramages or *kutunga*, each presided over by its own chief, the *launiu* or *aliki*, with the highest-ranked *kutunga* serving as the line of the district paramount. Every Futunan is automatically a mem-ber of the *kutunga* of both his father and mother. The *kutunga*, however, is not strictly speaking a land-holding corporate group, which is the function of the *kainga*. The term *kainga* denotes both a radial land seg-ment, and a group of persons resident on it. Generally, several *kainga* make up the ancestral lands of a *kutunga*, and affiliation with a particular *kainga* is thus a matter both of *kutunga* membership and of residence. In practice each *kainga* parcel is worked by its own residence group. *Kainga* are managed by the senior males of the minimal ramage, the *pule kainga*. The adaptive flexibility of this system of land tenure is obvious. Should the population of any *kainga* become too dense in relation to its land resources, the ambilateral nature of affiliation allows some of its members to exercise alternative options and affiliate by means of residence with other *kainga* of lesser population density.

Rank and stratification

The conical clan is, at every level, a ranked structure. Older and younger siblings, chiefs and commoners, higher and lesser ramages – all are positioned on a continuous scale with the fundamental criterion of seniority of descent. This principle of genealogical seniority may be viewed as a set of structural equivalents:

father : son :: older brother : younger brother :: chief : commoner.

Indeed, as Sahlins (1968:64) remarked, the ranked structure of Polynesian chiefdoms is mirrored within each household unit, 'the little chiefdom within the chiefdom'.

Like the great chief in his domain, the father is in his own house a sacred figure, a man of superior *mana*, his possessions, even his food, guarded by tabus against defilement by lesser familial kinsmen. Polynesians know innately how to honor the chief, for chieftainship begins at home: the chief's due is no more than elaborate filial respect (1968:64).

Yet, the gradation of rank within the Polynesian chiefdoms is not a continuous progression. A qualitative disjunction exists between chief and people, a disjunction clearly marked by differential access to sumptuary items, by prescribed behaviour, and by distinctive ritual behaviour (cf. Peebles and Kus 1977:422).

There is a strong ideological bias in Polynesian societies toward patrilineage and primogeniture in the hereditary succession to high rank. Nevertheless, just as ambilateral affiliation allows for flexibility in descent group membership, there is some flexibility in succession to high office. As noted earlier, maternal linkages may be used by persons of lower rank in order to associate themselves with those of higher rank. In some chiefdoms, such as Tonga, the female role in rank determination was to become extremely important, and pose potential contradictions to the political structure.

A second option for manipulation of the usual rules for succession to high office was that of usurpation. Sahlins observed that 'the contention between older and younger brothers is a celebrated condition of Hawaiian – indeed Polynesian – myth and practice' (1981a:56). In Figure 6A the theoretical rank of individuals declines progressively from left to right, with increasing genealogical distance from the founding ancestor. The actual political rank of the individuals, however, does not follow the same progression, since A1 and C1 are district paramounts, and A1, B1, C1, and D1 are sub-district chiefs. Thus, A2 is politically subordinate to B1, C1, and D1. Clearly, a junior brother can only look forward to increased diminution of his offspring's rank, as the conical clan continues to ramify. That junior brothers should seek to usurp the power and positions of their elder siblings is therefore not surprising, and the opposition between junior and senior is a 'structure of significance' that underlies status rivalry as a major force in Polynesian socio-political evolution.

Polynesian chiefdoms varied considerably in the degree to which differences in rank were formalized as distinct social strata. Given the common ancestry of all Polynesian societies, this range in degree of social stratification bespeaks major differences in pathways of political evolution. As Sahlins (1958:250) correctly recognized, such differentiation does not reflect regional cultural history, since the full range of minimal and elaborate stratification can be found in both West and East Polynesia.

A few ethnographic examples will illustrate the range in Polynesian systems of social stratification and political development. Representative of the least stratified chiefdoms is the atoll society of Pukapuka (Beaglehole and Beaglehole 1938). Pukapukans classified themselves into only two status levels, chiefs (*aliki*) and non-chiefs (*te tama*, lit. 'the children'), and as the Beagleholes state, 'status and rank grades... were not highly developed' (1938:234). Although the chief was sacred, and represented the people (his 'children') in rituals to the gods, no elaborate tabus or symbols of office separated him from the commoners who were also his kinsmen. His house was of the same type as others, and only a special sitting place, and private doorway, were reserved for him. 'During youth and boyhood, he, like his siblings, was without tapu and mixed freely with the other young people of the island' (1938:236). While the chief's word was not openly disputed, political control of economic production did not rest solely in his hands. Rather, such decisions were reached in village meetings (*wakapono lulu*) attended by all adult males as well as the chiefs.

Futuna represents a more elaborate and status-conscious level of society (Burrows 1936; Panoff 1970) in which the social ranks are more clearly distinguished and elaborated. In this case, a clear paramount (*sau*) existed, as well as lineage chiefs (*aliki*), and each of these was attended by a ceremonial adjutant (*mua*). Symbols of rank (such as feather crowns) were more developed, and so was deference behaviour and ritual accorded chiefs. In pre-contact times the chief's house was larger, and set off from those of commoners in a prominent position facing the *malae* or village plaza (Kirch 1975:365). A stylized *kava* ceremonial, still practised today, validated the relative rank of all chiefs to each other. Economic control, while still largely in the hands of the household heads (*pule kainga*), was impinged on considerably by the chiefs, especially in the mobilization of commoners for competitive feasts, clearing of communal gardens, or construction of large irrigation works.

Hawai'i represents an extreme of stratification in Polynesia, approximated also by Tonga and the Society Islands. Here the chiefs had become a conical clan superimposed upon a truncated class of commoners. The chiefs (*ali'i*) were internally ranked into seven or eight grades, with a paramount (*ali'i nui* or *mo'i*) at the pinnacle, and they practised sibling or half-sibling marriage to assure the highest rank of offspring. The symbols of *tapu* and rank were elaborate, the most sacred of chiefs holding the *kapu moe*, prostrating *tapu*. Feather cloaks and helmets, special eating bowls and spittoons, and so on, were made of the chiefs by craft specialists. The birth of a chief was celebrated by elaborate temple ritual. In the economic sphere, the *ali'i* not only closely regulated production through their stewards (*konohiki*), but regularly mobilized corvée labour. Most significantly, the direct control of land had passed out of the hands of the commoners, so that it was the chief, not the ramage, that was directly responsible for a territorial unit.

The search for an explanation of this range of social stratification among Polynesian chiefdoms motivated both Sahlins (1958) and Goldman (1970) in their comparative ethnographic studies. Though arriving at disparate conclusions – the one stressing ecological determinants, the other inherent status rivalry – both studies produced similar tripartite classifications of stratification. Table 2 lists the various societies treated by Sahlins and Goldman, with their corresponding typological statuses. Goldman described the differences between his three 'types' as follows:

> In the first, which I call 'Traditional', seniority is central. As the source of mana and sanctity, senior descent establishes rank and allocates authority and power in an orderly manner. The Traditional is essentially a religious system headed by a sacred chief and given stability by a religiously sanctioned gradation of worth. In the second system, which I call 'Open', seniority has been modified to allow military and political effectiveness to govern status and political control. The Open system is more strongly military and political than religious and stability in it must be maintained more directly by the exercise of secular powers. In the Open, status differences are no longer regularly graded but tend to be sharply defined. Finally, the third system, which I call 'Stratified', is characterized by clearcut breaks in status that are far-reaching in their impact on everyday life. In the Stratified system, status differences are economic and political. High rank holds the rule and possesses the land title: commoners are subject and landless. The Stratified represents a synthesis of Traditional and Open, combining respect and reverence for hereditary rank via seniority with necessary concessions to political and economic power (1970:20).

Since the spectrum summarized by Goldman encapsulates the full breadth of the chiefdom condition, Polynesia offers fertile terrain for the investigation of political evolution, with the most stratified of Polynesian societies bordering on the true 'state'. As Sahlins has written of Hawaiian society, the 'threshold which it had reached but could not cross was the boundary of primitive society itself' (1972:148).

Table 2. *Social stratification in Polynesian societies*

Island group	Approx. population of largest political unit	Degree of stratification	
		Sahlins	Goldman
Tonga	40,000	I	stratified
Hawai'i	30,000	I	stratified
Society Is.	9,000	I	stratified
Samoa	25,000	I	open
Mangareva	4,000	IIA	stratified
Easter Is.	3,500	IIA	open
Mangaia	3,000	IIA	open
Marquesas Is.	1,500	IIB	open
Niue	4,500	—	open
'Uvea	4,000	IIA	traditional
Maori (N.Z.)	3,500	—	traditional
Tongareva	2,000	—	traditional
Tikopia	1,250	IIB	traditional
Futuna	2,000	IIB	traditional
Pukapuka	500	III	traditional
Ontong-Java	2,000	III	traditional
Tokelau	500	III	traditional

Ritual, polity, and production

The principle of seniority of descent which associates rank with proximity to the founding ancestor also links Polynesian chiefs directly with the gods, themselves either deified ancestors or supernatural progenitors. Polynesian political systems cannot be understood separately from cosmology and religion, nor for that matter can their economic systems be divorced from their political and ritual contexts. As Goldman put it, 'whether we start with politics to explain the economy or with economics to explain the polity, we are involved in the same equation' (1970:509).

Closest to the gods, the chief is their earthly representative, the means by which supernatural efficacy, *mana*, is conveyed to the society at large. The chief is mediator, receiving and transmitting the offerings of the people to the ancestral and tribal deities. It is he who, on behalf of his people, recites the appropriate ritual formulae for securing rain, bountiful harvests, success in fishing, or victory in war. And since it is through the chief that these things are conveyed, he is imbued with the corollary of *mana*, sanctity or *tapu*. Not only is the chief tabu, but through his edicts certain crops, fish, activities, or indeed the whole 'land' may be made tabu in order that the gods shall grant his requests. (In certain societies, a class of priests developed, but never divorced the ritual apparatus from the chiefs. Indeed, the priests were usually members of chiefly families.)

Just as the degree of social stratification varied in Polynesian chiefdoms, so did the sanctity of the chief. All Polynesian chiefs were set apart from commoners by their *mana*, and by certain kinds of ritual deference. The most elaborate societies developed chiefly tabu to extreme levels. Consider the native historian Kamakau's description of a Hawaiian chief of *pi'o* rank (the offspring of a brother–sister union): 'The children born of these two were gods, fire, heat, and raging blazes, and they conversed with chiefs and retainers only at night' (1964:4). 'The kapu of a god was superior to the kapu of a chief, but the kapu of the . . . *pi'o* chiefs were equal to the gods' (1964:10). The elaboration of chiefly sanctity parallels that of social stratification, and is a critical aspect of Polynesian social transformation.

The wresting of food and material goods from nature was for Polynesians a fundamentally religious process, precisely because the natural world was the realm of the gods. 'When the native planted, tended his crops, and harvested, he did so psychically as well as physically, ritual including consecration, purification, prayers, charms, and offerings, accompanying every phase of his physical husbandry' (Handy 1927:6). Production was intimately tied to ritual sanction and control. 'The Work of the Gods', as the Tikopia called their annual religious cycle (Firth 1967), was for example a ritual codification of the island's production system. The chief, naturally, occupied the central role in this ritual regulation of production, and herein lies another vital clue to the evolutionary transformation of Polynesian societies. The chief, as Peebles and Kus maintain, is a 'ritually sanctioned homeostat' (1977:430) for the production system. But, he is more than the maintainer of a status quo, for it is precisely at the level of ritually controlled production that the political economy held sway over the domestic mode of production. Firth (1939:180) lucidly described the material advantage of ritual control: 'the effect of ritual is to maintain the association of the major instruments of production with the group of persons of higher social status, especially the chiefs of the clans. It is a conservative force, orienting the productive system towards the interests of the privileged group.' Thus, in Hawai'i, political tribute received by the chiefs from the people was ritually conceived as offerings to the gods (*ho'okupu*, literally, 'to cause to grow or multiply'), offerings which fell to the chiefs by virtue of their status as mediators between the society and its deities. Such tribute not only assured the chiefdom of supernatural support, it formed the material basis upon which the political aspirations of the chiefly class were realized.

Throughout Polynesia, a regular, ritual offering of tribute to the ramage chief in the form of first fruits suggests that this was an ancient pattern, which in the more developed chiefdoms reached elaborate proportions. The Tongan *'inasi* (Gifford 1929), Society Islands *parara'a matahiti* (Oliver 1974:259), and Hawaiian *makahiki* (Handy and Handy 1972) are major community-wide ritual presentations of first fruits and other products of the people to the ruling chiefs, which have their origins in a simpler first-fruits ritual.

We cannot close this discussion of the role of polity and ritual in production without at least a brief consideration of *redistribution*, which most theorists (Service 1967; Sahlins 1958, 1968; Fried 1967) have regarded as a fundamental characteristic of the chiefdom level of society. The tribute presented regularly to the chief was redistributed to other members of society, but not necessarily in the more-or-less equable manner sometimes assumed. In the less stratified societies, in which chiefs were intimately bound to the people through direct ties of kinship, first-fruits offerings and contributions of food and valued goods for major ceremonials were generally redistributed back to the individual households. In the increasingly stratified societies, however, this was not the case, and the goods rendered to the chief tended to concentrate near the apex of the socio-political pyramid. As Oliver (1974:1007, 1071–2) has shown for Tahiti, and Earle (1977) argues for Hawai'i, goods channelled into the redistributive network were used to support the chiefly hierarchy and to finance the political activities of the ruling elites. 'In some measure, goods and services contributed by the people precipitated out as the grand houses, assembly places, and temple platforms of chiefly precincts' (Sahlins 1963:299). The tribute given to the god in fact assured the glorification of the chiefly god-head. As it was said in a prayer of the Hawaiian *makahiki* harvest ritual,

> O Ku! O Kane! O Lono! . . .
> Here is an offering,
> A swine sacrificed for this visible rite
> The rite of *hula* for the *ali'i*,
> For the house of the god. . . .
> Life to the *ali'i*, life to the gods!   (Handy and Handy 1972:365)

Overview

This review of the main features of Polynesian social, economic, and political life, while necessarily brief, provides us with an ethnographic baseline from which to approach the linguistic and archaeological data directly relevant to a reconstruction of the ancestral form of Polynesian culture. I have tried to convey something of the range of variation in particular features, such as social stratification, as seen at the developmental endpoints represented by European contact. From such a review of structural variation and underlying similarity, it is possible to pose several hypotheses about the nature of the Ancestral Polynesian Society which gave birth to the region's protean cultures. First, this ancient society was centred around the pyramidal geometry of the conical clan, with its segmentary, ramage structure and ambilateral rules of affiliation. That such groups were territorially defined as much on the basis of land rights as on descent also seems highly probable .Within the conical clan, rank was determined on the basis of proximity to the founding ancestor, with the senior/junior distinction critical (a male/ female distinction less so). The inherent opposition between senior and junior is one that permeated the society, and was to form the basis for much of what transpired in the subsequent evolution of the varied daughter societies. The archaic society had for its titular head a hereditary chief, imbued with *mana* from the ancestral and primal deities, and who was *tapu* as a consequence. This person formed the critical linkage in the chain between gods and the earth and sea that provided sustenance. That the chief occupied the central role in the rituals of production seems to be significant to the later evolution of Polynesian polities, for in the ritually sanctioned control of production lay the seeds of a political economy. The opposition between a domestic 'strategy of underproduction' (Sahlins 1972:41–100) and the centrifugal demands of the chiefly, status-conscious armature is a vital aspect of the evolutionary process in Polynesia. 'The . . . potential of Polynesian chieftainship is precisely the . . . pressure it could exert on household output, its capacity both to generate a surplus and to deploy it out of the household towards a broader division of labor, cooperative construction, and massive ceremonial and military action' (Sahlins 1963:303).

These basic structural elements, and the contradictions and oppositions inherent in them, were carried as part of the 'cultural baggage' of every canoe-load of Polynesian voyagers who searched the Pacific for new landfalls. How such voyagers would apply these social and political structures to build new societies depended in part on the constraints, challenges, and opportunities presented by the particular island or archipelago they succeeded in finding and colonizing. Whether the new land was too isolated to maintain contacts with the homeland, whether it was vast or small, high or low, endowed with permanent streams, and so on, were factors that were to channel evolutionary pathways in certain directions. But the driving force in Polynesian technological and social evolution lay in the people, and in their concepts of themselves as members of a pyramidal society, as people of the chief, as descendants of the gods.

3
Ancestral Polynesia

The preceding chapter explored some structural principles characteristic of Polynesian chiefdoms, and the diversity of island settings in which they arose. While these data provide a baseline from which we may plumb the remoter periods of Polynesian antiquity, there are limits to the inferences one may draw from such a synchronic baseline, representing the endpoints of millennia of local evolution in several archipelagos. Comparative ethnographic analysis is important in reconstructing Ancestral Polynesian Society, but it is clearly desirable to rely on the direct, if sometimes meagre, data of archaeology. Fortunately, these archaeological data can be cross-checked and augmented by the evidence of historical linguistics, which aid in developing a fuller reconstruction of some aspects of the Ancestral society.

Origins

Over the years, the accumulated evidence of linguistics, physical anthropology, ethnobotany, and most recently, of archaeology have firmly convinced all but a few die-hards that Polynesian origins lie in the island realm of south-east Asia. Still ingrained in much of the Polynesian literature, nevertheless, is a 'migration mentality', an assumption that the ancestral Polynesians entered the Pacific more or less as a single ethnic unit, separately from other Oceanic peoples. Rather than viewing the peopling of the Pacific as a series of rapid and populous migrations that quickly led to an ethnic status quo, modern archaeology has contributed the perspective that the region's settlement history is both lengthy and complex. Man's progression into Oceania must be viewed as a gradual process of dominantly west-to-east movements (but with significant counter movements and 'eddies') beginning not long after the end of the Pleistocene, and completed only within the last millennium.

This gradual penetration of Oceania by man was more than the conquest of a great ocean: it encompassed a continual process of adaptation to an increasingly insular world. As the ancestral Oceanic

41

colonizers moved from the Melanesian island arcs into the remote tracts of the Pacific, they encountered more isolated, geologically simpler, and frequently biotically depauperate islands. They had to contend with new species of plants and animals, and with differing climates. These and other constraints led to the development of new cognitive and behavioural patterns, new technological and social adjustments. The cultural patterns characteristic of Ancestral Polynesia were not carried intact along migration routes, but developed in the islands themselves, in response to the challenges of oceanic existence. As J. Peter White observed: 'Polynesians were not strange newcomers to the Pacific: their roots lay in generations of adaptation to this island world' (1979:374). The Polynesians became Polynesians in Oceania, over the course of several thousand years of continual change.

In retrospect, it is surprising that the idea of a south-east Asian origin for the Polynesians did not gain widespread acceptance until the mid twentieth century, since one of the most compelling lines of evidence – language – did not need to await excavation. The linguistic position of the Polynesian languages has become clear as a result of the resurgence of interest in historical linguistics in the south-west Pacific since about 1950. The twenty-six languages of Polynesia (Biggs 1971:487) form a separate branch of the Austronesian language family, which together includes between 300 and 500 languages distributed from Madagascar to Easter Island (Dyen 1971). The Austronesian family, in the orthodox view, can be subdivided into two principal branches, a Western Austronesian group (including the modern languages of Indonesia and the Philippines) and an Eastern, or Oceanic group (Fig. 7). The Oceanic group itself may be divided with at least one major subgroup, Eastern Oceanic, composed of the languages of the South-east Solomons, North New Hebrides, Fiji, Rotuma, and Polynesia (and in some versions, Eastern or Nuclear Micronesian). Most culture-historians would associate the dispersal of the Eastern Oceanic languages with the archaeologically attested Lapita Cultural Complex, to be discussed shortly (Shutler and Marck 1975; Pawley and Green 1975). In any event, the position of the Polynesian languages as a subgroup of the Austronesian family unambiguously links the roots of Polynesian culture to its south-east Asian homeland.

The dispersal of the 'Austronesian horticulturalists' (Shutler and Marck 1975) from the area of island South-east Asia and western Melanesia and beyond required the development of appropriate technological skills and adaptive strategies. The human conquest of remote Oceania

required that man bring with him the plants and animals on which he was largely to depend; that he possess a maritime technology, including boats capable of distance voyaging; and finally, that his culture be capable of fully exploiting the products of sea, for at times he would be almost completely dependent on these resources if he was to establish himself in some parts of this island world (Green 1972:657).

The island-studded seas of south-east Asia were an ideal setting for the development of such critical pre-adaptations to oceanic existence. Linguistic reconstructions of Proto-Austronesian language (Dyen 1971; Pawley and Green 1975) indicate that these pre-adaptations – watercraft and voyaging ability, horticulture, and advanced fishing techniques – had all been achieved by perhaps 6000 BP. The Proto-Austronesian (PAN) lexical set includes terms for boats/canoes (PAN *wangka*), outriggers (*katiR*), and paddles (*besay*), for most of the Oceanic cultigens including taro (*tales*) and yam (*qubi(s)*), and for such fishing gear as traps (*buqubuqu*) and fishhooks (*kawil*). The stage was set for the Austronesian colonization of the Pacific.

Direct evidence of the early horticultural–maritime peoples of island South-east Asia has been slow to materialize, since archaeological investigation in the region is still in an embryonic state. Recent work in Taiwan (Chang 1969), and on mainland South-east Asia (Gorman 1971; Solheim 1969) has demonstrated the presence of earthenware, cord-marked ceramics associated with ground-stone adzes and other tools by *c.* 8000 BP. Furthermore, the plant evidence from Gorman's sites (Yen 1977) suggests that several of the Oceanic cultigens (*Areca, Aleurites, Canarium, Lagenaria, Piper, Terminalia*) were in use by Hoabinhian times. In the Philippines, Celebes, Halmahera, and Eastern Indonesia,

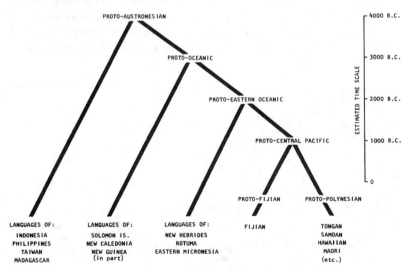

7. Generalized 'family tree' of the Austronesian language family, showing the relative position of the Polynesian language.

excavations by R.B. Fox (1970), Glover (1977), Bellwood (1976) and others are revealing a 'technocomplex' of ceramics, chert and obsidian flake tools, stone and shell adzes, and other shell implements that look very much like the kind of archaeological manifestation to be expected for ancestral Austronesian culture. This technocomplex appears throughout this area between about 5000–4000 BP. Although a great deal more excavation must be carried out, it appears that the 'neolithic' technocomplex being revealed in the middens and rockshelters of island South-east Asia represents the immediate ancestor of the Oceanic peoples.

The Lapita Cultural Complex

The material manifestations of the Austronesian dispersal across Melanesia to the gateway of Polynesia are much clearer than they are in the South-east Asia hearth, thanks to a greater intensity of archaeological exploration in Oceania. Polynesian origins may be traced to the Lapita Cultural Complex (Green 1978, 1979a), apparently representing the first major intrusion of man into the deeper reaches of Oceania (i.e., the island arcs that lie beyond New Guinea and its immediate neighbours, such as the Bismarks). Archaeological assemblages belonging to the Lapita complex are distributed from the Bismarks in western Melanesia, through the Santa Cruz Islands, New Hebrides, and New Caledonia, to Fiji, Tonga, and Samoa in West Polynesia (Fig. 8). Temporally, the complex spans the period from *c.* 1600 BC to 500 BC (Green 1979a:table 2.1). Lapita sites provide 'evidence of a community of culture in the South-west Pacific straddling the traditional boundary between Melanesia and Polynesia and antedating its appearance' (Golson 1972a:10).

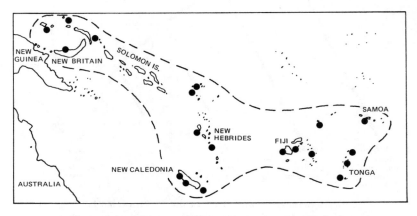

8. The distribution of Lapitoid sites in the south-western Pacific region.

Lapita sherds had first been reported by Father Otto Meyer, in 1909 from the Watom site in New Britain. Despite McKern's 1921 excavation of decorated Lapita ceramics on Tongatapu and 'Eua Islands (McKern 1929:102–19), their significance for Polynesian origins was not realized until three decades later when Gifford and Shutler (1956) excavated the site at Lapita (Site 13, which gave its name to the ceramic style) on the west coast of New Caledonia. Gifford and Shutler (1956:94) drew attention to the close resemblance between the ceramics from Watom, Site 13, and Tonga, as well as with sherds collected by Gifford at Sigatoka in Fiji. Two ^{14}C age determinations from Site 13 (2800 ± 350 BP, 2435 ± 400 BP) underscored the probable significance of Lapita pottery for Polynesian and eastern Melanesian origins.

Throughout the following two decades, various Lapita sites were investigated, in Watom, Santa Cruz–Reef Islands, New Hebrides, New Caledonia, Fiji, Tonga, and Samoa (see Green 1976a, b, 1978, 1979a). Unfortunately, most excavators focussed narrowly upon the decorated ceramics to the virtual exclusion of other artifact types, so that a broader definition of the Lapita Cultural Complex has been achieved only recently, largely as a result of Green's major excavations in the Reef–Santa Cruz sites of the South-eastern Solomon Islands (Green 1976b). Green (1979a) has provided the most thorough review of our present understanding of the Lapita Cultural Complex, of which the following discussion is a synopsis.

The Lapita Complex is minimally defined on the basis of its characteristic dentate-stamped pottery (Fig. 9). Since there is both spatial and temporal variability in Lapita ceramics, it has proved useful to employ a concept of a Lapitoid Ceramic Series (Golson 1971; Kirch 1978a, 1981a), emphasizing that Lapita assemblages partake of aspects of both *horizon* and *tradition*, as used in American archaeological terminology. Lapitoid ceramics are generally well fired, frequently calcareous-sand tempered, paddle-and-anvil finished, earthenware vessels (including shouldered pots, jars, bowls, flat-bottomed dishes, and plates). Although plain ware exists in substantial quantities, the decorative component is most distinctive. Mead and others (Mead *et al.* 1973; Donovan 1973) demonstrated that the Lapita design system is formed from a small set of design elements which are combined according to a set of syntactical 'rules' to form about 150 motifs. A certain number of these motifs are shared throughout the entire geographic extent of Lapita distribution, and testify to the cultural continuity of the complex (Green 1978).

Ceramics constitute only one aspect of the larger cultural complex. Other portable artifacts include a broad array of stone and shell adzes, flake tools (of chert and obsidian), coral and sea-urchin spine abraders, shell scrapers and peelers, slingstones, simple fishhooks, tattooing needles, awls, spear points, and various ornaments (shell rings, bracelets, and beads). Lapita sites range in size from 800–10,000 m² in area (Green 1979a:31), and display basin-shaped earth ovens, pits, and postmoulds indicative of permanent structures. The Lapita economy may be characterized as broad-spectrum, including horticulture, animal husbandry, and marine exploitation; more on this will be said shortly.

Among the most intriguing aspects of Lapita archaeology is the evidence for long-distance exchange. Ambrose and Green (1972) utilized emission spectrography to characterize obsidian excavated at the Ambittle and Gawa sites, demonstrating for both a source of Talasea on the Willaumez Peninsula of New Britain. The distance from Talasea to Gawa (Santa Cruz), some 2,000 km, testifies to 'the effective sea-faring ability of the region's earliest pottery manufacturers who were capable of transporting materials over long distances' (1972:81). Subsequent work has shown that, aside from obsidian, other items – including chert, metavolcanic adzes, oven stones, and pottery – were transported between Lapita communities from a variety of source areas. This evidence prompted Green (1976b:264) to suggest that 'the original Lapita adaptation was one to an *area* with a complex continental island environment which possessed a wide range of resources able to be assembled in individual communities through exchange'.

9. Sherd of Lapita pottery from the Reef Islands, showing characteristic dentate-stamped decoration (*photo courtesy R.C. Green, University of Auckland*).

Despite evidence – in ceramic design-system continuity and in transported materials – that the Lapita people were capabe of maintaining contacts over reasonably long distances by means of two-way voyaging, there were evidently limits to this capability. Most of Melanesia consists of inter-visible island chains, facilitating inter-island contacts. A major open-water gap, however, of 850 km, separates eastern Melanesia from the Fiji group to the east. Not surprisingly, the detailed analysis of Lapita design motifs undertaken by Green (1978, 1979a) revealed a fundamental distinction between Western and Eastern Lapita groups, the latter comprising the Fijian, Tongan, and Samoan sites (Fig. 10). This Eastern Lapita group seems, after initial settlement, to have become effectively isolated from its Western counterpart due to the large ocean gap between Fiji and the New Hebrides. It is this Eastern Lapita population which, over the course of some 1500 years of local adaptation, gave rise to Ancestral Polynesian Society.

Archaeological evidence for the breakup of the ancestral Lapita population into discrete Western and Eastern branches is paralleled by that of historical linguistics (Pawley and Green 1975). The breakup of Proto-Eastern Oceanic language (Fig. 7) was probably associated with the differentiation of local Lapita communities, itself a function of isolation due to sizeable ocean gaps. The Eastern Lapita population, which occupied Fiji–Tonga–Samoa, and continued to maintain inter-island voyaging within this triangle of archipelagos, may be associated with Proto-Central Pacific language. Central-Pacific diverged into Proto-Fijian and Proto-Polynesian branches over the course of several hundred years after the initial settlement of the region.

In short, archaeological and linguistic evidence are mutually supportive in pointing to an Eastern subgroup of the Lapita Cultural

10. Sorted matrix of Jaccard coefficients representing the number of shared Lapita design motifs between a set of Western and Eastern Lapita sites (from Green 1978). Note the tight coherence of the Western group, including Watom, SZ-8, and RL-2.

Complex as the ancestral population for Polynesians. By the time this founding population had arrived in the Fiji–Tonga–Samoa area, it reflected generations of adaptation to an island mode of existence. The further environmental and social challenges posed in the West Polynesian hearth were to mould from this Lapita progenitor an Ancestral Polynesian Society. It is on this Eastern Lapita population and the Fiji–Tonga–Samoa area that we must focus for evidence of the transition from Lapita to Polynesian culture and society.

The Eastern Lapita sequence

In crossing the water gap between the New Hebrides and Fiji and colonizing the Fiji–Tonga–Samoa triangle, the Lapita people crossed the threshold of Oceania proper. Here they were to encounter truly *oceanic* environmental conditions and constraints. The island arcs of Melanesia – the immediate homeland of the Eastern Lapita pioneers – consist of large, 'continental' islands, geologically old and complex, with a rich and varied biota. Fiji, too, is geologically complex but beyond it the island chains of Lau, Tonga, and Samoa consist only of recent volcanics or of coral islands (both atolls and uplifted limestone), with a correspondingly depauperate biota. This is a region of much geological activity, and the andesite line which divides the region (Fig. 11) marks the border between the Pacific Plate and the Fiji Plate. Along this subduction zone there is much tectonic activity and vulcanism. Not the least consequence of this geologic turmoil has been the displacement of Lapita sites in relation to their ancient shorelines. More importantly, however, 'on crossing the andesite line and entering the oceanic world of the geologist, the first people to settle Polynesia encountered a rather restricted suite of suitable rock types, continental equivalents of which they had largely ignored previously' (Green 1974b:142). The effects of this environmental transition we shall explore shortly.

Although Eastern Lapita pottery had been discovered by McKern (1929) in Tongatapu and 'Eua in 1921, its significance for Polynesian origins was not realized until Gifford's investigations in Fiji in the late 1940s (Gifford 1951), and Golson's discovery of plain pottery in Samoa in 1956, precipitated the emergence of a consistent culture-historical framework (Golston 1971). Subsequently, intensive excavation of sites with Lapitoid pottery in Tongatapu, Niuatoputapu, Samoa, 'Uvea and Futuna, Viti Levu, and Lau have provided a great deal of new evidence for the 1500-year transition from pioneering Eastern Lapita to Ancestral Polynesian Society.

The principal excavated sites containing Lapitoid pottery are listed in Table 3, with their associated ^{14}C ages (the earliest reliable age for each site is given). These sites, which include open middens and rockshelters, are either coastal, or associated with geomorphological features indicative of former shorelines. The Mulifanua site on Upolu is presently submerged, while the Niuatoputapu and Tongatapu sites are situated behind elevated shorelines now as much as 2 km inland. Figure 11 shows the geographical distribution of these sites, and their relation to the andesite line, as well as to known chert and obsidian sources. To date, the earliest dated Lapita site in the Fiji–Tonga–Samoa triangle is Natunuku, on the north coast of Viti Levu, with a ^{14}C age of 3240 ± 100 BP. A newly discovered site on Naigani Island, off the east coast of Viti Levu, may well prove to be older (S. Best 1981). By the end of the second millennium BC, we have clear evidence for the permanent colonization of Tongatapu and Samoa as well. Given that intensive surveys have yet to be conducted on most of the smaller islands, it seems certain that all three archipelagos, and probably the isolated islands of Futuna and 'Uvea, had been settled by 1000 BC.

The prehistoric sequence of the Fiji–Tonga–Samoa area from about 1500 BC to the first few centuries of the Christian era is most clearly represented in the sequence of ceramic change. Unlike many other areas of the world, in West Polynesia the ceramic sequence is one of gradual simplification of the Lapitoid Series, until the potter's art was completely abandoned *c.* AD 300. Green (1974c, 1979a) has divided

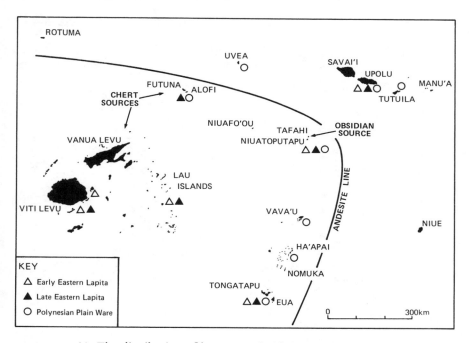

11. The distribution of known Lapitoid sites in the Fiji–West Polynesian region.

Table 3. Sites with Lapitoid pottery in West Polynesia and Fiji

Island and site	Type	¹⁴C age	Ceramic phase represented	Reference
Viti Levu (Fiji)				
Natunuku (VL 1/1)	Midden	3240 ± 100	Early Eastern Lapita	
Yanuca (VL 16/81)	Rockshelter	2980 ± 90	Early to Late Eastern Lapita	Hunt 1980
Sigatoka (VL 16/1)	Sand dune	2460 ± 90	Late Eastern Lapita	Birks 1973
Lakeba (Fiji)				
Unnamed	Rockshelter	2300 ± 170	Early Eastern Lapita to Plain Ware	S. Best n.d.
Tongatapu				
TO-2	Midden	3090 ± 95	Early Eastern Lapita	Poulsen 1968
Mangaia Mound	Midden	2630 ± 50	Early Eastern Lapita	Groube 1971
Vuki's Mound	Midden	2440 ± 110	Late Eastern Lapita	*Ibid.*
TO-6	Midden	2380 ± 51	Late Eastern Lapita	Poulsen 1968
Niuatoputapu				
Lolokoka (NT-90)	Midden	3210 ± 85	Early Eastern Lapita	Kirch 1978a
Lotoa (NT-100)	Midden	—	Late Eastern Lapita	*Ibid.*
Pome'e (NT-93)	Midden	—	Polynesian Plain Ware	*Ibid.*
Futuna				
Tavai (FU-11)	Midden (buried)	2120 ± 80	Late Eastern Lapita	Kirch 1981a
Samoa				
Ferry Berth	Submerged midden	2890 ± 80	Early Eastern Lapita	Green & Davidson 1974
Sasoa'a (SU-Sa-3)	Inland site	1840 ± 60	Polynesian Plain Ware	*Ibid.*
Vailele (SU-Va-1)	Mound site	1880 ± 60	Polynesian Plain Ware	*Ibid.* 1969
Potusa (SM17-1)	Midden	1800 ± 40	Polynesian Plain Ware	Jennings & Holmer 1980
Falemoa (SM17-2)	Midden	2030 ± 60	Polynesian Plain Ware	*Ibid.*

this sequence of ceramic change into three phases, as shown in Figure 12. Early Eastern Lapita pottery (as found at Natunuku, Lolokoka, and TO-2) includes the characteristic dentate-stamped decoration, and a wide range of vessel types. Late Eastern Lapita pottery loses certain early vessel forms, especially those exhibiting the dentate-stamped decoration (although notched rims are frequent). Polynesian Plain Ware, the endpoint of the sequence, is restricted to undecorated, simple bowls, often of crude manufacture.

The gradual decline and eventual disappearance of the potter's craft is one of the major technological changes marking the transition from Lapita to Ancestral Polynesia. Explanations for the unique loss of pottery in Polynesia remain at the level of speculation. Absence of raw materials can be ruled out, since both clay and temper are abundant on all high islands in the region. The process of ceramic change was doubtless complex, and may have included such variables as changing roles of pottery as objects of ritual or exchange, and food preparation methods (Irwin 1981).

It must be noted that while the sequence of ceramic change in Viti

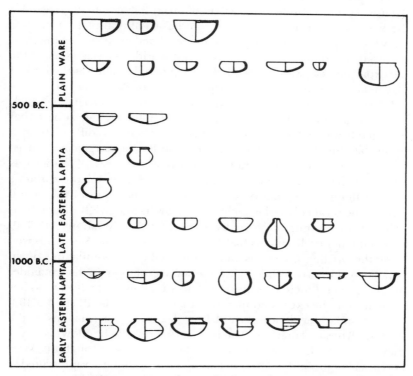

12. The sequence of ceramic change from Early Eastern Lapita to Polynesian Plain Ware, as reflected in vessel form (*courtesy R.C. Green, University of Auckland*).

Levu parallels that of the Polynesian islands through the Late Eastern Lapita phase, it is thereafter divergent, reflecting increased differentiation between Fiji and Polynesia. The later culture-history of Fiji is something apart from that of Polynesia, an intriguing and complex sequence (Frost 1979) requiring its own analysis beyond the purview of this book.

The transition from pioneering Lapita to archaic Polynesia is reflected in more than ceramic change, and Green (1971a, 1974c) has demonstrated that the early Polynesian adz kit developed gradually from a set of early Lapita adz prototypes. The range of isotropic rocks available for stone tool manufacture is severely restricted in the Samoan and Tongan archipelagos, which may have been a significant factor in the sequence of adz change. Among the major technological changes in adzes was the gradual abandonment of the use of heavy *Tridacna* shell, and an increase in the relative frequency of plano-convex forms.

The ceramic and adz sequences from *c.* 1500 BC to the first few centuries of the Christian era reflect the transformation of an ancestral Lapita technology to a truly Polynesian form. These changes parallel other economic and social developments as well as the increasing divergence and subsequent breakup of Proto-Polynesian language. By the first few centuries after Christ, the basic cultural pattern that we know as 'Polynesian' had been formed, moulded by the environmental constraints and possibilities of an oceanic world. The stage was set for the expansion eastwards of the Polynesian peoples, and for their rapid dispersal over some 20 million square miles of Pacific Ocean.

I have referred continually to Ancestral Polynesian Society, by which term I mean the social forms and supporting technological base that emerged from the Lapita transition just described. It is difficult to fix a lower date for the appearance of Ancestral Polynesian Society, for its development was clearly a gradual process, and the rate of change was unlikely to have been the same on all islands (even though these islands were evidently in regular or at least intermittent contact). In general terms, Ancestral Polynesian technology is archaeologically distinguishable from its Lapita ancestor by about 500 BC. By about AD 300, independent developments had occurred in Tonga and Samoa (as well as on the smaller, isolated islands) which led those populations down separate pathways of technological and social evolution. In the remainder of this chapter, I focus closely upon Ancestral Polynesian Society as it is evidenced in the excavated materials dated from *c.* 500 BC to AD 300, with secondary evidence derived from lexical reconstructions of the Proto-Polynesian language. The reconstruction which follows is a synthesis of data from a range of excavated sites throughout West Polynesia; items or data present at one site are often not represented at others. In presenting a generalized reconstruction for Ancestral Polynesian Society I do not mean to imply the absence of variability between individual settlements and their communities. Indeed, as I have recently argued (Kirch 1981a) there is increasing evidence for such variation. Nevertheless, sufficient consistency between sites and their assemblages exists so that the reconstruction made here should be generally valid throughout the region.

Ancestral Polynesia: a reconstruction

Technology

Excavations in a range of Eastern Lapita and Polynesian Plain Ware sites have provided a substantial collection of Ancestral Polynesian material culture, even though the acidic soils of most open sites have not been especially favourable to the preservation of bone and shell, let alone highly perishable wooden or fibre objects. Some aspects of Ancestral Polynesian technology, notably adzes and ceramics, have already been reviewed in terms of their roles in defining the Lapitoid sequence in West Polynesia. Ancestral Polynesian material culture clearly reflects considerable adaptation to the restricted range of raw materials available in an oceanic environment. The Ancestral Polynesian tool kit included a variety of adz forms, stone and shell chisels, hammerstones, abraders of branch coral and echinoid spines, rubbing or polishing stones, grindstones, and smaller whetstones (a sample of artifacts from the Niuatoputapu sites is shown in Fig. 13). These and other tools were utilized to manufacture a variety of implements and objects, not all of which are as yet archaeologically attested. In the household sphere, we have numerous examples of several varieties of vegetable peelers and scrapers, and of course the ubiquitous ceramics, which include such functional types as water jars, cooking pots, and serving bowls/dishes. The use of the earth oven (PPN *umu*) is well attested, with excavated examples in more than seven sites (Fig. 14). Fishing gear has been only sparsely represented to date, but one-piece shell fishhooks (cf. Kirch and Dye 1979), net weights, and *Cypraea*-shell caps for octopus-lure gear are attested; several possible trolling lures are also in evidence. In the way of clothing and personal adornment, we have a series of shell ornaments, including *Trochus*-shell armbands, a variety of shell beads and rings, and several kinds of 'bracelet' segment of *Tridacna* or *Spondylus* shell.

We may infer the presence of many kinds of perishable items from the lexical reconstruction of appropriate terms in the Proto-Polynesian language (Walsh and Biggs 1966; Biggs, Walsh, and Waga 1970; Pawley and Green 1971). Thus, the use of barkcloth is indicated by the term *tapa*. Likewise, a developed outrigger canoe technology is evidenced by a variety of technical and functional terms, such as canoe (*waka*), outrigger boom (*kiato*), paddle (*'alo*), sail (*laa*), cargo (*uta*), to voyage (*folau*), and seaman or navigator (*tautai*).

Beyond the technical–functional level of material culture, there are indications that the artistic styles expressed in contact-period Polynesian societies find their antecedents in Ancestral Polynesia. That the art of tattooing was practised is evident from the presence of tattooing chisels in Tongan sites excavated by Poulsen (1968:fig. 2). Moreover, Green (1979b) argues that a number of Lapita decorative motifs may be traced in ethnographically documented barkcloth and tattooing designs.

Production systems

An earlier debate as to the economic foundations of Lapita and Ancestral Polynesian societies, inspired principally by Groube's proposal (1971) that the Lapita populations represented 'oceanic strandloopers', has now been resolved by the accumulation of both direct and indirect evidence supporting the view of Ancestral Polynesian economy as a broad-based, generalist set of strategies including agriculture, animal husbandry, and marine exploitation. Certainly the excavated material-culture items enumerated above are in line with such a reconstruction. I will review the ethnobotanical, linguistic, and archaeological evidence for the two main facets of production – agriculture–animal husbandry

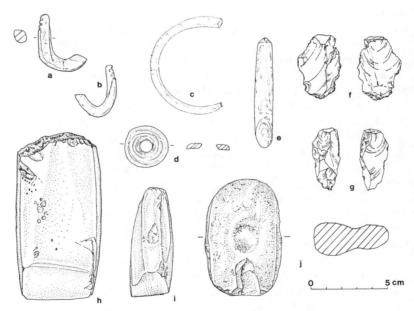

13. Artifacts from Lapitoid sites on Niuatoputapu, Tonga: a,b, one-piece fishhooks of *Turbo* shell; c, *Trochus*-shell armband; d, *Conus*-shell ornament; e, sea-urchin spine abrader; f,g, flakes of volcanic glass; h,i, *Tridacna*-shell adzes; j, hammerstone or nut-cracking hammer with pecked finger-grips.

and marine exploitation – and for the exchange of goods between communities.

The case for an agricultural subsistence base for Ancestral Polynesian Society could be built on ethnobotanical evidence alone. Polynesian agriculture, as witnessed by the European explorers, was clearly derivative (Yen 1973a), and set in the mould of south-east Asian-Melanesian tropical 'vegeculture' (Barrau 1965b, c). The roster of Polynesian crop plants, as well as domestic animals, is (with the significant exception of the sweet potato) south-east Asian and Melanesian in origin. Reconstruction of Proto-Austronesian language includes terms for many of the Polynesian cultigens, including the taro–yam complex. We may presume, with Yen, that the transfer of plant species in island colonization was accompanied by 'the *concepts* that underlie *method*' (1973a:70). Such fundamental ethnobiological concepts as that 'taro requires a wet edaphic medium and yam requires a dry' (Yen 1973a:70) have surely been part of the Austronesian view of agriculture for millennia, and are reflected in the significance of 'l'humide et le sec' (Barrau 1965a) in Oceanic cultivation systems everywhere.

Archaeological evidence for Ancestral Polynesian agriculture and animal husbandry is uneven, but convincing when analysed as a total complex. Settlement sites range in size from just over 1,000 m² to 7,000 m², and the depths of accumulated deposit bespeak continuous occupation for some term of years (perhaps as great as 300–400 years in

14. Earth oven, filled with fire-altered cooking stones, in the Early Eastern Lapita site of Lolokoka, Niuatoputapu Island, Tonga.

several instances). It is difficult to conceive of such settlements being maintained solely on the basis of hunting–gathering–fishing. Fortunately, we need not rely on these indirect arguments, for the presence of domestic animals is attested in the faunal components from excavated sites. Pig bone is reported from at least six sites, dog from four sites, and the domestic fowl (*Gallus gallus*) from five sites. The presence of pig, in particular, is strong indirect evidence for agriculture, given the close association between the two in all Oceanic subsistence systems. 'The dependence of animals, especially pigs, on agricultural systems seems to be an argument for the transfer of plant agriculture itself. Apart from household waste, pig husbandry is mainly conducted by the feeding of coconut, breadfruit, and sweet potato, with the support of foraging for natural products from the flora and seashore' (Yen 1973a:71).

Although the ideal direct evidence of cultigen macro-fossils (or pollen) is lacking (with the exception of carbonized coconut endocarp), artifactual evidence for crop plants comes from a variety of scrapers and peelers that appear to be designed for removing the skins of tubers and/or breadfruit. Similar implements were used throughout Polynesia in historic times. Furthermore, indirect evidence for the transfer of plant materials between island groups has come recently from the presence of terrestrial molluscs (Christensen and Kirch 1981a; Hunt 1980) recovered from archaeological sediments by fine sieving. Several *anthropophilic* snails, such as *Gastrocopta pediculus* and *Lamellidea oblonga*, have long been suspected by malacologists to be adventive, transported and introduced to the Pacific islands by prehistoric man (Cooke 1926; Cooke and Kondo 1960; Pilsbry 1916–18; Solem 1959, 1978). These species frequent food plants and disturbed vegetation surrounding human habitations, and their dispersal by man is thus presumed to reflect the transport of plant materials (and, probably, of soil) as well. As Cooke and Kondo (1960:251) note of *Tornatellides oblongus*, 'it was undoubtedly a lowland species disseminated accidently with food plants'.

In short, the introduction to the West Polynesian archipelagos of domestic animals and crops by the earliest Lapita colonizers seems indisputable, and is consistent with the linguistic reconstruction of terms for these items in the Proto-Polynesian lexicon (Table 4). But what of the cultivation *systems*, their agronomy and operation? Here we must depend increasingly on linguistic and ethnobotanical evidence. Swidden (slash-and-burn) farming is fundamental to Oceanic agriculture (Barrau 1965a; Yen 1973a), and was doubtless the basis of most Ancestral Polynesian cultivation. However, some rudiments of intensive systems, such as drainage and irrigation (particularly in association with the cultivation of taro) may well have been known to the earliest Austronesian settlers of the Pacific (Spriggs 1982).

Table 4. *Proto-Polynesian (PPN) lexical reconstructions relating to technology and production*

Gloss	Reconstruction
Material culture	
Canoe	*waka
Outrigger boom	*kiato
Sail	*laa
Paddle	*'alo
Cargo	*uta
Wooden bowl	*kumete
Cooking pot	*kulo
Kava bowl	*taano'a
Adz	*toki
Barkcloth	*tapa
Mat	*fala
Basket	*kete
Agriculture	
Pig	*puaka
Dog	*kulii
Domestic fowl	*moa
Taro (*Colocasia*)	*talo
Yam (*Dioscorea*)	*'ufi
Breadfruit (*Artocarpus*)	*kulu
Banana (*Musa*)	*futi
Chestnut (*Inocarpus*)	*ifi
Alocasia	*kape
Kava (*Piper*)	*kawa
To plant	*too
To harvest	*utu
Garden	*ma'ala
Fermented food	*maa/masi
Cook in earth oven	*ta'o
Fishing	
To fish	*faangota
To fish with torches	*rama
Fish trap	*fiinaki
Net	*kupenga
Fishhook	*ma(a)ta'u
Settlement pattern	
House	*fale
Ceremonial area	*mala'e
Canoe shed	*folau

Aside from the annual cultivated crops – centred around the taro–yam complex – Polynesian agricultural systems display an important arboricultural component. Breadfruit is the dominant cultigen, but other trees, such as the fruit- or nut-bearing *Inocarpus, Spondias,*

Terminalia, Barringtonia, Canarium, and others, are also important. Two lines of evidence indicate that arboriculture was one focus of Ancestral Polynesian agriculture. The first is the presence, in several excavated sites, of large pits inferred to have been used for the ensilage and fermentation of breadfruit paste, the terms for which (**maa/masi*) are again reconstructable Proto-Polynesian items. Such a pit, excavated at the site of Pome'e (NT-93) on Niuatoputapu, is illustrated in section in Figure 15. (The adaptive significance of such fermentation pits is explored in greater detail in Chapter 6.) A second line of evidence consists of a large number of ovoid stones, frequently with pecked finger grips (Fig. 13), interpreted as hammers for opening various hard-shelled nuts, such as *Canarium* or *Terminalia*. The degree of edge-damage evidenced on these stones is too slight for hammerstones used in lithic tool production, and they are furthermore virtually identical to ethnographically documented nut-cracking stones from the Solomon Islands. It is likely, therefore, that a full complement of tree species was also transferred

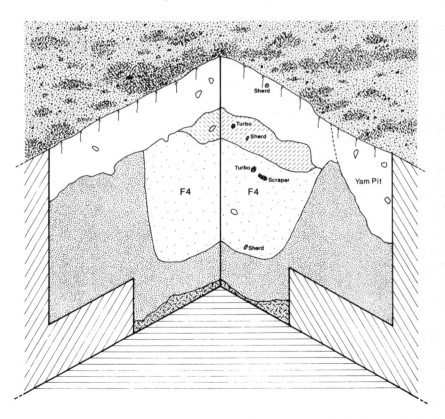

15. Excavated section through a probable breadfruit fermentation and storage silo, Site NT-93, Niuatoputapu, Tonga.

with the initial colonizers of West Polynesia. Whereas the nut–fruit species were to become dominant aspects of certain eastern Melanesian subsistence systems (e.g., Santa Cruz, cf. Yen 1974b), in Polynesia they were relegated to a minor role with only the breadfruit occupying a significant position in subsistence production.

Whereas uninhabited oceanic islands lacked much in the way of terrestrial food resources, the adjacent reefs, lagoons, and pelagic waters were characterized by extremely large populations of fish and shellfish, prior to initial human exploitation. Pioneering Lapita communities depended heavily upon marine resources while terrestrial production systems were being established. Tongan visitors to the site of Poulsen's Early Lapita excavations 'expressed surprise at the size of the biggest of the excavated *toʻo* [*Gafrarium* sp.] shells' (Poulsen 1967:292), and Swadling (ms.) found that initial Lapita sites in the Reef Islands likewise display a great species diversity and unusually large size range of edible molluscs. The same situation, moreover, obtained with the earliest occupation deposits in Tikopia (Kirch and Yen 1982), where the volume of shellfish deposited greatly exceeded the densities at any later sites.

Linguistic evidence (Table 4) implies that Ancestral Polynesians inherited from their Lapita ancestors a sophisticated knowledge of marine resources, and a variety of strategies for their exploitation. Fishhooks, traps, nets, spears and plant poisons are all indicated by lexical reconstructions. Unfortunately, artifactual evidence of Ancestral Polynesian fishing gear is sparse, although excavations in Tongatapu, Samoa, and Niuatoputapu have yielded simple one-piece fishhooks of *Turbo* shell, and *Cypraea*-shell caps probably for the octopus-hook. (Large collections of similar Lapitoid fishing gear were recovered from early levels on the outliers of Anuta and Tikopia.) Unambiguous evidence for the range of fish and shellfish taken by the Ancestral Polynesian fishermen derives from the excavated faunal components of these sites. Molluscs (both bivalves and gastropods) are abundant in all sites, as are the bones of marine turtles and elasmobranchs (sharks and rays). The range of fish species represented is illustrated by the three principal Niuatoputapu sites (Table 5). The fish bones from these sites are all common inshore reef genera, and in fact are by and large the same taxa that dominate in contemporary Niuan fish catches (Kirch and Dye 1979). Significantly, several of the taxa represented in Table 5 are not usually taken with hook and line, and thus provide indirect support for the contention that angling was only one component of Ancestral Polynesian fishing strategies. Based on ethno-archaeological comparisons (Kirch and Dye 1979), the bulk of the fish caught was probably taken by spearing and netting methods. In Figure 16, something of the diversity of indigenous Polynesian fishing strategies is displayed, as these are applied to the varied micro-environments of the

Table 5. *Minimum numbers of identified fish from Niuatoputapu Lapita sites*

Taxon	Site NT-90	Site NT-93	Site NT-100
Acanthuridae			
Acanthurus	4		2
Other	5	1	1
Balistidae	1		2
Carangidae			1
Diodontidae			
Diodon hystrix	18	4	1
Labridae	2	1	1
Lethrinidae	2		1
Lutjanidae			
Lutjanus	1		
Scaridae			
Calotomus	1		2
Scarus	13	2	9
Serranidae			
Cephalopholus			1
Sparidae			
Monotaxis grandoculis	6	6	6
Totals (MNI)	51	10	27
Total bones (E)	99	14	38
MNI/E ratio	0.52	0.71	0.71

contemporary Niuatoputapu marine ecosystem. All available evidence – linguistic, artifactual, faunal, and ethno-archaeological – suggests that a similar range of exploitation strategies was fully developed by Ancestral Polynesians.

While terrestrial production and marine exploitation provided Ancestral Polynesian settlements with the basis for economic self-sufficiency, there is some evidence for exchange relations between communities. Green argued that the original Lapita adaptation was to an environmentally diverse *area*, and that exchange permitted the distribution of scarce resources (obsidian, chert, adzes, clay, oven stones, etc.) among Lapita populations. Since the Fiji–Tonga–Samoa region is also characterized by an uneven distribution of natural resources (especially isotropic stone, and clay and temper for pottery manufacture), one might predict exchange to have been an important aspect of the Ancestral Polynesian economy. There is, in fact, some evidence for the importation of exotic items; chert from the NT-90 site on Niuatoputapu, for example, is probably from a Futunan source, while basalt adzes in Tongatapu are clearly imports from one of the high volcanic islands. On the whole, however, these items are represented in low frequencies, and then only in the earliest sites. While a clear statement on this point is not yet within our purview, the evidence suggests

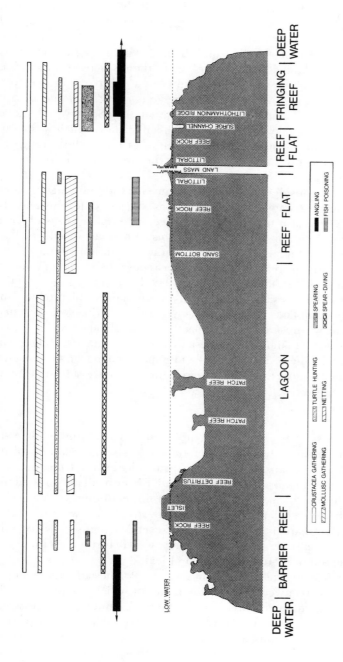

16. The micro-environmental distribution of indigenous fishing strategies on Niuatoputapu, based on contemporary ethnoecological studies (after Kirch and Dye 1979). Bar thickness indicates relative quantitative significance.

that exchange did not constitute a *significant* economic strategy for Ancestral Polynesians. Exotic items in the early sites may reflect continued contacts between 'mother' settlements and 'daughter' propagules which became less important once the pioneering settlements had become firmly established. Furthermore, as the Lapita descendants adapted lithic technology to the restricted rock suites of the oceanic islands, the need for imported chert or obsidian presumably declined. An hypothesis suggests itself, that the discontinuance of exchange in Ancestral Polynesian Society reflects an increasing propensity for economic self-sufficiency, which was to aid significantly in the successful colonization of the farthest flung and isolated island groups of Polynesia in the first few centuries of the Christian era.

It is worth considering that the evidence for wide-ranging exchange systems linking Lapita communities, as suggested for instance by Green (1979a), also implies the existence of complex forms of social and political organization. Such systems, moreover, need not have been based on hierarchic networks, but rather on horizontally structured networks of areal integration, such as described ethnographically by Schwartz (1963). Friedman (1981, 1982) has recently suggested that ancestral Austronesian social forms were indeed hierarchic, and involved long-distance trade in prestige goods, but this has yet to be tested. At any rate, we must not assume that the ancestral Lapita societies were any less *complex* than their Polynesian (or, for that matter, Melanesian) descendants. The course of social and political change in Oceania was one of *transformation*, and not of some kind of 'progress' from lesser to greater complexity.

Social relations

Nothing is so critical in our attempt to understand and explain the evolution of the Polynesian chiefdoms as the social relations of the Ancestral Polynesians. The structural principles by which the Ancestral Polynesians organized their social and political affairs formed the baseline from which the varied ethnographic endpoints of Polynesia – from relatively egalitarian to elaborately stratified – were ultimately derived. In Chapter 2, we developed several hypotheses based on a comparative ethnographic review. Here, we will further test these with a consideration of archaeological and lexical data.

The archaeological evidence of Ancestral Polynesian settlement patterns tells us relatively little of the nature of social groups *per se*. The basic unit of settlement was evidently the small hamlet or village, which on the size of Ancestral Polynesian sites would have incorporated several household units. Since no large areal exposures have as yet been excavated, we are still ignorant of the internal layout of such settlements. Certainly, however, there is no evidence of any significant public architecture such as is found among some of the later Polynesian chiefdoms. The Proto-Polynesian term *mala'e* does imply the existence of communal assembly grounds, though these were probably little more than open yards where religious rites and community feasts were held. (Such open spaces continued to form a part of West Polynesian settlement patterns, whereas in East Polynesia the *marae* was developed in the direction of elaborate and frequently megalithic religious structures.)

Artifactual evidence for social status is similarly lacking. Differential mortuary behaviour might provide valuable clues in this area, but to date no Ancestral Polynesian cemeteries have been located. None of the shell ornaments recovered from excavations can be unequivocally interpreted as insignia of rank, even though it is possible that they functioned in such a manner. Direct archaeological data, in short, imply only dispersed hamlet groups composed of several households each, with no direct evidence of social stratification.

The data of lexical reconstruction provide one of the most important sources for accurately interpreting the nature of Ancestral Polynesian social relations. In Table 6 are given a number of Proto-Polynesian lexemes pertaining to kinship terminology, social statuses, social groups, and ritual. Sibling terminology (Epling, Kirk, and Boyd 1973; R. Clark 1975) in Proto-Polynesian offers one clue, evident in the distinctions drawn between senior and junior siblings of the same sex:

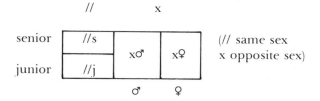

The senior/junior distinction, as we have noted, was fundamental to the Polynesian ideology of rank. While this pattern was to be simplified in certain Polynesian societies, it is significant that the ancestral sibling-term system was retained by all of the more highly stratified chiefdoms.

Of the several reconstructable Proto-Polynesian lexemes for social statuses, the most important is certainly *'ariki*, 'chief'. Among the Polynesian languages, semantic agreements for reflexes of *'ariki* are close, and confidently permit the attribution of a Proto-Polynesian gloss, 'chief, head of a lineage; first born in the senior line, who succeeds to the chieftainship of the lineage and has strong personal '*mana*' and '*tapu*' (Pawley 1979:20). Indeed, the associated terms *mana* and *tapu* are likewise reconstructable items. Pawley (1979, 1981) suggests that the term *'ariki* was derived from an older Proto-Oceanic contrast set *qa-lapa(s)* 'chief' (lit. 'Great One'), and *qa-diki*, 'first born son of chief' (lit. 'Little One'). Originally these terms were probably titles: 'Whereas in Proto-oceanic * qa-lapa(s) and * qa-diki were proper nouns, the titles of individual people, PPN * qariki is reconstructable as a common noun, occurring after the definite and indefinite articles, and designating a class of objects rather than a title' (1979:23). Pawley (1981:12) suggests that the principle of primogeniture 'led to the title of the chief himself, and ultimately becoming a common noun designating a class of people or a member of that class'. The lexical data clearly indicate that Ancestral Polynesian Society had already developed the institution of hereditary chieftainship.

The nature of chiefship in Ancestral Polynesian Society can be hypothesized in its broad aspects on. the basis of comparative ethnography. Some years ago, Williamson portrayed his notion of the ancestral type of Polynesian chief:

> We must, I think, believe that at one time the concentration in a head chief of sacred duties and secular rule was usual among the Polynesians or their ancestors, more or less remote; that the high priest was the head chief; and some of the islands offer . . . indications that this has been so. Presumably the foundation of his power was religious (1924:55).

Koskinen (1960) reached essentially the same opinion based on an extensive comparison of *ariki*-ship in Polynesia, noting that the original meaning of the term *ariki* was clearly 'first born' of the chief (thus presaging Pawley's lexical reconstruction). The 'more clearly sacerdotal' character of the 'oldest form of Polynesian *ariki* chieftainship' was also evident to Koskinen (1960:148). An ideology of direct, male descent from the gods, and of associated *mana* and *tapu* was the original mode of legitimation for Polynesian chieftainship.

Aside from the chief, a number of other Polynesian social statuses can be reconstructed from the lexical data (Table 6). Among these is *tufunga*, with a gloss of 'expert, specialist, craftsman'. The position of *tufunga* was probably not hereditary, but some ritual status may be implied by several Polynesian reflexes in which the semantic value is 'priest' (e.g., Hawaiian *kahuna*). *Tufunga* were the valued guardians of specialized knowledge, especially in areas concerned with production. Another social status of note is *toa*, 'warrior' (see also PPN *kaitaua*, 'to be warlike'), indicating that conflict may have been an important aspect of Ancestral Polynesian Society. To judge on the basis of the comparative ethnographic baseline, this was also an achieved status, based on prowess and skill. However, since success in war is a physical manifestation of *mana*, here is the germ of a potential conflict between *'ariki* and *toa* over their respective claims to the sources of *mana* or power. As we shall see in later chapters, this conflict was in some Polynesian societies to come to the forefront of political transformation.

One further lexical item of note is Proto-Polynesian *tautai*, 'seaman,

Table 6. *Proto-Polynesian lexical reconstructions relating to social organization and ritual*

Gloss	Proto-Polynesian reconstruction
Sibling kin terms	
Elder sibling, same sex	*tuakana
Younger sibling, same sex	*t(a,e)hina
Woman's brother	*tuanga'ane
Man's sister	*tuafafine
Social statuses	
Chief	*'ariki
Expert, craftsman, specialist	*tufunga
Warrior	*toa
Seaman, navigator	*tautai
Social groups	
Corporate, land-holding descent group	*kainanga
Minimal descent group, household (with land)	*kainga
Assembly of people	*fono
Gods, ritual, religion	
Sacred, prohibited	*tapu
Supernatural power	*mana
Deity	*'atua
Spirit, soul, corpse	*'anga'anga
Piper methysticum; ceremony	*kawa
To perform ritual	*fa'i
Offering, act of worship, remove tapu	*mori
Prayer	*lotu
Kava bowl	*taano'a
Pigment of *Curcuma domestica*	*renga

navigator, fisherman'. According to Pawley, from the existence of this term one may 'infer that there was some specialization of economic roles in PPN society' (1979:18). More, *tautai is matched by *tau'uta, 'landlubber', which raises the tantalizing suggestion of a land people / sea people distinction, as reflected for instance in traditional Fijian society (Hocart 1929, 1952; Sahlins 1976).

The ramage or cognatic descent group was throughout Polynesia the basic social and territorial unit. Lexical reconstruction allows us to specify the ancestral term for this group, *kainanga, which may be glossed as 'a land-holding descent group, under the authority of a chief' (Pawley 1979:6). Some modern reflexes of *kainanga are Tikopian *kainanga*, 'clan, non-exogamous descent group', Tongan *kainanga*, 'populace', Tahitian *mata'einana*, 'high order ramage', and Rarotongan *matakeinanga*, 'tribe' (note that the East Polynesian reflexes have the added prefix *mata-*). The term may have derived from a Proto-Oceanic root **kai(n)*, meaning the people of a place, local inhabitants (Pawley 1981:17). As Goodenough (1955) recognized, the **kainanga* group is actually an ancient 'Malayo-Polynesian' social structure, since it is found not only in Polynesia, but in various Micronesian communities as well (e.g., Trukese *kainang*, 'matrilineal sib'). That Ancestral Polynesian Society was organized on such a ramage system has important implications for the subsequent evolution of its daughter societies. Inherently segmentary and expansionistic, such a structure is well suited to a kind of 'radiation' into all of the primary ecological zones of an island. Despite this tendency, the pyramidal geometry of the conical clan allows the segmentary branches to retain their genealogical interrelations, thus facilitating the amalgamation of large political units under the leadership of a ranking chief.

In addition to the **kainanga* descent group, we can reconstruct a second Proto-Polynesian term, **kainga*, with reflexes in both Tongic and Nuclear Polynesian subgroups (e.g., Tongan *kainga*, 'relative', Futunan *kainga*, 'household group with associated land', Samoan *'ainga*, 'family group', Easter Island *kainga*, 'land segment', Mangarevan *kainga*, 'lands belonging to a family', and Hawaiian *'aina*, 'land'). The semantic values for these reflexes suggest that the Proto-Polynesian term referred to a minimal descent group or extended household, together with the lands occupied and cultivated by that group. Probably, residence was a criterion for group membership, which would not have been the case with the larger and more inclusive **kainanga*.

The **fono*, or political assembly of people (especially adult males), is also a term of Proto-Polynesian ancestry, which suggests that despite the hereditary chieftainship, decision-making in Ancestral Polynesia was based on consensus within the **kainanga* as a whole. (Such an interpretation is in keeping with the idea that the ** 'ariki* was more of a sacred, than secular, ruler in Ancestral Polynesian Society.) The physical space upon which such **fono* were held, and where the ** 'ariki* probably invoked the ancestral deities, was the **malae* or ceremonial plaza.

Finally, lexical reconstruction and comparative ethnography allow us to say something of the ancestral religion, and of the ritual forms that linked society to the supernatural and that validated social relations of production. The concepts of *mana* and *tapu* have already been mentioned. In Chapter 2 I noted that Polynesian ritual is intimately linked to the chieftainship, with the apotheosized ancestors of the chiefs constituting the principal deities. For Proto-Polynesian, we may reconstruct the term ** 'atua*, 'class of spiritual beings, deities'. Note that this term, like that for chief, begins with ** 'a-*, 'this form being the POC marker preceding proper nouns, personal names' (Pawley 1979:35), supporting the interpretation that, originally, deities were specifically *ancestral* gods. A second category of spiritual beings is indicated by Proto-Polynesian *'anga'anga*, probably best glossed as 'soul, spirit, or corpse' (Biggs, Walsh, and Waga 1970). Presumably, *'anga'anga* were not specifically deities, but rather the spirits of deceased persons, perhaps of low rank.

Several Proto-Polynesian terms refer to aspects of ritual: *mori*, 'offering, act of worship, to remove tapu'; *fa'i*, 'to perform ritual'; *lotu*, 'prayer'; and *kawa*, 'ceremonial involving the use of the narcotic *Piper methysticum*'. The last mentioned was throughout Polynesia an important kind of ritual, usually involving the invocation of ancestral spirits (cf. Firth 1967). That the ritual use of *P. methysticum* was already developed by the ancestral Polynesians is supported as well by the Proto-Polynesian term *taano'a*, a bowl for mixing and serving the narcotic *kava* infusion. Green (personal communication 1981) has speculated that the elaborately decorated, flat-bottomed Lapita ceramic dishes with out-turned rims might have functioned as such *kava* vessels (in Fiji, *kava* continued to be served in special ceramic vessels, *ndari*, until historic times).

One final Proto-Polynesian reconstruction with relevance to ritual is *renga*, the saffron-coloured pigment extracted from the root of *Curcuma domestica*. In almost every Polynesian society this pigment was an important accompaniment to ritual, used to decorate the bodies of participants, or to dye their barkcloth. Such ritual use of *renga* most probably began with the Ancestral Polynesians, or their ancestors.

Overview

The evidence of linguistics, ethnobotany, and archaeology all converge on a central theme: that the economic basis and structural principles characteristic of Polynesian societies developed gradually, in part through adaptation to the challenges of island life. This process began some five to six millennia ago in island South-east Asia, with the development of sophisticated outrigger canoes, marine exploitation techniques, and taro–yam horticulture. As the Oceanic-speaking peoples dispersed eastwards through the island arcs of Melanesia to the western gateway of Polynesia, new environmental constraints, such as reduced island size, greater isolation, biotic impoverishment, and geological simplicity, continued to influence the direction of change. Successful colonization of new islands came to depend increasingly upon the ability to transfer both biotic and cultural elements of the 'human landscape': cultigens, domestic animals, and the ethnobiological concepts and techniques that permitted their rapid establishment in new landfalls.

Following upon the colonization of the Fiji–Tonga–Samoa triangle, by about 1500 BC, this region became isolated, an 850 km ocean gap separating these archipelagos from eastern Melanesia. Developments in West Polynesia led to the formation of Ancestral Polynesian Society, concerning which we have advanced several propositions:

1. Ancestral Polynesians possessed a relatively elaborate material culture (well adapted to local raw materials), with most elements of the historically documented Polynesian material culture either archaeologically represented or inferred on the basis of lexical reconstruction. Ceramics were the significant element which did not persist to the ethnographic period.

2. Subsistence economy was based upon agriculture ('tropical vegeculture'), with the taro–yam complex of central importance. Arboriculture (especially of breadfruit) and animal husbandry (pigs, dogs, fowl) comprised significant elements in the agricultural production systems.

3. Marine resources (fish and shellfish) furnished the primary source of protein, and Ancestral Polynesians utilized a broad range of marine exploitation strategies, including netting, angling, spearing, and the use of plant poisons.

4. Small, generally coastal, multi-household hamlets constituted the basic Ancestral Polynesian settlement pattern. Lexical reconstruction specifies the existence of ceremonial plazas (*malae*).

5. The organizing principles of the society were those of the conical clan, with rank based upon genealogical distance from a founding ancestor. A system of hereditary chieftainship was already established, with clan deities consisting of the apotheosized chiefly ancestors. These chiefs were both sacred and secular rulers, whose perceived efficacy depended upon *mana* from the gods. The rank differential between chiefs and commoners was not, at this stage however, reflected in elaborate material or behavioural terms. Land was controlled and utilized by corporate, non-unilinear descent groups or ramages.

The structure of this ancestral social pattern was to play a fundamental role in directing the courses of evolution and societal transformation throughout Polynesia. For example the opposition between junior and senior, manifested in kinship terminology, but also in the whole ranking system, was to have great effects on the development of Polynesian polities. Likewise with the opposition between high and low *mana* which on the one hand correlated with distinctions in rank, but which was also manifest in efficacy and hence practical action. Chiefs were by definition the receptacles of *mana*, but theirs was not a monopoly, leaving open the possibility for rivals (such as the *toa*, warriors) to usurp some of the social and economic power that accompanied the control of *mana*. We can as well infer that the contradiction between domestic and political interests in the organization of production was already entrenched in Ancestral Polynesian Society. This opposition between the centripetal underproduction of the household, and the centrifugal demands of the larger polity is one that we see played out in all of the Polynesian islands.

The ethnographically witnessed spectrum of Polynesian chiefdoms – from relatively egalitarian to elaborate and highly stratified – all reflect transformations from this Ancestral Polynesian Society. In outlining the above Ancestral Polynesian model, we have thus laid bare the 'zero-point' from which Polynesian societies differentiated. To now understand the varied transformations of this ancestral base, we may begin by considering the dispersal to, and colonization by Polynesians of, the many widely separated islands. These processes of colonization and adaptation to new environments were the first stage in the evolution of the Polynesian chiefdoms.

> *All human action is carried on by knowledgeable agents who both construct the social world through their action, but yet whose action is also conditioned or constrained by the very world of their creation. In constituting and reconstituting the social world, human beings at the same time are involved in an active interplay with nature, in which they both modify nature and themselves.*
>
> Anthony Giddens (1981:54)

4
Dispersal, colonization, and adaptation

The westerly archipelagos of Fiji, Tonga, and Samoa – wherein Ancestral Polynesian Society developed from its Lapita ancestor – are but the threshold of greater Polynesia. In the mid first millennium BC, the Pacific waters rolling eastward from the ancestral homeland were a trackless unknown, as intergalactic space is to twentieth-century man. Having broken away from the inter-visible island arcs of Melanesia, and with continued improvements in canoe design and navigational skill, Ancestral Polynesians took the great voyaging leap eastwards (as well as northwards and southwards) into oceanic space, accomplishing the greatest purposeful dispersal in human history. Between some time in the late first millennium BC and the end of the first millennium AD, the most remote and lonely islands in the world, Easter Island and Hawai'i, along with several hundred others, were discovered and colonized.

In the previous chapter I reviewed linguistic, ethnobotanical, and archaeological evidence for the origins and development of Polynesian culture, and attempted a reconstruction of the broad outlines of Ancestral Polynesian Society. In the evolution of the Polynesian chiefdoms, the first steps toward differentiation from this ancestral society were those that accompanied dispersal: the inevitable reassortment of technology and society ('the founder effect') and the constraints of previously unencountered environments. In the present chapter, we shall look closely at the processes of adaptation that accompanied dispersal and colonization, processes that influenced the subsequent courses of evolution in particular archipelagos.

The Polynesian dispersal

The broad time-and-space framework for the dispersal of Polynesian peoples out of the Fiji–West Polynesian hearth is reasonably well established thanks to three decades of stratigraphic excavations. Nevertheless, some enigmas remain, and one of these concerns the initial eastward movement out of the western homeland. To date, the earliest known archaeological assemblages in East Polynesia are the sand dune occupation sites of Haʻatuatua on Nukuhiva, and Hane on Uahuka of the Marquesas Islands (Table 7). Both sites have yielded large artifact arrays, including a few Polynesian Plain Ware sherds, the only ceramics so far reported outside of West Polynesia. Some of these sherds may be from locally manufactured pots, but others derive from the Rewa Delta area of Viti Levu, Fiji (Dickinson and Shutler 1974). Also present at Haʻatuatua and Hane are adz forms characteristic of Polynesian Plain Ware contexts in Samoa and Tonga (e.g., Type V planoconvex sectioned adzes [Green and Davidson 1969b]), and other items that relate the early Marquesan sites with the terminal period of pottery manufacture in West Polynesia (Fig. 17). On the basis of these

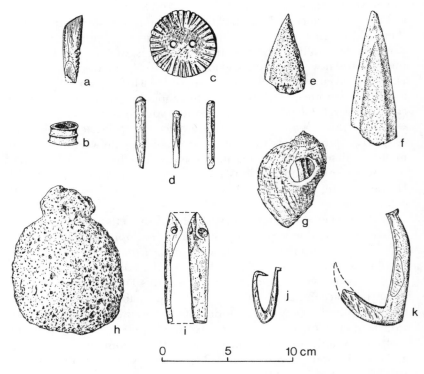

17. Early East Polynesian artifacts from the Marquesas Islands: a, shell chisel; b, bone reel ornament; c, pearl-shell ornament; d, three sea-urchin spine abraders; e,f, abraders of *Porites* coral; g, vegetable peeler of *Tonna* shell; h, stone plummet sinker; i, pearl-shell trolling lure; j,k, one-piece fishhooks of pearl-shell (after Suggs 1961).

materials, Y. Sinoto (1970, 1979a) proposed that the Marquesas archipelago was the first to be settled from the west, and subsequently served as the primary dispersal centre for East Polynesia.

The dating of the early Marquesan sites is unfortunately in a state of some confusion. From Ha'atuatua, Suggs (1961) originally obtained corrected ¹¹C age determinations of 2080 ± 150 BP and 1910 ± 180 BP. Sinoto (1970), however, questioned the precise cultural associations of Suggs's samples. For the Hane site, a series of seventeen ¹¹C dates were processed for the lower stratigraphic levels. Although Sinoto (1970) based his date of AD 300 for initial colonization of the Marquesas on this series, his reasons for selection of this age estimate are unclear. The seventeen determinations range from as early as 1915 ± 200 BP, to less than 250 years BP (Fig. 18). Upon close scrutiny, some ten dates, all by the Gakushuin Laboratory, form an overlapping group distinctly later in time than the cluster of determinations made by the Washington State University laboratory. It is likely that there were serious problems of contamination or insufficient pretreatment in the Gakushuin Laboratory, since their determinations are unacceptably late.

The above discussion of radiocarbon dates underscores the uncertainty of the present temporal framework for early Marquesan settlement. In my view, it is probable that Suggs's samples do date *in situ* cultural material (as Sinoto himself averred, 1970:113), and that an initial settlement of the Marquesas by the second century BC is likely.

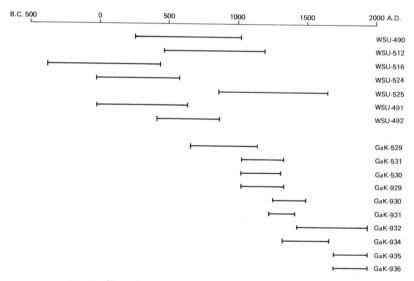

18. Radiocarbon age determinations for Layers V and VI at the Hane Dune Site, Ua Huka Island, Marquesas; bars represent 95 per cent confidence intervals based on Klein *et al.* (1982). See text for discussion.

Table 7. *Early East Polynesian sites*

Island and site	Type	^{14}C Age*	Reference
Marquesas			
Ha'atuatua (NHaal)	Dune site	2080 ± 150	Suggs 1961
Hane (MUH 1)	Dune site	1750 ± 140	Sinoto 1966
Societies			
Maupiti	Burial site	1090 ± 85	Emory and Sinoto 1964
Vaito'otia-Fa'ahia (ScH1-1)	Waterlogged site	1100 ± 70	Sinoto and McCoy 1975
Line Islands (Fanning)			
FAN1-7	Open midden	1560 ± 85	A. Sinoto 1973
Hawaiian Islands			
Bellows (O18)	Dune site	1600 ± 90	R. Pearson *et al.* 1971
Kawainui (Oa-G6-32)	Open site	1500 ± 145	Kelly and Clark 1980
Halawa (Mo-Al-3)	Dune site	1380 ± 90	Kirch and Kelly 1975
Pu'u Ali'i (H1)	Dune site	1660 ± 60	Emory, Bonk & Sinoto 1959
Waiahukini (H8)	Rockshelter	1195 ± 210	*Ibid.*
Henderson Island			
HEN-1	Rockshelter	790 ± 110	Sinoto ms.

Cook Islands			
Ureia (AIT.10)	Beach midden	969 ± 83	Bellwood 1978b
Kermadecs			
Low Flat Site (KO36/1)	Open midden	1035 ± 60	Anderson 1980b
New Zealand			
Wairau Bar	Midden with burials	940 ± 110	Duff 1956
Washpool	Midden	760 ± 41	Leach and Leach 1979

*Age BP (1950), T1/2 = 5568. Age given is usually only one of a series, and has been selected to best represent the age of *initial* occupation.

Geoff Irwin (1981) has recently gone further and suggested that East Polynesia may have been settled not long after Samoa and Tonga, early in the first millennium BC. He argues that since the rapid spread of Lapita colonizers throughout the western Pacific demonstrates their voyaging and colonizing abilities, there is no reason why they should have abruptly ceased their eastwards movement upon reaching Samoa and Tonga. It is possible, of course, that colonizing voyages did set off eastwards, but attempts to establish new settlements repeatedly failed until the Marquesas landfall late in the first millennium BC. Irwin's hypothesis is intriguing, although there is no concrete evidence as yet of East Polynesian settlement prior to that represented at Hane and Ha'atuatua.

In searching for evidence of early sites in any island group, serious sampling problems must be overcome. Early sites are never common, since initial population densities on any island were low. More important, these initial settlement sites have had the longest time for deep burial, erosion, submergence, or other disturbance by post-depositional processes. Spriggs (1981:125–42), for example, has recently claimed – on the basis of geomorphic evidence from the New Hebrides – that many early valley-bottom sites in Oceania are now deeply buried under alluvium resulting from human-induced forest clearance and erosion. Such a sampling problem may well exist in the Society Islands, another likely candidate for initial East Polynesian settlement. To date, only two relatively early sites, Maupiti and Vaito'otia-Fa'ahia, have been discovered in the Societies, and neither of these appears to be as old as Hane or Ha'atuatua in the Marquesas. It is noteworthy that both of these sites were discovered by *accident*, and that there has not been a systematic attempt at sub-surface sampling in those Society Island environments where initial settlement sites might predictably have been situated (e.g., on coastal plains near the larger, well-watered valleys and opposite passes through the barrier reef). This situation is compounded by the apparent recent subsidence of the Society group, so that early deposits may now lie up to 1 metre beneath sea level. At the coastal midden site of Te Amaama (Site ScMf-5) on Mo'orea, Green (Green *et al.* 1967:181–2) found that the lower 12″ of a 42″ thick deposit lay beneath the present water table. A charcoal sample from beneath the water table yielded a ^{14}C age of 760 ± 80 BP, indicating subsidence on the order of more than 0.3 metre since AD 1200. A similar stratigraphic situation obtained at the Hauiti Site (ScMf-2). In short, one suspects that the Society Islands could have been a locus of early East Polynesian settlement (cf. Bellwood 1970), and that for reasons of inadequate sampling strategy, we simply have not yet recovered the direct archaeological evidence.

At the present, we can with certainty state only that at least one central East Polynesian archipelago, the Marquesas, was settled by the last one or two centuries BC. The possibility of earlier sites in the Marquesas, or of other early settlements in the Society group (or even in the Cook Islands) remains unresolved on archaeological evidence. Linguistic data (Green 1966; Pawley 1966) indicate that whatever the location of the initial East Polynesian settlement (and whether over one archipelago or two adjacent ones) it remained an intact speech community long enough for certain lexical innovations to develop, prior to the further dispersal of colonists to the marginal extremes of East Polynesia: Easter Island, Hawai'i, and New Zealand.

There are good reasons to presume that the voyagers who colonized Easter Island were among the first to venture beyond the central East Polynesian homeland. Although the Rapanui language includes several Proto-East Polynesian lexical innovations, it also retains some archaic features, suggesting divergence of the ancestral Rapanui speech community earlier than other marginal East Polynesian groups. Among these retentions is the Proto-Polynesian glottal stop (*ʔ), noted by Green (1966:17). Ross Clark (1979:263) interprets the glotto-chronological evidence for East Polynesia as indicating 'about 1500 years of divergence' of Rapanui from the other central Eastern Polynesian languages. According to McCoy (1979:145) 'the agreement between glottochronological and radiocarbon dates place the settlement of the island at AD 400 to 500'. Such an age for initial settlement is further supported by the presence of early East Polynesian adz forms, as well as the absence of 'certain widespread materials items known to be of somewhat later origin than AD 500 in the primary dispersal centers of East Polynesia' (1979:145).

Several radiocarbon-dated occupation sites in the Hawaiian Islands document colonization of this northern Polynesian outpost by AD 300–500, probably not long after the settlement of Easter Island. The best-known early occupation site, at Bellows Beach, O'ahu, yielded several artifact forms closely related to those of the early Marquesan sites, including plano-convex adzes, pearl-shell, one-piece hooks with distinctive line-lashing devices, and an imitation porpoise-tooth pendant (Pearson, Kirch, and Pietrusewsky 1971; Kirch 1974). Only a few kilometres from the Bellows Site, Clark (Kelly and Clark 1980) tested buried deposits containing flaked stone, dated 1500 ± 145 BP. This site is situated on a slope adjacent to the present Kawainui Marsh, recently shown by the geologist Kraft to have been a marine embayment at the time of early human occupation of the area. The Pu'u Ali'i sand dune site on Hawai'i Island, also containing early East Polynesian artifact forms, may have been settled by the fourth century AD. The Halawa Dune Site on Moloka'i (Kirch and Kelly 1975) was settled by about AD 650, and contains archaic artifact forms. With regard to the initial Hawaiian colonization, it is worth noting that A. Sinoto (1973) recovered evidence of early East Polynesian occupation on Fanning

Island, just north of the equator and approximately half-way between central East Polynesia and Hawai'i. Site FAN1–7 yielded a corrected ^{14}C age determination of 1560 ± 85 BP, consistent with the Hawaiian data, and indicative of northerly voyaging by East Polynesians in the first few centuries of the Christian era.

Y. Sinoto (ms.), however, has recently disputed the evidence for settlement of Hawaii by AD 300–500, basing his argument on the absence, in the early Hawaiian sites, of diagnostic artifacts of his 'Archaic East Polynesian Culture', especially such items as shaped whale-tooth pendants, toggle-head harpoons, and *patu* hand clubs. There are, however, grounds for questioning Sinoto's attribution of these traits as 'archaic': they may in fact represent developments in central East Polynesia *after* the settlement of Easter and Hawai'i. Furthermore, these supposedly 'archaic' traits were notably absent in the earliest stratigraphic horizons (Layers VI and VII) at the Hane site (Y. Sinoto 1966:Fig. 3). Rather, the alternative hypothesis that these material culture traits represent *later developments* is consistent with the dating of Sinoto's 'archaic' site of Vaito'otia-Fa'ahia to *c.* AD 800–900 (Y. Sinoto 1979b).

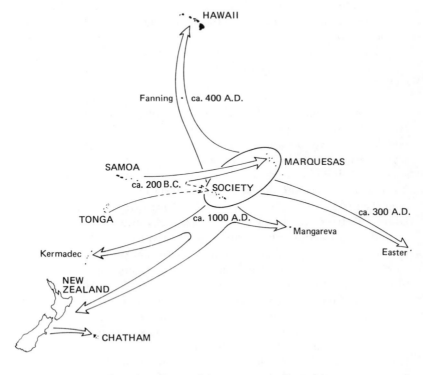

19. Polynesian dispersal patterns, as indicated by current archaeological and linguistic evidence.

While Polynesia's eastern and northern outposts were settled within the first few centuries of the Christian era, the southern extreme – New Zealand – did not witness man's arrival until about AD 800. The material culture of the early New Zealand sites – whale-tooth pendants, adz types, cloak pins, and so forth – clearly relates them to sites of the same age in the Society Islands (Y. Sinoto 1979a, b). A Society Islands origin for the Maori is further consistent with linguistic evidence, wherein Maori language is part of a Tahitian subgroup (Green 1966; Pawley 1966; R. Clark 1979).

The Chatham Islands, 860 km east of South Island, may have been first settled by drift voyagers from New Zealand not long after the latter was colonized. Sutton (1980:79) plausibly argues that 'a small founding population with little substantial chance of secondary settlement was involved'. Harsh environmental challenges in the Chathams must have placed remarkable pressures on the founding population.

Raoul Island in the Kermadec group, 1,000 km north-east of New Zealand, was evidently also colonized about the same time. A. J. Anderson (1980b) reports a midden site, with a basal radiocarbon age of 1015 ± 65 BP, containing the characteristic whale-tooth pendants and early adz forms. For unknown reasons, this Polynesian colony did not survive, and the island was uninhabited when rediscovered by Europeans late in the eighteenth century.

To sum up the current evidence for East Polynesian dispersals, it is likely that at least one successful ancestral East Polynesian settlement had been established in the Marquesas by the closing centuries of the first millennium BC (Fig. 19). From this (and possibly other) East Polynesian homeland(s), voyagers ventured eastward and northward to settle Easter Island and Hawai'i by AD 300–500. Another half-millennium later, the vast lands of New Zealand became the final outpost to be settled by the Polynesians. Beyond this archaeological and linguistic reconstruction of settlement events lies the fundamental issue of colonization strategies: what motives led the Polynesians to undertake these voyages of up to 4,000 km, and how were they able to so frequently succeed in founding viable communities in the new landfalls?

The challenge and strategy of colonization

The issue of colonization strategy raises the question of whether the Polynesian dispersal resulted from purposive voyages of discovery and settlement, or was largely the consequence of accidental drift of canoes. This question is the crux of a long-standing scholarly debate, fuelled in part by the writings of Andrew Sharp (1956), and dealt with at length by others (e.g., Golson 1962; Finney 1977). The answer is not an either/or proposition, and both purposive voyages of colonization and accidental drifts have actively influenced the geographical distribution of the Polynesians.

Computer simulations carried out by the geographers Levison, Ward, and Webb (1973) proved particularly enlightening in this debate. In essence, their computer experiments were designed to test the null hypothesis that all of the Polynesian islands could have been settled by successive drift voyages. The research approach was statistical, to assess the *relative probability* of drift from one island to any other, given our knowledge of Pacific Ocean winds and currents. Data on wind and current direction and force were compiled, for Marsden squares (5° of latitude and longitude) by month, and probability tables established. Using these stochastic data some 101,016 'voyages' were simulated from sixty-two different starting locations with three possible outcomes: (1) a landfall was reached; (2) the canoe was lost in a gale (wind Beaufort Force 9 or greater); or (3) the drift exceeded 183 days, the maximum length. The track of the canoe, as carried along by wind and current, was plotted each day. The end result of this truly mammoth simulation study is a set of drift contact probabilities, which allow a realistic assessment of the likelihood that certain island groups were ever settled by drift voyagers. For those islands with negligible drift-contact probabilities, we can be reasonably confident that colonization was a purposive matter.

While drift voyages could have resulted in the settlement of *some* islands, the initial movement from West to East Polynesia, as well as the settlement of such remote isolates as Hawai‘i, Easter, and New Zealand, was certainly due to intentional voyages against prevailing winds and currents. Not a single experimental voyage out of 16,000 drifts from 'starting points along the northern margins of central and eastern Polynesia' made a Hawaiian landfall (Levison *et al.* 1973:53). The authors were 'led to the conclusion that voyages from the Marquesas and Tahiti areas would have to be made by crews who intended to follow a northerly course, which implies a motive such as seeking new lands' (*ibid.*).

Given that the settlement of the Polynesian Triangle was predicated upon a purposive search for new lands, what motives could induce would-be colonizers to risk their lives in such an uncertain quest? The question may be more rhetorical than amenable to scientific testing, but it is worth posing. One possible motive for voyaging, suggested by a number of authors (e.g., Emory 1946:278; Suggs 1960a:106), is that of over-population, with resulting competition between local social groups leading to one or more of these departing the homeland, leaving those behind to take over its abandoned lands. Such scenarios are, indeed, witnessed in oral traditions, one of the best documented being the expulsion of the Nga Faea from Tikopia (Firth 1961:136–43). These people were driven from the Faea district by the rival Nga Ariki who, faced with land shortages, were desirous of the former's fertile garden lands. Rather than fall prey to the enemy, the Nga Faea elected to take to their canoes:

The women and children were in the canoes; many of the men swam alongside. According to one account, the canoes were decorated with barkcloth streamers, as if it were a gala ritual occasion. Wailing, the folk of Nga Faea abandoned the land, some of them supporting their chief on the deck of his vessel, holding him aloft in their arms, in the gesture of supreme respect which the Tikopia pay to men of rank (Firth 1961:139).

Whether this chief Tiako or any of his people ever settled new lands we shall never know. Handy (1930c:131) recorded another voyaging legend, from Hivaoa in the Marquesas, of a canoe named Kaahua, 'which made a voyage from Puamau in ancient times in search of lands'. An interesting detail is that the canoe is said to have carried 'a great quantity of breadfruit paste', evidently to sustain the party of men, women, and children during their quest.

One major objection voiced against population pressure and competition as a voyaging motive is that 'voyages left island groups much earlier than the stress of numbers is attested archaeologically' (Irwin 1980:328). While probably true for the larger islands, such as Upolu or Savaii in Samoa, we cannot assume that relatively high population densities were not reached on some smaller islands within a matter of a few centuries. In the first millennium BC, for example, the island of Niuatoputapu was less than one-half its present area, and a population of perhaps 1,000 persons might have put severe pressures on production, especially when compounded by the stress of periodic drought or cyclone. It is possible, then, that on some of the smaller islands population growth might have led to overcrowding, competition, and expulsion of a group within a comparatively short time after initial settlement.

Yen (1974a:75) alluded to extra-demographic inducements to migration when he wrote that, 'It will never be known whether the spurs to wider and earlier migrations were associated not merely with population considerations, but with the insufficiency of adjustments in some human ecosystems.' We know from archaeological evidence that Polynesian colonies were at one time established on some of the more tenuous habitats of the central Pacific, such as the drought-prone equatorial atolls. It is conceivable that colonists in such harsh environments, unable to produce at a constant subsistence level, chose to move on in search of better prospects.

Although demographic and ecological pressures probably motivated a goodly number of colonization voyages, one must question whether such pressures alone could have led to the extraordinary dispersal witnessed in Polynesia. The opposition between senior and junior siblings, or between branches of a descent group, may also have provided a motive for voyaging in search of new lands to colonize. The younger brother of a chief might well be enticed by the possibilities of establishing his line as foremost in a new island, and quarrels between rival siblings could have led the loser to flee with his followers. Such motives for colonization are not mere speculation, for just such scenarios are encoded in Polynesian myth. In the great cosmogonic myths of Polynesia, it is Maui – the younger brother – who goes fishing with his magic hook to pull islands from the sea (Luomala 1949). Another well-known instance is the Hawaiian legend of Pa'ao, who was forced to leave his ancestral homeland in Kahiki after a falling out with his older brother, Lonopele. Arriving in Hawai'i, the younger brother Pa'ao became a 'stranger king' (Sahlins 1981b), deposing the existing chief and establishing a new line of ruling paramounts. Whether the legend is historically 'true' matters not, for the structure it represents is real, and formed the basis upon which the actions of real men were formulated.

It might appear unscientific or incurably romantic to suggest that 'wanderlust' could have been a motive for migration, yet some culturally ingrained ethic of exploration and discovery may have played a vital role in Polynesian dispersal. Moving over the course of several thousand years through the island arcs of the south-western Pacific, Polynesian ancestors would have built up a conception of the Pacific as a sea of islands, more bridge than barrier. Thus the Polynesian explorer might well have 'set sail . . . in search of new land, confident in the belief that, as usual, islands would rise over the horizon to meet him' (Levison *et al.* 1973:64). Certainly, Polynesian mythology is replete with tales of the great culture heroes, like Ru, who went in search of new lands. The folklorist Luomala has claimed that 'one of the many reasons why Polynesians set out on hazardous voyages to other islands is the restless desire to visit strange places, to go sightseeing' (1955:27). Firth (1936:18–21) describes just such an attitude for the Tikopia. Too frequently, perhaps, Western anthropologists attribute the actions of 'primitive' peoples to environmental or utilitarian motives. But to the Polynesians, the 'undiscovered lands beyond the horizon' were a 'space frontier as the solar system is today' (Levison *et al.* 1973:4), and the simple desire to conquer this frontier may have dominated all other motives for voyaging and colonization.

A curious and unexplained aspect of Polynesian voyaging is that the purposeful expeditions which reached every habitable island by about AD 1000 seemed to have abruptly ceased not long after this date. In Hawai'i, New Zealand, Easter Island, the Marquesas, and other islands, canoe technology changed radically from ocean-going designs to those suited only for inshore sailing. Two-way inter-island voyaging did continue in central Polynesia, especially between and within the Society and Tuamotu island chains, and amongst the West Polynesian archipelagos, but here distances were much shorter. As Irwin notes, 'we are faced with the situation that once virtually every scrap of land in the Pacific had been settled, the process stopped' (1980:328). Since it is unlikely that there was any 'widespread underlying reason for the ending of voyages, it suggests that information that the islands had been successfully colonized was transmitted back to the sources' (*ibid.*). Whether this was so may prove to be an untestable proposition, but one that hints at the complexities of Polynesian dispersal and colonization.

Polynesian colonization strategies

The successful establishment of a human population on a remote and previously uninhabited Pacific island was surely neither a simple nor easy task. Successful colonization required a maritime technology to transport cultigens and domestic animals and methods for their establishment, strategies to exploit the natural resources of the new habitat upon arrival, and a reproductive strategy to ensure that the new propagule did not go to extinction within a few decades. The issue of colonization strategies is one that Polynesian prehistorians have not carefully considered, even though this initial phase was absolutely critical in influencing the direction of subsequent adaptation and evolution on any island or archipelago. Direct archaeological evidence for certain aspects of colonization strategy (such as reproduction) may admittedly be difficult or impossible to obtain. As in other facets of island pre-history, however, the first step in obtaining answers is to formulate appropriate questions.

The ocean-going capabilities of Polynesian double-canoes have been the focus of recent experimentation, most spectacularly the voyages of the *Hokule'a* (Finney 1977). Not only canoe design, but such factors as the social organization of the crew and their ability to withstand considerable psychological stress are at issue. Direct evidence of pre-historic canoe design and construction techniques has recently been forthcoming from excavations at the uniquely waterlogged site of Vaito'otia-Fa'ahia (Fig. 20) on Huahine, Society Islands, dating to AD 850–1200 (Sinoto 1979b). Anaerobic conditions have preserved adzed planks 'probably used on the front and back ends of the double canoe platforms' (*ibid*:13). Sinoto suggests an extrapolated canoe length of 24 metres (80 ft). By way of comparison, the experimental canoe *Hokule'a* is 18.9 metres (62 ft) long, and carried a crew of seventeen persons (Finney 1977). Also recovered at Huahine was a steering paddle 3.8 metres long. Clearly, vessels of this size were capable of transporting organized expeditions of as many as twenty to thirty colonists along with their stocks of domestic animals and crop plants.

Since the natural biota of the Polynesian islands lacked much in the way of edible plants, or terrestrial game other than birds, the establishment of imported vegetative stocks of crop plants and of breeding pairs of domestic animals would have received the greatest priority. Many of the earliest East Polynesian sites contain faunal evidence for one or more domestic animals, and evidence for the transport of plant materials exists in the form of anthropophilic land snails which were carried inadvertently in adhering soil (Christensen and Kirch 1981a, b). In a fledgling colony's first years, transplanted cultigens and animals could not have provided a sufficient basis for subsistence, and the settling party would have had to depend heavily upon naturally abundant resources, particularly shellfish, fish, wild birds, and wild plants (such as indigenous bracken fern rhizomes). Initial settlement sites, when archaeologically excavated, show the unmistakable signs of such intensive exploitation of natural resources. Site TK-4 on Tikopia, colonized about 900 BC, though only about 4,500 m² in area, and with a deposit averaging *c.* 30 cm in depth, contains an estimated 70 metric tons of molluscs (Kirch and Yen 1982). Also present are large quantities of marine turtle, fish bone, and a considerable range of land and sea birds (Fig. 21). The megapode, a galliform bird, was locally extirpated within the first few years of settlement doubtless due to predation. Similar emphasis on marine exploitation has been noted for the earliest stratigraphic horizons of the Hane dune site in the Marquesas Islands (Kirch 1973).

The most critical aspect of colonization strategy is certainly the reproduction of the human propagule. The size and age–sex composition of the population were essential in determining whether the colony would survive and grow, or head irreversibly toward extinction. MacArthur and Wilson (1967) and Richter-Dyn and Goel (1972) have discussed survivorship theory in general terms, noting that the critical

20. Two wooden canoe planks with lashing holes, and a wooden bowl, at the waterlogged Fa'ahia site, Huahine Island, Society Islands (*photo courtesy Y.H. Sinoto, Bishop Museum*).

factors are (1) the size of the founding propagule, N, (2) the per capita birth rate, λ (3) the per capita death rate, μ, and (4) the carrying capacity of the environment, K (see also Black 1979:65–6). With human populations, the matter of carrying capacity is complicated, since more than static environmental parameters are involved, including the level of technology. Ideally, N should be as large as possible, and a high rate of intrinsic population growth (r) should be 'accomplished by a small death rate rather than by a large birth rate' (McArthur and Wilson 1967:78). Thus the ratio $(\lambda-\mu)/\lambda = r$ should be large. Furthermore, 'when K is small ... the expected time to extinction is small, and colonists must reinvade frequently to maintain the species' (*ibid.*). Establishing precise λ or μ values for colonists is probably impossible on archaeological data, but our knowledge of canoe capacities suggests an upper limit of about thirty persons for N. Quantitative estimates of K are extremely difficult to calculate (cf. Glassow 1978), and the size of an island is only a very rough index of K. It is doubtless significant, however, that several rather small islands, with correspondingly low K values, once supported Polynesian colonies which subsequently went to extinction (these are further discussed below).

In an important study, McArthur, Saunders, and Tweedie (1976) used computer-generated simulation to assess the potential survival probabilities of Polynesian propagules of 6, 10, and 14 (formed of 3, 5, and 7 couples). The effects on survival probability of increasing N are obvious: with a propagule of 6 in which the only marriage rule was a

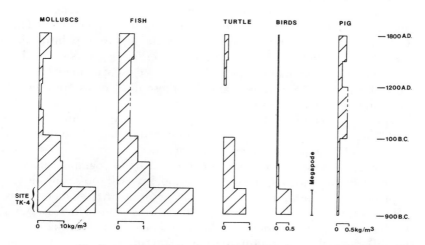

21. General trends in the exploitation of major faunal groups throughout the Tikopia sequence, as reflected in estimates of usable meat per cubic metre of archaeological deposit. Note the great reduction in all wild animal foods following the initial colonization phase represented by Site TK-4.

ban on incest, probability of extinction was as high as 77 per cent, whereas increasing N to 14 (7 couples) lowered the extinction probability to 19 per cent. As MacArthur and Wilson (1967:89–92) originally observed, reproductive value, determined by the age structure of females and their associated fertility rates, also has a significant effect on survival. For a propagule of 10 in which the females are between seventeen and twenty-one years, the extinction probability is only 28 per cent, whereas with females between the ages of twenty-six and thirty, this probability rises to 77 per cent (McArthur *et al.* 1976: Table 2).

In their classic study of island biogeography, MacArthur and Wilson (1967) argued that different selection pressures affect reproductive strategies of colonizing versus established populations. Their so-called r/K selection model takes its terms from the Verhulst–Pearl logistic difference equation that describes a sigmoid population-growth curve:

$$\frac{dN}{dt} = rN \left(\frac{K-N}{K} \right)$$

Population size, N, is a function of the intrinsic rate of increase, r, constrained by the carrying capacity or resource threshold of the environment. For humans, the latter is, of course, not an absolute parameter, but one that is dependent upon the technology and production strategy of the particular population under study. In the MacArthur–Wilson model, which Diamond (1977) among others has suggested is applicable to human populations, a spectrum of reproductive strategies is idealized as two dichotomized patterns. At one end of the spectrum are populations with a high intrinsic rate of increase, operating in the absence of substantial competition or other density-dependent effects. Colonizing species or populations, such as the 'supertramp' birds discussed by Diamond (1977) are characteristically r-strategists. On the other hand are populations in which growth is closely regulated in the face of intense competition. Naturally, these ideal types are merely endpoints on a continuum.

The r/K selection model as developed by MacArthur and Wilson (1967) was, however, applied to non-human populations, and to the selection of genetic determinants of reproductive behaviour. Despite the claims of Diamond (1977) and others that such biogeographic models are relevant to human groups, the r/K model is itself too simplistic to explain Polynesian adaptation to the reproductive challenge of colonization. In humans, for example, the intrinsic rate of increase, r, is closely regulated by a variety of cultural and behavioural mechanisms, including social organization (marriage patterns, tabus), post-partum tabu or other spacing mechanisms, infanticide, abortion, warfare, immigration, and so forth. Nevertheless, while the basic r/K model does not account for the complexities of human reproduction and demography, it does appear that human groups in Oceania responded

– *technologically and socially* – to density conditions. There are good reasons to believe that, over time, changes in population size and density of particular islands led to modifications in reproductive rates.

In general, groups of colonizing Polynesians probably exhibited rapid population growth (not constrained by such practices as abortion, infanticide, or warfare), generalizing and broad-based subsistence practices, and only weakly developed socio-political controls on production. In contrast, later populations that had achieved high levels of density appear to have shifted to conscious regulation of population growth, along with economic and ecological specialization, well-developed socio-political controls on production, and intense competition. This shift from density-independent to density-dependent adaptations seems to have occurred both on individual islands and over whole archipelagos, and is a basic feature of Polynesian technological and social evolution. Chapter 5 explores this shift in greater detail, and assesses certain archaeological and palaeodemographic data for testing the model outlined here.

Adaptation in new environments

Thus far, we have been concerned largely with the challenges and response strategies directly related to initial voyaging and successful transfer of cultural landscapes. As demonstrated in Chapter 2, the diversity of island environments within Polynesia would also have posed substantial adaptive challenges to founding populations. The process of adaptation to these new environmental conditions forms a critical part of the evolution of Polynesian societies.

Since colonizing parties of Polynesians were small, and therefore representative of only a portion of the cultural–behavioural variability inherent in the 'mother' population, something akin to the 'founder effect' known to geneticists (e.g., Mayr 1942; Dobzhansky 1963:71–2) may have operated to produce rapid change in island cultures. As argued by Vayda and Rappaport, 'if the migration to an isolated place, whether a small island or a large continent, is by a relatively small group of people who are unable to reproduce in full the culture of the population from which they derived, then the culture in the new place will be immediately different from the culture in the homeland' (1963:134–5). It is indeed likely that certain initial changes in technology, resource exploitation strategy, or even in religious practice, were due to this founder effect.

On the other hand, to the extent that the new environment differed in certain respects from the homeland – as it sometimes radically did (as in the case of New Zealand) – technology and behaviour patterns transferred from the homeland would have undergone an immediate reassortment or segregation. Yen (1973a) has emphasized this aspect of

Table 8. *Cultigens and domestic animals in various Polynesian island groups*

Island group	Farinaceous annuals	Tree crops	Other crops	Dog	Pig	Fowl
Western Polynesia						
Futuna	9	9	6	X	X	X
'Uvea	8	9	6	X	X	X
Tonga	9	8	6	X	X	X
Eastern Polynesia						
Societies	7	7	5	X	X	X
Marquesas	7	6	5	X	X	X
Easter Island	5	1	3	—	—	X
Hawai'i	6	3	4	X	X	X
Tuamotus	3	1	0	—	X	—
New Zealand	4	0	2	X	—	—

adaptation to new environments, with particular reference to agricultural systems. The 'detachable parts of former environments', such as planting stocks, tools, and cultural concepts, 'together with the elements of natural exploitation, have to undergo a *reassortment or resegregation* as a first step in the colonization of a new island' (1973a:76, my italics). The progress of this introductory-developmental sequence is 'dictated by the ultimate constraints offered by the new environment', and in the case of agricultural systems, by the 'genetic flexibility of the introduced species' (*ibid.*). The effect of such resegregation is evident in the distribution of plants and domestic animals throughout Polynesia (Table 8). East Polynesian groups suffered a reduction in the number of crop species and domestic animals, all of which are adventive to the region. This reduction may be due in part to a failure to attempt the transfer process, or to failure of planting stocks or breeding animals to survive lengthy sea voyages. It is clear, however, that where crop reductions were most severe, for example, the Tuamotus and New Zealand, these were due to particularly harsh environmental constraints. Polynesian crops were tropical in origin and in ecological template, and only four species were sufficiently adaptable to withstand the temperate climate of New Zealand. In the Tuamotus, atoll constraints of limited water and poor soils posed equally stringent challenges to an ancestral agricultural economy.

The reassortment and adaptation of technological systems is well illustrated in the case of fishing gear excavated from early Marquesan archaeological contexts. Early levels of the Hane and Ha'atuatua sites yielded an unusual range of one-piece fishhook types, both in form and size. This variability is explicable, however, when we contrast the Marquesan situation with that of the West Polynesian homeland. In the western archipelagos, angling with one-piece fishhooks evidently did not constitute a dominant fishing strategy, owing to the greater productivity of netting and spearing in lagoons and broad reef flats (Kirch and Dye 1979). When the first colonists of the Marquesas moved from their lagoon-reef homeland environment, they were confronted with a new set of environmental conditions – rocky headlands and deep bays with limited coral growth – not suited to the fishing strategies that had been developed in the western tropical islands. The adaptive response to these conditions was a rapid increase in experimentation and innovation with angling gear (Fig. 22). Fishing gear in later Marquesan sites again became less variable and highly standardized (with essentially one form of jabbing hook). This subsequent reduction in fishhook variability represents the effect of variety-limiting selection upon the earlier range of experimental behaviour, with the few forms that proved effective in the new environment ultimately becoming the only fishhook types manufactured (see also Kirch 1980b:115–17).

Processes of adaptation to environment are often best exemplified in situations where constraints are especially severe, or where the shift from one habitat to another is marked by unusual ecological differences. The Polynesian Triangle provides several instances of such conditions, with a number of marginal islands and with temperate New Zealand, particularly South Island.

Not all attempts at island colonization and adaptation succeeded. Within Polynesia are at least twelve islands that, while initially colonized by man at some point in the past, lacked Polynesian occupants when rediscovered by European voyagers in the eighteenth century. These 'mystery islands' as Bellwood dubbed them represent unsuccessful experiments in colonization and adaptation. As a perusal

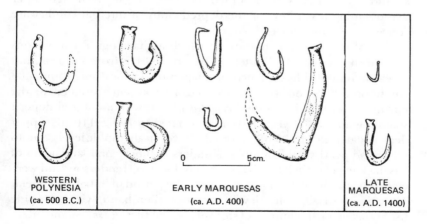

22. Adaptation and change in Marquesan angling gear; see text for discussion (after Kirch 1980a).

Table 9. *Polynesian islands unoccupied at European contact*

Island	Type	Area (km²)	Ecological constraints
Howland	Cay	1.3	Fresh water limited
Washington	Closed atoll	10.3	Fresh water limited
Fanning	Atoll	33.5	Fresh water limited
Christmas	Atoll	645.0	Fresh water limited
Malden	Closed atoll	10.0	Fresh water limited
Palmerston	Atoll	n.a.	n.a.
Suwarrow	Atoll	0.4	Fresh water limited
Nihoa	High volcanic	0.6	Fresh water limited; no timber; no fringing reef
Necker	High volcanic	0.2	Fresh water limited; no timber; no fringing reef
Pitcairn	High volcanic	5.2	No fringing reef
Henderson	Makatea	38.7	Fresh water limited
Raoul	High volcanic	29.4	Active volcano

of Table 9 indicates, all of these islands (with the exception of Christmas atoll) are rather small, with correspondingly limited carrying capacities. Most of them suffer additional constraints, such as limited sources of fresh water and absence of timber, or in the case of Raoul Island, from volcanic hazard. It is indeed likely that 'insufficiency of adjustments' to these harsh ecosystems led their colonizing populations to abandon them after a relatively short time (cf. Yen 1974a:75). On others, however, we have evidence that populations persisted for several hundred years at least (e.g., Pitcairn, see Gathercole 1964; and Raoul, see A.J. Anderson 1980b). Why such larger and fertile islands should have ceased to be occupied is indeed a mystery, though either demographic instability, or the depredations of internal conflict are conceivable causes for extinction.

One of the 'mystery' islands on which archaeological excavations have been conducted, Henderson Island (169 km from Pitcairn), has revealed remarkable evidence of adaptation to local environmental conditions. Y. Sinoto (ms.) excavated a rockshelter situated in the northern cliff of this uplifted, *makatea* island, with a cultural deposit spanning about 300 years (basal layer dated to 790 ± 110 BP, upper deposit dated 495 ± 105 BP). From the lower stratigraphic levels, Sinoto recovered pearl-shell fishhooks, abraders of block coral, and adzes of basalt. The pearl shell and basalt are not local to Henderson, and were evidently imported at, or not long after, the period of initial settlement. The upper stratigraphic levels, on the other hand, yielded crude fishhooks of local hammer-oyster shell, coral files of *Porites*, and adzes of fossilized *Tridacna* shell available in the island's upraised limestone (Fig. 23). As Sinoto writes, 'gradual material adaptation . . . is excellently

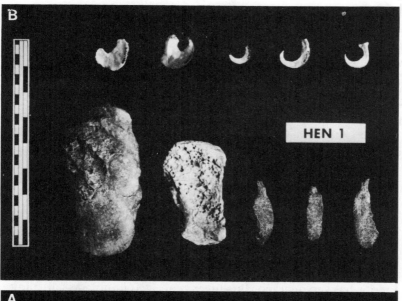

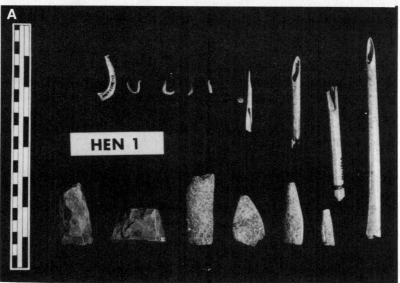

23. Artifacts excavated from upper and lower levels of a rock-shelter site (HEN 1) on Henderson Island, illustrating local adaptation in material culture. A. Artifacts from the lower level include adzes of non-local basalt, files of *Porites* coral, pearl-shell fishhooks of Marquesan type (possibly imports); and cut bird bone. B. Artifacts from the intermediate and upper levels include adzes of fossilized *Tridacna* shell, files of *Porites* coral, and fishhooks of local *Isognomon* shell (*photo courtesy Y.H. Sinoto, Bishop Museum*).

demonstrated. As the materials that were brought to Henderson were exhausted, the locally available resources were exploited' (ms.:4–5).

With the colonization of New Zealand, Polynesians from the tropical, central archipelagos of East Polynesia (probably the Society Islands) suddenly faced drastically different environmental conditions which truly challenged their ingenuity and ability to adapt. Even in the north, where the climate is milder, only four of the crop species transferred from the tropical homeland would survive the temperate climate (Table 8). Most interesting, however, are the adaptations undergone by those who settled the far southerly regions, south of the Banks Peninsula. A resurgence of archaeological work in Southland over the past decade has provided much new data on the processes by which colonizing tropical East Polynesian agriculturalists were transformed to temperate hunters-and-gatherers (A.J. Anderson 1982a, 1982b, 1983; Hamel 1982).

Though Southland is a vast region – especially for people used to relatively small islands – its constraints were formidable. The coast regions have a mean annual temperature of about 10°C, and the interior has very marked climatic extremes. Not only was agriculture impossible with the Polynesian crop inventory, but the range of naturally occurring starchy plants was limited, with the New Zealand *ti* (*Cordyline australis*) as the only major species. Southland's coasts are relatively exposed, and lack the coral reefs and great species diversity known to the colonizing East Polynesians in their homeland islands.

Despite such constraints, the land offered new possibilities for forging a subsistence regime on which to base stable, if not very dense, populations. The productivity of the southern ocean is quite high, and the coastal regions are rich in several species of fish (barracouta, red cod, blue cod, and groupers), in seabirds (penguins, albatrosses, petrels, shearwaters, and shags), and in sea mammals (fur seals, sea lions). Most remarkable, however, were the large ratite birds.

For the first Polynesian voyagers to step ashore, the luxuriant forest held a surprise at once familiar and bizarre: birds in form not unlike the tropical housefowls they called *moa* but here materialized in the size of dreams. Some, the height of a child, busily scratched at the litter on the forest floor; others, the height of a man, pecked and tore at the shrubbery; and still others, half as tall again, reached up into the foliage of the trees (Anderson 1983:8).

These 'marvellous fowls' ranged in size from the small *Megalapteryx didinus*, weighing perhaps 15–30 kg, up to the impressive *Dinornis giganteus*, with a body weight of 125–230 kg. In short, the pioneering East Polynesians had been thrust upon 'a land for hunting, fishing and gathering, more or less in that order' (A.J. Anderson 1982b:49).

These new and drastically different environmental conditions clearly put pressures upon the archaic Polynesian technology and subsistence strategies, requiring significant adaptation. Although much of the material culture in Archaic Southland sites retains its East Polynesian forms (as in the adzes and ornament styles), certain aspects of technology directly related to subsistence underwent significant change. As Anderson notes, 'one of the most striking features of the fishing patterns is the scarcity of evidence of the netting–trapping complex which is so prominent historically in northern New Zealand and elsewhere in Polynesia' (*ibid*:51). Angling gear, on the other hand, underwent a phase of experimentation and proliferation of forms, in a manner directly analogous to the Marquesan case described earlier. The new emphasis on hunting is also reflected archaeologically by the development of large silcrete and porcellanite blades and flake tools used for *moa* butchering, and of large earth ovens for processing *moa* flesh.

The early Archaic settlement patterns also reflect the process of adaptation to a hunting and fishing way of life. As shown in Figure 24, large multi-function bases, situated along the coast (frequently at the mouths of interior-trending rivers), were linked with a series of inland staging, transit, and base camps. *Moa* hunting proceeded from these base camps, where, as at the Hawksburn site (A.J. Anderson 1979a), large numbers of earth ovens and flake tools indicate the emphasis on *moa* processing. Other specialized sites linked into this settlement pattern were stone quarries (for silcrete and porcellanite in the interior, and for basalt and chalcedony on the coast), and coastal restricted-function sites, such as fishing camps. Despite the shift in subsistence from agriculture to hunting–fishing–gathering, the adaptation of settlement patterns did not lead to a fully transient pattern. Indeed, there was probably a strong desire on the part of the colonizing East Polynesians to lead a settled existence, such as is evidenced by the primary coastal multi-function bases (such as Papatowai, Little Papanui, Murdering Beach, Shag Mouth, and other well-known Archaic sites). Permanent settlement, however, required an effective means of food storage, and here again the adaptive ingenuity of the colonizing Polynesians is reflected. Methods were developed to preserve meat in kelp bags, sealed with fat and made airtight (A.J. Anderson 1983:21–2), which made it possible to 'organize food gathering activities to take the maximum advantage of seasonally abundant resources'.

While adaptations in material culture and settlement pattern are most clearly evidenced in the archaeological record, there are also suggestions of significant changes in social organization. Anderson has speculated that the Archaic period in Southland may have seen a 'restructuring of Polynesian society to New Zealand life':

A small population, and very probably an asymmetric one in terms of the social structure from which it derived, would have been intent upon establishing new systems of political power and prestige as the 'colonial effect' struck home: the release from traditional social stratification and sources of wealth. Competition by small groups, perhaps centered on the multi-function bases, for new

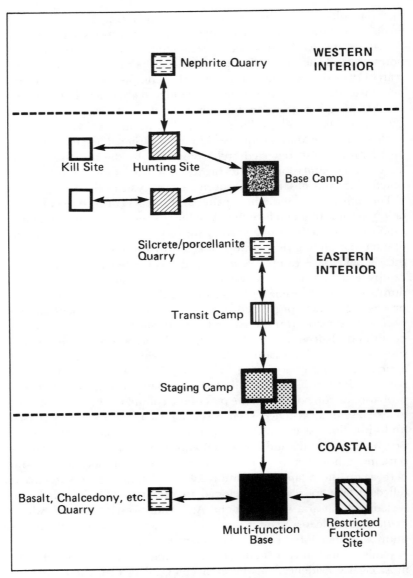

24. Archaic settlement pattern in the South Island, New Zealand, reflecting adaptation to a dominantly hunting–gathering and fishing subsistence mode (after A.J. Anderson 1982b).

territories, a different 'pecking-order' and a new scale of material values could have involved conspicuous consumption of big game, territorial marking by painting and the display of technological virtuosity (and thereby wealth) in decorative artefactual styles (1982b:69).

Overview

The differentiation of Ancestral Polynesian Society began with the dispersal of colonizing populations, first to the central eastern archipelagos, and later to the more remote, marginal outposts. Change was implicit in the colonization process, with the founder effect operative on various aspects of culture. Equally important were the environmental conditions and constraints featured in each island group, many of which required immediate adaptations or adjustments, in technology, subsistence strategies, settlement patterns, and social relations. Thus, the colonization phase in any island sequence may be regarded as a significant period of reassortment of social and technological systems. In some islands, especially the smaller ones, environmental challenges proved to be too severe, and pioneering groups either left in search of more hospitable lands, or failed to reproduce themselves. On most of the larger islands, however, the colonization process was successful, and the seeds of new societies became firmly rooted, their features now more closely adapted to local conditions, but still carrying the imprint of Ancestral Polynesian Society.

5
The demographic factor

Population growth – from small founding propagules to large and densely settled societies – is a fundamental aspect of all Polynesian developmental sequences. Jack Golson maintained that 'even though the colonizing groups were probably small, their capacity to increase would be enormous in the untouched and generally benign environments of the Pacific Islands and with the technology and economy' at the command of the Polynesians (1972a:29). In the previous chapter, I argued that a relatively high intrinsic rate of population increase would have been essential to a successful strategy of island colonization, and indeed, that rapid population growth helped to assure a propagule's permanence. In a study of historical data relating to population increase on three isolated islands, Birdsell (1957) demonstrated that small colonizing groups, such as those that settled the outposts of Polynesia, are certainly capable of growing at a very fast rate, with doubling times on the order of one generation. In the case of the *Bounty* mutineers, who with their Tahitian wives settled remote Pitcairn Island, the intrinsic rate of increase (r) approximated 0.04. There is no reason to suppose that growth rates among colonizing prehistoric Polynesians were appreciably lower than that of Pitcairn.

At the same time, it is clear that the exponential rates of population growth which characterized early phases of settlement on Polynesian islands were not generally operative when the European explorers arrived on the scene, one or more millennia later. These early observers reported large and relatively dense populations in which a variety of cultural and natural mechanisms served to maintain island populations at essentially static levels. The practice of infanticide for example, so abhorrent to missionaries and explorers, was endemic among the Society Islanders (Oliver 1974:424–6), and is reported for other Polynesian populations as well (e.g., Firth 1936; Kamakau 1961: 234). Thus, while initial population growth rates were high, a balance between human numbers and the capacity of their insular environments to maintain them had to be reached during the development of each Polynesian chiefdom. As Brookfield (1976) avers, a concept of *popu-*

lation thresholds is necessary, given that the resources – renewable and non-renewable – of any island ecosystem have finite limits. This is not the simple deterministic process it might at first appear, however, and the relationships between population, environment, and socio-economic and political structures were complexly interwoven.

These complex interrelationships are well portrayed in a model of island carrying capacity developed by Bayliss-Smith (1974), re-produced here as Figure 25. The size of an island population is regulated by two kinds of *constraint*: cultural and ecological. Ecological constraints comprise the total land area, the effects of periodic natural disasters, deterioration of the environment due to over-exploitation, limits on productivity, and basic nutritional requirements. Cultural constraints include controls on fertility and mortality, production beyond basic subsistence needs ('social' or 'trade' production; cf.

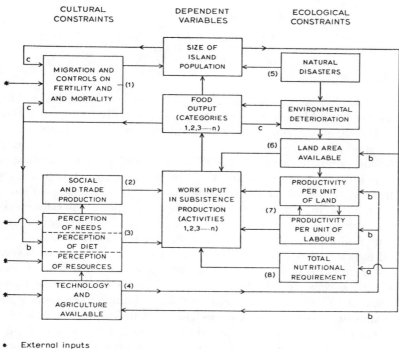

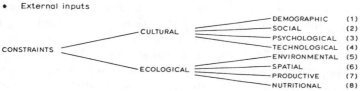

25. A model of cultural and ecological constraints affecting island populations (*courtesy of T. Bayliss-Smith, Cambridge University*).

Table 10. *Estimated populations of the principal islands and archipelagos at European contact*

Island or group	Total population*	Population of maximal political unit	Total land (km²)	Arable land (km²)†	Density (N/km²)††
Hawaiian Is.	200,000	30,000	16,633	1,663	120
Tongan Is.	40,000	40,000	696	487	82
Society Is.	45,000	9,000	1,535	460	98
Samoan Is.	80,000	25,000	2,829	810	99
Easter Is.	7,000	3,500	160	106	66
'Uvea	4,000	4,000	59	40	68
Mangaia	3,000	3,000	70	40	75
Marquesas Is.	35,000	1,500	1,058	529	66
Futuna	2,000	2,000	62	40	50
New Zealand	115,000	3,500	265,146	10,000	11

* Best estimate based on ethnographic and archaeological evidence.
† Estimate based on environmental data available.
†† Density per area of *arable* land.

Brookfield 1972), psychological perceptions of diet and needs, and the level of available technology and agricultural skills.

The significance of demographic variables for the evolution of the Polynesian chiefdoms is highlighted by a consideration of the contact-period populations of the major island groups (prior to the massive depopulation which occurred nearly everywhere as a result of introduced disease). Table 10 presents population estimates for ten of the main archipelagos and islands of Polynesia, along with estimates of the size of a maximal political unit (that under the control of a paramount chief). Also provided are data on total and arable land, and an estimate of population density in relation to arable land. Several significant conclusions may be drawn from these data. First, for all islands except New Zealand, there is a strong correlation between population and total land area ($R = 0.97$), reinforcing the proposition that most Polynesian populations had reached some threshold level of balance between numbers and resources. (The fact that New Zealand is something of an anomaly, supporting for example only slightly more than half as many people as Hawai'i on sixteen times the land area, is accounted for by the more severe constraints of the New Zealand climate acting upon the tropical Oceanic crops.) The correlation between population and arable land is also reasonably high ($R = 0.49$), suggesting that agricultural resources were a significant limiting factor to population increase.

Somewhat more suggestive are the relationships between population size, density, and the degree of social stratification in Polynesian societies (see Table 2). As shown in Figure 26, there is a reasonably consistent correlation between the degree of stratification, as measured by Sahlins's (1958) criteria, and the population size of the maximal political unit. A similar correlation, shown in Figure 26, obtains between population density per square kilometre of arable land and degree of stratification. Clearly, demographic variables relate significantly to socio-political complexity in Polynesia. We must let caution reign, however, and stop short of positing particular causal relationships between demography and socio-political complexity. Lacking direct historical evidence, one could argue either the primacy of population growth as a spur to increased stratification, or – conceivably – the reverse proposition, that increased stratification allowed chiefs to bring neighbouring groups under their sway thus swelling the size of the chiefdom. Indeed, these two scenarios are not necessarily mutually exclusive. Obviously, we need accurate diachronic data for prehistoric Polynesian populations, data which can be compared with parallel archaeological evidence for social stratification, from mortuary remains, settlement patterns, and the like.

Polynesian islands – and especially the more isolated ones such as Hawai'i, Easter, and New Zealand – provide unique opportunities for the study of demographic processes. This is due to several factors. First, the remote Polynesian islands were colonized relatively recently, providing short, controlled time-frames. Second, due to their isolation, such islands have been colonized only once or twice, by small founding populations. Third, and particularly important, the isolation of many

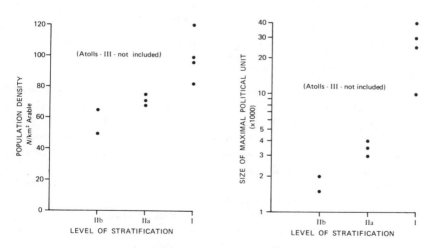

26. Population density and size of maximal political units for nine Polynesian societies, plotted in relation to Sahlins's categories of social stratification.

Polynesian islands has effectively barred both immigration and emigration, allowing one to discount the effects of exogenous population movements. Finally, being precisely bounded, islands are microcosms with sharply defined limits to the development and intensification of production. Because of these opportunities for analytical control, the remoter Polynesian islands are excellent localities in which to undertake archaeological investigations of the relations between demography, environment, and cultural systems.

Archaeologists and prehistorians have displayed varying attitudes toward the role of population growth and density in Polynesian culture history. Some have simply ignored demographic considerations, a reflection of the difficulties of obtaining accurate population estimates from archaeological data. A few, however, have recognized the fundamental role of demographic change in the evolution of Polynesian societies. Suggs, whose Marquesan work stands out for its forward-looking theoretical base, held population growth to be a major factor in Marquesan cultural change, leading to settlement expansion out of the favourable windward valleys to more marginal leeward habitats, and to inter-tribal warfare and competition (1960a:119, 128; 1961:182). Suggs argued that population growth and political intensification were intimately linked in the Marquesas:

> a large population was producing a sizeable food surplus which was appropriated by the upper classes of Marquesan society, the chiefs and priests, and utilized in supporting the population in large public works that of course also reflected the glory of the chiefs and priests, reinforcing their power   (1960a:128).

> The cause of the intense prestige rivalry may be seen in the relation of the population to the habitable land. As the population increased beyond the point at which all possible ecological niches became filled, intergroup conflicts over land would have increased . . . The need to acquire and hold the land necessary for existence and to increase the areas held to accommodate population increases intensified to an extreme the rivalry apparently present in most Polynesian societies   (1961:185–6).

Somewhat parallel views have been expressed regarding Easter Island and Hawai'i. McCoy (1976:141–7) suggests that in Easter Island rapid population growth after initial settlement led fairly quickly to high density levels. Ensuing environmental degradation, in part due to population pressure, led to internal strife and warfare, ultimately leading to a collapse of the political system (see Chapter 11). For Hawai'i, Tuggle and Griffin (1973:63) and Cordy (1974b:97–8) have posited population growth as an *independent* variable. In Cordy's words: 'the presence of complex chiefdoms in Hawaii requires an initiating independent variable; steady population increases within simple chiefdoms in one or many areas reaching the population pressure level is proposed as such an independent variable' (1974:98). Hommon, however, has taken issue with this stance, and regards population growth in prehistoric Hawai'i as an 'important phenomenon that interacted with the natural environment, agricultural technology and social and political organization in a systemic fashion' (1976:250).

The social anthropologist Oliver likewise attributed primary importance to population growth in the development of Maohi (Society Island) society: 'I believe that the principal influence upon social change in these Islands was population increase, and not so much by immigration as by steady internal increase' (1974:1123). This increase 'led people to spread out over all the Islands and, eventually, in some places (but not everywhere), to exert pressure upon the land – to compete for favorable territory, terrestrial and marine.'

Models of population growth on islands

Several lines of evidence all imply that the size and densities of Polynesian populations were closely related both to the level of agricultural production and to degree of social stratification. The demonstration of such correspondences, however, is not of much help in furthering our ultimate goal of understanding the evolution of Polynesian societies. To assess the evolutionary role of population, we must deal with demographic *change*, with patterns of growth over long periods of time. In Figure 27 I have diagrammed several kinds of population growth curves which might have actually occurred on one or more Polynesian islands. It may be instructive to consider these briefly in turn.

The first model (Fig. 27 A) is one we may term the *extinction* curve, and which we presume represents the scenarios of the 'mystery' islands discussed in Chapter 4. In this model, population increases at first, but never reaches a critical threshold, and after a time (ranging from a few generations to perhaps several centuries) declines to extinction.

In the *exponential* model (Fig. 27 B), population growth is a direct reflection of the intrinsic rate of increase (r), so that

$$\frac{dN}{dt} = rN$$

and,

$$N_t = N_0 e^{rt}$$

In the more isolated islands, where emigration and immigration were minimal, such exponential growth would directly reflect the excess of births (b) over deaths (d), since $r = b-d$. It is probable that exponential growth curves did characterize the initial phases of colonization on many Polynesian islands, as argued above and suggested by Birdsell's (1957) data. However, if a population continued to increase at a steady exponential rate, it would be a simple matter of time before the population size far exceeded the resources available for its biological needs.

(For example, a canoe load of twenty-five persons arriving in Hawai'i in AD 400, whose descendants proliferated at an annual rate of 2 per cent, well below the historically documented Pitcairn Island case, would have given rise to 2.32×10^{13} people by the time of Captain Cook's arrival in AD 1778!) This brings us to the theoretically critical but methodologically thorny issue of carrying capacity (K), the utility of which has been hotly debated in anthropology (Glassow 1978). The debate centres largely on the methodological difficulties of estimating K for human populations, yet as Brookfield (1976) pointed out, some concept of population thresholds is fundamental, given that resources

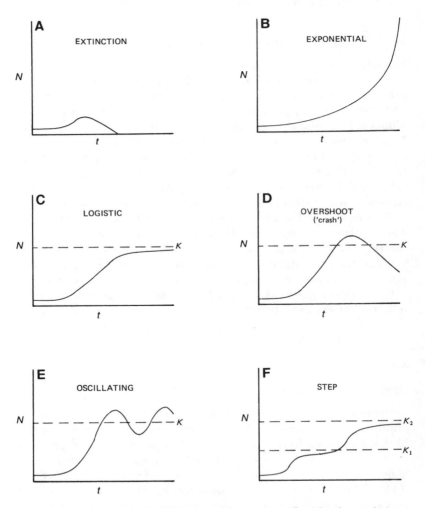

27. Hypothetical demographic scenarios for island populations (see text for discussion).

have certain finite parameters. Population biologists and evolutionary ecologists have long recognized the inverse relationship between growth rate and population density, noting that r decreases as the ratio N/K approaches unity (Pianka 1974; Wilson and Bossert 1971; Pielou 1977; Christiansen and Fenchel 1977). Carrying capacity, in this sense, can be defined in terms of growth, as the density of individuals at which the population ceases to grow ($r = 0$), whether or not the theoretical maximum population that can be supported on any given island has been attained.

The simplest model for natural population growth in which r decreases as N approaches K is that which assumes a *linear* relationship between r and N. This relationship is given by the well-known Verhulst-Pearl-logistic equation,

$$\frac{dN}{dt} = rN\left(\frac{K-N}{K}\right)$$

describing an S-shaped or sigmoid growth curve (Fig. 27 C). Such a model is frequently similar to actual growth curves empirically generated for animal populations.

Although the logistic often appears to give a close approximation to natural growth processes, its underlying assumptions may not accurately reflect a 'real world' situation. Pianka (1974) and Pielou (1977) among others have discussed some of these assumptions and possible modifications of the logistic model. Possible variations on the logistic model are, for example, portrayed in Figures 27 D to F. In the *overshoot* or *crash* model, population levels climb well above carrying capacity, and having exceeded their resource base, undergo a subsequent crash. There is thus a lead–lag time relationship between r and N. In the alternative *oscillating* model, the overshoot and crash are less pronounced, and population levels oscillate around carrying capacity. To complicate matters further, K itself does not have to be static (indeed, it probably is never static in real world situations), and fluctuations in population levels may be adjustments to fluctuations in resource levels. Variations in carrying capacity can result from a range of temporal processes, including environmental hazards such as periodic drought and cyclonic destruction of crops. The long-term effects of human use of an island, including deforestation and erosion, also certainly had a real impact on carrying capacity (see Chapter 6). In yet another variant, carrying capacity may be shifted upwards, as in the case of technological development or intensification (through irrigation, for example, or the introduction of a new, high-yielding crop), resulting in a *step* growth curve, as in Figure 27 F.

Some form of sigmoid or logistic process probably characterized population growth on all Polynesian islands. The archaeological problem is how to test this hypothesis, for any test requires that we be able to reconstruct with reasonable accuracy the magnitude of population changes in particular islands over time. To date, attempts to estimate prehistoric Polynesian populations have been limited to those of Green (1973) for Tonga, W. Shawcross (1970) for New Zealand, and Bellwood (1972a) for the Hanatekua Valley in the Marquesas. These studies were concerned with static or maximum population estimates for the period immediately prior to European contact, and did not attempt to analyse population change over time. Archaeological data potentially bearing on prehistoric population growth are of two general kinds: (1) material remains of human behaviour whose quantity per unit time and rate of deposition are proportionally related to population size; and (2) the direct evidence of human skeletal material. In the following pages I examine evidence for prehistoric population growth in the Hawaiian Islands, to test the hypothesis that such growth followed a sigmoid process. Our basic concern is with the *shape* of the prehistoric Hawaiian population growth curve (rather than actual numerical estimates), and its wider implications for human ecology suggested by the relationship between N and K.

Population growth: the Hawaiian case

Census-taking in archaeology is based on an assumption of correspondence between population size at a given time, and the number of objects or material remains used by that population (Ammerman *et al.* 1976:31). Among the classes of material remains commonly used to estimate past populations are food residues, artifacts, and habitation space (houses, packed house volumes, rooms, and so on; Cook 1972). The present analysis relies on a variant of the habitation space approach, assuming an allometric relationship between number of habitation sites and population size. In prehistoric Hawai'i, habitation sites were usually discrete physical structures, often stone platforms or stone-walled enclosures (sometimes rockshelters) associated with a household unit (for examples, see Green 1969, 1970; Kirch and Kelly 1975). Settlement patterns were dispersed, with some tendency toward nucleation around prominent geographic features, such as a sheltered bay, or major stream. Since most Hawaiian habitation sites are equatable with household units (the exceptions being certain early coastal sites that were evidently nucleated settlements with more than one household, e.g., the Halawa Dune Site on Moloka'i), the assumption of an allometric relationship between population size and number of habitation sites is probably reasonable.

To implement a census-taking approach in Hawaiian archaeology, we must of course have reasonably tight chronological control, and be able to specify time-spans for the occupation periods of each of the residential sites that comprise our sample. The development of hydration-alteration rind dating of volcanic glass artifacts (Barrera and Kirch 1973; Morgenstein and Rosendahl 1976), in conjunction with the more traditional ^{14}C dating, has permitted the age assessment of several hundred prehistoric Hawaiian residential sites over the past decade. Flake tools of volcanic glass are ubiquitous at all Hawaiian sites, and age assessment of multiple flakes from single habitation components permits the assignment of an occupation time-span. In many cases, these spans are cross-checked by ^{14}C dates from the same deposits. It would be misleading, however, to imply that the hydration-alteration rind dating of Hawaiian volcanic glass is problem free. Recent investigations have demonstrated that both chemical composition of the glass, as well as temperature variations, may affect the rate of hydration-alteration (Olson 1983). These factors may be partially controlled: (1) by the choice of sites from one geographic region, such as West Hawai'i, where nearly all volcanic glass was derived from a single, high-quality source (the Pu'u Wa'awa'a cone); and (2) by the selection of coastal or lowland sites, all within a relatively uniform temperature regime. These controls have both been applied here.

Population growth in West Hawai'i

The western leeward half of Hawai'i Island has been the scene of more intensive archaeology than any other part of the archipelago (Kirch 1979a:198–201; Clark and Kirch 1983:5–8), and is an excellent location to attempt a census-taking approach, using the temporal frequency of dated habitation sites. Somewhat arid and less optimal for Polynesian settlement than windward valleys, West Hawai'i was evidently not permanently settled until about the ninth century AD. By the time of European contact, however, the area had developed large and dense populations whose subsistence needs were provided for by extensive dryfield agricultural systems (see Chapter 7). To date, we have four well-dated samples of residential sites from West Hawai'i; the temporal distribution of these is given in Table 11, with the total number of sites occupied in each 100-year interval indicated.

The first sample consists of 51 sites from various parts of the West Hawai'i region (including Lapakahi and Anaeho'omalu), temporal data for which were synthesized by Hommon (1976) in his own attempt to model population growth in Hawai'i. The sites in Hommon's general sample include the initial settlements at Koaie (Tuggle and Griffin 1973) and at Anaeho'omalu (Barrera 1971). The second sample of 13 sites is from Kalahuipua'a, a coastal fishing community centred around a group of fishponds (Kirch 1979a). The Kalahuipua'a area was first settled in the thirteenth century and was abandoned before significant European contact. The North Kona sample, obtained by Cordy (1981), consists of 39 residential site complexes from Kohanaiki to Kukio. The temporal distribution of North Kona sites, given in Table 11, has been

Table 11. *Temporal frequency of dated habitation sites in the West Hawai'i region*

Time period	General sample (Hommon, N=51)	Kalahuipua'a (Kirch, N=13)	North Kona (Cordy, N=39)	Waimea–Kawaihae (Clark, N=10)	Total region (N=113)
AD 800–899	1				1
AD 900–999	1				1
AD 1000–1099	2				2
AD 1100–1199	4				4
AD 1200–1299	6	2			8
AD 1300–1399	14	1			15
AD 1400–1499	22	2		1	25
AD 1500–1599	31	10	11	3	55
AD 1600–1699	40	9	28	7	84
AD 1700–1799	30	6	20	10	66

derived from the original age estimates presented in Cordy (1981: Appendix E). For reasons explained in Kirch (1983), Cordy's own population reconstructions for the North Kona area are based on several unwarranted assumptions and suspect methods, and have been rejected here. The fourth sample of 10 sites consist of a recently excavated and dated series in the Waimea–Kawaihae road corridor (Clark and Kirch 1983).

The combined West Hawai'i sample of 113 dated residential sites is plotted as a site frequency histogram in Figure 28. Since the population of West Hawai'i at any given time should be reflected in the number of occupied residential sites, the growth curve indicated by Figure 28 is believed to reflect the general shape of the area's prehistoric population growth curve. The data synthesized in Figure 28 suggest a small population for the first four centuries of settlement in the region. By about AD 1200, a phase of rapid population expansion was underway, with population nearly doubling every century until about AD 1600. According to the data at hand, population growth then slowed considerably in the seventeenth century, and may have reached a peak by about AD 1650–1700, with a decline in total population in the century prior to European contact. Whether such a decline might have been due to an actual increase in deaths over births, or to emigration (to

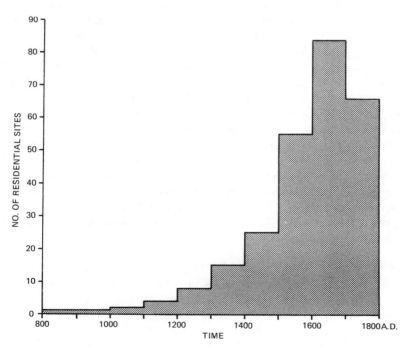

28. Site frequency histogram for the West Hawai'i region.

other parts of the island or archipelago), is not certain. Nevertheless, it is clear that we are dealing with a typical sigmoid curve.

A sigmoid growth pattern for the prehistoric West Hawai'i population is clearly indicated, and the mathematically simplest sigmoid model is the logistic. However, a strictly logistic model requires that we accept several assumptions (Pianka 1974; Pielou 1977) that may not be warranted. In particular, the logistic assumes a linear relationship between per capita rate of increase (r) and population size, N, so that r decreases monotonically with increasing N, becoming 0 when N/K equals unity. This assumption means that population growth is density-dependent *at all density levels*. As Pielou (1977:35) observes, 'it may be more reasonable to suppose that there is some threshold density below which individuals do not interfere with one another'. This is especially so in Polynesia, because we would not anticipate density-dependent growth in a population colonizing a previously uninhabited island or area, until such time as a sizeable population had built up and pressure on land and resources began to be contributing variables. In fact, an absence of density-dependent controls should characterize colonizing propagules. Thus, rather than assume a linear relationship between r and N, we may postulate a curve in which r decreases only after a threshold population size had been reached.

A second problem with a purely logistic model is that it does not fit the rapidly attained peak indicated in the West Hawai'i site frequency distribution. If the population peak was equal to K, then under the logistic, population growth should have begun to slow down considerably before it appears, in fact, to have done. Under a logistic model, a point of optimal yield would have been reached in West Hawai'i at about AD 1200, rather than in the fifteenth century, as suggested by Figure 28. In fact, the shape of the West Hawai'i site frequency distribution can be fitted to a logistic model *only* if we suppose that r was monotonically decreasing in response to a value of K somewhat higher than the actual population peak. The rapid attainment of a peak might have been due to a rapid decline in K, due possibly to environmental degradation. On the other hand, other factors such as warfare, infanticide, and so forth could also have precipitated a decline in population growth. This is a significant point, the implications of which we will consider further below.

Population growth on Kaho'olawe Island

The arid, leeward island of Kaho'olawe, whose archaeological landscape is relatively unscathed by agricultural or urban development, was recently the subject of a massive archaeological survey, covering the entire island and resulting in the identification of 2,337 features. Of these, some 655 features were dated by means of 1,120 hydration-rind age determinations on basaltic-glass flakes, and Hommon

(1980) has used these data to derive a preliminary model of the island's population growth curve. The frequency of dated residential features by 100-year time intervals is shown in Figure 29, based on data compiled by Hommon (1980: table 6). These data suggest a small founding population during the first three centuries after colonization, followed by a period of rapid population increase peaking in the sixteenth century. The last two centuries prior to European contact then witnessed a major decline in population and, according to Hommon, a retraction of settlement distribution from the upland plateau to a few small settlements along the coast. The Kahoʻolawe case thus appears to be an example of the overshoot or 'crash' model of population growth and decline, discussed earlier (see Fig. 27 D). This late prehistoric population decline, far more acute than that indicated for West Hawaiʻi, is believed to be the result of human-induced degradation of the island's rather fragile, xerophytic plant community, and consequent erosion of its arable soil cover.

Evidence from other islands

The West Hawaiʻi and Kahoʻolawe residential site frequency curves both suggest sigmoidal processes of population growth, and the Kahoʻolawe case a substantial reduction in local population prior to European contact. We must be cautious, however, of leaping to the assumption that these curves reflect the demographic situation throughout the archipelago. Both West Hawaiʻi and Kahoʻolawe are relatively dry, leeward areas where the limits to agricultural intensifi-

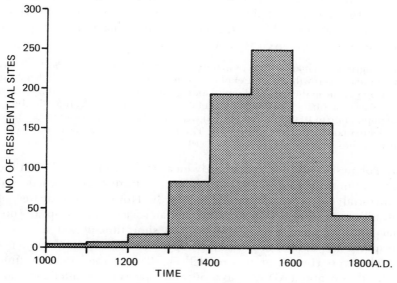

29. Site frequency histogram for Kahoʻolawe Island.

cation were much lower than those in the more optimal, windward regions, and where the possibilities for human-induced environmental degradation were more acute (see Chapter 6). Indeed, evidence from other parts of the Hawaiian group indicate that the archipelago's total population was still increasing at the time of Cook's arrival, and that there may have been considerable internal redistributions of population concentration. Certainly, the data from such areas as Halawa Valley and Kawela on Moloka'i Island (Kirch and Kelly 1975; Weisler and Kirch 1982), and from the Makaha and Anahulu Valleys on O'ahu (Green 1980; Kirch 1979b), support the notion of continued population increase up until European contact and the introduction of debilitating diseases. Clearly, we need to generate more local site population frequency curves, like those for West Hawai'i and Kaho'olawe, for other areas in different ecological situations throughout the archipelago, before the overall picture of prehistoric Hawaiian demographic change can be thoroughly understood.

The need for additional palaeodemographic research notwithstanding, the data obtained to date do, in my view, demonstrate that prehistoric Hawaiian population growth curves were sigmoidal, reflecting a shift from early, high rates of population increase, to later, decreased growth rates, with population reduction in at least some areas. The significance of such sigmoid growth sequences for Hawaiian prehistory, including structural changes in Hawaiian society and political organization, has been discussed by Hommon (1976) and Cordy (1981), and will be explored in greater detail in Chapter 10. At this point, I simply wish to draw attention to the important suggestion of Baker and Sanders (1972:162–3) that the rapid evolution of complex political systems may partially be accounted for by the 'steepness' of the later phases of population growth in a given system:

If we agree that a major stimulus in the evolution of large-scale political systems is population growth, then the explanation for the evolution within such a short period may lie in the nature of population growth. For societies organized on a tribal level, a tribal size up to 5,000–6,000 people is conceivable, but a doubling of population to 10,000–12,000 would require a chiefdom type organization in order to maintain it as a stable society. This means that chiefdoms would evolve from tribes within a single century (1972:162–3).

In Polynesia, societies were already hierarchically organized from the time of initial colonization, as we have seen from a reconstruction of Ancestral Polynesian Society (Chapter 3). However, the degree of stratification witnessed in some Polynesian societies at European contact may well have developed over a very short time period, in partial response to population growth, as suggested by Baker and Sanders.

The West Hawai'i growth model (Fig. 28) indicates that the time period from about AD 1250 to 1650, and especially the latter 200 years of that span, would have seen not only rapid population growth, and expansion into previously vacant environmental zones, but presumably also increased competition for local resources. As we shall see in Chapter 7, this period in West Hawai'i is also characterized by extensive archaeological evidence for the development and intensification of large dryfield agricultural systems. Such intensification of production must furthermore have had concomitants in the social mechanisms for control and distribution of agricultural and other products. The clear implication is that we must look to this period of rapid population growth for the evidence of change in socio-political structure leading to the unique degree of Hawaiian social stratification and political development. Similarly, it is quite likely that the elaboration of socio-political structures on other Polynesian islands was also associated with major episodes of population growth and expansion.

The Hawaiian population growth curves presented above demonstrate that empirical evidence for prehistoric demography can be generated with archaeological data from Polynesian sites, and that at least one major Polynesian society underwent a transition from rapid, density-independent to reduced, density-dependent growth. Since the Hawaiian case is unlikely to be unique, it may be taken as a model for population growth in other (though not necessarily all) Polynesian archipelagos. At this point, we may turn to several sets of palaeodemographic data obtained from analysis of skeletal populations, to further assess the level of density dependence in later prehistoric Polynesian populations.

Palaeodemography of Polynesian populations

Techniques for the analysis of palaeodemographic parameters based upon skeletal populations have developed rapidly in the past decade (Angel 1969; Acsadi and Nemeskeri 1970; Weiss 1973; Bennett 1973; Moore, Swedlund, and Armelagos 1975). There has, unfortunately, been virtually no application of these methods in Polynesia. At least four reasonably good-sized skeletal series – one from Tonga, one from the Marquesas, and two from Hawai'i – can be regarded as representative of former *populations*, and meet criteria necessary for the construction of life tables. (For a detailed discussion of life tables, and the methods for their construction from skeletal data, see the above cited references, especially Acsadi and Nemeskeri 1970; also Hassan 1981. An excellent treatment of life tables in population biology is provided in Hutchinson 1978.)

The Tongan sample derives from two adjacent *fa'itoka* burial mounds at 'Atele (sites TO-At-1 and -2) on Tongatapu Island, excavated by Davidson (1969), with an osteological study of the human remains by Pietrusewsky (1969). Both mounds were apparently used over a period of several centuries during the second millennium AD, and thus date to

Table 12. *Life table: 'Atele skeletal population*

x	D_x	d_x	l_x	q_x	L_x	T_x	e_x^0
0–1	12	19.67	100.00	0.197	180.33	1695.06	16.95
2–3	12	19.67	80.33	0.245	211.49	1514.73	18.86
4–7	7	11.48	60.66	0.189	219.68	1303.24	21.48
8–11	0	0.00	49.18	0.000	196.72	1083.56	22.03
12–17	6	9.84	49.18	0.200	265.56	886.84	18.03
18–21	1	1.64	39.34	0.042	154.08	621.28	15.79
22–31	10	16.39	37.70	0.435	295.05	467.20	12.39
32–41	9	14.75	21.31	0.692	139.35	172.15	8.08
42–51	4	6.56	6.56	1.000	32.80	32.80	5.00
Σ	61						

Explanation:

x = age interval; D_x = actual number of observed deaths at age x

d_x = number of individuals dying at age x based on cohort of 100 individuals

$$d_x = \frac{D_x}{\Sigma D_x}$$

l_x = survivorship at age x or number of individuals living at age x
q_x = mortality rate; probability of dying at age x ($q_x = d_x/l_x$)
L_x = number of individuals alive between age x and $x + 1$
T_x = total years lived from age x on

$$T_x = \sum_x^{t-1} L_x$$

e_x^0 = expectation of life at age x ($e_x^0 = T_x/l_x$)

a late phase of the Tongan sequence, when the population of the group had probably achieved a dense and possibly stable condition. The excavations provided a sample of 61 individuals assignable to age and sex (out of a total of 99 individuals), which has been used to construct the life table given here as Table 12.

The Marquesan population derives from the Hane Dune Site on Uahuka Island, excavated by Y. Sinoto (1966). Some 42 burials, mostly from Layer IV, were analysed by Pietrusewsky (1976), and the life table given in Table 13 is from this study (1976: table 3). The population dates to the Marquesan Expansion Period, which Suggs (1961) regarded as a time of population expansion into marginal areas of the archipelago (Sinoto [1970:125–8, figs. 13, 14] provides a brief discussion of the archaeological context of the Hane burials).

The two Hawaiian samples both come from communal sand-dune sepulchres. The largest of these, Mokapu on the island of O'ahu, consists of 1,163 individuals (probably the largest single cemetery in Polynesia), studied in detail by Snow (1974), whose age–sex distri-

Table 13. *Life table: Hane skeletal population**

x	D_x	d_x	l_x	q_x	L_x	T_x	e_x^0
0–1	1	2.6	100.0	0.026	987	2094.7	20.9
2–6	7	17.9	97.4	0.184	885	1996.0	20.5
7–11	5	12.8	79.5	0.161	731	1553.5	19.5
12–16	4	10.2	66.7	0.153	616	1188.0	17.8
17–21	1	2.6	56.5	0.046	552	880.0	15.6
22–31	9	23.1	53.9	0.429	424	604.0	11.2
32–41	11	28.2	30.8	0.916	167	180.0	5.8
42–51	1	2.6	2.6	1.000	13	13.0	5.0
Σ	39						

*After Pietrusewsky (1976: table 3).

Table 14. *Life table: Mokapu skeletal population*

x	D_x	d_x	l_x	q_x	L_x	T_x	e_x^0
0–1	51	4.39	100	0.0439	195.61	2395.37	23.95
2–3.5	95	8.17	95.61	0.0855	137.29	2199.76	23.01
3.6–5.5	38	3.27	87.44	0.0374	171.61	2061.71	23.58
5.6–10.5	65	5.59	84.17	0.0664	406.88	1890.10	22.46
10.6–16.5	50	4.30	78.58	0.0547	458.58	1483.22	18.88
16.6–20.5	26	2.24	74.28	0.0302	292.64	1024.64	13.79
20.6–30.5	454	39.04	72.04	0.5419	525.20	732.00	10.16
30.6–40.5	338	29.06	33.00	0.8802	184.70	206.80	6.27
40.6–50.5	43	3.70	3.94	0.9348	20.90	22.10	5.61
50.6–over	3	0.26	0.24	1.0000	1.20	1.20	5.00
Σ	1,163						

See Table 12 for explanation.

butions have been used to construct Table 14. Regrettably, the age of the Mokapu interments is unknown; the presence of early settlements along the windward O'ahu coastline near Mokapu (dating, as with the Bellows site, from the initial colonization of the archipelago) provides reason to suspect that the Mokapu series could be of some antiquity, but until radiocarbon or other absolute dates become available, such a conclusion remains speculative. (A programme of radiocarbon dating of the Mokapu skeletal series would seem to be a high priority for Hawaiian archaeology, given the potential significance of this population for the modelling and interpretation of demographic processes.) The second Hawaiian skeletal series, with 92 burials (Table 15), was excavated from the upper levels of the Pu'u Ali'i Sand Dune site at

Table 15. *Life table: Puʻu Aliʻi skeletal population*

x	D_x	d_x	l_x	q_x	L_x	T_x	e_x^0
0–9	39	42.39	100	0.4239	788.04	1904.89	19.05
10–14	1	1.09	57.61	0.0189	285.33	1116.85	19.39
15–19	11	11.96	56.52	0.2116	252.71	831.52	14.71
20–24	9	9.78	44.56	0.2195	198.37	578.80	12.99
25–29	6	6.52	34.78	0.1875	157.61	380.44	10.94
30–34	7	7.61	28.26	0.2692	122.28	222.83	7.88
35–39	10	10.87	20.65	0.5263	76.09	100.55	4.87
40–44	9	9.78	9.78	1.0000	24.46	24.46	2.50
Σ	92						

See Table 12 for explanation.

South Point, Hawaiʻi Island (Underwood 1969), and dates to about AD 1600–1780, that is, the two centuries preceding European contact.

Several palaeodemographic parameters have been graphed in Figures 30 to 32 for these four prehistoric Polynesian populations. We may consider first the survivorship curves of Figure 30. In overall pattern, the populations are similar, particularly the rapid decrease in l_x after about age thirty-five. There is considerable variation, however, in the younger portions of the curves, which may reflect certain demographic conditions of these populations. Survivorship is lowest for the Tongan population, which in late prehistoric times had achieved a high level of density in relation to arable land (and possibly, lower nutritional status than the other populations represented). The Puʻu Aliʻi population fared only slightly better, and this too represents a late period in the local prehistoric sequence, a phase of high population density and intense inter-group conflict for resources (see Chapter 11). Next in order of increased survivorship is the Hane population, which – perhaps significantly – represents a phase of the Marquesan sequence prior to the achievement of maximum density. Finally, there is the Mokapu population, for which we have (regrettably) no accurate age estimates. If the Mokapu population does date (even in part) to a relatively early phase of the Hawaiian sequence (as the nearby presence of early sites might imply), we would have in Figure 30 a significant ordering of survivorship according to the relative positions of these populations in their local island sequences, with later populations which had achieved high density levels being marked by the lowest survivorship. The implications for density-dependent controls on population growth are obviously considerable.

The patterns of age-specific mortality shown in Figure 31 evidence further correlates of this putative association between density and palaeodemography. The Puʻu Aliʻi and ʻAtele populations have the highest levels of infant and child mortality, which is what would be expected given reduced nutritional status of dense, agricultural populations (also those for which the intake of animal protein was likely to be lower, for reasons explained in Chapters 6 and 7). This general trend is also reflected to a degree in the life expectancy curves shown in Figure 32.

The palaeodemographic data provided by these skeletal populations are tantalizing in their suggestion that Polynesian populations were re-

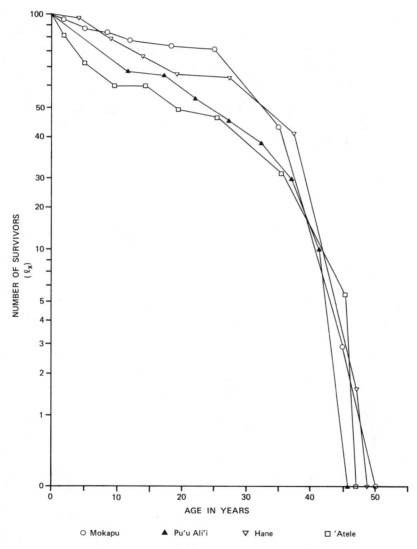

30. Survivorship in four prehistoric Polynesian populations.

sponding to certain density-dependent effects. Unfortunately, archaeological and osteological data are mute when it comes to understanding
the behavioural patterns by which late prehistoric Polynesian populations were regulated, and how the islanders themselves viewed the
relationship between population size and resources. For this purpose
we must again turn to ethnographic materials.

Population regulation: the case of Tikopia

Sir Raymond Firth's richly textured ethnographic monographs have
made Tikopia, one of the Polynesian Outliers, the most thoroughly
documented of any Oceanic society. A small volcanic high island (4.6
km²), Tikopia supports a population very close to carrying capacity,
under a traditional agricultural regime. In 1929, there were 1,281
Tikopians, or a density of 278 persons per square kilometre, a high
value not only for Polynesia, but for any 'primitive' agricultural society
(by way of comparison, the population density of Tikopia rivals that of
the most densely settled areas of Ifugao, in central Luzon, Philippines,

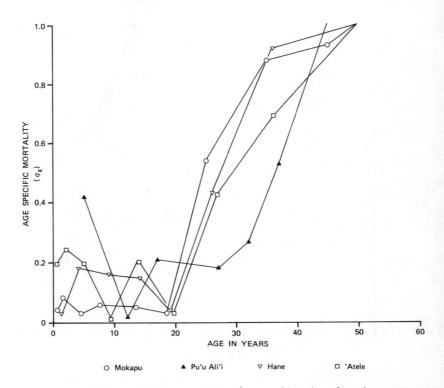

31. Age-specific mortality in four prehistoric Polynesian
populations.

noted for their magnificent, intensively irrigated rice terraces [Conklin 1980:6, 72]). By 1952, the population had increased even further to about 1,750 (density 380/km²), due in large part to the relaxation of traditional cultural controls on population size (Firth 1936; 1959b; Borrie, Firth, and Spillius 1957). As we shall see, this level of density actually exceeded the island's carrying capacity under conditions of environmental stress.

The Tikopia, who at the time of Firth's 1928 fieldwork (and to a large degree even today) operated under a traditional Polynesian economic system, unaffected by plantation agriculture or cash cropping, are acutely aware of the close relationship between population, land (and agricultural) resources, and the quality of life. They 'realize the existence of a food problem in general as well as in individual terms' (Firth 1939:39). Thus, 'not only is there a tendency for families to be regulated in size according to the quantity of their orchards and other ground, but there is a conception of a total population for which food has to be

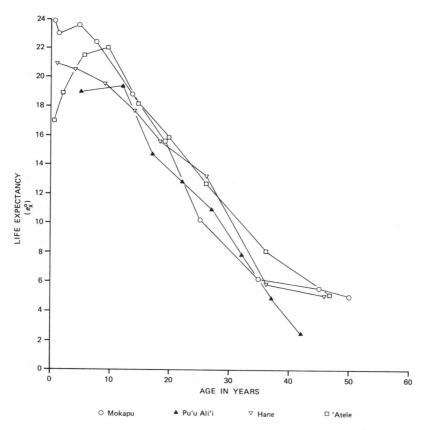

32. Life expectancy in four prehistoric Polynesian populations.

provided' (1939:39). *Fakatau ki te kai*, 'measured according to the food' (1939:43) is the fundamental concept underlying a variety of cultural controls used by the Tikopia to maintain population at an acceptable level – acceptable not merely in terms of bare subsistence necessity, but in terms of culturally specified standards. Among these controlling mechanisms are celibacy, *coitus interruptus*, abortion, infanticide, sea-voyaging, and ultimately, war. Should these cultural mechanisms fail, there is always the threat of natural disaster – drought or cyclone – which brings the inevitable *onge* famine.

Tikopia population is regulated largely at the family (*paito*) level, but cultural sanctions against over-population are also encoded in the most sacred rituals of the traditional religious system, the 'work of the gods' (Firth 1967). A critical part of the monsoon-season ritual, following upon the complex yam rites, was the *fono* or proclamation at Rarokoka, in the sacred district of Uta. The *fono* took the form of a ritually pre-scribed public address by the Ariki Tafua to the entire populace. 'Not only was it picturesque in setting – the glade in the forest, the rising sun, the expectant silent crowd, and the towering figure of the chief of Tafua rolling out the phrases – but the speech itself was remarkable for its dignity and rhythm and for the moral code which it promulgated' (Firth 1967:263). The *fono* ended with the following lines:

> The man who slept with his wife
> And feels thus let him rise
> One male and one female
> That is the plucking of the coconut and the carrying of the water bottle
> The man who will persist in creating himself a family
> Where is his basis of trees he will create his family for?
> He will make a family merely to go and steal.   (1967:269)

This is, as Firth notes, a 'remarkable injunction', embodying several Tikopia concepts of population regulation. First is the idea that the ideal family size consists of two children (one male and one female) with their parents – the concept of *fai tama fakangamua*, 'producing foremost children'. The question is posed, where is the 'basis of trees' (*tafito i rakau*), the productive orchards, that will feed an increasing household; if the productive basis is lacking, the result will clearly be anti-social. Finally, the *fono* also refers – in the opening lines – to one of the favoured methods of contraception, that of *coitus interruptus*.

A variety of other methods were used to keep population in check. One of the most important was the celibacy of junior males of a 'house', who were frequently expected to refrain from marriage and the pro-duction of offspring, since the children of 'their elder brothers will occupy all the food resources at command' of the descent group (1936:414). The limitation of offspring, not only of these celibates (who were not, however, denied sexual activity), but by married couples was accomplished by *coitus interruptus*, abortion, and infanticide. In addition, the common practice of young men to set out on overseas canoe voyages, on which many of them were inevitably lost, also helped to reduce the general population level.

The efficacy of these measures has been demonstrated, in a negative fashion, by the great increase in population since the advent of Christianity when abortion and infanticide were outlawed, and since the government discouraged overseas voyaging. Between 1929 and 1952 the island's population grew by 37 per cent (an average intrinsic rate of 0.014). This increase was accommodated in large part by outmigration to new communities in the Solomon Islands, and by certain adjustments in the agricultural system (including the adoption of steel tools and the cultivation of high-yielding manioc). Nevertheless, the increase was such that when disaster struck in 1952 and again in 1953, only the relief supplies of rice provided by the government in Honiara helped to alleviate the severity of the resulting famine, and even then at least seventeen persons succumbed to famine-induced deaths (Firth 1959b:59).

Disaster-induced famine (*onge*) is a powerful force in periodically trimming the Tikopia population, as it was for many of the tropical Polynesian societies (see Chapter 6). Here we must note a significant point concerning the concept of carrying capacity – that measured over a sequence of decades, rather than annually, an island's carrying capacity is the population capable of surviving a severe disaster-induced famine. Thus, carrying capacity is not a static variable, but one that fluctuates over time in a stochastic fashion. In the case of Tikopia, it is clear that by 1952 population had grown to a level well above the low point on the carrying capacity curve; had government relief not been provided to the Tikopia, the demographic consequences would have been grimmer.

Like other Polynesians, the Tikopia have a well-developed set of responses to disaster-induced famine, both to alleviate the severity and impact of the famine itself, and to speed the process of recovery of the agricultural sector. Food shortages are alleviated in part by drawing upon the surplus reserves of pit-ensiled breadfruit and other starch (*masi*). Among other adjustments observed by Firth (1959b) are: (1) a shortening of the fallow period; (2) the restriction of planting rights by non-kin on kin-group property; (3) a similar restriction on rights to collect wild food plants; and (4) a concern with the precise demarcation of land boundaries.

We cannot leave this analysis of Tikopia demography without discussing one final, cultural means of population regulation. War between social divisions of the island was an ultimate means of relieving the stress of over-population, and according to Tikopia tradition (Firth 1961), was practised twice within the last four or five centuries. A more detailed discussion of these traditions will be found in Chapter 8; here I note simply that the Tikopia themselves openly recognize warfare, and the extermination or expulsion of one segment of the population, as a real, albeit ultimate, means of demographic control. (During the course of the 1952–3 famine in Tikopia, the ancient tales of the expulsion of the Nga Ravenga and Nga Faea groups by the ancestors of the present chiefs were frequently re-told, and there was at one point some apparent concern that history might repeat itself [Firth 1959:93].) Furthermore, the ethnographic literature for Polynesia as a whole tells us that Tikopia was certainly not unique in this respect. As we shall see, the links between population and competition were tightly forged in the Polynesian chiefdoms.

Overview

K.B. Cumberland once wrote that 'the future of Polynesia is bound up above all with the growth of population in physically confined and precisely bounded island areas' (1962b:388). The same may be said for the past. In this chapter, I have explored several lines of evidence – archaeological, palaeodemographic, and ethnographic – relating to Polynesian demography. At the most general level, there can be no doubt as to the importance of population growth in the evolution of Polynesian societies; the close correlation between population and social stratification is merely one indicator of this relation.

A general consideration of population biology on circumscribed islands is in itself sufficient to suggest that the sequence of population change on any Polynesian island would be characterized by a gradual transition from an initially small, but rapidly growing population, to a more stable, density-dependent population regulated by a variety of cultural and natural controls (Table 16). To judge from the ethnographic data, virtually all Polynesian populations had reached such high-density levels by the time of European contact. In some islands, this level may have been reached even a millennium or more before European incursions, while in the large archipelagos of East Polynesia, there is evidence that populations could have expanded to yet higher levels of density. As Golson noted, 'the demographic prehistory of the Pacific Islands' was very likely 'complex with different islands at different stages of the [demographic] cycle when Europeans first attempted to number their inhabitants' (1972a:30).

Utilizing archaeological evidence for Hawai'i, I have attempted to demonstrate that sequences of population growth can indeed be empirically validated. In the Hawaiian case, rough population growth curves for some areas have been approximated, supporting the contention of a sigmoid growth process. With the Tikopia ethnographic data, we have glimpsed something of the varied cultural and natural

Table 16. *Probable characteristics and cultural correlates of early and late popu-lations on Polynesian islands*

Variable	Early, colonizing population	Late populations
Demographic characteristics		
Population size	Well below carrying capacity; non-equilibrium	At or near carrying capacity; equilibrium or oscillating
Intrinsic growth rate	High	Low
Population density	Low	High
Mortality	Density-independent	Density-dependent
Cultural regulation	Limited	Important; abortion, infanticide, celibacy, warfare and other controls
Cultural correlates		
Subsistence	Broad-based, non-intensive	Intensive production; emphasis on specialization
Inter-group competition	Variable, usually lax	Frequently intense; warfare common
Social controls on production	Weak	Highly developed regulatory apparatus; ritual and secular controls

controls that served to regulate Polynesian populations once they had expanded beyond the initial, colonization phase of density-independent growth.

I cannot overstress the caveat that the demographic sequences of the Polynesian islands were not identical, and each of the possible variations shown in Figure 27 will doubtless be evidenced once additional empirical analyses of population growth are forthcoming. In Tonga, for example, it is likely that an oscillating steady-state population was achieved more than one thousand years prior to European contact. The population of Easter Island on the other hand appears to have seriously overshot the carrying capacity of that remote isle, with a major demographic crash in the late prehistoric period. These variations are significant for the understanding of particular evolutionary sequences.

On the broad canvas of the Polynesian region, however, it is the similarities in these demographic sequences that stand out in terms of the evolution of particular societies. As witnessed by the European explorers, Polynesian chiefdoms were by-and-large densely settled, agrarian societies, in which competition for land and other resources was a fact of life. In the chapters to follow, the linkages between the demographic factor and other variables, such as settlement patterns, agricultural intensification, and political organization, will be further explored. It should already be clear that in the course of evolution in the Polynesian islands, population was never solely a dependent or independent variable. The views of Malthus and of Boserup must both find their place in our models.

6
Changing environments

The stereotypic notion of Pacific Islands as ecologically monotonous, with the same reefs, lagoons, and jungle-clad hills could not be farther from the truth. As we saw in Chapter 2, the island ecosystems of Polynesia exhibit a remarkable range of environmental variability, with significant consequences for technological and behavioural adaptation. Colonizing fishermen arriving in the Marquesas, for example, were constrained to modify their fishing strategies from those previously used in the tropical lagoons of West Polynesia. More dramatic yet were the adaptations required of the tropical agriculturalists who settled temperate New Zealand. These and other changes in environment faced by colonizing groups of Polynesians were significant in initiating processes leading to differentiation of the region's chiefdoms. The role of environments in culture change is, however, more complex than that of geographic variability between islands. Increasingly, archaeologists in Polynesia have come to realize the dynamic aspect of island ecosystems, and it is on such changes over time that I will focus in this chapter.

Environmental dynamics in Polynesia resulted as much, or more, from man's own actions as from natural processes. In certain academic as well as popular circles, the thesis has arisen that prehistoric Oceanic peoples avidly practised a 'conservation ethic' towards their island habitats, and that major ecological changes did not occur until after the advent of Europeans. Recent evidence shows this view to be false, and one suspects that the true scale of prehistoric human impact on the Pacific Islands is not yet fully grasped either by prehistorians or natural scientists (Kirch 1982a; 1982b; 1983b; Spriggs 1981). As the French geographer Ravault has said with regard to Tahiti: 'le milieu physique est plus ou moins doué, plus ou moins fragile, mais dans une large mesure, ce sont les hommes qui en décident' (1980:52). In this chapter, archaeological and palaeo-environmental data are marshalled to demonstrate that the Polynesians actively manipulated, modified, and, at times, degraded their island habitats, producing ecological changes which were fraught with major consequences for the evolutionary direction of the Polynesian chiefdoms.

123

Directional change in island environments

Given the brief period of time – in geological terms – that humans have occupied Polynesia, one tends to assume that island landscapes may be taken as a relative constant. Yet, even disregarding for the moment human-induced modification of landscapes, we now have evidence for first-order transformations of environment wrought by natural processes that take place over a time-scale measured in centuries. Consider the case of Niuatoputapu, a small volcanic island situated along the edge of the deep Tonga Trench, an active tectonic zone where the Pacific Plate is subducting beneath the Fiji Plate. Archaeological investigations on the Tongan island of Niuatoputapu (Kirch 1978a) revealed that Lapita sites were restricted to a narrow zone or band, situated immediately inland of a former shoreline (Fig. 33). This shoreline is now as much as 2 km inland of the present beach, the intervening

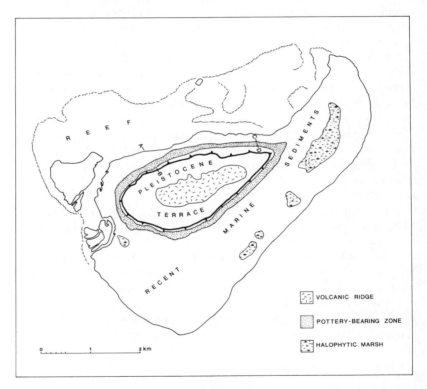

33. Geomorphic map of Niuatoputapu, Tonga, showing the distribution of Lapitoid sites in a concentric zone at the base of the central volcanic ridge. The land seaward of the pottery-bearing zone consists of former reef and lagoon tectonically uplifted since the time of initial human colonization (*c.* 800 BC).

terrain consisting of low-lying, uplifted coral reef platform and sandy flats (former lagoon floors). Thus, at the time of initial human settlement, *c.* 800 BC, Niuatoputapu was considerably smaller than at present and surrounded by a much more extensive reef–lagoon ecosystem than today. Gradual tectonic uplift (which continues today) elevated these reefs and lagoons, more than doubling the terrestial area. Since the uplifted, 'new' land, lacking in soil development, is virtually worthless for subsistence agriculture, the adaptive consequences of this environmental change were largely negative; the island's marine resources were vastly reduced, without a concomitant increase in the potential for terrestrial production.

Tikopia provides evidence of a similar transformation of environment (Kirch and Yen 1982). In this case, changes in the island's shoreline may have been initiated by tectonic uplift, major storm-wave activity, or a combination of these forces. Whatever the ultimate causes, the modifications of landscape were striking (Fig. 34), with gradual accretion of calcareous lowlands amounting to a 41 per cent increase in total land area. Furthermore, accretion of a sand spit or tombolo resulted in the conversion of a salt-water bay to a brackish lake. This closure of the bay, a rather recent event (post AD 1400) in Tikopia prehistory, had serious adaptive consequences for the former bay shore occupants, as major shellfish and fish resources of the former bay were extirpated due to salinity changes. As argued by Kirch and Yen (1982:365–8), these environmental transformations were a major factor in the inter-district rivalry and warfare related by Tikopia oral traditions (Firth 1961).

Parallel instances of long-term landscape change will likely be revealed in the course of additional archaeological work in the Pacific. In Hawai'i, for example, the large Kawainui Marsh on O'ahu was an open marine embayment about 1500 years ago (Kraft, personal communication, 1980), which would explain the presence of early Polynesian sites along its inland margins (Kelly and Clark 1980). Certainly, it is incumbent upon Polynesian prehistorians to actively seek the evidence for major landscape change, and not to accept a static view of environment simply because man has occupied these islands for only a few millennia.

Long-term climatic change is another kind of gradual environmental transformation of potential significance to Polynesian prehistory, but one that has been largely ignored outside of New Zealand. In the large temperate islands of New Zealand, the physical evidence for climatic change is more evident, and the relevance of even minor climatic shifts for Polynesian adaptation were recognized early by prehistorians. In a seminal article, Yen (1961) advanced the hypothesis that a slightly warmer climate in the period prior to AD 1200, as suggested by Raeside (1948) and Holloway (1954), might have permitted the initial introduction of

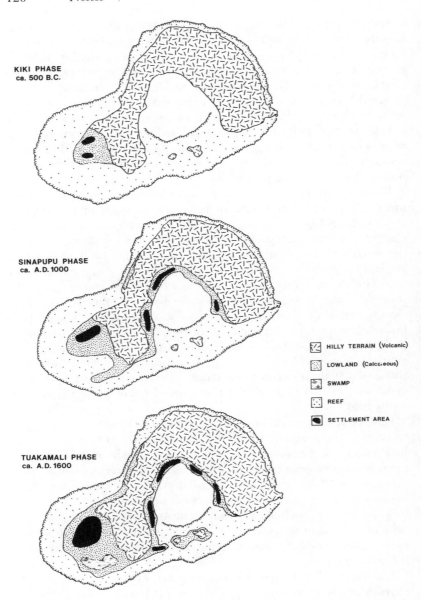

KIKI PHASE
ca. 500 B.C.

SINAPUPU PHASE
ca. A.D. 1000

HILLY TERRAIN (Volcanic)

LOWLAND (Calcareous)

SWAMP

REEF

SETTLEMENT AREA

TUAKAMALI PHASE
ca. A.D. 1600

34. Palaeogeographic maps of Tikopia Island at three points in time; note the expansion of the calcareous lowlands and closure of the marine embayment (from Kirch and Yen 1982).

the sweet potato from tropical East Polynesia to New Zealand. 'The subsequent deterioration of climate would have provided the stimulus and *time* for the Maori to invent the technical methods to preserve his plants' (Yen 1961:342), that is, to adapt the cultivation of the sweet potato from a perennial to an annual basis, with over-winter storage of the tubers. Yen's climatic model was subsequently adopted by several prehistorians (e.g., Green 1963), and a debate has ensued over the degree and role of climatic change in New Zealand prehistory (Cumberland 1962a; Holloway 1964; Gorbey 1967). Recently, Leach and Leach (1979b), drawing heavily on the work of Wardle (1973) and other natural scientists, have argued that a 'climatic optimum' between *c.* AD 900 and 1500 allowed the successful cultivation of *kumara* and gourds in the Wairarapa region (North Island). Subsequent 'climatic deterioration was a prime cause of virtual abandonment of the Palliser Bay settlements' (Leach and Leach 1979b:238). This position is not accepted by all New Zealand archaeologists, however, and we may expect the debate to continue.

Unfortunately, we know virtually nothing of possible climatic shifts on other Polynesian islands during the past two or three thousand years. The glacial record of Mauna Kea, Hawai'i (Porter 1975) indicates significant climatic cycles on the order of thousands of years, and it is entirely possible that higher-order frequency cycles existed as well. Even a minor increase in winter rainfall in arid, leeward portions of Hawai'i would make the difference between one or no crops of sweet potato, and could account for the presence of agricultural features recorded by archaeologists in presently marginal lands (e.g., the flood-water irrigation features recorded by Rosendahl [1972b] in South Kohala, or certain ephemeral agricultural features at Kawela, Moloka'i [Weisler and Kirch 1981]). Certainly, the problem of long-term climatic change in the Pacific Islands deserves more attention than it has hitherto received.

The significance of environmental hazards

Those who have not experienced the Pacific Islands at first hand, may find the concept of 'environmental hazards' incongruous in a region popularly stereotyped as a tropical paradise. Recurrent environmental perturbations or oscillations are indeed a fact of life throughout most of Polynesia, and posed significant challenges of adaptation for pre-historic island populations. The distribution and frequency of major hazards is given for the different islands and archipelagos in Table 17.

The most pervasive and significant enviromental hazards in Polynesia are drought and tropical cyclones. The major impact of both of these is on agricultural production, with famine a likely consequence,

Table 17. *Incidence of environmental hazards in the principal islands and archipelagos of Polynesia*

Island/group	Cyclone	Drought	Tsunami	Volcanic eruption	Valley floods
Tonga	F	F	R	—	—
Samoa	F	F	R	C	C
Futuna	F	F	R	—	F
'Uvea	F	F	R	—	—
Cook Islands	C	C	R	—	C
Society Islands	C	C	C	—	C
Marquesas Islands	R	F	C	—	C
Hawaiian Islands	R	C	C	F*	C
New Zealand		C	R	R	C
Tuamotu Islands	C	C	C	—	—
Mangareva	C	C	C	—	—
Easter	R	F	C	—	—
Tikopia	F	F	R	—	—
Anuta	F	F	R	—	—

Key: F, frequent; C, common; R, rare; —, absent.
*Hawai'i Island only.

though cyclones also are destructive of property, and at times, human lives. Pronounced wet and dry seasons characterize many Polynesian islands, and when the low rainfall period is drier or more extended than usual, the consequences for indigenous agricultural systems can be disastrous. In 1976, I witnessed the effects of a three-month drought on Niuatoputapu, from late July through October. Hardest hit were the aroid cultivations, especially taro (*Colocasia esculenta*); what had been luxuriant gardens in July had turned to fields of brown, withered stalks (Fig. 35) three months later. Pig herds were affected as well – wallows dried up, and the yearlings died of heat exhaustion. By October, the drought had become a topic of serious discussion and concern. Fortunately, a supply of flour sent by the government from Tongatapu averted disaster, but traditionally, the island would have had to rely upon its own resources.

The Marquesas were especially prone to drought, and in Handy's view, 'the uncertainty of rainfall and these occasional droughts have affected directly the native culture' (1923:8). Adamson (1936:17) notes that drought results in 'extreme aridity' in the lower elevations, and agricultural crops doubtless suffered immensely. Drought-induced famine served as a check on population growth, and Suggs relates that a famine between 1803 and 1813 is reputed to have 'wiped out two-thirds of the population' of Nukuhiva (1961:191). The beachcomber Robarts experienced this famine directly, noting that its 'dreadfull effects' were 'severely felt in all parts of the Island' (Dening 1974:121). Robarts calculated that during his residence in a single valley over the course of one year, 200–300 persons perished (Dening 1974:273–5). Not surprisingly, therefore, it was in the Marquesas that a major Polynesian method of buffering against famine – the pit-ensilage of breadfruit – was developed to an apogee.

Tropical cyclones in Polynesia have a more restricted geographic occurrence than drought, with the area of greatest frequency (about 2 per year, on the average) being the Tonga–Samoa archipelagos (Visher 1925:27). Farther east, the Society and Tuamotu groups receive cyclones less frequently (about 0.2/yr on the average), and these storms are quite infrequent in the peripheral parts of Polynesia. In Tonga and Samoa, however, as well as among the Outliers such as Tikopia and Anuta, cyclones are greatly feared for their destructive power. The French missionary Père Chanel witnessed the fury of a tropical cyclone that struck Futuna in 1840:

The night of the second or third of February, a tempest, announced for several days by a dark sky and a strong eastern wind, broke suddenly with furor. The lightening, the thunder, the torrents of rain, an incredible noise from the sea, the cries of the islanders who invoked their gods, such was the scene which confronted us throughout the night . . . The coconut palms, the banana plants, the breadfruit trees, all the productions of the island were so maltreated, that after this great disaster, we were once again menaced by famine (Chanel 1960:301–2).

35. A withered taro plant in a drought-affected garden on Niuatoputapu Island. If adequate rainfall had been available, the plant would be 2–3 times this size.

Whether a drought or cyclone induces famine or merely disrupts production is closely related to the timing of these hazards in relation to local cropping cycles (Currey 1980:451). Throughout West Polynesia, the period of seasonally low rainfall also coincides with a phase of minimal production in the agricultural calendar. Yams and breadfruit are out of season, and subsistence may depend upon aroids, the crops most susceptible to drought. This cropping cycle–ecological rhythm relationship is illustrated in Figure 36 for 'Uvea Island. Even in a good year, the months from August through October are relatively lean. If a drought affects the growth of the new yam crop, then famine may carry over into the new year. Should a cyclone also hit the island, generally in the period between November to April, this potential for disaster is compounded. Firth (1939:73–7, fig. 2) provides a similar analysis of seasonal variations in Tikopia food production, noting 'a marked scarcity of almost every kind of food' during May–June. 'I gathered from native opinion that such scarcity is not uncommon at this time owing to an interval between crops, assisted by a lower rainfall' (1939:75).

While drought and cyclone were the dominant environmental hazards faced by the prehistoric Polynesians, several other perturbations also posed adaptive challenges at various times and places.

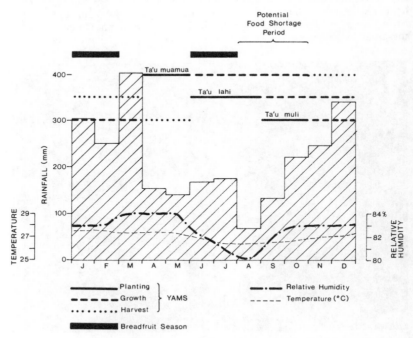

36. Annual ecological rhythms and agricultural production in 'Uvea Island, showing the period of potential food shortage (from Kirch 1975).

Tsunami certainly struck various islands in the past, as they have in historic times, with considerable destruction of coastal habitations, fishponds, and gardens. In some areas such as the windward valleys of Kohala, Hawai'i, periodic flooding due to exceptionally heavy rains destroyed irrigated fields constructed on alluvial terrain. Volcanic eruptions were important in a few regions, such as Kilauea, Hawai'i, where the entire surface of the shield volcano has been inundated with lava flows at least once since Polynesian colonization. Handy and Handy (1972:274) report that a 'volcanic upheaval' in Ka'u, Hawai'i in 1868 resulted in famine. In temperate New Zealand, a unique hazard for tropical Polynesian agriculture was posed by annual frosts, requiring major adaptation of agronomic practice (Yen 1961, 1974a).

Thus, contrary to the popular image of the Pacific Islands as an abundant paradise, a combination of annual seasonality in crop production, with stochastically recurrent hazards, render famine a significant challenge to island life. Currey (1980:447–8) notes that the recurrence interval for famines in Hawai'i is about twenty-one years, an interval 'no less frequent than the historical record of famines in Bangladesh'. Certainly, the theme of famine pervades Polynesian mythology, as in Mangareva (Buck 1938a:24, 34, 39, 40, 44). In Hawai'i, 'the theme of mythical lands rich in foods reflects the constant anxiety in the native mind in those early times arising from the ever-present specter of famine' (Handy and Handy 1972:273). The term for famine in many Polynesian islands – *onge* (Mangareva, Samoa, Futuna, Tikopia), *honge* (Tonga, 'Uvea) – reflects an ancient concept, with cognates in many Melanesian and Micronesian languages (e.g., *songe*, Rotuma; *songe*, Roviana; *rongo*, Gilberts; *kwole*, Marshalls). The significance of famine in the development of Polynesian societies is clear. Famines served as a critical natural check or control on population increase (see Chapter 5). Once the population of any island had reached relatively high density levels, moreover, famines may have triggered competition and conflict between social groups. In the political traditions of Futuna, for example, the protohistoric conquest of neighbouring Alofi Island by the paramount chief Veliteki is attributed to food shortages resulting from a cyclone (Burrows 1936:36; Kirch 1975:346).

War was generally an ultimate recourse, often utilized only after a series of other cultural buffering mechanisms had failed to return a famine-ridden island back to normal subsistence production. During the period following an environmental disaster, when intensive efforts were devoted to re-establishing the agricultural system, food consumption often depended upon a range of wild or famine foods (see Currey 1980:table 3 for a list of the more noted famine plants). Many of these famine plants were not elements of the indigenous flora, but rather adventive species introduced by Polynesians, and maintained in a feral state throughout large tracts of secondary vegetation. Of particular note are the bitter yam (*Dioscorea bulbifera*), the ti plant (*Cordyline fruticosa*), and the *aka* (*Pueraria lobata*). In 'Uvea, these species are distributed throughout a large tract of edaphically degraded land in the island's centre (the *toafa*, Kirch 1978b:160), land which will not support regular cultivations. During *honge* periods, this *toafa* is burned over to induce the sprouting of feral arrowroot and yams, facilitating the collection of the subterranean tubers (Kirch 1978b:179). Needless to say, such an adaptation to famine conditions had both positive and negative effects – positive in providing the needed feral tubers, but negative in that it maintained the anthropogenic *toafa* in a degraded condition through repeated burning.

The most important and sophisticated Polynesian methods of buffering against famine were several techniques of preserving and storing staple starch foods (Barrau and Peeters 1972; Yen 1975). One method involved the grating of arrowroot (*Tacca leontopetaloides*) tubers, and in some western islands, sago pith (*Metroxylon* spp.), filtering out the starch grains in fresh or sea water, with the result after decanting and drying being a storable flour (Fig. 37). More widespread and significant in tropical Polynesia was the technique of pit-ensilage and semi-anaerobic fermentation of starchy food pastes (Table 18), especially breadfruit (Cox 1980; Kirch 1979c:303). In a tropical environment, where the edible products of the dominant crop plants are generally

37. A work group on Niuatoputapu Island filters starch from *mahoa* (*Tacca leontopetaloides*) tubers, using sea-water. The starch is carried in solution into the canoe hull; water is then decanted and the flour dried for storage.

Table 18. *Pit-storage of starch staples in Polynesian societies*

Island/group	Name of stored product	Breadfruit	Taro	Banana	Alocasia	Cyrtosperma	Sago	Burckella	Manioc[*]
Anuta	*ma*	X	X	X	X	X	X	X	X
Tikopia	*masi*	X	X	X				X	X
Tonga	*ma*	X	X	X	X				X
Samoa	*masi*	X		X					
Futuna	*masi*	X	X	X		X			
'Uvea	*mahi*	X		X					
Society Is.	*mahi*	X							
Marquesas Is.	*ma*	X							
Mangareva	*ma*	X							

[*]An American cultigen adapted to pit-storage after European contact.

tubers, corms, or fruit (rather than easily stored seeds), storage of staple starches posed a real problem of technological adaptation. The ingenious Polynesian solution was to take advantage of natural fermentation, using a sort of 'controlled rotting'. Breadfruit (and other starches, including taro, banana, and certain fruits, e.g., *Burckella*) was placed, uncooked, in leaf-lined underground silos (Fig. 38). Bacterial fermentation in these silos created waste alcoholic by-products, gradually resulting in a steady-state system. Renewal of the leaf-linings every year or two permitted the fermented farinaceous contents to be stored for periods of a decade or more. The fermented product is called *ma, masi,* or *mahi,* and the term is reconstructable to Proto-Polynesian language. As noted in Chapter 3, archaeological evidence of fermentation pits has been reported in Lapita contexts (see Fig. 15).

Storage of *ma* reached a developmental peak in the Marquesas Islands, a reflection of the severity of drought and consequent need for a reliable buffering mechanism against famine. Robarts, who participated in the preparation of *ma,* gives a clear description of the process, and notes that 'the large pitts are Kept against a scarce time, as is frequent the case in these Isles' (Dening 1974:272–3). He was told that with proper care and replacement of the pit linings, *ma* could be kept in storage for as long as forty years. Storage pits with volume as great as 216 m^3 are reported (in Taipivai, Nukuhiva; Linton 1925:103). *Ma* pits are frequently found on the Marquesan ridge-top fortifications (Suggs 1961), and the association between famine, storage of surplus, and warfare is obvious.

The practice of *ma* storage and its role in Polynesian economies, offer some further clues regarding the relationships between household production and the chieftainship. As Yen (1975:162) pointed out, *ma* preparation and storage is one form of *intensification of production* (see also Chapter 7). 'Centralization, or at least concentration of these resources, and partability are factors contributing to the possibilities of distribution along communal lines, but the agency of leadership is implied in such organization' (1975:156). In the Anutan case described by Yen (1975:159–61; see also Yen 1973b), *ma* is prepared in individual households, as part of the 'domestic mode of production' (Sahlins 1972). However, in the distribution of the fermented product to alleviate famine, 'direct control of. . . distribution passes into the hands of the chiefs' (Yen 1975:161).

In many Polynesian societies, particularly those of the larger high islands, the preparation and distribution of *ma* formed a part of the economic intensification 'deployed to political organization' (Sahlins 1972:147). Such deployment took the form of distribution of *ma* for alleviation of famine as already noted, or at times, for feasts accompanying major ceremonies. In Mangareva, Buck comments that:

large pits were owned by the chiefs of districts commanding a large quantity of fruit. In seasons of plenty (*'ou*), people contributed to the contents of the district pits to build up a reserve for important social occasions. The district pits had proper names applied to them, and their full utilization depended on abundant seasons   (1938a:207).

38. A woman on Tikopia refills a *masi* storage silo after renewing the leaf lining.

Handy (1923:188) reports that large Marquesan *ma* pits were constructed and filled as a 'tribal' operation. Linton adds that:

many of the great communal pits were built in the village and were placed as a rule in or near the tribal assembly place. Additional pits were built high up in the hills, in secluded places, where they would be safe from an enemy and could provide food for the tribe if it were driven out of the valley (1925:103).

One of the clearest accounts of the relationship between *ma* production and chiefly power is that of James Morrison, boatswain's mate on the infamous *Bounty*, in Tahiti in 1788:

if a Chief wants a Supply [of breadfruit] for the purpose of Making Mahee [*mahi*] he sends a Bit of Cocoa Nut leaf to all, or as Many of the Inhabitants of his district as he shall think proper, and on the appointed dy they Bring each a load, which is generally accompanied with a hog and some fish by others according to their several abilitys . . . when supplys are raised this Way the people bring it in such a Manner as bespeaks at once their regard for their Chiefs & fear of displeasing them . . . (quoted in Oliver 1974:238).

In sum, environmental catastrophes, a recurrent part of island life, played a significant role in the evolution of the Polynesian chiefdoms. Famine resulting from natural disasters such as cyclones, drought, or volcanic activity was a powerful control on large populations. On the other hand, Polynesians developed a variety of cultural buffering mechanisms to alleviate the more severe effects of such disasters. Most technologically ingenious and developed of these mechanisms was the fermentation and storage of starch pastes, especially that made from breadfruit. In the application of this buffering mechanism, we see the critical interplay between environment, economy, and political organization. Polynesian chiefs not only organized the production and distribution of *ma* for the welfare of their people, but in the process enhanced their own status and power. In Chapter 7 we shall explore further the mobilization of the productive forces of society in the service of a greater political economy.

Man's transported landscapes

The valleys and plains of any Polynesian island, as viewed by the early European explorers, were already, in Edgar Anderson's delightful phrase, 'transported landscapes'. Anderson developed his bold concept based upon research with the adventive, ruderal floras of North America: 'unconsciously as well as deliberately man carries whole floras about the globe with him . . . he now lives surrounded by transported landscapes' (1952:9). Although Anderson was concerned primarily with weeds and cultigens, his concept of transported landscapes epitomizes the effects of human colonization of natural ecosystems. By means of both purposeful and accidental transport of adventive plants and animals, man transforms the biota of his new habitats, creating a new, and in many respects, artificial landscape. On Oceanic islands, the introduction of highly competitive weeds and predators had drastic effects on the vulnerable endemic biota (cf. Fosberg 1963a:5). Murdock expounded on the consequences of man's actions in the transport of artificial landscapes:

Transplanted to islands where their respective ecological niches were either unfilled or filled by weaker indigenous forms, and where the forms on which they preyed were unprotected and vulnerable, the introduced species must repeatedly have wrought havoc on the native fauna and flora, extinguishing many species and greatly restricting the distribution of others. The resulting changes in the island ecosystems must often have been substantial and not infrequently spectacular (1963:150).

Direct archaeological evidence for the introduction of several animal species with initial Polynesian colonizers has come from a variety of sites. Skeletal remains of domestic dog, pig, and fowl have been recovered in Lapita contexts, as well as in early East Polynesian sites. Of this domestic triad, the pig – which frequently went feral on Polynesian islands – had the most significant impact on native vegetation. Of course, a range of crop plants also accompanied the Polynesians as purposeful introductions.

Just as significant as these purposeful introductions – and perhaps with a greater impact on the native biota – were a variety of inadvertent stowaways transmitted across the Pacific in Polynesian voyaging canoes. Skeletal remains of a small rat (*Rattus exulans*) are ubiquitous in Polynesian archaeological sites. Concerning this species, Tate wrote: 'It regularly enters houses and lives in the thatch of native huts. It was probably carried about the Pacific in big canoes which it entered at night while they were loaded with provisions in readiness for long voyages' (1951:97). Several species of geckos (Gekkonidae) and skinks (Scincidae) were likewise stowaways on Polynesian canoes (Stejneger 1899; Adamson 1939:26, 63). Skeletal remains of these diminutive lizards have not yet been reported from early settlement sites (doubt-less because excavators rarely use the 0.5 mm mesh screens necessary for their recovery!), but gecko and skink mandibles have now been found in later prehistoric deposits at Barbers Point, O'ahu, and in a cave deposit at Keopu on Hawai'i Island (A. Schilt, personal communication 1982). Several species of synanthropic arthropods were probably prehistoric Polynesian dispersals, including centipeds (Adamson 1932), cockroaches, fleas, and mites (Adamson 1939:26, 39, 59, 61).

Malacologists have long regarded several widely spread Pacific snails to be dispersed by prehistoric Oceanic peoples (Pilsbry 1916–18; Cooke 1926; Cooke and Kondo 1960; Solem 1959). Cooke maintained that 'about a dozen species were carried by Polynesians in their migrations' (1926:2279). These anthropophilic species 'are abundant in the native villages and in the plantations' (*ibid.*), frequently living on coconuts, breadfruit, and other economic plants. Such snails were probably transported by the Polynesians while 'sticking to native impedimenta, cocoanuts, or other food materials, in the thousand years or more of inter-island canoe voyages' (Pilsbry 1916–18:140–1). One such species is *Lamellidea pusilla*, whose typical widespread distribution is shown in Figure 39.

Christensen and I demonstrated that the shells of these anthropophilic snails are recoverable from archaeological contexts, and provide evidence relating to early Polynesian transport of the vegetative and/or edaphic materials on which the snails were carried. For example, three species, *Lamellidea pusilla, Gastrocopta pediculus*, and *Lamellaxis gracilis*, were established in Tikopia within the first few decades after colonization, *c.* 900 BC (Christensen and Kirch 1981a). At the early Lapita site of Yanuca in Fiji, dated to *c.* 1300 BC, *Gastrocopta pediculus* and *Lamellaxis gracilis* have also been reported (Hunt 1980:192). Christensen (1981) reports six anthropophilic species, including the above three, from the Vaito'otia-Fa'ahia site on Huahine, in the Societies, while Kirch (1973) found *Lamellidea oblonga*, and *Gastrocopta pediculus* to be present at the Hane site in the Marquesas. In Hawai'i, *L. gracilis* has been recovered from several prehistoric contexts.

Polynesian dispersal of adventives was by no means limited to the fauna, and there is evidence that a host of competitive weeds were transported from island to island (Merrill 1939). These include such species as *Ludwigia octivalvis*, a dominant weed in irrigated taro fields, and *Digitaria setigera*, which frequents pig pens (Kirch 1982a:3). M.S. Allen (1981) reported on the preserved seeds of four weedy species from a prehistoric rockshelter at the Mauna Kea adz quarry site on Hawai'i Island. The increased use of flotation in archaeological excavations can be expected to yield considerable data on the distribution of weeds by the Polynesians (see Clark and Kirch 1983 for a recent application in Hawai'i).

The introduction of all of these adventive species, both purposeful and inadvertent, amounted to a 'gigantic, unplanned ecological experiment' (Bates 1956:796), with important consequences for the native biota of islands. Most of the species introduced by man were highly competitive, and would have rapidly made inroads on the endemic, vulnerable fauna and flora of Oceanic islands, particularly in the lowland elevations, where man's activities were concentrated. As Fosberg maintained, 'perhaps the thing that most distinguishes islands, at least oceanic islands . . . is their extreme vulnerability, or susceptibility, to disturbance' (1963b:559).

The impact of Polynesian colonization on island biota went beyond the transport of a large associated group of domestic, synanthropic, and anthropophilic species, and their ecological impact upon the

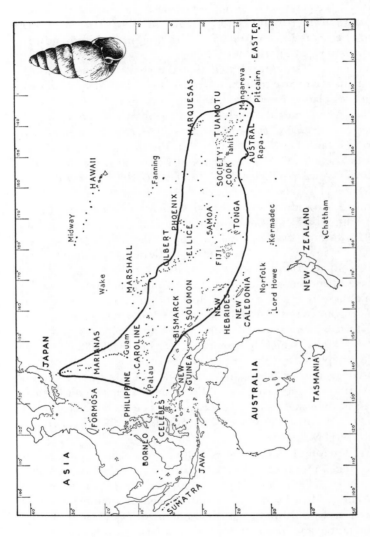

39. The distribution of the anthropophilic land snail *Lamellidea pusilla* (adapted from Cooke and Kondo 1960). Such widespread distribution patterns are characteristic of land snails transported by human agency.

native biota. Anderson's concept of transported landscapes can logically be extended, for humans carry with them a cultural concept of landscape, and actively modify new environments according to that mould. As Sahlins (1976:209) maintains, 'nature is to culture as the constituted is to the constituting'. Thus, the 'action of nature is mediated by a conceptual scheme' (1976:210), a cognitive 'map' of how the world – or an island – was to be ordered. For the Polynesians, this scheme included such concepts as the efficacy of fire in clearing forest for garden land, the diversion of streams to feed irrigated pondfields, and even such notions as a 'proper' political division of the landscape (into radial, segmentary units, see Chapter 2). Thus, having arrived in a particular island group, Polynesians did not simply adapt passively to its constraints and limitations. They actively modified and moulded their insular world, with – as we shall see – often dramatic consequences for their own mode of existence.

Human impact on island ecosystems

Vegetation change and erosion

The transport and introduction of a variety of cultigens and weeds resulted in a radical replacement of the lowland vegetation of nearly every Polynesian island. More far-reaching in its implications was the action of Polynesians in clearing – primarily with the aid of fire – large tracts of native forest. Prior to man's arrival, Oceanic islands were as a rule reasonably well forested; by the time of European discovery, these forests had been greatly reduced, and were frequently replaced with degraded fern–grassland savannahs. Since the scale of such deforestation and its probable significance for human adaptation have not been widely recognized by Polynesian prehistorians, it may be well to review some of the relevant evidence for a variety of islands.

A large number of the *tropical* Polynesian islands are distinguished by a highly characteristic vegetative association (termed *toafa* on several), of which the dominant species is a fern, *Dicranopteris linearis*. The *toafa* of Futuna Island (Kirch 1975) is typical, and covers a large percentage of the interior plateaux and ridges of that high island (Fig. 40). Along with the *Dicranopteris* fern are abundant terrestrial orchids (*Spathoglottis pacifica*), and scattered scrub *Pandanus*, with an occasional ironwood tree (*Casuarina equistifolia*). This *toafa* was created, and is being maintained and continually expanded, by the use of fire. Clearing of native forest for swidden gardens is a major impetus, though fires are lit for other purposes as well (e.g., to flush birds or wild pigs, and simply for the fun of watching the conflagrations).

The development and spread of *toafa* is related to the thin, easily eroded volcanic soils of most Polynesian tropical high islands. These soils frequently consist of little more than an organic A horizon developed over weathered basalt or andesite (saprolite). When native

40. Degraded fernland savannah (*toafa*) on the interior ridges of Futuna Island, with remnant patches of indigenous forest.

41. View of Mangareva Island, showing the totally deforested interior ridges. The fertile alluvial plains, to which cultivation is largely confined, have probably been enriched by the deposition of soil eroded from the ridges (*photo courtesy Bishop Museum*).

forest is fired and the thin soil exposed to sheet wash, especially for more than one season, the A horizon may be removed, resulting in a laterized oxisol. The *Dicranopteris* fern is one of the few species that will successfully colonize such terrain.

Geomorphic evidence for the clearance of native forest, subsequent erosion of ridges, and creation of *toafa* was obtained at the Late Eastern Lapita site of Tavai on Futuna (Kirch 1975; 1981a). Here, a former village site at the foot of a bluff, inland of which is a large *toafa*-covered plateau, is buried under up to 2.5 metres of erosional debris. Radio-carbon dating indicates that erosion began as early as the first few centuries AD.

Dicranopteris-fern savannah is found on the interiors of many other tropical Polynesian islands (I have already mentioned the *toafa* which covers much of the interior of 'Uvea Island). On Mangaia, in the Cook Islands, most of the interior ridges are covered with this vegetation (Buck 1934:5). Fernland is characteristic of large areas in the Society Islands, where it is again found on degraded, lateritic soils (Papy 1954–5:154, 207). Regarding *Dicranopteris* savannah in the Papeari District of Tahiti, Ravault remarked that *'l'homme est partout responsable de cette radicale transformation du paysage végétal'* (1980:51). The fires, purposeful or accidental, that maintain this degraded vegetation were described by several early European visitors to Tahiti, such as Davies, in 1807: 'For several days and nights past there has been a strong great fire in the lower hills of Matavae, which consumed almost every tree and shrub before it . . .' (quoted in Oliver 1974:43).

The island of Mangareva exhibits an extreme degree of human-induced deforestation, with the entire interior covered in grassland savannah (Fig. 41). As described by C.M. Cooke: 'Nearly all the islands have been continuously burned over for years. The ridges are entirely bare of trees and are covered with coarse grass. . . Probably the disappearance of the native fauna [and flora] has been caused chiefly by fire' (1935:41). Many of the Marquesas Islands also have large tracts of fern and grass savannah, such as the Tovii Plateau of Nukuhiva (Adamson 1936:59).

The consequences of this widespread process of savannah creation on many Polynesian islands cannot be overestimated. Most important was the reduction in total arable land, for these degraded tracts were no longer suitable for cultivation. Since the savannahs were probably expanding at the same time that the human populations of the islands were burgeoning, the potential for population pressure was greatly heightened. In particular, the degradation of ridges and plateaux indirectly placed a higher value on the increasingly important valley lands and coastal plains, upon which agricultural production was dependent. Not that the degradation of the uplands was entirely negative, however. As Spriggs (1981) has shown for the Melanesian island of

Aneityum, erosion of the interior volcanic slopes of a high island may significantly add to alluvial deposition in valley bottoms, thus enriching and increasing the prime arable land. A similar process of erosion adding to fertile lowland agricultural soils has been documented for Tikopia (Kirch and Yen 1982:147–60). Nevertheless, the gains from increased alluvial deposition did not always outweigh the negative consequences of environmental degradation.

Easter Island provides another example of drastic vegetation change induced by a Polynesian population. As McCoy notes, 'beginning with the explorers' descriptions in the eighteenth century, observers have consistently commented on the almost treeless landscape of Easter Island' (1976:7). Whether this 'oceanic steppe-like meadow or grass heath', as Skottsberg (1956:422) described it, was natural or anthropogenic has been the subject of some debate. Intriguing evidence for former forest was provided by numerous root casts or moulds revealed by Mulloy and Figueroa's excavations under the large temple site of Ahu-a-Kivi (1978:22). The excavators concluded that 'the area was once covered with significantly more vegetation than has been reported in historic times. Some of this vegetation must have been quite large' (1978:22). Recently, Flenley's (1979, 1981) palynological investigations of cores from Rano Raraku, Rano Aroi, and Rano Kau crater lakes have provided conclusive evidence that the pre-human vegetation of Easter comprised a 'scrubby rainforest'. Although Flenley's analyses are not yet complete, the Polynesian occupants of Easter Island are clearly implicated in the radical conversion of the island's flora (1979:39).

McCoy (1976:145–6) has discussed the probable adaptive consequences of the 'hypothesized deterioration of the [Easter Island] landscape through radical reduction of forest, shrub, and grassland communities, following over-exploitation and misuse by man'. Among these were erosion of the precious soil mantle, and loss of wood for construction. Chapter 11 will explore in greater detail the close relationships between environmental change, demography, and socio-political development in Easter Island.

Vegetation change resulting from Polynesian actions was no less pronounced in sub-tropical Hawai'i than in the tropical archipelagos (Kirch 1982a). Early European visitors to Hawai'i frequently remarked on the barren and unwooded character of the lowlands. Vancouver, visiting Kaua'i Island, noted that 'a space comprehending at least one half of the island, appeared to produce nothing but a coarse spiry grass [probably *Heteropogon contortus*] from an argillaceous soil, which had the appearance of having undergone the action of fire' (1798, vol. I:170). Archaeological and geomorphic studies have begun to demonstrate that these barren lowlands were, in fact, the consequence of extensive forest removal by Polynesians. In the Halawa Valley on Moloka'i, a large colluvial fan with stratified erosional deposits containing endemic subfossil land snails and abundant charcoal, is silent witness to a cycle of slope erosion set off by firing of an original native forest cover (Kirch and Kelly 1975:55–64). In the upper Makaha Valley on Oʻahu, clearance of steep hillsides led to erosion and slumping that partially buried a valley-bottom taro irrigation system (Yen *et al.* 1972). Dramatic evidence of vegetation removal by fire, and subsequent erosion, has also been claimed for Kahoʻolawe Island (Hommon 1980).

Nowhere in Polynesia was the destruction of native forests so extensive and consequential as in New Zealand. As late as the 1950s, scholarly doctrine held that extensive areas of grassland savannah, particularly in the South Island, resulted from post-glacial climatic change. This picture was soon reversed, however, through detailed studies of subfossil evidence for former forests (Molloy *et al.* 1963; Molloy 1967; Molloy 1969). This evidence consists of 'surface logs and forest windthrow hummocks and hollows in now-treeless areas; buried wood, charcoal, and other plant remains; buried soil profiles; and a number of relic plants and soils' (Molloy 1969:341). Most importantly, a large series of subfossil wood and charcoal samples were radiocarbon dated, with the resultant ages almost always falling within the period of prehistoric Polynesian occupation (Molloy *et al.* 1963: table 1; Molloy 1969: table 1). These studies allowed both a reconstruction of the former composition and distribution of forest, and of the sequence of its destruction – through fire – by the Polynesian occupants of New Zealand.

More recently, our understanding of the Polynesian deforestation of New Zealand has been amplified by pollen sequences obtained and analysed by McGlone (1983) from various parts of both North and South Islands. The sequences from Porter's Pass and Longwood Range, shown in Figure 42, are both typical, with a rapid decrease in the local forest tree dominants (*Nothofagus, Podocarpus*), and concomitant increase in grasses and *Pteridium* fern. McGlone notes that 'at most sites when the main forest clearance phase began it proceeded very rapidly indeed; (*ibid.*), and 'between 800 and 500 yr BP there is abundant evidence from both North and South Island for the beginning of forest clearance on a grand scale' (*ibid.*).

In general terms, prior to Polynesian colonization, New Zealand was 'essentially a forested land', with the largely endemic forest 'consisting of mixed podocarp-dicotyledonous (subtropical) or *Nothofagus* (subantarctic) species' (Cumberland 1961:139). Destruction of this forest mantle began with the arrival of Polynesians, from fires ignited probably for a variety of purposes (to flush game, especially *moa* birds; for agricultural clearance, and so forth). By the time of European arrival, some thousand years later, the results of this '*Brandwirtschaft*' (Cumberland 1962a:163) were dramatic indeed. According to Cumberland's estimate, 'not less than eight million acres of forest had been replaced by grass and scrub and many more acres had been disturbed and diversified' (1961:142). The approximate extent of this forest destruction is conveyed in Figure 43.

Such massive vegetation change had serious consequences for soils and erosion. Molloy described the effects of Polynesian burning of about 75 per cent of the Waimakariri catchment in central South Island:

The destruction of the forest and grassland mantle changed the dynamic soil system from a dominant wasting regime to an active 'drift regime' . . . in dramatic fashion . . . the soils of the steeplands were removed wholly or in part, screes were extended to lower altitudes, and fans and flood plains were rejuvenated by a fresh supply of detritus . . . It is no coincidence that the most spectacular examples of soil erosion and scree development lie within the boundary of Polynesian burning (1967:66).

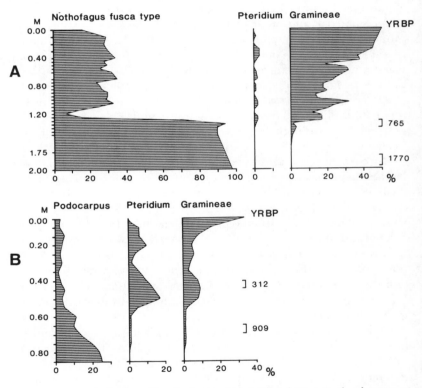

42. Pollen profiles from two South Island New Zealand swamp sites, showing the impact of prehistoric forest clearance (from McGlone 1983). A. Porter's Pass, inland Canterbury (unpublished data of N.T. Moar, DSIR, New Zealand). B. Longwood Range, Southland. In both profiles, note the rapid decline in forest trees (*Nothofagus*, *Podocarpus*), and relative increase in ferns (*Pteridium*) and grasses (Gramineae).

In the North Island, where milder temperatures permitted the development of *kumara* agriculture (Best 1925), much of this forest destruction was related to clearance for cultivation. Once cleared and initially cultivated, the terrain tended to be re-vegetated, not by forest species, but by the bracken fern (*Pteridium esculentum*). This pyrophytic species was, in fact, a major food source for the Maori, having a large, starchy rhizome (K. Shawcross 1967). Helen Leach (1980) has recently argued that the succession to bracken fern was largely irreversible, and that land covered in fern could generally not be reclaimed again for *kumara* cultivation. As Leach points out, several 'important cultural implications' follow 'from the progressive and sometimes irreversible transformation of forest and shrub land into fern' (1980:144). A sedentary, agricultural community would, over time, be faced with a progressive loss of suitable garden land, and 'might eventually abandon horticulture entirely and adopt the bracken rhizome as their sole source of starch'. This is a trend which finds some resonance in the archaeological record (Leach and Leach 1979a; Houghton 1980). However, given the high cultural value placed upon *kumara* (especially

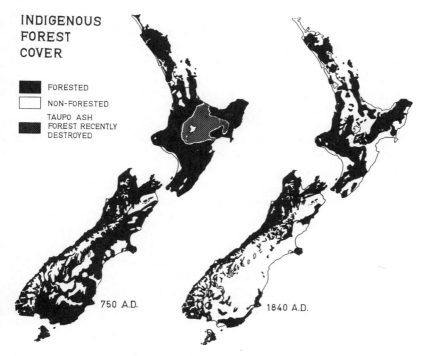

INDIGENOUS
FOREST
COVER

■ FORESTED

□ NON-FORESTED

▨ TAUPO ASH
FOREST RECENTLY
DESTROYED

750 A.D.

1840 A.D.

43. Prehistoric reduction in indigenous forest cover in New Zealand as shown by estimated extent of forest at the time of initial Polynesian colonization (*c.* AD 750) and just prior to European settlement (AD 1840) (after Cumberland 1961).

its role in feasting), the loss of status that would accompany such an economic shift would likely have been unacceptable, at least to a powerful group. 'Their alternative would have been to acquire new areas of lowland forest, initially by migration and later by conquest' (Leach 1980:144). Leach's thesis provides an especially clear case of the complex interactions between land-use patterns, environmental change, cultural values, and social conflict, themes that recur throughout.

Human impact on native fauna

It would be strange indeed if the tremendous impact of the Polynesians in greatly reducing the native forest cover of the Pacific Islands did not also have a correspondingly intense effect on island faunas. Oceanic islands are, after all, noted for the speciation and evolution of endemic birds, land snails, and insects – species vulnerable to competition and predation once the barrier of isolation is broken (Fosberg 1963a). Until recently, archaeological evidence for major human impact on Poly-nesian island faunas was largely confined to New Zealand, where the extinction of the large, flightless *moa* birds provided a spectacular case (and one that had inspired nearly a century of scientific debate). The picture is now rapidly changing, especially due to spectacular extinct avifaunal discoveries in Hawai'i. Our only certain conclusion at this stage of research is that we have but scratched the surface with regard to prehistoric human effects on island biota.

Although human impact on any landscape is cumulative, the major effect on island faunas often appears at the earlier end of an occupation sequence. Lapita colonization in the south-western Pacific left its mark on local populations of birds, shellfish, turtles, and fish. From several Lapita sites (Reef Islands, Tikopia, Naigani in Fiji) we now have osteological evidence for the rapid extinction of the megapode (*Megapodius freycinet*, and possibly other spp.), a large galliform bird. Studies by Swadling (summarized in Green 1976b:256–7) of shellfish remains in the Reef Islands Lapita sites have demonstrated that initial human exploitation of these molluscan populations led (1) to a decline in local species diversity, and (2) to a significant reduction in the maxi-mum size attained by individuals of various species.

The faunal sequence from Tikopia (Kirch and Yen 1982:274–310) provides an especially clear example of the impact of humans on a pre-viously uninhabited oceanic island. Site TK-4, occupied about 900 BC and representing initial settlement, is marked by: (1) an extremely high density of shellfish remains, including large individuals, many at the upper size limit known for their respective species; (2) the presence of *Megapodius*, as well as a possibly extinct species of rail; (3) a high density of turtle bones; (4) a broad range of terrestrial and sea birds; and (5) large numbers of fish bones, from a wide range of taxa. At the time of their initial arrival on Tikopia, the human colonists exploited dense populations of all these animals. Subsequently, the impact of the first few decades of human exploitation is reflected in the extirpation of the megapode, a great reduction in turtle, a decline in the quantity and sizes of shellfish, and in a reduction in numbers of birds and fish represented in later midden sites. The situation from Tikopia is by no means unique; the faunal sequence of the early Hane site in the Marquesas Islands exhibits a roughly parallel pattern (Kirch 1973).

New Zealand has long been famous for its extinct *moa* (Dinornithiformes) and the earliest Polynesian colonizers there have been dubbed 'moa hunters' in recognition of the role of *moa* hunting in their economies. These flightless birds, with their 'tubby' bodies and massive legs (Fig. 44), ranged in size from the towering *Dinornis giganteus*, perhaps 13 ft tall, to *Anomalopteryx oweni*, about the size of a bush turkey (Cassels 1979:31). The exact number of species of *moa* has been a matter of some controversy, with Archey's (1941) twenty species reduced by Cracraft (1976) to thirteen. More controversial has been the cause of *moa* extinction, with climatic deterioration and human impact being the two main contenders (Fleming 1962; Cumberland 1962a; Archey 1941; Cassels 1979; ms., n.d.).

The weight of scientific evidence now solidly backs the argument that the Polynesians were the primary agent in the extinction of this marvellous group of birds. Direct predation was doubtless a factor, but probably of far greater importance was the widespread destruction of the native habitats of the *moa*, due to fire. Ambrose (1968) vividly pre-

44. Reconstructions of four species of New Zealand *moa*, left to right: *Dinornis maximus, Aptornis* sp., *Euryapteryx gravis*, and *Cnemiornis* sp. (from Cumberland 1962a).

sented the archaeological evidence for what Jones called a 'cameo of man's destructive march through the countryside' (1975:31), the rapid entry of Polynesians into the inland plains of South Island, and the 'catastrophic' alteration of the region. As Ambrose states: 'the only interpretation necessary is that moas ceased to exist in the area after the first entry of fire and man . . . the first arrival of man marks the last appearance of moa' (1968:592). As Cassels (1979; ms., n.d.) notes, there is 'a fairly definite and striking absence of moa bones [in sites] later than the 1600s' (1979:32), suggesting that human impact had led to the birds' extinction within the first 600–800 years of Polynesian occupation in New Zealand. Moas were by no means the only birds affected by the arrival in New Zealand of the Polynesians. Some fourteen to sixteen other endemic species also went extinct during the early phase of Polynesian occupation. These include ducks, geese, a crow, an eagle, a coot, and others (Cassels, 1978–9). In addition, a number of species were extirpated in local areas.

Until recently, the New Zealand case appeared to be without parallel in Polynesia. In the late 1970s, however, investigation of several sand dune and cave localities in the Hawaiian Islands began to yield skeletal remains of previously unknown species of extinct, and often flightless birds (Olson and Wetmore 1976). Particularly rich concentrations of extinct bones in limestone sinkholes at Barbers Point, O'ahu (A. Sinoto 1978) raised the question of whether these species had coexisted with Polynesian man, and whether the latter was in any way implicated in their extinction. Investigations of non-marine molluscs from stratigraphic columns in these sinks, by Kirch and Christensen (1980) provided tantalizing evidence: massive numbers of extinct bird bones appeared at the same levels with the Polynesian-transported snail *Lamellaxis gracilis*, and with the bones of *Rattus exulans* and skinks, also Polynesian-introduced species. Further, these stratigraphic levels also showed dramatic changes in the relative frequency of the endemic land snail species, indicative of major environmental change (Fig. 45). The hypothesis could now be advanced that man was present prior to the extinction of the birds, and that his activities were possibly responsible for the changes in habitat.

Subsequent work at Barbers Point (Davis 1978) and elsewhere in Hawai'i has now left little doubt that habitation destruction, especially of lowland dry forests, by the Polynesians, resulted in the extinction of no less than forty species of birds (Olson and James 1982). One can only wonder that it took three decades of intensive work in Hawaiian archaeology before such a significant discovery was made!

Polynesian impact on island faunas was by no means restricted to birdlife. The destruction of large tracts of forest certainly resulted in the extinction of countless species of endemic insects, land snails, and other invertebrates. In Hawai'i, numerous species of endemic snails

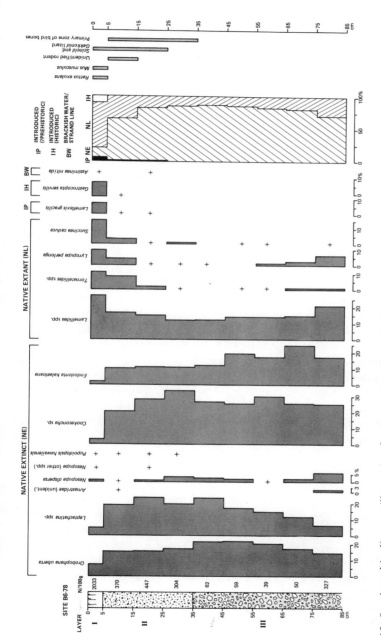

45. Stratigraphic diagram illustrating frequency changes in land snails in a limestone sink at Barber's Point, Oʻahu Island. The middle stratigraphic unit contains large numbers of bird bones, including extinct species; changes in the land snail profile indicate that this was a period of substantial environmental change.

were extinct within the period of Polynesian occupation (Kirch 1982a; 1983b). Nor was the impact of humans restricted to terrestrial animals. Swadling (1976) and A.J. Anderson (1979b, 1981) have both documented changes in the population structures of marine shellfish due to exploitation by man, though these changes did not result in extinction. It is certain that future work in Polynesian archaeology will continue to add to our knowledge of just how extensively the Polynesians modified, and often degraded, their island environments.

Overview

The dynamism of island environments operates at several levels, each with its own consequences for human adaptation. Long-term natural processes, such as tectonic uplift or climatic change, may radically alter an island's configuration or its possibilities for a particular kind of economic exploitation. Precisely because such processes occur so slowly, however, they do not invoke sudden stress, and may be countered through gradual, incremental adaptation. Quite the opposite is true of natural disasters, which as we have seen, occur repeatedly throughout Polynesia. These hazards, especially drought and cyclones, figured prominently in the evolution of Polynesian societies, for two reasons. First, they served as critical regulators for human populations, especially populations that had reached a relatively high density. Second, and equally important, such disasters – precisely because they recur stochastically and are thus in one sense predictable – encouraged the development of several forms of buffering, such as *masi* storage. Not only did these buffering mechanisms serve to offset (in part) the devastating effects of disasters, but they enhanced the economic, managerial role of the chiefly class. And, in times of relative abundance, stocks of preserved food provided a surplus that might well be put to political, rather than merely subsistence, ends.

More important than either low- or high-frequency cycles of natural environmental change, however, were the cumulative impacts wrought on island ecosystems by the Polynesians themselves. Ramon Margalef observed that 'the evolution of man has not been in the direction of passive adjustment to more mature ecosystems but is actively sustained through a regression of the rest of the biosphere' (1968:97). The history of man in Polynesia certainly lends credence to this proposition. The extremely high level of exploitation of natural resources by colonizing populations, which led fairly quickly to the extinction of many species and had a serious impact on the ecosystem as a whole, may have been a quite efficient strategy of colonization. It was, however, to have serious consequences for the colonists' descendants, who – faced with declining sources of natural protein, with degraded fernland savannahs, and frequently serious erosion – were encouraged to develop intensive forms of agricultural production.

Rhys Jones asserted that the main theme of New Zealand prehistory was 'dynamic linkage between economic experimentation and ecological tolerance, itself driven by the demographic engine of a human population' occupying a large empty island (1975:32). We may extend Jones's assertion, for New Zealand – despite its continental proportions – is but a mirror of parallel trends common to all of the Polynesian chiefdoms. Having now explored the demographic and environmental trends that underlie cultural change in Polynesia, let us turn to an analysis of the development of production systems in the course of island evolution.

7
Development and intensification of production

The dual horticultural–marine exploitation subsistence base of Ancestral Polynesian Society, transferred by intrepid colonists to a range of varied island environments, provided the foundation for indigenous production systems throughout Polynesia. Initial reassortment and adaptation of these systems was, however, only the first stage in the development of each island's productive base. Far more significant to an understanding of the evolution of the region's chiefdoms is the analysis of the longer-term intensification of production, and the relationship of such intensification to social and political structures.

The present chapter examines in greater detail the evidence for the development of production systems in several Polynesian societies. The term *development* must be understood here in a broad sense, as encompassing three major components: (1) adaptation (2) expansion, and (3) intensification. Local development of production systems required adaptation to particular environmental conditions and constraints. As noted in Chapter 4, the adaptive component of development is markedly evident in the colonization phases of most island sequences, although later adaptation to new or changing conditions also occurred regularly. Assuming successful adaptation, the development of production systems usually proceeded as a matter of simple *expansion*; forest was cleared for shifting cultivation, breadfruit and coconut groves planted, pig herds enlarged, and so on. Perhaps the most significant component of production development, however, is *intensification*, which unlike expansion, involves an increased labour input (either for the construction of permanent facilities, such as pondfields, or in the daily labour input to agriculture and fishing) to achieve a relative increase in yields. The intensification of production systems characterizes all Polynesian developmental sequences, even though particular forms and emphases vary from place to place. Moreover, this was 'intensification of domestic production by political means and for public purposes' (Sahlins 1972:148), a critical aspect in the evolution of Polynesian chiefdoms.

Development of production systems

For many Polynesian societies, the historical development of local production systems is only sketchily known from direct archaeological evidence, and reconstruction is largely a matter of inference and speculation. In several cases, however, recent archaeological studies provide reasonably good data with which to reconstruct the development of production. I will briefly review the evidence for two of these cases – Tikopia and the Marquesas – with an emphasis on certain underlying regularities.

Tikopia

A Polynesian Outlier with only 4.6 km² of land area (plus 1.1 km² of brackish lake), Tikopia has been continuously inhabited by descendants of Lapita potters since about 900 BC. In previous chapters, I mentioned the dynamic landscape changes witnessed during the period of human tenure on the island, and examined the ethnographic evidence for the contact-period population of Tikopia as one close to carrying capacity, and regulated by a variety of cultural controls. The island's rich archaeological record (Kirch and Yen 1982) permitted a detailed reconstruction of the development of production, from initial colonization through to recent changes influenced by Western contact. This evolutionary sequence is graphically portrayed in Figure 46, in which environmental change, agro-environmental adaptations, and production system transformations are shown in relation to both 'absolute' and cultural time-scales.

The transference and establishment of an agricultural subsistence base by the initial colonizers is demonstrated by a range of evidence from the early TK-4 site, including the skeletal remains of domestic pig, dog, and fowl, anthropophilic snails, and such implements as vegetable peelers. It is not possible on archaeological grounds to be more specific about the nature of the cultigen roster, although we presume that the dominant Oceanic crops – aroids, yams, bananas, and breadfruit – were among those transported to the island. We can, however, say something regarding agronomic practice: excavations in the intensively cultivated Rakisu tract (Kirch and Yen 1982:147–60) have shown that fire was an integral part of early agricultural practice on Tikopia, and we would argue that the primary method of gardening for the first 1500–2000 years of the Tikopia sequence was shifting cultivation. Restricted in area at first, shifting cultivations gradually expanded to encompass virtually the entire island, replacing the natural rainforest. Among the archaeological signals of this expansion of agriculture is the stratigraphic evidence for increased rates of hillslope erosion, and deposition of soil in colluvial fans.

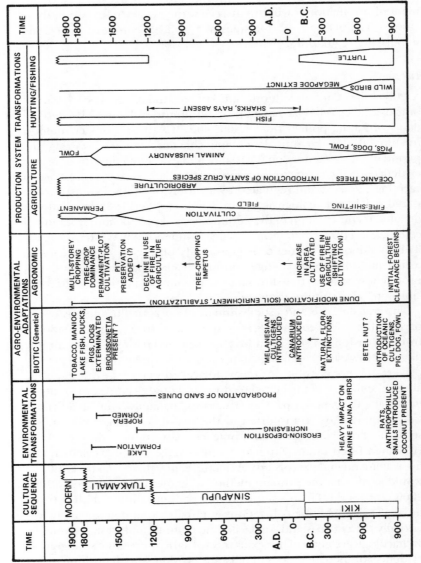

46. The development of the Tikopia production system, shown in relation to major environmental transformations (after Kirch and Yen 1982).

In a pattern common to the colonization phases of most oceanic islands, the initial subsistence base of Tikopia was marked by heavy exploitation of indigenous birds and marine fauna. The quantities of bird, fish, turtle, and shellfish in the early TK-4 site reflect the natural abundance of an indigenous fauna prior to human exploitation (Fig. 21). Such high resource levels did not long withstand the sustained pressure of human predation, leading to a dramatic reduction over time in both the variety and quantity of meat in the Tikopia diet. Most striking in this regard was the local extinction of the largest land bird, a megapode. The reduction in wild meat intake was to a degree (though not totally) offset by the development of animal husbandry, particularly of pigs. Given the integration of pigs and agriculture throughout Oceania (Yen 1973a; Kirch 1979c), increasing importance of pig husbandry can also be regarded as a reflection of the island's expanding agricultural base.

In the final phase of the Tikopia sequence – the Tuakamali – the island's production system underwent a series of radical changes, some relatively sudden in onset, others reflecting trends initiated in preceding phases. These transformations were played out against a sequence of dramatic landscape change, including the conversion of a large saltwater bay to a closed, brackish lake. The previously dominant shifting cultivation was replaced gradually by a system of permanent orchard gardening in which tree crops were arrayed in multi-storeyed association (e.g., *Cyrtosperma, Antiaris, Artocarpus, Metroxylon,* and *Cocos* forming ascending levels). This had the further effect of restricting yam–aroid field cropping to relatively permanent, intensive tracts (such as Rakisu). Among the adaptive features of this arboricultural system are its ability to reduce the risk of crop destruction from cyclones (by sheltering the lower-storey crops, especially *Cyrtosperma*) and its retardation of hillslope erosion. A more dramatic change of the Tuakamali Phase was the sudden extermination of the island's pig herd, a decision with obvious social as well as dietary implications. Since pigs are a major item of group exchange in virtually all Oceanic societies, their elimination may also have occasioned a re-ordering of exchange valuables (today, barkcloth and mats are the principal articles of exchange between kin groups). The expunging of this high-quality food source, which had an effect of reducing the overall meat intake in the local diet, was most likely a response to an intolerable level of human-husbanded animal competition, itself implying a high human population density (see Chapter 5).

While the evolution of the Tikopia production system can be read as a set of complex interactions between demography, technology, and natural resources, it is important to stress that the cultural factor is by no means absent in the archaeological reconstruction (Kirch and Yen 1982:355–9). As we have argued, several changes in local resource use can only be explained with reference to decisions based on cultural values. The clearest instances of this are the absence, for 1300 years in the Tikopia sequence, of turtles, sharks, and rays, and later in time, the removal of eels and puffer-fish from the diet. All of these animals have associations, in contemporary Tikopia or in surrounding islands (e.g., the Santa Cruz and Banks Islands groups), with totem and *tapu*. We have argued that their long absence from the Tikopia faunal record cannot be due either to local extinction of the species, or to sampling error, and must therefore reflect culturally prescribed valuations of these foods as edible or inedible (cf. Sahlins 1976:171).

The long-term development of the Tikopia production system was thus marked by two dominant, gradual trends: an expansion of the terrestrial, agricultural sector, matched by a reduction in the quantity as well as diversity of animal food. In agriculture, the initial expansion of a slash-and-burn cropping mode shifted to an arboricultural emphasis, with its risk minimization. The addition of pit fermentation late in the sequence may reflect some intensification of agricultural production, as does the labour-intensive cultivation of Rakisu. In the exploitative sector of subsistence, the pressures of continued human harvesting reduced dramatically initial high yields of wild resources: birds, fish, turtles, shellfish. This reduction in available protein was only partially offset by the development of pig husbandry, itself ultimately eliminated.

The Marquesas

The Marquesas Islands contrast in several important respects with Tikopia. On the one hand, we have a single, small island – on the other a large archipelago; whereas Tikopia has broad reef flats and a diverse tropical fish fauna, the Marquesas lack extensive coral reefs and have correspondingly depauperate fish resources. In terms of human settlement, Tikopia was settled at least 600 years earlier than the Marquesas. Yet, despite these contrasts, the development of production systems exhibit, in both cases, a number of significant regularities. Figure 47 is a graphic synthesis of the available data bearing on the temporal development of Marquesan production systems, drawing largely from the work of Suggs (1960a, 1961), Sinoto (1966, 1970, 1979a) and Kirch (1973).

Sites of the Settlement Period (Hane, Ha'atuatua) reflect the same dominant emphasis on exploitation of the abundant wild resources of land and sea evident in the colonization phase of Tikopia, a pattern evidently characteristic of Oceanic colonization in general. Several lines of evidence indicate that the first settlers did establish an agricultural base, but the importance of agriculture is not evident archaeologically until near the end of the Settlement Period. Interestingly, the faunal data from the MUH1 site (Kirch 1973) suggest that

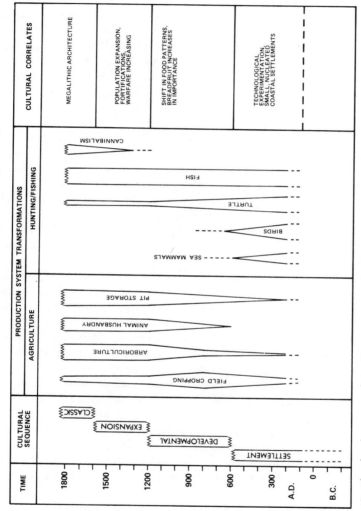

47. The development of the Marquesan production system.

domestic pig and dog may not have been introduced until later during this period (we must, however, be cautious of possible sampling error in this case).

As in Tikopia, the early emphasis on exploitation of wild resources led to a reduction in the natural abundance of several species populations, notably sea mammals (especially porpoise), birds, and turtles. By the end of the Settlement Period, both birds and sea mammals had ceased to be regular items in the Marquesan diet.

Suggs's choice of the term 'Developmental' for the succeeding cultural period was apt, for this stage saw the establishment of a basic production system that was only further elaborated in succeeding periods. After an early phase of technological experimentation, fishing gear for the exploitation of deep bays and rocky shorelines characteristic of the Marquesas had become standardized (Kirch 1980a, b; see Chapter 4). The early heavy reliance on birds and sea mammals had, however, ceased. In their stead, we now see the evidence of animal husbandry, of both pigs and dogs. The Marquesan agricultural pattern, with its emphasis on arboriculture, and especially breadfruit, was firmly established during the Developmental Period, witnessed archaeologically by an increased frequency in peelers of *Cypraea* shell (Suggs 1961:181–2). Suggs opined that 'large breadfruit groves, such as those described in historic sources, were probably in this period first planted in the valley bottoms' (1961:182). Arboriculture did not, however, totally supplant other forms of field cultivation, and small irrigated terrace systems for *Colocasia* culture are reported from many Marquesan valleys (Handy 1923; Kellum-Ottino 1971; Bellwood 1972a).

I noted in Chapter 6 that the Marquesan emphasis on tree cropping of breadfruit, coupled with the local frequency of drought and consequent famine, led to a remarkable development of *ma* storage capacity. Two settlement pattern studies have been carried out in the Marquesas, in the Hane Valley of Uahuka (Kellum-Ottino 1971) and in the Hanatekua Valley of Hiva Oa (Bellwood 1972a), and these provide some indication of the scale of *ma* storage. In Hanatekua, Bellwood recorded eighteen pits, with a total estimated storage capacity of 67 m^3 of preserved breadfruit paste. The Hane Valley has some thirty-three pits dispersed in clusters throughout the valley (but concentrated in the interior portions); in addition, there are thirteen pits constructed into house platforms. The total storage capacity of these forty-six pits may be estimated at about 292 m^3. Both of these valleys are rather small, and were politically unimportant. In the densely settled large valleys which were centres of political power, such as Taipivai on Nukuhiva, *ma* storage capacities were evidently greater still. Linton reports that a single pit in Taipivai had a volume of 216 m^3 (1925:103).

The Expansion and Classic Periods were marked by further expansion of the basic production patterns established during the Developmental Period, spurred on by a major increase in population and expansion of settlement into marginal lands. That the archipelago's population began to approach some form of limit conditions is suggested by the proliferation of ridge-top fortifications, and other evidence for inter-valley warfare and competition.

One development of the late Expansion and Classic Periods, chilling in its implications, was cannibalism. In the Hane Dune Site faunal sequence, the archaeological evidence for consumption of human flesh is irrefutable: scattered, broken, and often charred human bones were found in the upper levels of the dune (Kirch 1973). Suggs (1960a:122; 1961:25) reports the 'remains of a young child who had been cooked and partially eaten' in one of the Uea Valley rockshelters (Site NBM 4), occupied from Expansion through Classic Periods. Ethnographic information on cannibalism (Handy 1923:138–40, 218–21) indicates that the victims (called *ika*, 'fish', as in Fiji) were enemies from warring tribes, and that revenge – rather than malnutrition – was the principal motive. Nonetheless, the institutionalization of cannibalism in late prehistoric Marquesan society must be taken as a symptom of tensions which had developed between social groups, exacerbated by dense populations and recurrent famines.

Comparison

Despite differences in scale, in aspects of local environment, and in length of human tenure, both the Tikopia and Marquesas sequences exhibit parallel trends in the development of production. Archaeological evidence from other Polynesian islands would support the notion that these two evolutionary trajectories reflect, in their general trends, those of most Polynesian islands. To be sure, local differences exist and must be taken into account. The emphasis in Tikopia and the Marquesas on arboriculture, for example, is replaced in other archipelagos by dryfield cropping or irrigation, as we shall see further below. In New Zealand, harsh environmental conditions necessitated a greater readaptation of the agricultural subsistence base than elsewhere. In spite of these caveats, we can use the Tikopia and Marquesas cases to illustrate several major trends in the development of Polynesian production systems:

1. A discrete colonization phase is recognizable, marked by a heavy exploitation of and dependence on wild resources. The effects of such heavy predation were to greatly reduce certain food species populations within a few centuries of initial settlement. This phase is also characterized by a high rate of technological experimentation and adaptation (see Kirch 1980a, b) in both the agricultural and hunting–fishing components of production.

2. Once a human population had become permanently established,

and initial adaptations to local environmental conditions achieved, an increasing dominance and expansion of agricultural production was undertaken, a trend which continues throughout the sequences. Expansion of agricultural production was further marked by an increase in animal husbandry.

3. Despite the above trend, production of domestic animals never appears to fully replace the protein available from natural resources during the colonization phase, so that production systems reflect a gradual reduction in available meat over time.

4. As the natural vegetation was cleared and wild animals exploited (some species to the point of local extirpation), and with the expansion of agriculture, the local ecosystems underwent a successional 're- gression' to a simpler form (Margalef 1968; Odum 1969). Thus the development of production systems reflects increasing management of the environment, which may include considerable alteration and even degradation of local landscapes.

5. Finally, there is evidence for increasing intensification of pro- duction later in island developmental sequences. In Tikopia, and more clearly in the Marquesas, this is exhibited in pit storage of breadfruit. Local forms of intensification vary from locality to locality, but the underlying trend appears consistent. Of the several trends that we have isolated, this is doubtless the most significant for an evolutionary analysis of the Polynesian chiefdoms.

Production and the chieftainship

The Tikopian and Marquesan sequences reveal an increasing develop- ment and intensification of production, and the same general trend can be demonstrated, to greater or lesser degrees, for all Polynesian societies. The simple determinist explanation would be to label popu- lation growth and 'pressure' as the cause for such intensification, seeing the latter as a direct response to the former. While population growth is surely one factor in the development of production, this explanation is unacceptable on several counts. First, elevating population growth to independent variable status ignores the evidence for cultural regulation of population throughout Polynesia. Second, and more serious, it takes no account of the social relations of production, of the dominant struc- tures that organize production. A more dynamic model is called for, one that can incorporate demography, technology, environmental conditions and constraints, and the social relations of production into a system that does not reduce to simplistic linear causality.

Ancestral Polynesian Society did not operate at the theoretical 'domestic mode of production', or of *underproduction* as Sahlins (1972) has characterized the DMP. Demand of goods for exchange, for meeting ritual obligations, and for the maintenance and aggrandizement of the chiefly line, impelled production beyond the minimal level sufficient for reproduction of individual households. Particularly when we consider the demands of status-conscious and competitive chiefs (dependent for their prestige upon the successful production and redistribution of food and status goods), it is evident that we need to analyse production in terms of both *necessary production* as well as *surplus*. As H. Pearson (1957; see also Harris 1959; Dalton 1960; Orans 1966) pointed out some time ago, the term 'surplus' can only be understood in its institutional context, and does *not* imply some superfluous entity with an inherent capacity to cause the development of social stratification. Rather, by surplus we mean that portion of production which extends beyond the sphere of individual households, and which therefore finances the general public economy, and especially, the political actions of the chiefs. We should also note that this surplus production is dominantly agricultural, although non-agricultural products (e.g., prestige goods such as mats and barkcloth) are also involved. However, as indicated in Chapter 2, the production of food was the key to Polynesian economies, and the control and distribution of surplus food the key to larger social and political relations. Indeed, it was such surplus food which (in the larger societies at least) fed the chiefs and their retainers, who constituted a non-food-producing class.

The production of an agricultural surplus, and its appropriation and distribution by *ariki*, was doubtless an important part of the economy of Ancestral Polynesian Society. We have already noted the pan-Polynesian practice of first-fruits tribute, one of the important mechanisms for surplus appropriation. Thus, whereas certain earlier studies (e.g., Sahlins 1958) attributed the appearance of Polynesian chieftainship to the development of surplus production, the relationship is 'at least mutual', if not largely the other way around (Sahlins 1972:140). 'Leadership continually generates domestic surplus. The development of rank and chieftainship becomes, *pari passu*, development of the productive forces' (1972:140).

It is important as well to consider surplus as a dynamic variable, in relation to changing demands both from the socio-political system, and from demographic and techno-environmental conditions. The work of Sachs (1966) and of Friedman (1979) on the notion of the production function provide a basis for such an analysis. Given the nature of Ancestral Polynesian Society, a constant or increasing level of surplus was vital to the successful reproduction of the society as structurally constituted. We can portray this in a simple diagram (Fig. 48) where for any given labour force or population, L_x, yield (Y_x) must be sufficient to produce not only for necessary consumption (V_x, subsistence production at the household level), but a surplus (S_x), where $Y = V + S$. Given an increasing population, production must maintain a positive rate of surplus increase ($dS/dt > 0$), as well as a positive ratio between yield and labour input $(dY/dL > 0)$ (cf. Harris 1959:198). Further, since the chiefs were inherently status conscious and competitive, there would have been a tendency to increase the ratio of S/V over time (assuming, for the moment, that no limiting conditions impinged on the development of the productive apparatus).

While the continued reproduction of the society required this concomitant production of a surplus, a variety of limiting conditions impinged. We can begin to understand these by considering the production function, as developed by Sachs (1966) and elaborated by Friedman (1979), shown here in Figure 49. Considering a given technology for production (T_x), in a particular environment, the relation between L and Y takes the form of a curve, indicated in the diagram (the

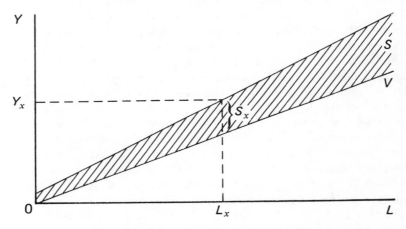

48. The production of surplus (S) over subsistence production at the household level (V). See text for discussion.

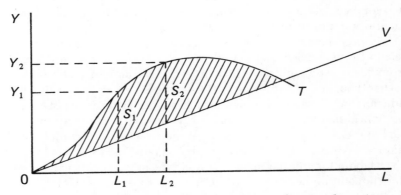

49. A graphic model of the production function for a given technology (T). The shaded zone represents surplus yield over necessary production (V). See text for discussion.

surplus at any given time is indicated by the shaded zone). For a constant area of land, an increase in L will produce, at first, a relatively rapid increase in Y, which, however, gradually tapers off, and ultimately declines past a point of diminishing returns. When we analyse the situation with respect to time, that is, when increasing L is the result of a growing population, we see that there are several critical points on the function $0T$. The first critical point (L_1, Y_1) is reached when the rate of increase in surplus relative to yield begins to drop $(d^2S/dY^2 < 0)$. The second critical point (L_2, Y_2) occurs later when surplus actually begins to decline relative to yield $(dS/dY < 0)$. The operational threshold of the system, of course, is reached when $Y = V$, at which point no surplus exists at all. It is most unlikely that any social system will get to this third point, however, for critical and untolerable pressures will build up much earlier, as surplus begins to decrease, threatening the existent social relations of production and authority of the polity.

Following Friedman (1979:171–4), we can divide the production function into a series of regions which correspond to a hierarchy of increasing, additive constraints (Fig. 50). Region I 'is the sector of maximal expansion where surplus is forthcoming at an increasing rate' $(d^2S/dY^2 > 0)$, and would be characteristic of Polynesian island systems following initial colonization and adaptation, but prior to the achievement of limits in land area or of degradation of resources. Both yield and surplus increase faster than labour (population), and chiefs are able to easily appropriate surplus to meet competitive and ritual demands. In Region II, however, the cost of producing a surplus begins to increase, even though the ratio of surplus to yield is positive $(dS/dY > 0)$. At this stage, competition between chiefs for surplus may intensify. In Region III, the situation becomes acute, for now surplus is declining

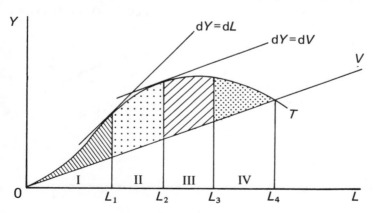

50. The production function divided into a series of regions characterized by a hierarchy of constraints; see text for discussion (after Friedman 1979).

relative to yield ($dS/dY < 0$), even though $dY/dL > 0$. Since the absolute
surplus is now diminishing, even though demand is not, the tension
between chiefs and the cultivators may become critical at this stage.
Finally, in Region IV, we are 'over the hill', and the system is in general
decline, since yield is decreasing relative to labour input ($dY/dL < 0$).

The above analysis held both the technology of production and the
environment constant, an unrealistic condition. In any real Polynesian
system, steps would have been taken to intensify production well
before the critical Region III was entered; likewise, cultural controls on
population growth may have served as a brake on development. The
effect of intensification of production, such as through irrigation or of
construction of fishponds, can be diagrammed in Figure 51. A shift
from one level of technology (T_1) to a more intensive one (T_2) will shift
the productive function to a new curve (such a shift being made with a
certain cost in labour input).

The process of intensification, in short, results both from the
increased demands for necessary consumption posed by a growing
population, and the demands of the chiefs for surplus sufficient to
underwrite their political actions and enhance their prestige. The
proximate cause for intensification frequently lies in the demands of
the prestige or public economy, rather than in direct population pressure, since the impetus for increased surplus will arise well before Y
approaches V (the limiting condition for population growth being $Y = V$).
At the same time, population increase provides the dynamic context for
the changing equations between L, Y, and S. Population growth, in
short, is an ultimate rather than proximate cause.

While intensification of agriculture or of fishing can shift the production function to a new curve, thus meeting the increased demands
for surplus, the role of a dynamic environment cannot be ignored. In
Chapter 6, evidence for environmental change of several kinds was

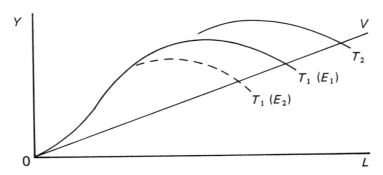

51. The effects of intensification (T_2) and of environmental
degradation (T_1 in E_2) on a production function; see text for
discussion.

marshalled, and stochastic perturbations and longer-term modifications of ecosystems were shown to be significant in Polynesia. Figure 51 diagrams the potential effect of environmental degradation (e.g., erosion of formerly arable hillslopes) on a particular production system: the production function is lowered once the process of degradation sets in. Thus, environmental degradation may offset, partially or wholly, gains made by intensification. Similarly, an environmental hazard – cyclone, drought, and so on – may have the effect of suddenly lowering yield and reducing available surplus, throwing the system into a crisis. Of course, not all environmental changes were deleterious, and some modifications such as valley-infilling may have enhanced the potential for further intensification (Spriggs 1981).

Having argued that the social relations of production and especially the demands of the *ariki* for surplus were a major impetus to intensification, some ethnographic data on the economic role of Polynesian chiefs is in order. Three points are important here: (1) the role of chiefs in controlling and directing production; (2) the means by which a surplus product was appropriated; and (3) the particular uses which chiefs made of surplus production.

In all Polynesian societies, individual households comprised the basic units of production, consumption, and exchange, but the larger economic system was far more than a mere summation of these units, and the chiefship played a dominant role in the integration of the whole. We noted in Chapter 2 that religious activity formed an integral part of Polynesian economic practice, and it was in his control of ritual that the chief exercised significant power over production. The timing of agricultural calendars, for example, depended upon a seasonal cycle of ritual activity, determined by the chief. In Tikopia, for instance, the 'work of the gods' (Firth 1967) regulated such economic activities as yam planting, canoe repair, and turmeric extraction. Not only does 'the imperative of the ritual' provide a 'safeguard to production', but economic ritual 'helps in the perpetuation of the system of production and distribution in vogue in the society, and in particular, *in the maintenance of the economic position of people of rank*' (Firth 1939:182, 171, my italics). In ritually directing production at a certain level of effort, the chiefs assured the continuance of the established political order.

The *tapu* associated with Polynesian *ariki* was not merely a passive indicator of rank, it was actively used as an economic tool. By the imposition of a *tapu* or interdiction on the use of terrestrial or marine resources, the chief not only 'reserved their yield for collective purposes'; the dual effect was also to raise domestic production levels, since 'in the absence of a prohibition on standing crops further labor would not have been necessary' (Sahlins 1968:91). The imposition of chiefly interdictions on the use of resources is ubiquitous in Polynesian ethnography. Throughout central East Polynesia, such restrictions go under the term *rahui* or a cognate reflex. Handy (1923:59) reports that in the Marquesas, chiefs anticipating a large tribal feast might impose an *ahui* on a significant portion of the standing crop for as long as one year. In Mangareva, 'closed seasons (*ra'ui*) were declared in connection with food, and putting them into effect was the ruler's privilege' (Buck 1938a:161). In the Society Islands, *rahui* were enforced not only by supernatural sanctions, but by the threat of land dispossession for those who disobeyed (Oliver 1974:633). *Rahui* have been interpreted by some anthropologists as primitive 'conservation' measures, and in some cases they may have had that effect, but as Oliver points out, they were 'deliberately imposed for the benefit of the imposers' (1974:1072), and such was their primary intention. *Tapu* allowed the Polynesian chief 'to take charge of the economic forces . . . in the interests of the community' (Firth 1939:212), as well as in the interests of the chiefs.

The role of Polynesian chiefs in production extended further, to the development of permanent facilities, as, for example, with the irrigation complexes and fishponds of Hawai'i. Earle (1978:183) observes that a Hawaiian chief could greatly increase the productive capacity of his lands by improving irrigation facilities, and invested surplus agricultural produce in such works by feeding the large labour force enlisted to carry out such projects. I'i (1959:68–9) describes how Kamehameha, following his conquest of O'ahu, set about expanding the irrigation facilities of the fertile leeward valleys of Nu'uanu, Manoa, and at Waikiki (see also Kirch and Sahlins, in preparation). The large coastal fishponds of Hawai'i were likewise the product of corvée labour, initiated by chiefs (Summers 1964:2). Even in the less stratified societies, such as New Zealand Maori, the chief assumed the initiative in the construction of large public works (Firth 1959a:133).

Turning to the chiefly *appropriation* of surplus (both property and labour), we again note the religious ideology, summarized by Goldman: 'The ariki stands to the people as a god. As the deity is the primary source of food and must therefore receive back a portion of it – a divine economic circulation – so the chief, the divine exemplar, must occupy a parallel place as a center of circulation' (1970:485). The ancestral mode of appropriation of surplus was probably that represented by sacrificial offerings, first fruits, presented to the chief in his ritual capacity as representative of the deities. As Firth (1939) shows for Tikopia, first fruits (the term, *muakai*, is literally 'foremost foods') are used by the chiefs to further their place in the economic hierarchy, recycled in the elaborate system of group exchange in which the chief is expected to play the dominant role.

As the power of the chieftainship expanded in various Polynesian societies, the ancestral pattern of first fruits and similar ritual tribute developed into various systems of regular taxation, though still retaining their ritual guise. 'In the system of tributes', Goldman writes, 'the transformation was from voluntary giving within a pattern of mutual honoring to compulsory giving within a pattern of unequal reciprocity' (1970:511). The Hawaiian *makahiki*, with its elaborate associated cult of Lono, and the Tongan '*inasi*, represent peaks within Polynesia of the transformation of first fruits to regularized taxation. To a lesser degree, however, the same process occurred in many island societies. In both Mangareva and Mangaia, for instance, tenant cultivators owed regular tribute to the landed chiefs and warriors (Buck 1938a, 1934). Nor was surplus appropriated solely in the form of food or material property, for in some societies (especially Hawai'i) corvée labour became a formalized institution.

Finally, we may consider the varied uses to which chiefs put the appropriated surplus. In the less stratified societies, the majority of such surplus was returned to the producers by redistribution, whether by exchanges with chiefly families, or by the sponsorship by chiefs of large communal feasts. Such was, probably, the pattern in Ancestral Polynesian Society as well. While feasts served to redistribute the surplus, they also provided the chief an opportunity to assert his rank and prestige, and to demonstrate the efficacy of his *mana* (Firth 1939:222), which in turn enhanced his ability to direct production and to appropriate surplus. In many societies, accumulated surplus was used to alleviate famine following natural disasters. Such was one function of the large communal breadfruit pits of the Marquesas, under chiefly control (Handy 1923).

As the degree of social stratification increased in various Polynesian societies (in part, as a function of the chiefly ability to control production and accumulate surplus), the proportion of surplus actually redistributed to the people at large decreased. Thus, in societies such as Hawai'i, Tonga, and Tahiti, large quantities of food, and a considerable degree of corvée labour, were invested in the support of large chiefly establishments and entourages, in the construction of major public works (both economic, such as irrigation systems and fishponds, and ceremonial, such as temples and chiefs' tombs), and in the support of craft specialists. Oliver reports that construction of a major temple (*marae*) in the Society Islands might be preceded by a *rahui* lasting two or three years, in order to accumulate the necessary surplus to feed the labourers and to 'provide food for the marae consecration ceremony' (1974:996). Even in these highly stratified societies, however, chiefs were still expected to work for the communal welfare, and an overly bloated chieftainship might raise the spectre of rebellion. While the more advanced Polynesian societies pushed the evolution of the chiefdom economy to its organizational limits, they never fully divorced the system from its ancestral kinship ideology.

Intensive production: the wet and the dry

Variability in indigenous Polynesian agricultural systems, displayed in the ethnographic record, is evident in the different emphases of particular, intensified systems: one may cite, as examples, the water-control (irrigation/drainage) cropping systems of Hawai'i, Futuna, or 'Uvea (Kirch 1976, 1977a, 1978b), the intensive tree cropping of breadfruit with concomitant pit-storage in the Marquesas and Mangareva (Handy 1923; Buck 1938a), and the dryfield rotational cropping system of Anuta (Yen 1973b). As Jacques Barrau (1965a) pointed out, Oceanic agricultures incorporate a fundamental wet/dry dichotomy, evident not only in crop plants, and in edaphic–hydrologic modifications of environment, but in ritual and symbolic systems as well. This contrast between the wet and the dry is inherent in the ecological templates of the two dominant cultigens of Oceanic agriculture: taro (*Colocasia esculenta*) and the greater yam (*Dioscorea alata*). Taro, while not restricted to wet situations, responds most favourably under inundation, specifically by means of pondfield irrigation or in some similar aqueous environment. The tropophytic yams, on the other hand, require well-drained soils, inspiring the agronomic mirror-image of taro cultivation, elaborate mounding or drainage techniques. The sweet potato (*Ipomoea batatas*), as an additive element in Polynesia (Yen 1974a), has further strengthened the dry half of the contrast, particularly in East Polynesia, where its entry can be ascribed to prehistoric times.

This wet/dry dichotomy is not merely an operational perspective of the ethnographer, but forms an essential part of indigenous folk agronomy. A Hawaiian informant of the nineteenth century began an account of local agriculture with the statement: '*Elua ano a ka aina, he maloo a he wai . . .*'; 'of two kinds is the land, the dry and the wet' (Fornander 1919:160). Because the distinction is so fundamental in Polynesia, it provides a basis for discussing the archaeological evidence for prehistoric cropping systems.

Irrigation and drainage

The taro irrigation systems of Polynesia, and especially those of Hawai'i, have attracted considerable attention as witnesses of former agricultural intensification, and have figured in the debate over the 'hydraulic hypothesis' (Wittfogel 1957; Goldman 1970; Earle 1978). Such systems are perhaps more correctly conceived not as irrigation in the narrow sense, but as *water control*, incorporating both inundated pondfields and raised garden beds in naturally swampy terrain. Technical variation in hydrology, edaphic modification, and agronomic practice was in fact considerable in Polynesian water-control systems, but in all cases the underlying objective was the same: the creation of a suitable hydromorphic medium for the production of *Colocasia*.

Simplest of all water-control taro cultivation systems was that developed primarily on atolls, such as in the Cook Islands and the Tuamotu archipelago (e.g., Chazine 1977). A pit or trench was excavated through the coral sand of a large atoll islet, to a depth sufficient to allow the taro tubers to tap the shallow Ghyben–Herzberg aquifer of fresh water. Such taro fields were frequently mulched with organic debris to create a fertile planting medium.

On many Polynesian high islands, the coastal alluvial plains or lowlands are in places swampy and, if adequately drained to permit the flow of water (and to counter stagnation), these naturally hydromorphic soils are well adapted to intensive taro culture. The agronomic technique in these situations is to dig a network of reticulate ditches separating slightly raised garden beds upon which taro is planted. Such drainage systems are known ethnographically for 'Uvea (Kirch 1978b), and the Society Islands (Handy 1930b), whereas Ishizuki (1974) reports on a prehistoric drainage system in the Falefa Valley, Samoa. A set of drained beds in 'Uvea is illustrated in Figure 52.

The third category of Polynesian water-control taro systems are those utilizing true pondfields (generally terraces, though also sunken fields in some instances), irrigated from a water source such as a spring or

52. Intensive swamp cultivation of taro (*Colocasia esculenta*) on raised garden beds on 'Uvea Island.

stream. Such irrigated complexes range considerably in their complexity and scale, and at least four major types may be distinguished: (I) simple terrace systems situated in stream channels; (II) systems fed by a single ditch or spring which debauches directly into the uppermost field; (III) systems with peripheral ditches providing multiple feed into a number of fields, and sometimes with ditch bifurcations; and (IV) systems fed by more than a single ditch or spring (Kirch 1977a:260). These types are diagrammatically portrayed in Figure 53. Not surprisingly,

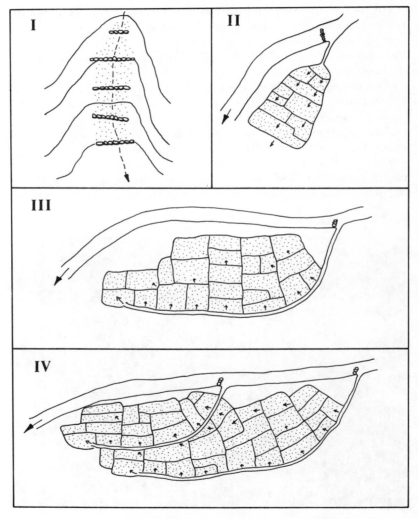

53. A diagrammatic classification of prehistoric Hawaiian pondfield irrigation systems; see text for discussion (from Kirch 1977a).

Table 19. *Wet cultivation of taro (Colocasia) in Polynesia*

Island/group	System types*	Agricultural significance**	References
Futuna	P, G	D	Kirch 1975
'Uvea	G	S	Kirch 1978b
Samoa	G	S/M	Ishizuki 1974
Rarotonga	P, G	S	Buck 1944; Bellwood 1978b
Mangaia	P, G	D	Buck 1934; B. Allen 1971
Society Islands	G, P	S/M	Green 1961; Oliver 1974
Marquesas	P	M	Handy 1923
Tuamotu Islands	S	S/M	Chazine 1977
Mangareva	P, S	M	Buck 1938a
Rapa	P	D	Stokes ms; Hanson 1970
Rurutu	P	S	Vérin 1969
Tubuai	P	S	Aitken 1930
Raivavae	P	D	
Pitcairn	P?	?	
Hawaiian Islands	P, G	S/D	Handy and Handy 1972; Kirch 1977a; Earle 1980

*Key: P, irrigated pondfields; G, drained garden beds; S, sunken pits.
**Key: D, dominant; S, significant; M, minor.

there tends to be close correlation between type and scale, as we shall see with regard to the Hawaiian examples.

The distribution of water-control systems throughout Polynesia is summarized in Table 19, which also provides data on the scale of individual systems and on the importance of irrigation/drainage in the total agricultural production complex. Among the most developed and intensive irrigation complexes are those of Futuna and Hawai'i. The Futunan systems (Fig. 54) have been studied both ethnographically and archaeologically (Kirch 1975), though absolute dating has only been able to project their age back into the late prehistoric period. It is in Hawai'i that the most detailed archaeological investigations of taro irrigation have been conducted.

The geographic distribution of taro irrigation in Hawai'i reflects the local availability of surface water and, to an extent, the degree of landform dissection, so that the greatest development of irrigation took place on the older, western islands of Kaua'i and O'ahu (Handy 1940; Handy and Handy 1972; Earle 1980). Nevertheless, the windward zones of all islands supported substantial tracts of irrigated pondfields, and recent archaeological surveys have demonstrated a remarkable extension of irrigation practice even on leeward slopes, as at Lalamilo, Hawai'i Island (J. Clark 1981; Clark and Kirch 1983).

Intensive archaeological studies of prehistoric and early historic irrigation in Hawai'i have focussed on five areas: the Halele'a District of Kaua'i Island (Earle 1978; Schilt 1980a; Athens 1983); the upper Makaha Valley, O'ahu (Yen *et al.* 1972); the Anahulu Valley, O'ahu (Kirch 1979b; Kirch and Sahlins, in preparation); the Halawa Valley, Moloka'i (Kirch and Kelly 1975); and the Kohala valleys, Hawai'i (Tuggle and Tomonari-Tuggle 1980). As a result of these studies, the scale, complexity, and agronomy of indigenous Hawaiian irrigation are now relatively well understood (for summaries, see Kirch 1977a and Earle 1980). The Hawaiian irrigation systems include all four types listed above, and range from small sets of a few terraces covering as little as 0.07 hectare to extensive complexes blanketing alluvial floodplains and covering as much as 53 hectares. The lengths of irrigation ditches likewise range from as short as 20 metres to one, in Halele'a District, 3.7 km long. The small systems were evidently cultivated by single domestic units, while the larger systems incorporated landholdings of many commoners, as well as groups of fields (*ko'ele*) cultivated for the chiefs and their stewards (*konohiki*). The layout of irrigated fields on the lower floodplains of Halawa Valley, Moloka'i, is shown in Figure 55.

The concept of water control for taro cultivation was doubtless introduced to Hawai'i by the initial Polynesian colonizers, but it is likely that water-control systems were limited in size and distribution until population began expanding after about AD 1200. The earliest

54. Irrigated taro pondfields at Nuku, Futuna Island. The field in centre view is partially planted; note the main irrigation ditch to the left of the photo.

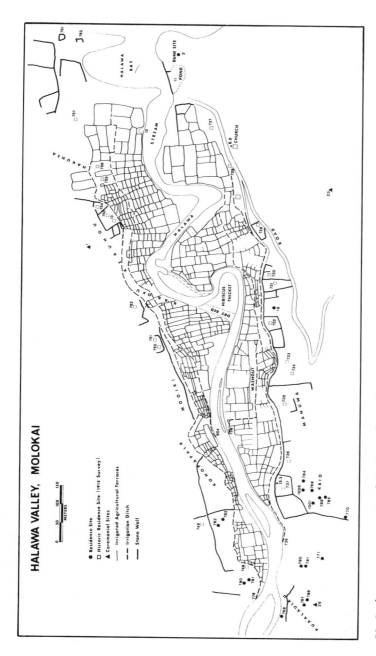

55. Settlement pattern map of the lower floodplains of Halawa Valley. Moloka'i Island, showing the extensive grid of irrigated pondfields (after Kirch and Kelly 1975).

securely dated irrigation site is that in the upper valley of Makaha, with a radiocarbon age of 565 ± 110 BP (Yen *et al.* 1972:89). In Halawa Valley, Moloka'i, the stratigraphic superposition of a Type III system over a Type II system (Kirch and Kelly 1975) suggested to Riley that the main floodplain complexes (Types III and IV) may have been constructed later in time than those utilizing side-stream watercourses. Earle, however, argued the reverse proposition: 'the probable sequence would have been first to construct systems on the alluvial floodplains and later to use the irregular and more steeply sloping terrain found inland' (1978:24). Aside from the stratigraphic evidence from Halawa (and the relatively early date for the Makaha Type III system), there is another reason to suspect that the larger floodplain complexes were relatively late developments. As argued in Chapter 6, much of the valley-bottom alluvium in Hawaiian valleys may be the result of human-induced erosion on higher slopes. Initial work by P. Beggerly (personal communication 1980) in the Kahana Valley, O'ahu, certainly suggests this as does the comparison with Spriggs's research in the New Hebrides (1981). If so, then some alluvial floodplains may not have become suitable environments for irrigation until relatively late in the Hawaiian sequence.

Recent work in the upper Anahulu Valley, O'ahu (Kirch and Sahlins, in preparation) suggests that large pondfield complexes found on the alluvial flats were constructed over a short period of time, in the late prehistoric–early historic era. In fact, the upper valley may have undergone a radical shift in settlement pattern and production system at this time. The probable impetus for this change, and for the construction of the irrigation systems, was the conquest of the area by Kamehameha, ruling paramount of Hawai'i, in AD 1795, and his subsequent efforts at intensification of production. Kamehameha awarded Anahulu to Keeaumoku, one of his warrior chiefs, and throughout the first half of the nineteenth century the valley was subject to heavy demands for the support of the chiefly establishment on O'ahu. The Anahulu case clearly demonstrates the link between intensive pondfield agriculture and the demands of chiefs for surplus production.

Hawaiian and other Polynesian taro irrigation systems reflect agricultural intensification in two ways, both in the labour requirements of construction and maintenance of the hydrologic facilities, and in the increased yields per unit of land. Annual yields of irrigated taro range from 30 to as many as 60 metric tons per hectare, a productivity level considerably exceeding that of even the more intensive dryfield cultivation systems. The potential of irrigation to produce higher yields, and thus respond to the demands of increased population, as well as those of a political economy, is considerable, a point we shall explore further below.

Wittfogel (1957) originally proposed that the construction and maintenance of complex irrigation systems necessitated a managerial apparatus, and thereby stimulated the development of social stratification in irrigation-based societies. The possibility that irrigation was so linked to the rise of a hierarchical society in Hawai'i was addressed by Earle (1978), who found the thesis wanting, noting that 'centralized management would not have been required by the scale or complexity of the [Hawaiian] systems' (1980:22). While Earle's contention is sound, there is evidence that the *allocation of water* was one aspect of Hawaiian irrigation that did provide an opportunity for chiefly control.

The Hawaiian lexeme for water is *wai*. Significantly, the term for 'wealth, prosperity, ownership, or possession' is *waiwai*, the reduplicated form of *wai*. More important, the lexeme for 'law', *kanawai*, literally translates 'pertaining to water' (Handy and Handy (1972:57–8). Linguistic evidence aside, there is clear evidence that allocation of limited water resources was necessary at various periods for Hawaiian irrigation systems. In Halawa Valley, the seven irrigation complexes would have required about 0.07 m^3/sec of water flow. During normal periods of streamflow, such a volume poses no problem for the capacity of Halawa Stream. However, during the dry summer months, stream discharge may drop as low as 0.021 m^3/sec, and irrigation requirements could not be fully met. Managerial control would obviously need to be instituted during such periods.

Further evidence for the social and political appropriation of water supply has been forthcoming from studies in the Anahulu Valley (Kirch 1979b; Kirch and Sahlins, in preparation). As shown in Figure 56, the arrangement of ditches in two carefully mapped systems closely reflects social relations. In the one case, direct access to water is provided to the fields of three *kama'aina* cultivators of independent status. In the other ditch structure reflects affinal relationships. In Hawai'i, the old adage would seem to have been reversed, for water *was* as thick as blood! A close relationship between water allocation and social structure is evidenced for other Polynesian societies as well. In Futuna, ditch layout is organized to assure the fields of each descent group (*kainga*) direct access to the main water channel. For Rarotonga and Mangaia in the Cook Islands, Buck observed that 'a good deal of supervision is needed to ensure the various families on different terraces of their share of water, and sometimes quarrels break out' (1944:249–50).

Despite the relatively low level of managerial control required to operate Hawaiian irrigation systems, chiefs had a major investment in irrigation, upon which much of their surplus depended. Earle (1978) argued that the intensification of irrigation in the Halele'a District of Kaua'i was primarily a function of competition between chiefs. The early ethnohistoric records for all the islands demonstrate the degree to which chiefs relied upon irrigation to support their political ambitions. The Halawa Valley case is illustrative (Fig. 55); approximately one-third of the taro fields were under the control of the *konohiki* and chiefs. Labour to cultivate these fields was provided by the common people on a corvée basis. Commoners in Halawa reported that they worked regularly on the *po'alima* days (one out of every five days), during which the *ko'ele* pondfields of the chief were cultivated. Indeed, in both Halawa and Halele'a, it is clear that 'the right to hold land relied on an individual's ability to work for the konohiki' (Earle 1978:187).

Dryfield cultivation systems

Counterposed to the intensive wet cultivation of taro and other aroids in Polynesia is the dryland cultivation of field crops, of which yams (*Dioscorea alata* and other species, including *D. esculenta* and *D. pentaphylla*) are the archetype. Throughout Oceania including the tropical Polynesian islands, such dryfield cultivation in its non-intensive form consists of the well-known 'slash-and-burn', 'swidden', or 'shifting cultivation' method of agricultural production (Spencer 1966). Forest or secondary growth is cut, dried, and fired to create a garden clearing. Generally such a garden undergoes a succession of crops, often begin-

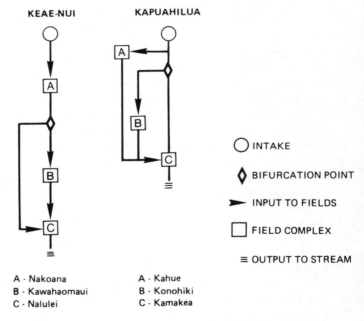

KEAE-NUI   KAPUAHILUA

◯ INTAKE

◊ BIFURCATION POINT

➤ INPUT TO FIELDS

▢ FIELD COMPLEX

≡ OUTPUT TO STREAM

A - Nakoana   A - Kahue
B - Kawahaomaui   B - Konohiki
C - Nalulei   C - Kamakea

56. The allocation of water in two early historic irrigation systems in the Anahulu Valley, O'ahu Island. In the Keae-Nui system, a by-pass ditch assures direct water feed to Nakoana's brother-in-law Nalulei. At Kapuahilua, three independent cultivators each share direct access to the main intake ditch (after Kirch 1979b).

ning with mixed yam-aroid plantings, and terminating with bananas (e.g., the 'Uvean swidden cycle, see Kirch 1978b). The plot reverts, after three or four years, to secondary growth and a fallow period of anywhere from three or four years up to twenty or more years. Such non-intensive forms of dryland cultivation were, and in a few instances still are (e.g., Futuna, Samoa), practised in tropical Polynesia. In many island groups, however, this non-intensive mode of integral swidden cultivation had – by the time of European contact – been transformed to some degree of permanent, rotational cropping. Such intensified forms of dryfield cropping reflect the demographic pressure of dense populations in circumscribed island ecosystems, as well as the demands made on production by island polities. While the literature on Polynesian production systems has emphasized irrigation, however, these intensive dryfield cultivation systems have been largely overlooked. As we shall see, they had a significance clearly equal to that of irrigation.

The isolated Polynesian Outlier of Anuta (Yen and Gordon 1973) has, up until the last decade, maintained a 'closed', indigenous subsistence production system, providing an ethnographic example of intensive field cropping. The Anutan agricultural system (Yen 1973b) integrates components of aroid pit cultivation, arboriculture (particularly of breadfruit and coconut), and intensive field cropping. The latter component is most notable for its intensity, also reflected in the island's population density of 432 persons/km^2 (in 1971). The exceptional aspect of this field cropping is the almost continuous rotation of taro and manioc (Fig. 57) on the volcanic hill, an area of *c*. 8.6 hectares. Yen (1973b:125) describes the crop-rotation sequence as a 'continuous planting cycle of taro–manioc–taro without a significant fallow period'. (Manioc, an American cultigen of post-European introduction to the Pacific, has replaced yams in the Anutan cropping system. Bananas are also a minor component of the rotational system.) Yen goes on to stress that 'the Anutan crop rotation is one of the most intensive recorded in Oceania, at least by this investigator. It is rivalled only by the irrigated terracing systems for taro-growing, *e.g.* in East Futuna' (1973b:125). Dominant agronomic features in this hilltop system are stone-faced, slope terraces which serve both as soil retention devices and as social plot boundaries. Yen observes that these boundaries reflect 'the inflexibility of field placement in successive cultivation cycles conferring definition on land parcels in terms of use rights' (1973b:124), not usually typical of shifting cultivation systems. Also significant in this rotational cropping scheme is the constant application of mulch, conserving soil moisture and enriching soil nutrients.

The intensiveness of the Anutan agricultural system is indicated not only in the reduction of fallow and in agronomic practice (terracing and mulching), but in labour input. Yen's analysis suggests a rough labour input of 7,000 man-hours per hectare/year (1973b:139). This compares for example, with only 3,000 hours/hectare/year for the non-intensive Hanunoo swidden system studied by Conklin (1957:151).

While the Anutan example is perhaps the only surviving ethnographic instance of intensive dryfield cultivation in Polynesia, recent archaeological work has revealed that similar systems were formerly operative in various island groups. In New Zealand, work by H. Leach (1979), Sullivan (1972, 1981), Lawlor (1980, 1981a, b) and others has documented a range of intensive walled-garden complexes throughout various parts of North Island. These field-cropping complexes focussed on the cultivation of sweet potato. Lawlor's (1980, 1981a) intensive archaeological investigation of a portion of the prehistoric field systems at Puhinui (Site N42/17, Oyster Point, South Auckland) demonstrated remarkably parallel trends in the adaptation of *Ipomoea* field cropping in New Zealand and Hawai'i (see below). In both cases, old lava substrates were utilized; the principal difference lies in the harsher climatic regime of the Auckland area, which set more severe constraints on the possible range of crops, and necessitated a change from perennial to annual cropping (cf. Yen 1961, 1974a). At Puhinui, which radiocarbon dates have shown to be intensively cultivated in the sixteenth century AD (Lawlor 1981b), the dominant agronomic features are linear 'stone rows', and stone mounds and heaps, with

57. Intensive dryfield cultivation of taro (*Colocasia esculenta*) on the volcanic hill of Anuta Island. Note the heavy mulch visible between plants in the foreground.

deeper garden soils filling depressions at the junction between scoriaceous and pahoehoe lava flows.

In West Polynesia, Kirch (1975) observed that parts of Alofi Island in the Horne group are characterized by abandoned dryland field systems. These are marked by field borders constructed of limestone cobbles, and presumably indicate former intensive cropping of yams and associated field crops.

On Easter Island, large tracts were intensively cultivated, with an emphasis on the sweet potato. Métraux (1940:151–2) refers to the heavy use of grass mulch, as in Anuta and Hawai'i. Unfortunately, the Easter Island dryland fields were not permanently delineated with stone rows or borders, and so have left no archaeological trace. Another form of intensive horticultural feature, the walled-garden plot or *manavai*, is however, very much in evidence throughout the island (McCoy 1976).

Other aspects of production

In virtually all Polynesian societies, food was classified as starch staples on the one hand, and certain socially or ritually valued foods on the other. These latter include special puddings, and especially, the flesh of either wild or domestic animals. Animal husbandry was an integral and culturally valued component of the indigenous production systems of every island group; not surprisingly, many of the intensive irrigation and dryland field systems described above also supported large numbers of domestic pigs, dogs, and fowl. In Hawai'i, the association of pig husbandry with dryland field systems is clear, and the journals of Cook and other early European visitors contain frequent references to the ability of the Hawaiians to supply large quantities of hogs.

Easter Island provides an instance of the intensive production of fowl (pigs and dogs were unknown on the island, apparently not surviving the initial voyage of colonization). Métraux (1940:19) remarked on the significance of chickens in Easter Island social and economic life: 'chickens were the usual gifts to people who must be honored; they were raised for feasts and appear as a favorite motif in art. The feathers were used in making circlets, eyeshades, and hats.' Fowl were husbanded in unique stone houses (*hare moa*) with interior passageways, the primary function of which was thwarting theft (McCoy 1976:23–6, 87). McCoy regards thievery of fowl as the result of rather severe population and environmental problems that beset Easter Island in the late prehistoric and protohistoric periods. 'The adjustment made by the society was containment of chickens, implying also, intensification of production. The *hare moa* . . . are speculated to have been an adaptive response to a major change in cultural values imposed earlier by population pressure' (1976:146).

Reefs, lagoons, and open pelagic waters were the other great source of flesh food throughout Polynesia. Generally, fishing remained at the level of exploitation of natural populations, but in Hawai'i a significant-technological advancement was made in aquacultural production. This was facilitated by the development of fishponds of several types, for the capture and husbanding of brackish water fish, notably mullet (*Mugil cephalus*) and milkfish (*Chanos chanos*). Such a pond, with its massive stone enclosing wall constructed on a broad reef flat, is shown in Figure 58. The archaeological remains of at least 449 ponds have been recorded on all of the major islands (Stokes 1909b; Summers 1964; Kikuchi 1976).

Kikuchi (1976) stressed the close relationship between Hawaiian fish-ponds and the level of socio-political complexity. Not only did ponds require large, organized labour forces for their construction, but traditional dates for pond construction suggest that most ponds were built after the fourteenth century AD, when the Hawaiian chiefdoms were undergoing rapid political changes (see Chapter 10). 'Fishponds became symbols of the chiefly right to conspicuous consumption and to ownership of the land and its resources. They were manifestations of the chief's political power and his ability to control and tap his resources' (1976:299). Most ponds were under the direct control of *konohiki*, land overseers of the chiefs, and their production went directly to feed the retinue of the chiefly households. Kikuchi (1976:298) estimated the annual yield of all fishponds in Hawai'i at contact as about 1,052 metric

58. A *loko kuapa* type fishpond constructed on the southern reef flat of Moloka'i Island (*photo courtesy M. Weisler, Bishop Museum*).

tons of fish. As status food, used primarily for the support of the chiefly bureaucracy, such a volume of fish production was a significant technological achievement of the late prehistoric Hawaiian chiefdoms.

Yet another significant component of Polynesian production systems was the storage of starch foods, especially the ensilage of breadfruit (*masi*), discussed at length in Chapter 6. Here we need only reiterate the importance of storage technology in allowing the accumulation of foodstuffs. While such surpluses were often directly converted to sub-sistence needs following natural disasters, they were also frequently put to political ends. As with Hawaiian fishponds, the storage facilities pro-vided a means for the support and aggrandizement of chiefly establishments.

Throughout the preceding discussion, I have stressed the agricultural and subsistence aspects of production, in part because the archaeological evidence of agricultural intensification is abundant. This emphasis should not, however, be construed as denigrating the significance of non-subsistence aspects of production, especially in the more stratified chiefdoms. Indeed, degree of craft specialization was closely correlated with the level of socio-political complexity (Sahlins 1958), a reflection of the ability of chiefs to channel surplus food production toward the sup-port of specialists. In Tonga, such skills as tattooing, stonemasonry (for the construction of chiefly tombs), canoe building, and navigation were the privileged domains of hereditary groups, themselves under the aegis of ruling paramounts. A similar situation obtained in Hawai'i, noted among students of Polynesian art for its range of material insignia produced for the chiefly class – feather cloaks and helmets, beautifully carved bowls and other implements, and so on (Buck 1957). Limitations of space do not allow me to pursue an in-depth analysis of status goods in Polynesian societies, but for present purposes it is suf-ficient to note that the relative importance of such goods in any chief-dom can be positively correlated with the degree of development and intensification of the productive forces, and their control by the chiefs.

Intensification in West Hawai'i: a case study

The best-known and well-studied dryland field systems of Polynesia are situated on the leeward, western side of Hawai'i Island. Within this region of relatively undissected flow slopes and lack of streams were three extensive zones of dryland cultivation (North Kohala, Lalamilo–Waimea, and Kona), corresponding to three areas where soil develop-ment and rainfall were adequate for cropping of taro, sweet potato, yams, sugar cane and other cultigens (Fig. 59). The region attracts anthropological interest for yet another reason: it was the hearth of the most powerful Hawaiian chieftainship, the line of chiefs descended from 'Umi and Liloa (Kamakau 1961), among whom the famous Kamehameha was but one descendant. Given that West Hawai'i was the setting for some of the most intensive socio-political development in Polynesia, the productive basis of these chiefdoms may repay detailed examination.

The earliest European explorers to Hawai'i Island, beginning with Cook's 1778–9 expedition, described agricultural field systems in operation, displaying admiration for the intensity of cultivation. Typical of such statements is Archibald Menzies's (botanist with Vancouver in 1793) concerning the Kona field system:

> we soon lost sight of the vessels, and entered their breadfruit plantations . . . The space between these trees did not lay idle. It was chiefly planted with sweet potatoes and rows of cloth plant. As we advanced beyond the breadfruit plantations, the country became more and more fertile, being in a high state of cultivation. For several miles around us there was not a spot that would admit of it but what was with great labor and industry cleared of the loose stones and planted with esculent roots or some useful vegetable or other. In clearing the ground, the stones are heaped up in ridges between the little fields and planted on each side, either with a row of sugar cane or the sweet root of these islands [*Cordyline fruticosa*].
> The produce of these plantations, besides the above mentioned, are the cloth plant, taro, and sweet potatoes (1920:75).

The Kohala field system covers a leeward slope between about 150 and 760 m elevation, with a total land area of perhaps 57 km^2 (Fig. 59). Menzies viewed this region from the sea, and noted that

> it bears every appearance of industrious cultivation by the number of small fields into which it is laid out, and if we might judge by the vast number of houses we saw along the shore, it is by far the most populous part we had yet seen of the island (1920:52).

The entire Kohala field system has yet to be defined archaeologically, but a segment, the *ahupua'a* of Lapakahi, was archaeologically investigated from 1968–70 (Newman n.d.; R. Pearson 1968; Tuggle and Griffin 1973), with an emphasis on the prehistoric agricultural system (Rosendahl 1972a; Choy 1973; Sugiyama 1973; Smith and Schilt 1973; Umebayashi 1973; and Rosendahl and Yen 1971).

The prehistoric agricultural zone at Lapakahi is dominated by low, stone and/or earthen field borders which lie perpendicular to the gentle, undissected flow slopes. Abutting these field borders are long trails, defined by parallel stone alignments (*c.* 1–2 m apart), which run from the coast to the top of the agricultural zone. These trails facilitated communication between coast and uplands, and served as boundaries between continuous socio-political units such as the *ahupua'a* and *'ili* (Cordy and Kaschko 1980). As seen in Figure 60, the field borders and trails break up the agricultural landscape into a regular grid, with individual field units of rectangular shape.

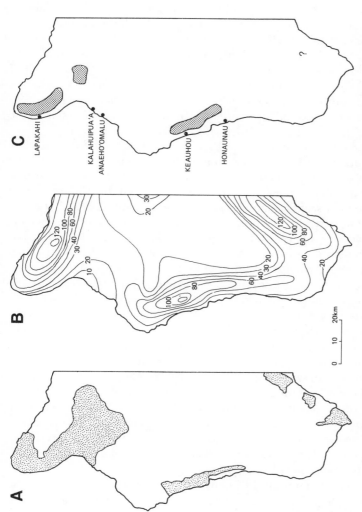

59. The West Hawai'i region. A. Distribution of arable soils. B. Annual rainfall in inches. C. Known extent of prehistoric field systems (north to south: Kohala field system, Lalamilo field system, Kona field system). The question mark indicates the probable presence of an as yet unsurveyed field system.

Within this grid of field borders and trails are a plethora of minor features, both agricultural and residential (and, in some cases, religious or ceremonial). These include stone mounds, low stone alignments, agricultural windbreaks, planting circles, small clearings, simple terraces, and animal enclosures or pens, as well as such residential features as C- and L-shaped structures and platforms. Rosendahl's excavation (1972a) of nine residential sites yielded significant data on the age and operation of the system, especially the integration of the upland fields into the larger production system, including marine exploitation. The residential sites produced direct evidence of crop plants, including carbonized tubers of *Ipomoea batatas* (Rosendahl and Yen 1971), *Dioscorea* tubers, *Cocos*, and *Lagenaria*. The high frequency of pig, dog, and chicken bone in the faunal components suggested to Rosendahl that 'animal husbandry was an important component of the Lapakahi horticultural complex (1972a:454).

Rosendahl characterized the Lapakahi and general North Kohala field complex as a 'modified integral swidden system' (1972a:502). 'The principal cropping scheme involved a system of shifting, slash and burn cultivation' (1972a:504), 'of sweet potato and dryland taro on an intensive field scale utilizing permanent field units' (1972a:511). The system thus derives from the extensive shifting cultivation characteristic of Malayo-Oceanic agriculture (Spencer 1966; Barrau 1961), but has been intensified in the direction of permanent cropping units. Such intensification evidently included a reduction of fallow length (although not necessarily to the level of permanent crop rotation), and the application of labour-intensive practices (such as the mulching mentioned in Menzies's account of Kona), which offset the potentially deleterious effects of fallow reduction on soil fertility (cf. Nye and Greenland 1960). Yen (1974a:311–17) similarly portrayed the Lapakahi system as 'derivative from a valley cropping pattern, in its extension of the nonirrigated, swidden portion into dry-land areas' (1974a:314). Yen stressed the role of the sweet potato, with its adaptable ecological template, in the intensification of the Kohala system: 'The impact of the sweet potato on agriculture was in the phase of dry-land development, and, in the new environment, was able to show its superiority, in respect to food-yield in its short-term attainment, and in its propensities for pig production' (1974a:315).

Since Lapakahi reflects the intensification – over some period of time – of an integral shifting cultivation regime, there ought to be archaeological manifestations of the temporal, as well as spatial, axes of this process. On the basis of fifty-four age determinations, Rosendahl (1972a) showed that the field complex developed over a period of about 350 years (AD 1450–1800) followed by decline and eventual abandonment in the early historic period. Some reflection of the increasing permanency of use is contained in the residential site data: 'the dominant occupation pattern throughout the prehistoric period was one of shifting residence, involving the recurrent extended occupation of residential features, while the pattern of permanent residential occupation seemed to be a late development, possibly becoming dominant only during the historic period' (1972a:482).

An analysis of the pattern of field units provides striking evidence for continued intensification of the system over time. Rosendahl (1972a:510) observed that 'various examples of field border embankments were constructed before the defined trails', and that 'matching and mismatching patterns of trail and field border interactions' could define a general sequence of field unit construction (though he neglected to follow through with the requisite analysis). In Figure 60, utilizing Rosendahl's detailed map data, I have separated out three phases of field-unit border and trail construction for a portion of the Lapakahi system. Two parallel trends are evident: (1) the breakup of originally intensive field units into successively smaller parcels; and (2) the division of one trail-defined unit into two, and later three, sub-units. This subdivision carries certain socio-political implications, since trail-defined

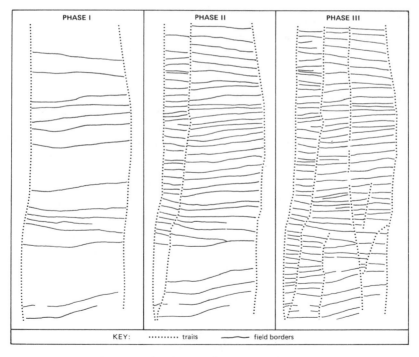

60. The temporal development of agricultural field borders and trails in one segment of the Lapakahi area, Hawai'i Island. Note the progressive division of the area into smaller units.

units were of sociological significance (Cordy and Kaschko 1980). That the intensification of the Lapakahi agricultural system was linked to socio-political changes is a point of inference to which we shall return shortly.

A second major agricultural field complex lay in the area of Lalamilo–Waimea, on the saddle between the Kohala Mountains and Mauna Kea, at between 750 and 900 m elevation (Fig. 59). Intensive archaeological study of the Lalamilo–Waimea system began only recently (Clark and Kirch 1983; J. Clark 1981), and modern land-use changes in Waimea have obliterated some fields, so that only dis-connected portions remain for archaeological study. Some 120 hec-tares of the largest intact field complex, between 693 and 753 m ele-vation, were mapped photogrammetrically with the use of low-level false-colour infra-red photography (J. Clark, 1981). Here, the dominant agricultural features are rectangular fields, either slope-terraces, or fields bordered by soil-and-rock ridges, as at Lapakahi. Unlike Lapakahi, however, these fields do not form a continuous grid, but are grouped in swales with deeper soil development. The Lalamilo field complex contrasts with Lapakahi in another significant respect: throughout the area is a reticulated network of irrigation ditches, feeding off the Waikoloa and Kahakohau Streams. These ditches differ from the typical valley irrigation channels discussed earlier, both in the num-ber of bifurcations, and in the degree of inter-connectivity. Further-more, the field plots do not appear to have been pondfields, since their surfaces are sloping. Rather, the Lalamilo system represents a type of intermittent irrigation, not previously reported for Hawai'i. It rep-resents the extension and modification of valley-bottom techniques of water control to a leeward slope environment. An initial series of radiocarbon age determinations suggests that the system is comparable in age with Lapakahi.

The third major system is at Kona, as described by Menzies (above). Soehren and Newman (1968) used aerial photos to map an area of *c.* 140 hectares situated on the gentle slope above Kealakekua Bay, and provided the first archaeological definition of the Kona field system. Long stone-wall segments (*kuaiwi*) there are oriented with the gentle slope and not perpendicular to it as in Kohala and Lalamilo. The cleared strips between these walls (10–15 metres wide) are 'periodically cross-sectioned by short field walls connecting two or more major field boundaries' (Soehren and Newman 1968:5). The general pattern is one of 'very narrow and greatly elongated rectangles oriented on an axis that is both northeast–southwest and sea–mountain' (1968:5). Soehren and Newman note that there is no evidence for irrigation of these fields, the crops evidently depending upon rainfall.

Unique to the Kona field system was an extensive belt dominated by breadfruit trees, referred to in the native land claim records of the mid nineteenth century as the *kalu'ulu* or *maloko'ulu* zone (Barrère and Kelly 1980:36). This arboricultural component, absent at Kohala and Lalamilo, correlates with higher annual rainfall in the Kona area, meeting the basic ecological requirements for *Artocarpus* (rainfall *c.* 1,320–2,500 mm; Purseglove 1968:380). Above the breadfruit zone were *kula* lands, dominated by the field cultivation of taro and sweet potato.

Schilt (1980b; personal communication) recently completed survey and excavations at the northern margin of the Kona field system, where the *kuaiwi* walls are infrequent and discontinuous, and irregular 'garden plots' dominate the agricultural pattern. Crozier (1971) had earlier investigated a small section of the field system in the land division of Kahalu'u (elevation *c.* 170 metres) where several residential features (platforms and terraces) were integrated with the agricultural field borders. Age determinations for these sites indicate utilization of the area by *c.* AD 1350, with intensive use in the sixteenth to seventeenth centuries.

Within the *ahupua'a* of Kealakekua, at an elevation of about 450 metres, a relatively undisturbed parcel with seven parallel *kuaiwi* walls and several habitation features has been studied intensively (Kirch, unpublished field notes, 1978–82, Bishop Museum). Aside from the obvious function of the *kuaiwi* walls (1) for clearing stone from the adjacent plots, and (2) for demarcation of fields for sociological purposes, these walls may have served a planting function, especially for *Cordyline* or other perennial species. Feral *Cordyline* still grows abundantly along the *kuaiwi* walls. Age determinations from residential features at Kealakekua indicate use of this part of the Kona field system from about AD 1650 to 1725.

The three field systems described above coincide geographically with the areas of West Hawai'i where rainfall and soil development permit the cultivation of Oceanic cultigens (Fig. 59). Thus, by late prehistoric times, all primary arable land below about 800 metres had been converted to agricultural production, and there is evidence of limited attempts to extend cultivation even into extremely marginal zones outside the extensive field systems. Rosendahl (1972b) studied two small sites (Complexes A and C) in lower Lalamilo and Waikoloa *ahupua'a*, both about 60 metres above sea level and receiving, on the average, less than 250 mm rainfall annually. Both sites consist of temporary, residential features adjacent to small alluvial basins, the soils of which could be cultivated if there were sufficient water, perhaps during the October–March season when more than 75 per cent of the precipitation occurs. At Complex A, the slopes surrounding the basin had been burned, perhaps intentionally, to facilitate the erosion of soil and deposition in the alluvial basin, as revealed in a section through the basin fill. At Complex C, a substantial wall was constructed across an intermittent drainage channel to divert runoff onto an adjacent alluvial basin; otherwise, there is little structural evidence for cultivation. These complexes represent temporary 'flood-water farming, or dryland-irrigation horticulture dependent on intermittent seasonal flows of surface water and on the extensive subsurface retention of soil water' (Rosendahl 1972b:88).

Such marginal sites would probably not fall within the usual definition of *intensive* agriculture, with its connotation of permanence. Yet, when considered as part of the whole agricultural landscape of West Hawai'i, these temporary, marginal sites reveal that agricultural intensification here involves not only development of ecologically favourable areas, but attempts at expansion to marginal limits. In extreme cases, these limits obviously lay beyond the ecological templates of even the most adaptable of the oceanic cultigens.

Another instance of attempts at expansion into marginal lands is provided by Reeve (1983) in his study of agricultural and residential features on the periphery of the Lalamilo–Waimea field system. In this case, Reeve argues that the attempt at marginal expansion outside of the zone of optimal rainfall and soil development (and requiring the construction of an intermittent irrigation channel several kilometres long) was undertaken between AD 1790 and 1794, as a direct response to local political events. During this period, Kamehameha established his base at Kawaihae on the coast, constructed the massive Pu'ukohola temple site, and maintained a sizeable standing army in preparation for the conquest of the westerly islands. Reeve believes that the marginal expansion of agriculture was undertaken by the Waimea chiefs, 'faced with this sudden demand for agricultural goods' precipitated by the military actions of the paramount (1983:236).

The evidence from the Hawai'i Island field systems suggest some general propositions regarding the temporal and spatial axes of agricultural intensification in the region:

1. Dating of agricultural fields, and of associated residential sites, indicates that the inland field systems were begun about AD 1300, even though coastal settlement in West Hawai'i dates to as early as AD 900. Most dates fall into the period *c.* AD 1600–1800, indicating that these two centuries witnessed the most intensive development of the field systems. This time period closely matches the region's period of peak population growth (see Chapter 5). However, population growth may not have been uniform with regard to local environment. A lag between inland and coastal site populations correlates closely with 'inland expansion' (Hommon 1976) and with the development and intensification of the large agricultural field systems. Despite this close temporal correspondence between agricultural intensification and increasing population, we need not assign the latter the status of an independent variable. For one thing, it is likely that population growth in the area had reached a plateau, or was actually even on the decline, prior to European contact.

2. The development of these dryland field systems involved fairly rapid lateral expansion, as well as intensification (cf. Hammond 1977, 1978). By the late 1600s, lateral expansion appears to have reached its limits, with nearly all suitable land having been brought under cultivation. Even the marginal alluvial basins at Waikoloa, described above, were in use by the mid-to-late 1600s (Rosendahl 1972b:100). Tuggle and Tomonari-Tuggle, reporting on their studies of late prehistoric agricultural systems in the windward valleys of Kohala, state a similar finding: 'The extent and intensity of the complexes in Kohala lead to the conclusion that agricultural growth had reached its limits in the Kohala–Hamakua region, under the constraints of a simple irrigation technology and probably a comparable level of dry-field technology' (1980:311).

3. The overall trend in intensification of all three systems was from an extensive form of shifting cultivation to an increasingly formalized system of permanently defined fields. This intensification comprised several parallel processes: (a) A reduction in fallow length probably took place as the fields became more formalized. Whether or not fallow was eliminated altogether is debatable, though Menzies (1920:76) remarked that fields were replanted immediately after harvesting. (b) An increase in labour input per unit area is also likely, associated with the increased use of various agronomic techniques such as mulching, terrace and mound construction, and so on, requiring increased labour. Both (a) and (b) are aspects of what Hammond (1977, 1978) has referred to as temporal intensification. (c) The construction of permanent facilities is abundantly evidenced in the archaeological remains. These facilities include the permanent field borders, stone mounds, *kuaiwi*, dry terraces, and – at Lalamilo – the irrigation networks. Such facilities reflect both agronomic practice, and attempts at social delineation of plots as the systems became increasingly permanent and formalized. (d) A further direction of intensification is suggested for the Kona field system, where a permanent zone of breadfruit was developed. Arboricultural intensification was limited to Kona because the lower rainfall at Lalamilo and Kohala was below the ecological tolerance of the tree. (e) Concomitant with the intensification of the agricultural production systems was the development of animal husbandry, especially of pigs.

The emphasis on dryland cultivation in Hawai'i Island (and in Maui Island) was accompanied by a concomitant demand for intensive labour, and provides a significant contrast to the agricultural systems of the westerly islands (Kaua'i, O'ahu, Moloka'i), where taro irrigation dominated. Kamakau noted that whereas women never performed agricultural labour in the westerly islands, 'on Maui and Hawaii the women worked outside as hard as the men ... tilling the ground' (1961:239). This inter-island difference in the role of women in agriculture corresponds well with the dominance of taro irrigation in

Kaua'i, O'ahu, and Moloka'i, and of dryland cultivation in Maui and Hawai'i. The major difference in labour requirements between the two sorts of agricultural system is the much greater need for intensive weeding and mulching in the dryland systems, work that presumably was performed largely by women, as is the case in many other parts of Polynesia (e.g., Anuta, Yen 1973b). Outside of Polynesia, the absorption by women of additional labour costs incurred during agricultural intensification has been noted by Spriggs (1981:32–3, 63, 66, 179) for late prehistoric Aneityum in the New Hebrides.

4. Finally, the expansion and intensification of these field systems had permanent effects upon the local ecosystem. For Kohala and Lalamilo, the evidence of sub-fossil land snail assemblages and of remnant vegetation indicate widespread clearance of an original mesic forest/parkland and creation of terminal grasslands over much of the area (Clark and Kirch 1983). The consequences for microclimate, runoff, erosion, and so forth are as yet unspecified, and remain important questions to be resolved in further investigations.

It is now possible to relate the process of agricultural intensification in West Hawai'i to the production function model presented earlier in the chapter. Figure 61 diagrams the West Hawai'i case in general terms, with T_1 representing the ancestral, integral swidden mode of cropping, and T_2 the developed, permanent-field, rotational-cropping system witnessed at contact. (The model simplifies the situation, since the change from T_1 to T_2 was clearly a *process* requiring several centuries, and not a sudden, qualitative shift.) Intensification permitted the production systems to meet continued demands both for increased necessary consumption at the household level (occasioned by increasing population in the region), and for surplus. All of the data reviewed

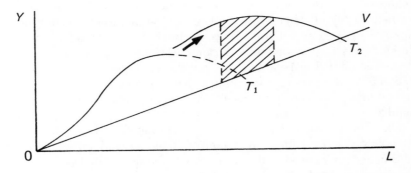

61. Diagram representing the effect of agricultural intensification on the production function for the Lapakahi production system. T_1 represents the initial system of shifting cultivation, T_2 the intensified system of dryfield cultivation with permanent plot boundaries and labour-intensive agronomic methods.

above, however, suggest that by the time of European contact, the systems had not only reached limits to lateral expansion, but probably limits to intensification as well.

The extent of chiefly demands for surplus is indicated by a consideration of Hawaiian ritual. Competition, including warfare, was not engaged in without a heavy investment in ritual activity, which itself translated into real demands on production. The pressure point of these demands for ritual prestation may have been the husbandry of pigs, for these were the necessary sacrificial accompaniments to successful supernatural support. Malo (1951:172) records that the consecration of a *luakini* type temple (dedicated to the war god, Ku) required as many as 800 hogs. One part of the elaborate ritual is described as follows: 'When the chiefs and the people had finished feasting on the pork, the king made an offering to his gods of 400 pigs, 400 bushels of bananas, 400 cocoanuts, 400 red fish, and 400 pieces of *oloa* cloth' (1951:174). These figures are probably not exaggerations, for the capacity of the West Hawai'i agricultural systems to produce swine was remarked upon by all the early explorers, who frequently re-supplied their stores with salt pork. Excavations by Ladd at the large temple of Pu'ukohola in Kohala district have yielded the faunal evidence of numerous pig sacrifices (A. Ziegler, personal communication, 1981).

It seems, therefore, that West Hawai'i was somewhere in the Region II–III area referred to earlier (Fig. 49), in which surplus was diminishing relative to yield ($dS/dY < 0$), or, at least, the system was rapidly approaching this condition. Since the late prehistoric Hawaiian polity was among the most demanding of all Polynesian societies, what really counted was the demand for surplus to be appropriated by the chiefship (S_c). West Hawai'i may have approached the state where such demand exceeded the ability of the production base to supply it ($dS_c/dt > 0 > dS/dt$). As Friedman points out, 'this is an unbearable political situation. While before, the chief was accumulating an increasing portion of an increasing surplus, he is now accumulating an increasing portion of a decreasing surplus' (1979:170). This situation would explain two aspects of late prehistoric Hawaiian society: (1) the drive toward expansionistic warfare and conquest of adjacent political (and economic) territories; and (2) the cycle of expansion, rebellion, and contraction of chiefdoms that characterized Hawaiian political history (see Chapter 10).

Ethnohistoric and traditional accounts of Hawaiian political history leave no doubt that competition between various lines of ruling chiefs was a hallmark of late prehistoric Hawaiian society. The pattern is a cyclical one, of expansion of one chiefly line, either by peaceful means or by conquest, over neighbouring domains: a 'tendency, on which traditions discourse at length, for chiefly domains to enlarge and contract, extended once by conquest only to be repartitioned again by rebellion' (Sahlins 1972:144). The incessant demand for surplus production led chiefs to undertake the conquest of adjacent territories; ultimately, however, when the burden on the common people became too great, the opportunity for a junior line to usurp the paramountship – with the support of the people – was seized, and demand lessened, at least for a time. As Malo put it: 'Many kings have been put to death by the people because of their oppression of the *makaainana*' (1951:195).

This intensity of chiefly competition has obvious and significant implications for agricultural expansion and intensification. As Hommon (1976:281) states, 'the prestige and power of the administrators of a Hawaiian primitive state were funded by a portion of the goods and services produced by the commoners . . . of the realm'. The ability to engage in conquest and other political enterprises was in large measure dependent upon the productive capacity of the economic infrastructure. Earle (1978) has argued that Hawaiian agricultural intensification 'was therefore an outcome of political competition, and *not* of population pressure' (1978:183). In West Hawai'i, although Earle's negative view of the role of demographic change may be overstated, there is no doubt that political competition was a significant driving force behind the expansion and intensification of the indigenous field systems. In fact, the traditions suggest that competition may have been even more intense in the more marginal, leeward regions such as West Hawai'i than in the windward valleys studied by Earle (Kirch 1980a). Sahlins has noted the same point: 'Competition probably accounts for a remarkable tendency to invert by culture the ecology of nature: many of the poorer regions of Polynesian high islands were more intensively exploited' (1972:141).

Sahlins (1972:140) rightly observed that 'the development of rank and chieftainship becomes, *pari passu*, development of the productive forces'. The case of West Hawai'i bears this out amply. Yet, there were limits beyond which the economic infrastructure could not be pushed – limits set by the natural environment itself. Archaeological and traditional evidence hint that such limits may have been approached by the mid 1600s. 'If Hawaiian society discovered limits to its ability to augment production and polity, this threshold which it had reached but could not cross was the boundary of primitive society itself' (Sahlins 1972:148). It may also have been a boundary of a more fundamental sort: a developmental endpoint of Oceanic agriculture.

Overview

The Polynesian islands present the prehistorian with an excellent opportunity to observe the conversion of natural ecosystems, from which humans were formerly absent, to managed environments, a regression of the biological process of succession. This conversion of nature into culture took a variety of divergent pathways in different islands, due to the processes we have isolated: the reassortment of production systems upon transfer from one homeland to a new island, and adaptation to local constraints. Despite such island-to-island variation, however, the evolution of Polynesian production systems can be readily divided into two phases.

The first phase is best characterized as one of *adaptation*, whether occasioned by the failure of particular cultigens or animals to survive overseas transport, or by new and harsh conditions of local climate, topography, soils, reefs, or water sources. In all those islands for which we now possess good archaeological data pertaining to the colonization phase, a heavy exploitation of naturally abundant wild resources helped to assure the survival of the human propagule through what may have been a difficult period of adjusting agronomic practice to local circumstance.

The later emphases and particular characteristics of local production systems were basically formulated and established during this adaptational phase. Once established, developmental pathways gradually entered the second phase, that of *expansion* and *intensification*. The particular form of intensive production developed in any local system reflects to a large degree the result of initial adaptation: whether of arboriculture as in the Marquesas, irrigation as in parts of Hawaiʻi and Futuna, or dryfield cultivation as in West Hawaiʻi and the Auckland region of New Zealand. The process of intensification itself, however, must be understood in terms of wider demographic, social, and political changes in each island situation.

That population growth was a spur to the intensification of production in all Polynesian islands would seem hardly to require lengthy argument. The correspondence between population increase and the expansion and intensification of leeward dryfield systems in West Hawaiʻi provides empirical documentation of the relationship between human numbers and caloric needs, and Hawaiʻi may be regarded as typical in this regard. The issue, therefore, is not whether population increase or pressure was a factor in the intensification of island production systems, but rather, whether such demographic pressure was the only significant force leading to the expansion and intensification of production. Again, the Hawaiian data indicate that the development of production in Polynesian societies was far more complex than a simple intensification of agriculture and fishing to meet increased caloric demands. Aside from necessary consumption, the hierarchical structure of Polynesian societies encouraged the production of a surplus, to support the broader political demands of the chiefs. More importantly, these complex interrelations between demographic pressure, level of production, and demands of the political economy were never static. The intensification process is one in which the variables constantly change their values. It was not only population growth that necessitated increased levels of production over time, for the same can be said of the demands of increasingly political societies. Sahlins remarked that 'as the [kinship] structure is politicized, especially as it is centralized in ruling chiefs, the household economy is mobilized in a larger social cause' (1972:130). Yet, the production system itself was not without its own effects, both on population and on the social relations of production. If intensification meant the construction of a floodplain irrigation system, the allocation of scarce water resources, the filling of communal bread-fruit pits, or the fabrication of village seine nets, the social and political apparatus for production was itself affected. Starting at an arbitrarily defined point, the political economy makes demands on production, only to have intensified production provide further opportunities for the dominant political group, whether over the control of irrigation water, the timing of agricultural rituals, the distribution of scarce resources, or whatever.

In this manner, Polynesian production systems might appear to have been capable of an endless progression towards increased intensity, subject only to the limitations of technology. But the limits to growth in ancient Polynesia were in fact more immediate, and lay in the cir-cumscribed nature of islands, and especially, in the finite quantity of arable land (and of exploitable reefs and lagoons). To be sure, some sys-tems – in particular, those based upon dryfield cultivation – were prone to a more rapid achievement of limit than others (based on water con-trol), and to a greater potential for environmental degradation. In time, however, the finite nature of islands posed limits to every sort of pro-duction system. Thus, we are brought to a consideration of one additional and highly intrinsic aspect of Polynesian societies: com-petition.

8

Competition and conflict

Warfare – ranging from simple raiding aimed at restoring the honour of an insulted party to major wars of territorial or inter-island conquest – was ubiquitous in Polynesia. Niue was 'in a state of more or less incessant warfare' (Loeb 1926:128); Buck (1932:54) describes 'constant fighting and warfare' in Tongareva; 'the Marquesas tribes were in a continual state of warfare' (Handy 1923:123); and, in Easter Island, 'there was constant rivalry between the tribes, particularly those of the eastern and western parts of the island' (Métraux 1940:149). Similar statements, readily extracted from the ethnographic accounts of virtually every Polynesian society, demonstrate that competition and armed conflict were fundamental aspects of these societies. As we shall see, warfare played a significant role in the transformation of Polynesian political and economic systems. Neither the causes nor functions of warfare in Polynesia, however, can be explained or understood from purely demographic or ecological perspectives. War, as the overt form of competition between greater and lesser powers, higher and lower status, indigene and invader, was thoroughly ingrained in Polynesian concepts of society.

Warfare surely characterized Ancestral Polynesian Society, for the term *toa*, 'warrior', can be reconstructed for Proto-Polynesian language. (The term is an interesting one, applied also to the ironwood tree, *Casuarina equisitifolia*, from which clubs and other weapons were commonly made in many islands.) *Toa*, though they need not have been of noble birth, rivalled the power and status of *ariki* in many islands. Buck notes that in Mangareva, 'the influence of tried warriors was very great' (1938a:189), while in Easter Island, 'some of the *matatoa* seem to have procured for themselves privileges usually reserved for the *ariki*' (Métraux 1940:138). Papa, a famous warrior of Futunan tradition, was so 'arrogant' that he established his *malae* on a site overlooking that of the Lalolalo chiefs, and 'had his kava served in the fashion appropriate to kings' (Burrows 1936:32). Indeed, the achievement of *toa* status provided an alternate route to power than that of the hereditary succession to *ariki*-ship (see Connelly 1976).

195

The significance of *toa*, and their ability to challenge the authority of *ariki*, was bound up with the Polynesian concept of *mana*. For the *ariki, mana* 'flowed' from the gods through a succession of sacred ancestors. However, since *mana* was manifest in prowess, power, and especially, in an ability to challenge the established order and succeed, it could also be demonstrated in practical action. A chief who was also an accomplished warrior would have greatly enhanced status, for his *mana* would be unquestioned. Should he suffer defeat, the stigma of low *mana* would attend him, and his authority and power might well be

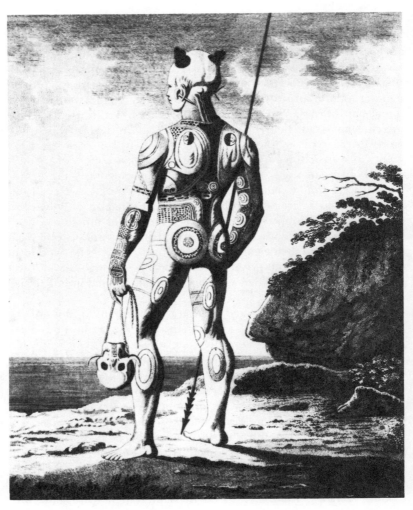

62. A Marquesan warrior with trophy skull, as sketched during the voyage of Krusenstern in 1803 (*photo courtesy Bishop Museum*).

challenged by another, either from within his group or from outside. Thus, as Goldman notes, 'the prominence of war, the adulation of sheer power, not to mention the immediate political consequences of victory or defeat, almost inevitably elevated the warriors to a level where they could challenge the ariki' (1970:14).

The usurpation of power, by prominent warriors and particularly by junior collaterals of a ruling chief, is a recurrent theme of Polynesian political traditions. The ascendancy of the famous Kamehameha, keeper of the war god Kukailimoku ('Ku-the-snatcher-of-chiefdoms'), over his senior collateral Kiwala'o (to whom the previous paramount, Kalaniopu'u, had bequeathed temporal overlordship) is but one instance of such usurpation. In Mangaia, the Temporal Lord was the most powerful war leader (Buck 1934). The theme recurs throughout Polynesia, and as Sahlins observes, 'usurpation itself is the principle of legitimacy' . . . Hawaiians say, "Every king acts as a conqueror when he is installed", for if he has not actually sacrificed the late king, he is usually presumed to have poisoned him' (1981b:113).

Warfare in Polynesia was therefore a means of preserving the *mana* and status of chiefs, as well as an opportunity for their rivals to usurp that same *mana* and status, and for *toa* to achieve a position in society not open to them by birth. Given this cultural context of warfare, it is easy to understand that the proximate causes of conflict were numerous; Williamson provides a partial catalogue of these:

struggles of rival chiefs for power, disputes as to succession, insubordination or rebellion of a subchief, or his resentment at the domination of his superior, lack of respect to a chief, disputes as to land, boundaries and property generally, the need of food and consequent raids, abduction of or elopement with women, vengeance for the death of a relation or insult or injury inflicted upon him, or theft or damage to his property, and the need of victims for human sacrifice to the gods (1937:3).

Polynesian warfare varied considerably in scale and intensity. At one end of the spectrum we have relatively simple raiding, such as that described by Buck (1932:55) for Tongareva, when 'the proclaiming of a *masanga* [ban on coconuts] forced the people of closed territory to make raids on their neighbor's plantations'. Raiding was a frequent means as well of avenging insults against one's person or tribe, a means of restoring *mana*. From the wider perspective of political evolution in Polynesia, however, it is the larger conflicts that are of special interest, particularly those that involved territorial conquest. Goldman rightly observed that 'war made lands and produce instruments and rewards of power' (1970:556). Having examined the cultural background of warfare in Polynesia, we may now look more closely at conflict in relation to island ecology and political systems.

Demographic and ecological correlates of competition

Vayda, in several studies of Maori warfare (1960, 1961, 1976), was perhaps the first to produce a model of Polynesian warfare in terms of 'direct ecological functions or consequences as the expansion of population and an increase in the extent of the environment being exploited' (1961:350). Vayda recognized that in situations of rapid population growth and expansion, such as evidently occurred in prehistoric New Zealand, 'sooner or later there would have been groups whose territory adjoined only the territory of other groups rather than any virgin land suitable for agriculture' (1961:348). Given continued population growth, the only viable alternative would be to expand the territory of the group by forcibly taking over the lands of one or more neighbouring groups. Furthermore, Vayda argued that the annexation of cleared agricultural land was preferable to expansion into virgin forest, 'because the labor involved in clearing the primary forest was so great' (1960:113). In the model, such territorial conquests not only allowed stronger local groups to expand, but the displacement of conquered groups led to a general population redistribution, and settlement of previously unoccupied lands. 'The expansion of one group, by means of warfare, into the contiguous territory of another could lead the second group to expand into the contiguous territory of a third – and so forth until finally there would be displacement of a group having territory contiguous to unoccupied land' (1976:77–8).

Vayda further argued (1976) that Maori warfare may be analysed as a *war process*, with distinguishable phases of fighting. Thus, raids and smaller-scale conflicts may have been a means for groups to continually 'test' each other's relative strength. Ultimately, such small-scale encounters would escalate to full-scale territorial conquests. Given the deeply ingrained cultural background of war in Polynesia, Vayda's model may appear demographically and ecologically deterministic. Nevertheless, his model in general terms is supported by a considerable array of ethnohistoric data, and provides an important perspective on the ability of territorial conquest to respond to pressures of population and land distribution (whether 'real', or simply perceived as such by the groups involved).

Roger Duff (1967) similarly stressed the role of population pressure and competition for arable land as the primary stimulus to warfare in New Zealand. In his words,

If we have to assign a specific reason for the evolution of warfare in the North Island rather than in the South or the Chathams, we can find it in the buildup of population which followed the adaptation of *kumara* growing to a still marginal environment. If we have to explain the distinctively chronic nature of Classic Maori warfare, we may seek it in the inherent competition for good *kumara* land and in the one-crop season   (1967:116).

Cassels (1974) while also acknowledging that population pressure was likely the primary stimulus to the development of Maori warfare, has stressed the need to be cautious about such models. Citing Kelly's (1968) important work in New Guinea, he rightly notes that very local population pressure or resource imbalances could trigger warfare, long before the entire region had approached a level of 'carrying capacity'.

The relationships between population growth, land (both limited area, and marginal versus fertile areas), and warfare have been noted for other Polynesian island groups as well. Suggs (1961) considered rapid population increase during the Marquesan Expansion Period to have led both to the settlement of marginal parts of the islands, and to an intensification of warfare. Suggs applied Vayda's model to the Marquesan situation, and indeed, carried it further, suggesting that the local population 'explosion' led to the settlement of other East Polynesian islands, by 'groups fleeing from the Marquesas' (1961:183–4). Ultimately, as all marginal lands were occupied, 'intergroup conflicts over land would have increased' (1961:186), a process serving to intensify 'to an extreme the rivalry present in most Polynesian societies'. McCoy (1976:143–5) also drew upon Vayda's model in his analysis of Easter Island warfare. He notes that 'it is clear that warfare was intended to force withdrawal from the land, thereby leaving it for exploitation by the victorious party' (1976:144). At the same time, however, McCoy recognized that while warfare served an adaptive function in the dispersal of population to unexploited land, it also had maladaptive aspects which in the long run prompted socio-political disintegration.

In Hawai'i, the role of war as the dominant factor in local sociopolitical development was argued by Cordy (1974b). In a rather linear chain of causation, Cordy proposed that population pressure acted as an independent 'initiating variable' to cultural change: 'one simple chiefdom (perhaps several) continued to grow in population, and this chiefdom(s) was surrounded by neighboring chiefdoms creating a full-land situation' (1974b:101). War for land, as an adjustment to this pressure, in turn 'required greater social complexity and integration' (1974b:102).

There seems to be little doubt that territorial conquest was a significant response to population increase and pressure on circumscribed lands throughout Polynesia (one would question, however, the 'prime mover' status that Cordy appears to attribute to warfare [cf. Friedman 1979:250, 258]). A general model is perhaps useful in outlining the process of competition and conflict; this is illustrated in diagrammatic form in Figure 63. We may envision this process as a series of phases (each grading into the next), the entire process taking several hundreds, or even a thousand or so years. In Phase I, our hypothetical island is colonized by a small social group, A, and a settlement is established in one of the fertile valleys on the south-east side of the island. (As is typical throughout much of Polynesia, this 'model' island has a well-watered, windward side, with permanent stream valleys and alluvial soils, and a drier, leeward side, more marginal for agricultural production.) Population growth within the next several generations gradually leads to fissioning of the original social group, with junior collateral lines establishing new groups in valleys farther along the coast (B, C). In this manner, the most favourable local environments come to be settled relatively rapidly.

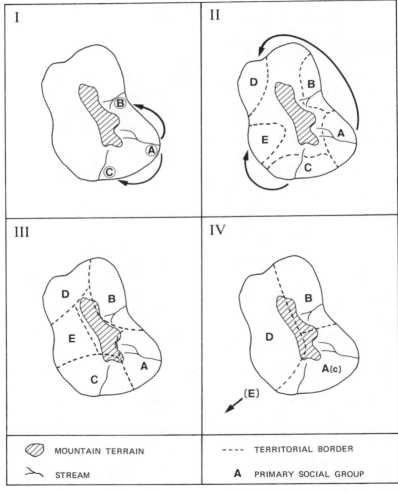

63. A diagrammatic model of the colonization of a hypothetical island, segmentation of social groups, and expansion leading to territorial conflict (see text for discussion).

By Phase II, continued population growth has led to fairly dense settlement in the windward valleys, with the territories of groups, A, B, and C now contiguous. Some degree of local agricultural intensification is initiated, particularly in the development of water-control systems for *Colocasia* cultivation. Nevertheless, the process of fissioning off of junior lines still continues, with the establishment, by this phase, of settlements in the more marginal, leeward side of the island (Phase II would, in essence, be equivalent to Suggs's Expansion Period in the Marquesan sequence). Competition and conflict between the densely settled windward groups (A, B, C) may be expected by Phase II, particularly with regard to boundary disputes.

In Phase III, population increase has now led to a 'full-land' situation, where the boundaries of all five political groups are contiguous. The windward groups have intensified irrigation production, while the leeward groups have adapted shifting cultivation to a short fallow regime. Under these conditions, boundary disputes have escalated, and inter-group raiding becomes common. The situation is easily exacerbated by environmental perturbations, such as drought or cyclone. In addition, degradation of the environment is occurring in local areas, for example, erosion on leeward ridges, and reduction in populations of wild birds, fish, and shellfish; these also tend to heighten the pressure on food resources.

By Phase IV, we have reached the level where territorial conquest has become full-fledged. Group A has conquered the territory of adjacent Group C, and incorporated the populations of both into one chiefdom polity. On the leeward side of the island, Group D has expanded into E's territory; in this scenario, the populace of E (those who were not felled in war) fled the island in search of new lands. Basically, a process of political consolidation has begun, with a monopoly of force as its principal instrument.

The general model or scenario sketched above is, of course, hypothetical. It is, nonetheless, closely reflected not only by ethnographic and archaeological evidence, but by indigenous oral traditions of local political history from several island groups (e.g., Mangareva, Buck 1938a; Mangaia, Buck, 1934; Society Islands, Oliver 1974; Easter Island, Métraux 1940; Hawai'i, Hommon 1976; Kamakau 1961). By way of ethnohistoric validation of this general model, I will briefly cite just two cases, those of Tikopia and Futuna. (Archaeological evidence supporting this model will be given in Part III.)

The demographic situation in Tikopia has already been discussed (Chapter 5), and it was briefly noted that war was an ultimate cultural control on over-population. In fact, a set of oral traditions (Firth 1961), tied to a genealogical framework and pertaining to the last few centuries of the Tikopia prehistoric sequence, provides a coherent account of war in relation to population pressure, food shortage, and competition for land. Although some anthropologists have dismissed such traditions as pure 'myth' (E.R. Leach 1962; Hooper 1981), archaeological investigations in Tikopia have corroborated many key aspects of the oral accounts, and confirmed Firth's view that these traditions constitute a 'quasi-history' which, if not entirely accurate from a Western historical viewpoint, at least is correct in its overall treatment of historical *process*. A detailed discussion of these traditions, and their archaeological corroboration, has been presented elsewhere (Kirch and Yen 1982:362–8), and here I summarize only certain highlights.

According to Tikopia tradition, by about the mid seventeenth century AD (based on genealogical calculation), the island was in a 'full-land' situation, with three major social and political groups. The first of these, Nga Faea, occupied the fertile western lowlands, while Nga Ravenga had control of the southern coast and adjacent hills. The third group, Nga Ariki (relative late arrivals to the island) were hemmed in along the inner shore of a marine embayment, with only steep talus for their agricultural land. These three groups were in a state of competition for limited agricultural resources, manifested by continual boundary disputes and the like. The problem of food shortage, acute for Nga Ariki, is explicit in the oral traditions, as in this metaphorically stated account:

time and again, I was told how day by day they and their households saw the scrapings of giant yam from the cooking houses of their Nga Ravenga neighbors float past them on the waters of the lake. Feeling the pinch of hunger they collected these scrapings, and baked them for food in their own ovens   (Firth 1961:131–2).

Unable to tolerate this situation, and provoked by land boundary disputes, Nga Ariki ultimately fell upon Nga Ravenga in a war of conquest, and virtually exterminated the latter, appropriating their lands. Nga Ariki were satisfied for a time, but after a generation or so, the scenario was repeated. This time Nga Faea fled before the Nga Ariki onslaught, leaving them sole masters of the island (see Chapter 4).

What the traditions do not discuss, but our archaeological investigations revealed (Kirch and Yen 1982), was that the seventeenth to eighteenth centuries in Tikopia were also a period of radical environmental change, the most dramatic manifestation of which was the closure of the salt-water bay to form Lake Te Roto (see Chapter 6, Fig. 34). Thus, not only did Nga Ariki originally possess the most marginal agricultural land on the island, but the creation of Te Roto eliminated their direct access to the sea (and to pelagic fish), and killed off the rich bivalve beds that had formerly been a major source of protein (as indicated in the midden deposits of Nga Ariki habitation sites). In short, archaeology has provided a solid ecological context for the political events discussed in Tikopia oral traditions. (As a footnote to the Tikopia case, it is worth noting that rivalry between social groups did not cease with Nga Ariki's mastery over the entire island. Rather, a division has developed between two districts, Faea and Ravenga, again manifested by frequent land disputes. Were population pressure not released by emigration (to Waimasi, Vanikoro, and other islands in the Solomons), it is probable that inter-district warfare would again erupt, as indeed was threatened as recently as the severe famine of 1952–3; Firth 1959).

The Futuna case involves a somewhat more complicated series of inter-group conflicts, again resulting in political consolidation, and related to competition for agricultural resources. Full analyses of the Futunan traditions may be found in Burrows (1936) and Kirch (1975). Figure 64 presents a summary of the political history of the Asoa–Alofi region of Futuna, beginning with five independent political units, and ending with the consolidation of the entire area by the paramount chief Veliteki, immediately prior to European contact. The underlying, recurrent themes in these political traditions are unmistakable: those of conquest and political amalgamation, resulting from desire for land, as seen for example in the founding tradition of the Mauifa line at Loka (competition for gardens between the Asoa people and the Fale Tolu), or in the conquest of Alofi, after the devastating effects of a cyclone and subsequent famine (Kirch 1975:342–7).

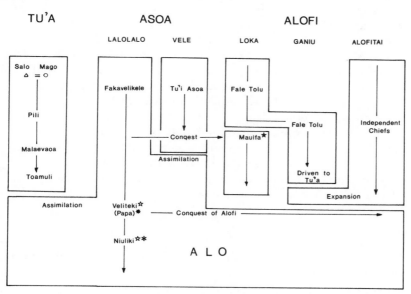

64. Graphic representation of the political traditions of the Asoa–Alofi region of Futuna and Alofi Islands, showing the succession of conquests and progressive amalgamation of the area under the authority of the Lalolalo line of paramount chiefs. Starred names are associated with known archaeological sites.

The Futunan case is significant in another regard, for it highlights the particular intensity of land competition in environments where shifting cultivation is the dominant agricultural mode. In Futuna, the sequence of inter-group conflict over land was strongest in the eastern part of the island (Asoa), which lacked permanent watercourses (unlike Sigave District, where irrigation was highly developed). Widening our perspective to include other Polynesian islands, there is considerable evidence to suggest that war for land was prominent in areas characterized by shifting cultivation, or its intensified dryfield forms (Kirch 1980a:47). This tendency is not surprising, when we consider that the limits to agricultural intensification are more severe in these environments, usually leeward areas lacking suitable water supply for irrigation or drainage. In areas where irrigation was feasible, local population pressure could be relieved (for a longer time, at least) through continued development of the pondfield infrastructure. The intensification of shifting cultivation, however, had more severe constraints, since reduction in fallow beyond a point will lead to decreased yields, or worse, permanent degradation of a landscape. With continued population increase, the only viable recourse in leeward, marginal environments was expansion to adjacent lands.

It is a fact of some significance that in Hawai'i, the most politically powerful and highly competitive chieftainships developed, *not* in areas where large-scale irrigation was feasible, but on the leeward sides of the islands, especially in the Kohala–Kona region of Hawai'i Island. (Curiously, this point has been overlooked by those who have discussed Hawaiian irrigation in terms of its evolutionary implications, e.g., Earle 1978, 1980.) Likewise, in the Society group, it was the smaller, more marginal islands such as Raiatea and Borabora that came to dominate the political scene in the late prehistoric period. Oliver (1974:1124) has suggested that Borabora's poor agricultural resources were, in fact, a direct stimulus to inter-island conquest. Sahlins as well (1972:141) has remarked on this important aspect of Polynesian production, 'the occupation and improvement of once-marginal areas effected under the aegis of ruling chiefs'.

Warfare and political development

Among the war songs intoned by the *rauti* during the course of battle in Tahiti was the following:

> War is growth (extension) to the land,
> Establishment of rock strata (great men),
> Spreading out of land (population) . . .
> War is fertile soil;
> Soil that will produce seeds (extension),
> Soil that will be verdant (produce power).

Soil spread out,
Soil for leaning slabs (increase of priests),
Soil for pavings (for marae [temples]).   Henry (1928:307)

As an indigenous statement, the chant is of particular interest, for it illustrates the political benefits that accrued to those victorious in war. While the use of coercive force as a dominant strategy in Polynesian islands was doubtless stimulated by the demographic and ecological factors discussed above, it was also spurred on by political motives. The association of victor with high *mana* and attendant status has already been discussed; here I wish to simply point out a few of the implications of intensive warfare for the evolution of complex polities.

The case of Mangaia (Buck 1934) is instructive, for though a relatively small high island, it is a sort of microcosm for a Polynesian society in which politics, as well as economics and religion, had come to be thoroughly bound up with warfare. In Buck's words,

In the course of history the prestige of the *toa* (successful warrior) began to overshadow that of the *rangatira* (chief). Successful leadership in war determined whether the tribe kept its own lands and acquired other . . . The war leader of the successful tribe became Temporal Lord of Mangaia . . . A hereditary chief could not rely on his seniority alone, but, to maintain his power in the tribe, he had to be a warrior as well   (1934:110).

In essence, the basis of political power had undergone a fundamental transformation, from one dependent upon descent and relationship to senior lines, to one in which the ability to apply coercive force was critical. Koskinen has referred to this change as a 'new type of *ariki*ship', noting as well that the 'chief became a political factor, and only remnants of his earlier priestly duties were retained' (1960:148–9). This transformation occurred, to varying degrees, in all of the larger island groups, and especially in the Society Islands, Hawai'i and Tonga. Not that the original emphasis on high rank and descent from the gods was entirely lost. In Hawai'i, for instance, while forceful usurpation of the reins of power by junior collaterals had become a recurrent pattern, the efforts of the usurpers to engage in marriages with high-ranking women were remarkable. Kamehameha was exceedingly disappointed that his child by Keopuolani, a chiefess of the highest (*ni'aupi'o*) rank, could not be born at Kukaniloko, ancestral temple of the ancient (indigenous) O'ahu paramounts, for this would have assured his heir of the highest status.

Burrows (1939b) long ago recognized the evolutionary significance of this shift in emphasis from a political apparatus based primarily on a kinship model of descent ('breed') to one in which power was defined on more directly practical, and overt, grounds, and in which territory ('border') was essential. As he wrote, 'progressive encroachment of border over breed seems to have been the rule in Polynesia. As territorial units grew larger and stronger, kinship grouping became simpler or vaguer' (1939b:20). Significantly, and I believe, correctly, Burrows pointed to 'warfare arising from rivalry over land or ambition for enhanced status' as the most powerful process favouring the transition from 'breed' to 'border' (1939b:21). Goldman, too, stressed this transformation from a political order rooted in the organic imagery of kin-group segmentation, to one based on territoriality. 'Kin groups bud, branch, and unfold. Territorial groups are created by chiefs. They express human agency. In this expression, they assert a radically new social idea' (1970:545).

The shift from descent to overt force as a basis for the attainment of political power also had major repercussions on local systems of land tenure and economic organization, and on religion. The Mangaian case is again instructive. Whereas originally the tribes 'occupied definite continuous areas' (Buck 1934:107), continued warfare led to a system wherein choice lands, especially the irrigated taro lands (*puna*), were redistributed as spoils of victory. 'Land tenure came to depend on conquest, which obliterated the rights of previous occupation and cultivation' (1934:129). In the Society Islands, paramount chiefs established personal estates in each of the territorial subdivisions under their suzerainty, placing their own stewards in charge of these lands (Oliver 1974:1209). Referring to Hawai'i, Hommon stressed that the significance of territorial acquisition lay, not so much in the land itself, but in the capture of a 'complete productive unit, consisting of terrestrial and marine resources and the resident producers' (1976:291). The benefit to the victorious chief was considerable, since surplus production could be redirected to his own entourage and political purposes. As we shall explore more fully in Chapter 10, the Hawaiian case witnessed the most radical shift in land tenure of any of the Polynesian groups, for the common populace came to be totally disenfranchised, working the land for chiefs who themselves held segments and districts at the pleasure of the paramount.

Clearly, warfare in Polynesia had more than one 'function': it was a means to relieve population pressure and obtain land for agricultural expansion, but was also a route to power and aggrandizement of status. Earle's argument that warfare should be understood as a 'capital investment . . . a feature of political competition over the means of production' (1978:183) has considerable merit. In Hawai'i, Mangaia, Tahiti and elsewhere throughout Polynesia war was indeed a means for chiefs to capture the productive apparatus of adjacent territories so as to put these to political uses. At the same time, however, we cannot ignore the real demographic and ecological pressure and constraints that provide a context for such political competition. Thus, I believe Earle was in error in rejecting outright any relationship between warfare and 'expanding population and subsistence requirements' (1978:183–4, 192).

Repercussions of the increased emphasis on coercive power can also be followed in the religious systems of the larger and more stratified chiefdoms. Buck tells us that in Mangaia, the war god Rongo became the 'national' god, and that 'change of government and the allocation of office and land had to be inaugurated by human sacrifice and ratified on the marae of Rongo with religious ritual' (1934:161–2). This is notable, for elsewhere throughout Polynesia Rongo is the god of agriculture and peace (e.g., the Hawaiian Lono; cf. Handy 1927:107–13), and was evidently so at an earlier time in Mangaia as well. According to Buck, it was the precedent set by the Ngariki clan, who first offered a human sacrifice to Rongo after a great victory, which established Rongo as a national god of war. In any event, the dominance of war cults, and associated human sacrifice, is clearly associated with the rise of militaristic chieftainships, notably in the Society Islands (the 'Oro cult) and in Hawai'i (the Ku cult). In Hawai'i, the worship of Ku became what Sahlins (1968:112) calls 'a religion of tribal dimensions', in which the pivotal figures were the ruling chiefs and a class of high priests (themselves of chiefly descent). As we shall see in Chapter 10, the material manifestations of the cult were massive stone temples, demanding considerable labour to construct and even more to supply the prodigious offerings needed for their consecration (see Chapter 7). In the worship of both Ku and 'Oro, human offerings enforced the absolute power and authority of the ruling chiefs. As Oliver observes, 'here is a case par excellence wherein religious commitment and politics were mutually supportive of an ideal condition for aggrandizement by either one or both' (1974:908).

Archaeological manifestations of warfare

Archaeological evidence for prehistoric warfare in Polynesia consists of occasional weapons (slingstones, spear points, etc.) found on the surface or in excavations, and of fortifications. Of these two classes of evidence, the second is far and away the most important, providing critical data on the age, development, and degree of armed conflict. Polynesian fortifications (and especially those of New Zealand), are the subject of a considerable literature, and here I can only review a few highlights of direct relevance to the arguments presented above. A good overview of the field is Daugherty (1979), to whom the reader is referred for an in-depth survey.

Several attempts have been made to classify Polynesian fortifications, and for New Zealand in particular there are a number of differing typologies (e.g., Best 1927; Golson 1957a; Groube 1965, 1970; A. Fox 1976). For our purposes, a modified version of Daugherty's simple functional classification (1979:5) will suffice to indicate the major kinds of fortification found throughout Polynesia. Three major categories were indicated by Daugherty's scheme: I, homeland defences; II, strategic defences; and III, refuges. Homeland forts, situated within an occupied territory, were the most substantial, and basically consisted of fortified, defended hamlets or villages, that is, permanent residential sites. In general terms, we can divide this category into two morphological classes: IA, those which utilized natural ridges, volcanic cones, headlands, and the like (usually with additional, often substantial modification, like pallisades and fosses), which were easily defended; and, IB, forts constructed on flat terrain (or in swampy ground), utilizing ditch-and-bank or pallisade construction. Type IA is epitomized by the Maori *pa*, while IB is well represented by the Tongan *kolo* (McKern 1929).

The second major class (II) of fortification is the *strategic*, designed to 'deny the enemy access or entrance into the territory' (Daugherty 1979:5). Such forts are most frequently sited on ridges or other high points, though there are exceptions, such as the great Poike Ditch on Easter Island. This latter construction, actually a linear series of ditches (each about 100 metres long and 10–15 metres wide, and 2–3 metres deep) with associated spoil banks, runs for nearly 3 kilometres, and would have blocked access to the Poike Peninsula from the rest of the island (Heyerdahl and Ferdon 1961: fig. 2, 385–91).

The final class of fortification (Type III) is that of *refuges*, places to which a group would flee in time of war. These are naturally defensive positions, such as ridges or peaks, with some artificial structural modification, which I have labelled as Type IIIA. A distinct subtype, IIIB, consists of caves or lava tubes modified for use as refuges.

Table 20 shows the distribution of each of these major classes of fortification throughout the various island groups, and lists some primary references to archaeological surveys and excavations of fortified sites. While strategic defences and refuges are found in virtually every island group, homeland sites are conspicuously absent in certain areas, even though warfare itself was endemic. Daugherty (1979:173) attributes the lack of elaborate fortifications in Hawai'i and the Society Islands to the 'openness and obviousness' of their war tactics, though other factors (such as the size of the territorial unit) may also be important.

Early discussions of Polynesian fortifications (e.g., Best 1927) tended to view these large artifacts in diffusionist terms. It is clear, however, that Polynesian forts must be viewed, in the main at least, as *local* developments, and that morphological similarities have often developed convergently, due to use of similar natural terrain, the same level of technology, and fighting tactics. It is probably significant that there is no general Polynesian term for fort. Rather, in West Polynesia forts are called *kolo* (or *'olo* in Samoa), whereas in East Polynesia they are termed either *pa* or *pare*, a term derived from the Proto-Polynesian word for 'enclosure'.

Table 20. *Distribution of fortifications in Polynesia*

Island/group	Types					Primary references
	IA	IB	II	IIIA	IIIB	
Tonga		X	?			McKern 1929; Davidson 1971
Samoa		X	X	X	X	Green and Davidson 1969, 1974
Futuna			X	X		Burrows 1936; Kirch 1975
'Uvea		X	?			Burrows 1937; Kirch 1975
Marquesas			X	X		Suggs 1961; Sinoto 1970
Easter Island			X		X	Heyerdahl and Ferdon 1961; McCoy 1976
Society Islands			X	?		Emory 1933; Green 1967
Raivaevae	X					Heyerdahl and Ferdon 1961; Green 1967
Hawai'i				X	X	McAllister 1933; Bonk 1969; Schilt 1980b
Rapa	X		X	X		Stokes ms; Ferdon 1965
New Zealand	X		X	X		Best 1927; A. Fox 1976; Groube 1970

Polynesian fortification reached its apogee in New Zealand, where the total number of forts has been estimated at 4,000–6,000 (Groube 1970:133), and this, as A. Fox (1976:9) admits, may be an under-estimate. The vast majority of *pa* sites are situated in the North Island, and their distribution closely reflects the prime agricultural settlement areas. Likewise, the less numerous *pa* of South Island are nearly all found along the north-east coasts (from Murderers Bay to the Banks Peninsula), also in association with agricultural areas (Brailsford 1981). Despite an early ethnographic interest in *pa* sites (Best 1927), it was not until fairly recently that archaeologists began to tackle the problems presented by excavation of such large-scale field monuments. There are now, however, several detailed investigations of *pa* sites, among these Fox's work at Pawhetau and at Tiromoana Pa (1974, 1978), Bellwood's excavation of Otakanini (1971, 1972b), Harsant's study of Oue Pa (1981), Fox and Green's excavation of the defended settlement of Maioro (1982), and Peters's of Mangakaware (1971). The recent synthesis by Fox (1976) concisely surveys the current state of knowledge of *pa* variation and development.

Groube (1970) distinguished three major classes of the Maori *pa* on the basis of their defences: Class I, terraced sites; Class II, sites defended with transverse ditches and banks; and Class III, sites defended with both transverse and lateral ditches and banks, including wholly enclosed forms. Fox (1976) suggests the addition to this scheme of

Class IV, swamp *pa*, defended only by wooden pallisades. Figure 65 is a plan of Tiromoana Pa at Hawke's Bay, showing many of the features characteristic of New Zealand fortifications. To the west and north, the *pa* is naturally defended by steep slopes, whereas ditches and banks, and pallisades, strengthen the *pa* from attack on the south and east. On the lower slopes are numerous terraces, many of which would have supported habitations. A ubiquitous feature of any *pa* site, sunken storage pits (for sweet potato, *kumara*), with raised rims and external drains, cover much of the level top of the site. Storage pits were often elaborately constructed, with internal drains and racks for holding the *kumara* tubers. Taniwha Pa, in the lower Waikato, is a rather unique site, in which fully 60 per cent of the flat area within the *pa* is taken up by a series of forty-four storage pits (Fig. 66), capable of holding about 370 cubic metres of *kumara* tubers (Law and Green 1972:265). Taniwha essentially consists of a 'fortified store, one which can be retreated to from other dwelling places if danger threatened' (1972:265).

Fox (1976:27–30) has presented a working model for the evolution of the Maori *pa*, based on the excavations and radiocarbon evidence obtained thus far. At several sites, such as Skipper's Ridge, Tiromoana,

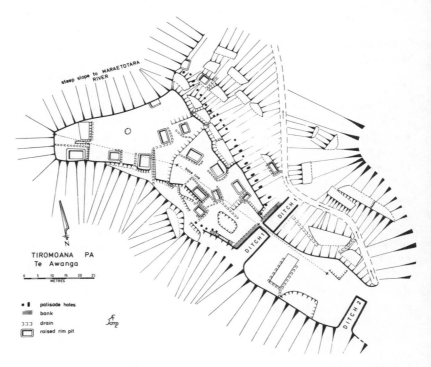

65. Plan of Tiromoana Pa, New Zealand (*courtesy R.C. Green, University of Auckland*).

Maioro, and Kauri Point, there is evidence for unfortified, hilltop agricultural settlements preceding the construction of *pa* defences. Such settlement sites, incorporating subterranean storage pits, had evidently become common by the twelfth and thirteenth centuries throughout parts of the North Island. The transition to earthwork or pallisade defences occurred at several excavated sites during the fifteenth and sixteenth centuries, and in some cases, successive stages of construction of increasingly sophisticated defences are discernible (e.g., at Otakanini and Tiromoana). Fox summarizes the origin of the *pa* as follows:

> fortification in New Zealand was an insular development, arising from the need to defend existing hilltop settlements where basic foodstuffs were stored. A stock of *kumara, taro*, and fern root was essential to feed the growing communities through the wet winter and to enable them to plant the new crops in the spring. Raiding a neighbor was a quick way to overcome a shortage, and hence the need and reason for defense (1976:28–9).

Archaeology has thus begun to provide concrete support for the theoretical speculations of Vayda and others regarding the close relationships between population growth, agriculture, and the development of warfare in New Zealand.

The island of Rapa, in the Austral group, though only 39 km² in area, presents a marvellous example of the development of homeland fortifications, elaborate ridge-top village sites with sophisticated defences.

66. Aerial view of Taniwha Pa, New Zealand, a fortified group of storage pits (*photo courtesy R.C. Green, University of Auckland*).

Vancouver (1798, vol. I:215) saw some of these villages from the sea in 1791, but a detailed survey was not conducted until Stokes's work in 1920 (ms.). The Rapan forts, locally known as *pare*, number about twenty-five, and are distributed over the island, occupying elevated points along the central mountain crest (Fig. 67). Stokes collected a wealth of oral traditions concerning clan history, including the relationship of these social groups to the forts, and some of this has been summarized by Hanson (1970:23–6). Clearly, the emphasis on fortified settlement reflected a phase of intense rivalry between social

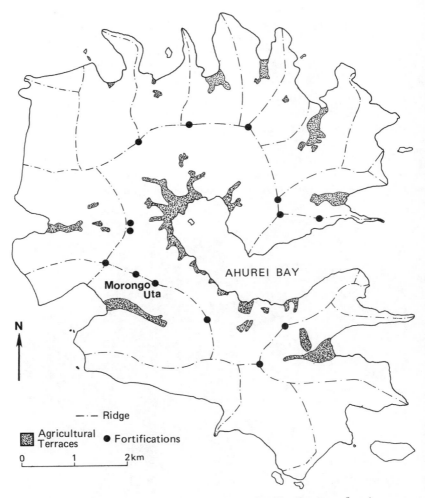

67. The island of Rapa, showing the distribution of major ridge-top fortifications and of irrigated agricultural terraces in valley bottoms (adapted from Heyerdahl and Ferdon 1965).

groups, spurred by competition for limited agricultural resources (especially the irrigated valley bottoms, see Fig. 67). It is probable that environmental degradation, induced by human burning of the vegetation on the steep hillsides, was also a factor which exacerbated the resource problem. Stokes summarized the development of the Rapan fortified villages as follows:

I assume . . . that the original use of refuges began at a period of great internal disturbance. It seems to suggest the period of the Tipi wars for ascendancy . . . It is paralleled by the interleaved situation of the clans in all parts of the island which seems to tell a story of conquests, part or whole, and reconquests which has left the plan of clan distribution exceedingly mixed (ms., p. 443).

To date, archaeological investigation of Rapa has been limited to the work of the Norwegian Expedition (1955–6), whose primary thrust was the excavation of Morongo Uta, the largest fortified village site on the island (Mulloy 1965). On this site, 'evidence of debris of daily living was plentiful' (1965:22), and it functioned both as a permanent or home-land village as well as a citadel against attack. As seen in the reconstruction (Fig. 68), the *pare* consists of a central tower, with surrounding terraces levelled into the narrow ridge lines extending out from the tower in three directions. Fosses across the ridges aided in defence, and the village was probably pallisaded when in use. Mulloy's excavation, unfortunately, failed to provide any evidence for the sequence of construction at Morongo Uta. The problem of the development of warfare and fortification in Rapa, along with the intensification of irrigation in the valley bottoms (and of environmental change and erosion), is one that will greatly repay future attempts as in-depth archaeological study.

In striking contrast to New Zealand or Rapa, the Hawaiian Islands – despite the endemic warfare that characterized late prehistoric Hawaiian culture – generally lack fortified sites. Nevertheless, mountain refuges are probably more common than previously thought. Several examples seen by the author on Oʻahu Island have fosses cut across steep ridges, although there is no evidence that such sites were ever permanently occupied, or even used by fleeing groups for extended periods of time. At Kawela, on Molokaʻi Island, is a particularly interesting refuge site situated on a narrow ridge between two branches of the Kawela Gulch (Weisler and Kirch 1982). The ridge-top plateau is accessible only along the narrow crest, and this was fortified with small terraces, which probably served as crude fighting stages. At one point on the ridge line, a cache of carefully selected water worn slingstones (Fig. 69) was located. What makes the site especially interesting is the presence of a major religious structure, of the type called *puʻuhonua*, farther inland along the ridge. This temple, constructed of stacked stone masonry, served as a place of refuge to which *tapu* breakers or defeated warriors could flee and be safe from their pursuers. Within the

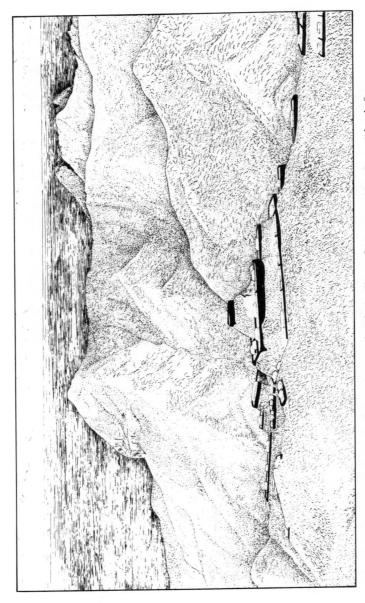

68. Conjectural reconstruction of the ridge-top fortified village of Morongo Uta, Rapa Island (from Heyerdahl and Ferdon 1965, *courtesy of T. Heyerdahl*).

confines of the *puʻuhonua* such persons were under the protection of the gods and, after appropriate rituals of purification, could go forth again with impunity. In the Kawela refuge site, therefore, we see the close relationship between religious belief and practical action (such as warfare), which is typical of Polynesian cultures.

On the leeward side of Hawaiʻi Island (in the districts of Kona,

69. A cache of slingstones situated on the fortified ridge at Kawela, Molokaʻi Island (*photo courtesy M. Weisler, Bishop Museum*).

Kohala, and Ka'u), where warfare was particularly intense, are found large caves of refuge, utilizing natural lava tubes. Five of these have been investigated: Lua Nunu (Bonk 1969), Keopu cave (Schilt, 1980b), the Keahole refuge cave (Hammatt and Folk 1980), Waikoloa Cave 16 (Bevacqua 1972), and Cave 900 (Rosendahl 1973). All of these sites have extensive modifications for defence, such as walled entrances and narrow crawlways, where an attacking enemy would be forced to enter single-file. At Keahole and Keopu, stratigraphic evidence suggests earlier use of these sites for habitation, with construction of defences only later. In fact, available dating indicates that these sites were used for refuge beginning about the sixteenth century, correlating with traditional evidence for a heightening of inter-district competition and conflict.

Overview

The archaeological evidence for warfare, from several island groups, reinforces a significant point regarding competition and conflict in Polynesia – that the use of coercive force developed *locally*, in distinctive patterns peculiar to each society. Yet, despite such variation, it is still possible to isolate several dominant factors closely related to the escalation or intensification of Polynesian warfare everywhere. Population growth, limited agricultural resources, chiefly demand for surplus and a consequent need for territorial expansion were clearly fundamental to the larger process. Environmental change – both stochastic perturbations and longer-term degradation induced by human land use – also had a role, and acute disasters may frequently have precipitated armed conflicts. Still, it is important to stress that the development of Polynesian warfare cannot be explained solely on a demographic–ecological model. Just as significant a variable in the process of war were ancestral Polynesian social and political relations, including cultural definitions of *mana* and status. As a socially defined category, *toa*-ship existed long before the colonization of most Polynesian islands, and the potential for political rivalry between *toa* and *ariki* (as between high and low grades of *ariki*) was latent in Ancestral Polynesian Society. Population increase and land shortage did not cause endemic warfare in Polynesian islands; they provided a context and stimulus wherein *ariki* and *toa*, striving for domination over people and resources, created through conflict, alliance, subversion, and persuasion, social and political systems never before realized in Polynesia. In these struggles for power, legitimated by myth and past actions, we see the evolution of island chiefdoms.

History is always structured by society; there are only more or less dynamic modes of effecting this.

Marshall Sahlins (1976:220)

9
Tonga

The preceding five chapters explored the dominant factors in the evolution of the Polynesian chiefdoms: the reassortment and adaptation of cultural systems following initial colonization, the growth of large and densely settled populations, stochastic perturbations and long-term environmental change, development and intensification of the productive forces, and competition and conflict between social groups. In examining each of these factors, I have drawn widely upon ethnographic and archaeological data for supporting examples and illustrations, avoiding an island-by-island culture historical treatment. While extended case studies of particular phenomena have been presented, we have yet to trace the evolutionary course of any particular Polynesian society from settlement to European contact. Such an objective is the aim of the next three chapters.

In Part III, I apply the theoretical orientation and analytical procedures developed in the preceding chapters to three specific societies. In so doing, I hope to further illustrate how the dominant evolutionary processes have, in the context of local conditions, resulted in the emergence of three societies which, although divergent in some respects, all share certain underlying structural similarities. The societies which I have chosen – Tonga, Hawai'i, and Easter Island – each have characteristics of special interest. Tonga not only reached a remarkable level of political development in Oceania, but is virtually unique within Polynesia for its elaborate external voyaging and exchange network. Hawai'i represents a case of equally great political transformation, but within a remote, isolated, yet large and fertile archipelago. Easter Island, perhaps the most intriguing of the three cases, is like Hawai'i truly isolated, and its fascination lies in the development there of a complex society which was in the end only to exceed its developmental limits and collapse upon itself.

From 'Eua to Vava'u, the Tongan archipelago extends 300 kilometres along a roughly northeast–southwest axis, incorporating about 160 islands, the largest being Tongatapu, 'Eua, and Vava'u, all uplifted

217

limestone, with fertile, developed soils (Fig. 70). The Ha'apai group comprises numerous low coral islets and atolls, the largest of which are Nomuka, 'Uiha, Foa, Lifuka, and Ha'ano. The active volcanic islands of Tofua and Late, west of the main archipelago, were never regularly inhabited, but were visited for stone and timber. Beyond this main

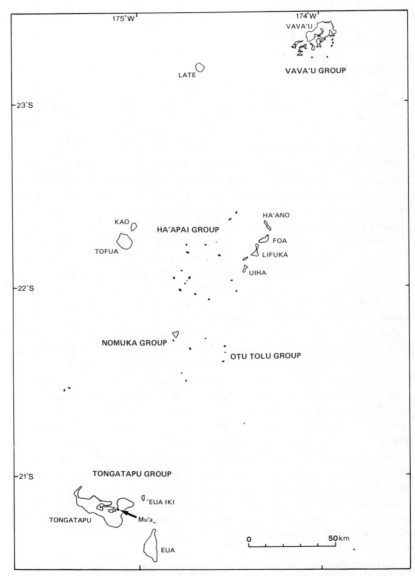

70. The Tongan archipelago, excluding the northerly islands of Niuatoputapu and Niuafo'ou.

group, some 300 kilometres north of Vava'u, lie Niuatoputapu and Tafahi, small high islands, and a further 190 kilometres north-west is Niuafo'ou, an active ring-shaped volcano with a central crater lake. Farthest-flung of the former Tongan dominions was 'Uvea, some 850 kilometres north-west of Tongatapu.

The complexity of the Tongan political system was evident to the early European explorers (indeed, the complexities confounded Cook for a time), and later ethnographers have invariably classified Tonga as one of the most stratified of Polynesian societies (e.g., Sahlins 1958; Goldman 1970). The entire archipelago was controlled by a pair of sacred and secular paramounts (the Tu'i Tonga and the *hau*), whose main seat was on the island of Tongatapu ('Sacred Tonga'). The truly unique feature of Tongan society, in contrast with other Polynesian chiefdoms, was the integration by the Tongan polity of an extensive geographic region, extending far beyond the limits of the Tongan archipelago itself. Guiart stressed this topological structure of the Tongan system: 'A l'échelle de l'Océanie, l'ensemble tongien pourrait être décrit comme un empire insulaire' (1963:661) . . . 'seul peut-être des pays polynésiens, l'archipel tongien s'était rallié autour d'une autorité centralisée' (1963:667).

The archipelago's northeast–southwest orientation facilitated inter-island contacts, for during the trade-wind season two-way voyaging up or down the chain is comparatively easy. We may readily distinguish between a group of 'core' islands ('Eua, Ha'apai, and Vava'u) closely linked to the central polity on Tongatapu, and the more distant 'outliers' of Niuatoputapu, Niuafo'ou, and 'Uvea (not to be confused with the Polynesian Outliers of Melanesia). Ultimately, this system of political and economic activity extended to Samoa and to eastern Fiji, from whence certain prestige goods, and chiefly spouses, were obtained (Hjarnø 1979–80; Kaeppler 1978). The development of this complex, stratified, and geographically extensive socio-political system may be traced through a combination of archaeological and ethno-historic materials.

The archaeological sequence

Archaeological investigations on Tongatapu, though limited in scope and uneven in their treatment of certain site types, provide the skeleton of a prehistoric sequence (Poulsen 1967, 1968, 1976, 1977; McKern 1929; Davidson 1969; Groube 1971; Golson 1957b). Lapita coloniz-ation was accomplished no later than about 1200 BC, based upon radiocarbon dated ceramic-bearing sites at Ha'ateiho and Pea. For the first millennium of Tongan prehistory, settlement was closely concen-trated along the shores of the inland lagoon (Groube 1971). A steady increase in the island's population, over the 1500 or so years that pottery was in use, is indicated by the distribution and density of ceramic-bearing sites. Sites containing Early Eastern Lapita, with well-decorated vessels, are relatively scarce, whereas the later Polynesian Plain Ware sites are so concentrated as to form an essentially continuous zone of pottery-bearing soils bordering the lagoon. As Groube argued, 'this coastal profusion' of pottery 'conforms to a prehistoric settlement pattern of villages situated along the lagoon shore' (1971:291). There is no obvious archaeological evidence, from this early period, of major differences in social status; elaborate mortuary practices, large-scale public architecture, or other evidence of status differential are lacking.

The first millennium AD has been termed the 'Dark Ages' by Davidson (1979), owing to the dearth of excavated sites from this period. Pottery manufacture ceased early in the first millennium AD, and non-ceramic habitation sites have not as yet attracted archaeological attention. As Davidson reports, 'there is little evidence until late in the first millennium AD of the monumental sites, particularly the earthen and stone mounds, that are now such a feature of the archaeological landscapes of both Samoa and Tonga' (1979:95). These include communal burial mounds, shared by members of a local ramage (Davidson 1969), chiefly sitting mounds (*'esi*), specialized mounds where chiefs practised the sport of snaring pigeons (*sia heu lupe*), and burial mounds of the highest-ranking paramounts and their immediate relatives (*langi*). Many of these mounds, especially the latter, are large and impressive structures, with facings of quarried and dressed coral limestone slabs up to 7.5 metres long. These monuments were constructed with corvée labour, and a class of stone-cutting specialists (*tufunga ta maka*) also developed (Martin 1818, II:91).

The profusion of these mounds throughout the Tongan landscape signals a significant shift in settlement patterns, from the earlier distribution of lagoon-shore villages to one of dispersed settlement inland – the pattern observed at European contact. Most likely, this shift was correlated with continued population increase and demand for agricultural land. The founding of the great ceremonial centre at Lapaha, Mu'a, is attributed to the 12th Tu'i Tonga Talatama, which on the basis of genealogical reckoning would date the initial constructions there to the thirteenth century AD. Most of the fortifications and larger burial mounds at Mu'a were, however, built after the reign of the 23rd Tu'i Tonga Takalaua, about 250 years later (mid sixteenth century). Two communal burial mounds (*fa'itoka*) excavated by Davidson (1969) at 'Atele have been ^{14}C dated, and tend to confirm the hypothesis that construction of large mounds dates to the second millennium AD. Site To-At-1 has an age of less than 1200 years, while To-At-2 dates between about the twelfth and sixteenth centuries AD.

Environment, agriculture, and population

Several significant environmental conditions constrained the direction of socio-political development in the archipelago: (1) environmental circumscription – islands are small and with precisely fixed boundaries, yet they are large enough for populations in the tens of thousands to build up; (2) lack of permanent watercourses, and consequent impossibility of irrigation, agricultural intensification therefore being restricted to dryland field systems; (3) recurrent environmental perturbations, the most devastating being cyclones and drought. These aspects of the Tongan ecosystem have had a major influence on the course of socio-political change, particularly in heightening the role of inter-group competition and warfare.

Despite these constraints, the Tongan islands – and Tongatapu in particular – are richly endowed with unusually fertile soils that permitted an intensive level of dryland agriculture. Tongatapu consists of relatively old *makatea* whose organic-coralline surface has been enriched periodically with volcanic ashfalls from the active volcanoes of Kao and Tofua. Annual rainfall, between 1,500 and 1,800 mm, is also at an adequate level for Oceanic crops. At European contact, the agricultural system consisted of a short-fallow swidden system, in which yams (especially *Dioscorea alata*), aroids (especially *Alocasia macrorrhiza*, but also *Colocasia esculenta*), and bananas were the principal field crops. A secondary arboricultural emphasis was represented by fruit trees such as breadfruit and the Tahitian chestnut (*Inocarpus fagiferus*); animal husbandry was also well developed. The dominance of yams in Tongan agriculture is noteworthy, since *Dioscorea* tubers may be stored for reasonably long periods, and thus provided an easily appropriated surplus product for the chiefly class. It is no coincidence that yams were the primary and mandatory item given as tribute to the Tu'i Tonga at the annual first-fruits ceremony (*'inasi*).

The intensity of Tongan agriculture is well documented in the journals of early European explorers, and we can do no better than to quote Cook's observations on Tongatapu in 1773:

I thought I was transported into one of the most fertile plains in Europe, here was not an inch of waste ground, the roads occupied no more space than was absolutely necessary and each fence did not take up above 4 Inches and even this was not wholly lost for in many of the fences were planted fruit trees and the Cloth plant, these served as a support to them . . . Nature, assisted by a little art, no were [*sic*] appears in a more flourishing state than at this isle (Beaglehole 1969, Book II:252).

Two aspects of this intensive dryland agriculture are of note: (1) the shortness of the fallow period; and (2) the stress on permanent land division. Cook noted that Tongatapu was 'wholly laid out in Plantations in which are some of the richest Productions of Nature' (1969:261), and while 'some old Plantations lay uncultivated or in fallow' (1967, Book I:139), it is quite clear that fallow periods were very short, on the order of a few years. The unusual fertility of Tonga's ash-rich soils, combined with intensive agronomic practices such as mulching made such a short-fallow cycle possible. The emphasis on fencing of gardens, and indeed the degree to which the island was carved up into walled parcels, bespeaks a permanency of land division which further reveals the intensity of Tongan agriculture. Thus, at the time of European contact, the Tongan landscape was an intensely agrarian scene, and densely settled.

As Green (1973) argued, population density in prehistoric Tonga was quite high for a productive system based upon such an intensified form of shifting cultivation, and a plateau of relatively high density may have been reached not long after the end of the Lapitoid Period (*c.* AD 300), if the widespread distribution of Plain Ware sites is any indication. The significance of population growth in Tonga can be illustrated using Carneiro's (1972) formula for calculating the time required for shifting cultivators to achieve a state where all available land is utilized:

$$t = \frac{\log \left(\dfrac{W}{C\,(Y + R)/Y} \right) \log P}{\log (1 + r)}$$

On Tongatapu, the total arable land (W) is 55,398 acres, and under ethnographically documented methods of shifting cultivation, about 0.4 acre/year is necessary per capita for subsistence (C). If we then assume an original fallow period (R) of 10 years, and a productive life of individual swidden plots (Y) of 2 years, we can calculate the time (t) required to reach a 'full-land' situation, under varying rates of population growth (r), given an initial population size (P). For example, given a founding population of 100 persons, and an intrinsic growth rate of 0.005,

$$t = \frac{\log \left(\dfrac{55,398}{0.4\,(2 + 10)/2} \right) - \log 100}{\log 1.005} = 1,091 \text{ years}$$

Even with a growth rate as low as 0.003 the elapsed time to a full-land situation would be 1,817 years, or well before the period of European contact. Roughly, all of the arable land on Tongatapu would have come under agrarian use and territorial control between one to two millennia after initial colonization, that is, between about 300 BC and AD 700. As noted above, this conclusion fits well with the evidence for the profusion of Plain Ware pottery sites by *c.* AD 300.

Such a full-land situation provided a context for inter-group competition as analysed in Chapter 8, leading ultimately to assimilation of weaker groups by stronger and larger ones. The process would have been more intense on the larger islands, such as Tongatapu and Vava'u, where early lineage segmentation had led to the development of several independent and subsequently competing chiefdoms. Assuming that this process of competition, and the aggrandizement of local polity that accompanies it, was in full swing during the first millennium AD, it is not surprising that the archaeological evidence for political hierarchization – in the form of the large monument sites – first appears about AD 1000.

A linguistic clue is further suggestive of the direction of political development in Tongatapu. Whereas reflexes of the ancient term for 'chief', **'ariki* are found throughout Polynesia, there is in Tonga a second term, *tu'i*, as in the titles Tu'i Tonga and Tu'i Ha'apai. This term generally takes the compound form Tu'i-(of a)-Place, and may be glossed as 'Lord of the Place'. This term is restricted in its geographical distribution to West Polynesia and Fiji, and therefore was probably an innovation local to the region. We may hypothesize that the term *tu'i* represents the development of a second level of chiefly hierarchy, that of the district paramount, the head either of the highest-ranking ramage within the conical clan, or of the strongest local group in warfare. It seems that by the beginning of the second millennium AD one such lineage on Tongatapu had gained hegemony over several formerly independent chiefdoms into which the island had been divided. The chief of this ascendant line assumed the title Tu'i Tonga: Lord of Tonga.

Rise of the dual paramountship

The more recent stage of socio-political evolution in Tonga is elucidated by a particularly rich ethnographic and traditional corpus. The renowned Polynesian obsession with genealogy – essential to the legitimation of chiefly titles – was nowhere more developed than in Tonga. The genealogical relations of the dominant political lines are well known, and provide a basis for analysing Tongan socio-political structure, and its development. Figure 71 displays the core genealogy of the principal lines of Tongan ruling chiefs, and reference to this figure should be made throughout the following discussion.

The first mythological ancestor of the Tu'i Tonga line, and – by extension – of all titled chiefs, was 'Aho'eitu, the half-man, half-god progeny of a union between the god Tangaloa 'Eitumatupu'a and a mortal woman. From this divine origin the line of the Tu'i Tonga, the sacred paramounts, reputedly continued in unbroken patrilineal succession through thirty-nine title-holders, ending with the Tu'i Tonga Laufilitonga who died in 1865. While the earliest part of this genealogy is mythical, the latter portion, shown in Figure 71, may be regarded as historically valid.

Prior to the 23rd Tu'i Tonga Takalaua, about the fifteenth century AD, the Tu'i Tonga served as both sacred and secular paramount. The assassination of Takalaua, however, precipitated a radical structural change in the Tongan polity: the development of the dual paramountship. According to the oral traditions (which are richly detailed and internally consistent on this point), the sons of Takalaua pursued their

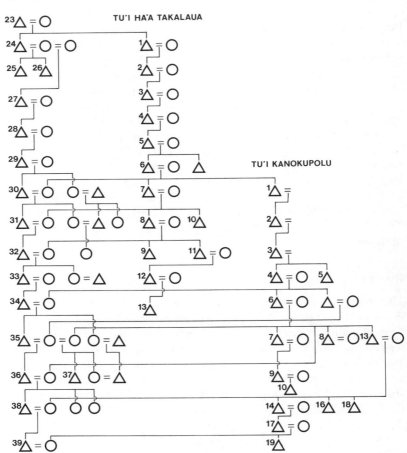

71. Genealogical relations between the principal ruling lines of Tonga. The succession of titles within each of the three ruling lines is indicated by the numbers.

father's assassins throughout the length and breadth of the Tongan archipelago (a metaphor for conquest), extending the quest to the outlying islands of Niuatoputapu, Niuafo'ou, Futuna, and 'Uvea, which they subjugated in turn. Following the apprehension of the murderers in 'Uvea, the senior son Kauulufonuafekai (Tu'i Tonga 24) assumed the title of Tu'i Tonga, and created a new title of Tu'i Ha'a Takalaua, transferring the secular power of the chiefdom to the latter, known henceforth as the *hau*. The first *hau* and Tu'i Ha'a Takalaua was Moungamotu'a, younger brother of Kauulufonuafekai.

Seven generations following the creation of the *hau* title, a second and structurally parallel collateral segmentation took place, with the formation of the Tu'i Kanokupolu line, the first title-holder being the junior brother of the Tu'i Ha'a Takalaua (Fig. 71). The Tu'i Kanokupolu gradually assumed the position of *hau*, temporal lord. Thus at the time of European contact with Tonga, the central polity consisted of a dual paramountship, summarized by Basil Thomson as follows:

there were in Tonga a spiritual and a temporal king. The former – the Tui Tonga – was lord of the soil, and enjoyed divine honours in virtue of his immortal origin; but he had an ever-diminishing share in the government . . . The temporal king [*hau*] – the Tui Kanokubolu – was the irresponsible sovereign of the people, wielding absolute power of life and death over his subjects, and was charged with the burden of the civil government and the ordering of the tribute due to the gods and their earthly representative, the Tui Tonga (1894:291).

The structural relationship between the Tu'i Tonga and the *hau* is diagrammed in Figure 72. To understand these relations, we must, as Kaeppler (1971a:174) avers, conceptually distinguish principles of social status from those governing societal rank. The most significant

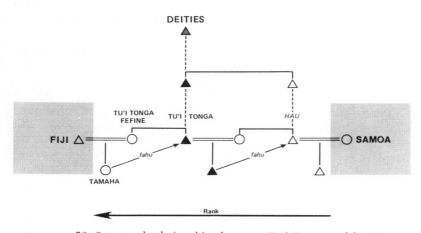

72. Structural relationships between Tu'i Tonga and *hau* (see text for discussion).

principle of social status is that within a group of siblings of both sexes, 'females have higher status than males' (1971a:176). The second principle is that among siblings of the same sex, age determines rank. Thus, the Tu'i Tonga is outranked (in terms of social status) by his sister, the Tu'i Tonga Fefine, or female Tu'i Tonga. The eldest daughter of the Tu'i Tonga Fefine was the Tamaha, the 'sacred child' of the Tu'i Tonga, who stood in the *fahu* relation to her mother's brother (see Gifford 1929; Kaeppler 1971a), with the right of appropriation of certain of the latter's possessions and privileges.

Figure 71 shows that the line of the *hau* frequently served as wife-givers to the Tu'i Tonga (this occurred nine times). Due to these hypergamic marriages, the Tu'i Tonga stood as 'sacred child' to the *hau*, with all of the obligations implied by the *fahu* relationship.

A potential dilemma for the principle of patrilineal succession to the Tu'i Tonga title was the higher social rank of the Tu'i Tonga Fefine. Since the son of the Tu'i Tonga Fefine would outrank his mother's brother the Tu'i Tonga, the potential for a conflict of succession is obvious. The problem was resolved ingeniously: the Tu'i Tonga Fefine was espoused to a Fijian chief, the Tu'i Lakemba, who as a foreigner was 'outside' of the line of descent of the Tongan paramounts. On the other hand, the problem of obtaining a suitably high-ranked spouse for the *hau* was resolved by marrying him to the Tamaha, or, by importing chiefly women from Samoa, again outsiders to the Tongan ruling house. This pattern of the Tongan paramount lineages serving as 'spouse takers' from Fiji and Samoa (Kaeppler 1978) is important in the larger structure of the Tongan chiefdom, a point to which I shall return below.

Assimilation of the outer islands into the Tongan political armature meant that the population tributary to – and to a degree dependent upon – the Tu'i Tonga increased several fold. The direct result of the Tongan expansion throughout the archipelago was to greatly increase the administrative burden on the central polity. The functional separation of sacred and secular, and the increased bureaucratization of the polity are probably logical consequences of the expansion process.

One of the archaeological indicators of stratified societies is a two or more tiered settlement pattern, with large ceremonial centres surrounded by villages or dispersed hamlets, and smaller centres (Peebles and Kus 1977; Renfrew 1973; Friedman and Rowlands 1978). Although we know relatively little of the development of Tongan settlement patterns, it is certain that the last thousand years of Tongan prehistory was marked by a major increase in the construction of large mounds of varying function (Kirch 1977b, 1980c; McKern 1929). The most important ceremonial centre, Lapaha at Mu'a, Tongatapu, provides further archaeological clues as to the transformation of Tongan society.

Lapaha: Tonga's central place

The most important archaeological complex in Tongatapu is situated at Mu'a, on the eastern shore of the central lagoon, near the pass. Lapaha, ancient seat of the paramount chiefs, was the central place upon which the entire chiefdom focussed. There the Tu'i Tonga and *hau* resided, and at their death, were buried. The annual tribute ceremonial, *'inasi*, was held there and shares were laid in front of the royal tombs on the *malae* Fanakava. Although no excavations have been conducted at Mu'a, McKern (1929:92–101) mapped the area, and provided descriptions of the principal features (Fig. 73). Some features, particularly the *langi* or burial mounds, are associated with particular ancestral chiefs, and a relative chronology can be established on the basis of the genealogies.

A relative *event sequence* for the construction and growth of Lapaha is set out in Figure 74, based upon the known genealogical associations. The growth of the central place mirrors the sequence of socio-political transformation analysed above on the basis of the oral tradition. The specific events referred to in Figure 74 are as follows:

1. The founding of Lapaha is attributed to the 12th Tu'i Tonga Talatama, who on the basis of genealogical reckoning dates to about the thirteenth century AD. It is noteworthy that the tradition regarding Lapaha's founding attributes the move to the need for a secure canoe anchorage (Gifford 1924:30). On Figure 73, it will be noted that the fortification ditch surrounding Lapaha ends abruptly at a former shoreline, suggesting that this ditch was constructed prior to aggradation of the lagoon edge (the island of Tongatapu is known to be undergoing gradual tectonic uplift).

1a. McKern (1929) notes that the 23rd Tu'i Tonga Takalaua either built, or rebuilt, the fortification ditch and bank surrounding Lapaha. This need for fortification implies the importance of competition and warfare even after the consolidation of political power by the Tu'i Tonga.

2. The spatial structure of Lapaha was reorganized by the 24th Tu'i Tonga Kauulufonuafekai, reflecting the structural change in the central polity. The area inland of the old shoreline remained the dwelling area of the Tu'i Tonga, while a new area on the lower filled land of the former lagoon, Moalunga, was created for the *hau*, at that time the newly created Tu'i Ha'a Takalaua. This spatial division reflects a moiety division in the settlement, between Kauhalauta ('people of the inland road') or Tu'i Tonga with his kinsmen, and Kauhalalalo ('people of the lower road'), the Tu'i Ha'a Takalaua and his kinsmen. It also reflects a spatial division of the central place into secular and sacred precincts.

3. Contemporaneous with the division of Lapaha into two precincts was the construction of the great dock, Mounu, reflecting the increased

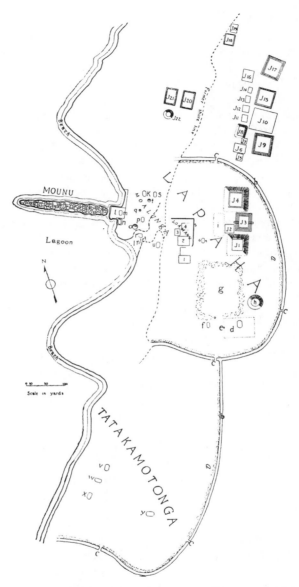

73. Archaeological plan of the ceremonial centre of Lapaha at
Mu'a, Tongatapu Island, the seat of the Tu'i Tonga (from
McKern 1929).

importance of inter-island voyaging that accompanied the integration of the outliers.

4. The great *langi* or burial mound Paepae o Telea (J20 on McKern's map, Fig. 73) is the first such structure which can be placed in the relative event sequence. This mound, with its massive, fitted facing blocks of quarried limestone, stands outside the fortified area.

5. Langi Leka (J9) is reported to be the burial place of Sinaitakala I, sister of the 30th Tu'i Tonga, and must have been constructed shortly after Paepae o Telea.

6. Langi Tuofefafa (J4) was the first of two great mounds to be raised inside of the fortified enclosure at Lapaha, adjacent to the *malae* Fanakava. This structure is the sepulchre of the 33rd Tu'i Tonga, Tu'i Pulotu I.

7. A relatively small mound (J8), the burial place of Tokemoana, the brother of Tu'i Pulotu I, was constructed outside of the fortification wall.

8. Langi Tuoteau (J1), very close to Tuofefafa (J4) in form, was built for Tu'i Pulotu II (Tu'i Tonga 35), like J4 within the fortified enclosure.

9. Sometime after the reign of the 30th Tu'i Tonga, with the rise of the Tu'i Kanokupolu line as *hau*, the capital seat was again expanded, with

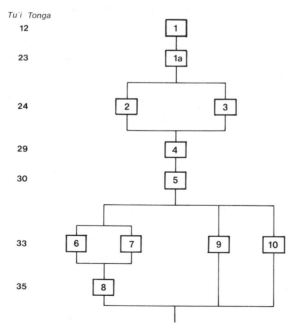

74. Event sequence for the construction of major features and monuments at Lapaha; see text for explanation.

the construction of a new fortified enclosure abutting Lapaha, named Tatakamotonga. This became the residence of the Tuʻi Kanokupolu and contained the house of his priest and other functionaries.

10. The *langi* known as Nukulukilangi (J19) and Namoala (J21), and the circular mound near the latter (J22), are all burial places of the Fale Fisi, and were constructed some time after the rise of this line to prominence, that is, after the 30th Tuʻi Tonga.

In short, the relative event sequence reveals a gradual expansion and increasing complexity of Lapaha that parallels the political transformation of the chiefdom. The testing of this sequence by means of stratigraphic excavation and radiocarbon dating would be highly desirable.

Structure of the protohistoric chiefdom

The Tuʻi Tonga and *hau* constituted the pinnacle of a hierarchical, decision-making structure which ramified throughout the geographic extent of the chiefdom. The general structure of this organization is diagrammed in Figure 75. With the creation of the *hau* title, the functions of the paramount were split. The role of the Tuʻi Tonga was mediation with the great ancestral deities, thus assuring the fertility of the land. As Mariner (Martin 1818, II:134) observed: 'we are to regard Tooitonga as a *divine* chief of the highest rank, but having no power or authority in affairs belonging to the king [*hau*].' The significance of this sacred role should not be underestimated, since the annual first-fruits ceremony (*ʻinasi*), at which the Tuʻi Tonga presided, served as a ritual cement binding the outlying districts and islands to the central political core.

In secular matters, such as assuring that tribute would be received from all districts for the *ʻinasi*, the *hau* was the ultimate authority, and evidently was under no compulsion to consult the Tuʻi Tonga. Gifford summarized the functional relations between the Tuʻi Tonga and *hau* as follows: 'The Tongan conception of the Tui Kanokupolu was a "working king", the one who supervised planting and other activities for the real king or Tui Tonga' (1929:98).

Attached to the Tuʻi Tonga was a group of four great chiefs and their ceremonial attendants (*matapule*) who constituted the Falefa ('four houses'); this body served as a 'sort of permanent court to the Tui Tonga' (Gifford 1929:63). The Tuʻi Kanokupolu had his own Falefa, probably an imitation of that of the Tuʻi Tonga. In effect, these chiefs were the descendants of younger brothers of the paramount lines, since all chiefly titles were ultimately derived from the ancestral Tuʻi Tonga line by collateral segmentation. Each chief was represented by a *matapule* (Gifford 1929:140–3), most of whom were of foreign origin (from Fiji, Samoa, Rotuma, or Tokelau). The great chiefs each controlled a major land section or island, which they held in fief from the paramounts. Administrative decisions passed down the hierarchy from paramount to the great chiefs and their *matapule*, and were proclaimed to the commoner class (*tu'a*) at public assemblies called *fono* (Gifford 1929:181).

Below the landed chiefs were a large body of lesser chiefs (*hou'eiki*) and *matapule*, followed by ranks of hereditary craftsmen (*tufunga*), and finally the commoners (*tu'a*). Certain *tufunga* were of considerable rank and importance, particularly canoe-builders (*tufunga fou vaka*) of the

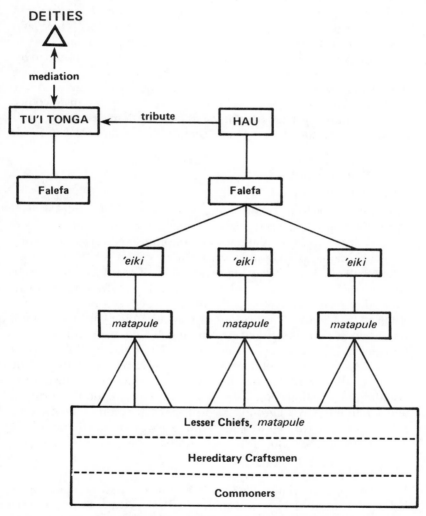

75. Hierarchical organization of the protohistoric Tongan chiefdom (see text for discussion).

paramount lines (Martin 1818, II:87–91). Since voyaging was essential to maintaining the political network, it is not surprising that navigators (*toutai vaka*) of the paramount lines were themselves *matapule* (Gifford 1929:142–3).

The division between commoner and chiefly classes was, at the time of European contact, sharply drawn. Contrary to the statements of Sahlins (1958) and others that Tongan society was organized on a ramage structure throughout, it is clear that ranked lineages (*ha'a*) pertained only to the class of chiefly title-holders and their immediate descendants (Korn 1974, 1978; Bott 1982:157). Commoners were affiliated with chiefs *not* on the basis of descent from a common ancestor, but through residence on the lands or estate (*tofi'a*) of the chief. Thus, land was no longer the joint property of a ramage group, as it had been in Ancestral Polynesian Society, but was allocated by the paramount to his subordinate chiefs, who in turn respected the use rights of commoners in exchange for regular tribute, and for labour when required. As we shall see in Chapter 10, the development of such true class distinctions, and the control of land by chiefs rather than descent groups, were transformations also found in late prehistoric Hawai'i.

Inter-island relations

The core islands

After his subjugation of the outer islands, Kauulufonuafekai (Tu'i Tonga 24) appointed a series of local chiefs (sometimes referred to as 'governors' or 'viceroys'). A junior son of the murdered Takalaua, bearing the same name as his father, was put in charge of 'Eua (Gifford 1924:62). For Ha'apai, two representatives of the Tu'i Tonga were appointed, Matauvave and Kolomoeuto (Gifford 1929:135; 1924:62). Two other chiefs, Haveatuli and Niutongo, were seconded to Vava'u (1929:134; 1924:62). The pattern of placing junior kinsmen as local representatives of the ruling paramount did not end with Kauulu-fonuafekai, but was continued by the *hau* (Tu'i Kanokupolu) who sent various junior kinsmen of the Ha'a Ngata line as representatives to the outer islands (Bott 1982). Among these were Takaihouma ('Eua Island), Ikahihifo (Ha'apai group), Fakateli'ao (Ha'apai), Maluhou (Ha'apai), and Tuituiohu (Vava'u group). A corollary to this pattern involved the sending of local women to Tongatapu as wives or concubines of the Tu'i Tonga and *hau* (Bott 1982).

Niuatoputapu

Whereas the core islands have been an integral part of Tonga since before the dawn of historical tradition, the northern 'outliers' were integrated into the Tongan political sphere only within the past 500 years. The evidence of linguistics is thoroughly convincing on this point; although the speech of Niuatoputapu is today Tongan, it was not so in AD 1616, when the Dutch explorer Le Maire recorded a brief word list (Kern 1948). As Biggs (1971) recognized, this list contains numerous Nuclear Polynesian lexical innovations, indicating that in the early seventeenth century the language of Niuatoputapu belonged to the Samoic-Outlier subgroup of Polynesian languages, and not to the Tongic group. Even today, terms referring to local aspects of environment (e.g., plant and fish names) are often different from the corresponding Tongan terms and contain several Nuclear Polynesian reflexes. Thus, the speech of Niuatoputapu became Tongan only after about AD 1620, through intensive lexical borrowing due to social intercourse with the main Tongan islands.

Archaeological evidence reinforces this linguistic picture. The archaeological signals of Tongan chiefly dominance on Niuatoputapu consist of several score large field monuments – burial mounds, chiefly sitting platforms, and pigeon-snaring mounds – distributed over the island's landscape. A relatively recent age for most of these structures is evidenced by their location on recently emerged ground (the island is undergong active tectonic uplift; Kirch 1978a, 1980a). Excavation of a large, cut-coral slab-faced burial monument of typical Tongan style, at Houmafakalele, yielded a radiocarbon age determination of 270 ± 85 BP, further indicative of the late period during which such sites were constructed on Niuatoputapu (Fig. 76).

76. A chiefly burial mound (*fa'itoka*) at Houmafakalele, Niuatoputapu Island. The facing is constructed of quarried and dressed slabs of reef conglomerate.

According to oral tradition, after Niuatoputapu was subjugated during the epic conquests of Kauulufonuafekai, Talapalo was appointed 'governor' (Gifford 1924:62). Until this century, when the title lapsed due to absence of a legitimate heir, the ruling chief of Niuatoputapu was called Maʻatu (Gifford 1929:135, 284–5). The first Maʻatu bore the name Latumailangi ('chief from heaven'), corroborating Le Maire's statement of April 1616 that 'this king or chief was called Latou by his people' (Villiers 1906:203). Bott (1982) states that Latumailangi was the son of Fonumanu by the Tuʻi Tonga Fefine 'Ekutongapipiki (sister of the 31st Tuʻi Tonga).

The tributary relationship of Niuatoputapu to Tongatapu is indicated in an account of some iron nails left by Captain Wallis on Niuatoputapu on 13 August 1767 (Carrington 1948:251). One of these nails was seen at Tongatapu in October 1773 by Captain Cook, and was evidently held in some regard (Beaglehole 1969:206), and had been carefully hafted to a bone handle. This was collected by the botanist Forster, and is illustrated by Kaeppler (1971b:Pl. 4b). Cook was told on his third voyage that the nail 'came from Onnuahtabutabu [Niuato-putapu], and on asking how the people of that island came by it, he [Fattafee the King] said one of them sold a Club for five Nails to a Ship which came to the island [Wallis in 1767], and these five Nails after wards came to Tongatapu and they were the first they had seen' (Beaglehole 1967:162). Such nails were surely a prized item, and it is significant that they were dispatched from Niuatoputapu to Tongatapu, seat of the paramount chiefs.

Niuafoʻou

Linguistic evidence indicates that Niuafoʻou was also brought under Tongan domination only within the last few hundred years, and this Tongan influence has yet to totally obliterate the original Nuclear Polynesian speech of the island. Studies of the language of Niuafoʻou by Collocott (1922), and by Dye (1980) confirm that a strong Nuclear Polynesian component is still recognizable. Unfortunately, no intensive archaeological work has been conducted on Niuafoʻou.

According to one tradition, Kauulufonuafekai appointed Makauka and Hakavalu as 'governors' of Niuafoʻou (Gifford 1924:62). In another version, his eldest son Fotofili was appointed (1924:67); Fotofili remains the title of the ruling line of Niuafoʻou. Bott (1982) states that the first Fotofili was the offspring of Tatafu (a son of the Tuʻi Haʻa Takalaua and *hau* Fotofili) and Tokanga-fuifuilupe, a daughter of the Tuʻi Tonga.

ʻUvea

Burrows (1937:169) reported that 'traditional history points to Tonga as the main source of 'Uvean culture'. The close relations between Tonga and 'Uvea are indicated in such cultural aspects as place names (33 per cent in common), kinship terms, the system of rank and *matapule* titles, material culture, and so forth. Nevertheless, studies of 'Uvean language by Biggs (1980) have shown that, as with Niuafo'ou, 'the language of Wallis Island, which has been suspected of being a third Tongic language, is in fact a Nuclear Polynesian language that has borrowed very heavily from Tongan' (1980:115–16). Biggs asserts that 'approximately half of the total EVU ['Uvean] vocabulary is borrowed from TON' (1980:120), and suggests that ' 'Uvea was colonized by Tongans perhaps five hundred years ago' (1980:124–5). Limited archaeological survey on 'Uvea (Kirch 1975; 1976) revealed the presence there of distinctly Tongan-style field monuments, including walled fortifications, large chiefly burial mounds, and pigeon-snaring mounds.

Both Tongan and 'Uvean oral traditions refer to relations between the islands. The first paramount of 'Uvea, Tauloko, was said to be of 'Tui Tonga family' (Burrows 1937:18; Henquel n.d.). Following the subjugation of 'Uvea by Kauulufonuafekai, Ngaasialili (or 'Elili, his Tongan name) was sent from Tonga to be lord over 'Uvea (Burrows 1937:19; Gifford 1929:68; 1924:62). Further, the Ha'avakatolo and the Ha'amea, two 'Tongan lineages' were sent to 'Uvea to guard Ngaasialili. The 'Uvean story of the land dispute between Liaki and Huka reports that the protagonists went to the Tu'i Tonga Telea to adjudicate the dispute. Probably the most famous traditional connection between the two islands also involved Telea, who used the great canoe Lomipeau to transport stones from 'Uvea for the construction of his *langi* or burial mound at Lapaha (Burrows 1937:24; Gifford 1929:67–8). Two 'Uveans, Tua and Fafie, are reputed to have constructed the *langi* Tuofefafa (Burrows 1937:36).

By now, the logic of alliances underlying the political network which bound the Tongan 'maritime empire' together should be clear. *Tehina*, junior brothers or kinsmen of the ruling lines, were placed at critical points on the outer islands, where they would marry into local chiefly lines and supplant the former, now conquered, autochthonous chiefs. This strategy was ingenious on several counts. First, it removed the direct threat of usurpation of the chiefly title by a junior sibling, at the same time that it offered the *tehina* considerable local autonomy (an appealing situation for a junior collateral, the rank of whose descendants would otherwise only be assured of geometrical decrease in relation to the senior line). Second, by marrying a local chiefly woman, the new chief and representative of the Tu'i Tonga or *hau* effectively became *fahu* or 'sacred child' to the indigenous inhabitants (Fig. 77).

Figure 78 displays the more prominent kinship connections between the various ruling chiefs. Initially, control over local governments was established by placing junior members of the Tu'i Tonga lineage as local representatives. This pattern was repeated by successive *hau* so that representatives of the new paramount would supplant the older line established by the Tu'i Tonga. It appears also that daughters of the local ruling lines were sent to Tongatapu to become wives and concubines of the Tu'i Tonga and *hau*. Sometimes, as in the case of the fifth Ma'atu of Niuatoputapu, a daughter of the *hau* was espoused to the

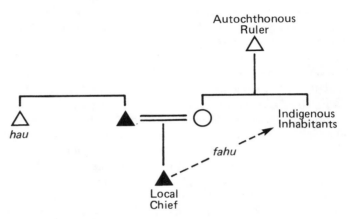

77. Through a marriage alliance with a daughter of the autochthonous ruling line, the conquering Tongan chief (shaded) assures that his offspring will stand in the *fahu* relationship to the indigenous population.

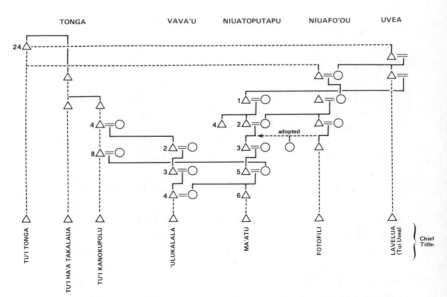

78. Marriage alliances between the ruling lines of the principal Tongan islands.

local ruling chief. As a general principle, however, marriage alliances between the central and local ruling lines were hypergamic.

Voyaging and tribute

A maritime chiefdom such as Tonga depended vitally upon developed canoe building and navigation. The high rank of canoe builders and navigators of the *hau* and Tu'i Tonga reflects the importance attached by the ruling polity to sea transport. Lapaha, the seat of the Tu'i Tonga, was reputedly chosen because of the advantage of its safe anchorage (Gifford 1924:30).

Early European explorers were duly impressed with the size and sailing qualities of the Tongan double canoes. Circumnavigator Cook referred to the large voyaging canoes as 'Vessels of burdthen . . . fit for distant Navigation' (Beaglehole 1969:264), noting that 'they carry from forty to fifty people, and some sixty or seventy' (1967:938). West (1865:48–9) described the impressive arrival of fourteen canoes belonging to the ruling line at Mu'a in 1846; each was able to carry between 100 and 150 men.

The political ties between the central polity of Tongatapu and the outer islands were ritually manifest in the annual first-fruits ceremony – the *'inasi* – and the *kava* ceremony performed with it (Martin 1818, II:196–204 provides a first-hand description). Actually, there were two *'inasi* each year, that of the first yam crop (*'inasi 'ufimui*, June–July), and one for the subsequent yam crop (*'inasi 'ufimotu'a*, about October–November) (Urbanowicz 1973:82–3). The alleged function of the *'inasi* was the mediation of the Tu'i Tonga with the great deities, especially Hikuleo, in order to assure the fertility and prosperity of the chiefdom. In reality, the bringing of first fruits and tribute from all parts of the chiefdom validated the claims of the Tu'i Tonga and *hau* to supreme political power, and provided the material basis for support of the non-food-producing chiefly class. As described by an eyewitness, Lawry, in 1822:

That part of the island where we live is called Mooa, or metropolis of Tonga: and to this place the chiefs of Vavaou and the Hapais bring their machee [*'inasi*], towards the end of the last moon the fleet of canoes and crowds of people by land rendering the Mooa a moving scene of universal bustle and stir (quoted in Urbanowicz 1973:83).

Tribute was not limited to agricultural produce, though yams were clearly required. Eyewitness missionary accounts report pearl shells from 'Uvea, 'iron wood of a superior kind' and fine mats from Niuafo'ou, 'the young of a sea bird' from Tofu, and 'fish from the sacred lake carefully prepared' from Nomuka (Urbanowicz 1973:81–2). Mariner lists dried fish, *mahoa'a* (flour made from *Tacca leontopetaloides*), mats, barkcloth, and bundles of dyed *Pandanus* leaves as 'other articles that form part of the *Inachi*' (Martin 1818, II:202).

Long-distance exchange

Tonga stands unique among the indigenous Polynesian chiefdoms for its extensive and regular long-distance exchange relations with societies beyond its own geographic and political borders. This long-distance exchange had political consequences which were far greater than any immediate, utilitarian gain due to the importation of exotic material items. Long-distance exchange of chiefly spouses as well as of material items was fundamentally a political strategy, and played a vital role in binding the core islands and outliers to the central polity.

Kaeppler (1978) presents a careful analysis of the exchange patterns between Tonga, Samoa, and Fiji, noting that these three 'form a larger social system, while each is culturally distinct'. In Figure 79 the underlying structure of social relations between Tonga, Fiji, and Samoa is portrayed diagrammatically from the Tongan viewpoint.

As discussed earlier, the potential contradiction in the Tongan social system, wherein the offspring of the Tu'i Tonga Fefine could potentially outrank the Tu'i Tonga (and hence lay claim to the title), was solved by marrying the Tu'i Tonga Fefine to a Fijian chief. This 'Fijian' line in Tonga became institutionalized as the Fale Fisi ('House of Fiji'). On the other hand, Samoan women were sought by high-ranking Tongan males, who 'might not want to marry into other Tongan lines for fear of their own line falling in importance and eventually being overshadowed' (Kaeppler 1978:249). The classic example of such a Tonga–Samoa marriage was that of the first Tu'i Kanokupolu, Ngata (son of the sixth Tu'i Ha'a Takalaua), who espoused the Samoan chiefess Tuhuia (Limapou in Tongan), of the Fale'ula lineage of 'Upolu, Samoa. Thus, underlying the more overt exchanges of goods was a system of kinship relations, with both Fiji and Samoa serving as spouse-givers to Tonga.

On the whole, relations with Fiji were more frequent and of greater significance than those with Samoa. Although it is well known that there was extensive intercourse between Tongans and the occupants of the Lau group of eastern Fiji (Hocart 1929; Thompson 1940), the Tongan

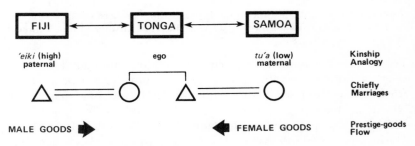

79. Structural relationships between Tonga, Fiji, and Samoa.

Table 21. *Goods exchanged among Tonga, Samoa, and Fiji*

	From Tonga	To Tonga
Fiji	Whale's teeth	Canoes
	Fine mats (Samoan)	Red feathers
	Ornaments	Decorated barkcloth
	Barkcloth	Mats
		Baskets
		Sandalwood (for oil)
		Sails
		Pottery
Samoa	Barkcloth	Fine mats (*kie hingoa*)
	Sleeping mats	
	Red feathers	

penetration of Fiji extended to the latter's political core – Thakaundrove (centred around the capital of Somosomo in Taveuni). The Tongans at Vava'u gave a clear description of Taveuni to Cook's astronomer Bayly (ms., 107), and named the paramount chief of Thakaundrove, Tui Thakau (Lord of the Reef).

Bayly noted that the 'Tonga men get all their red feathers for making their ornaments & all their fine painted cloth, & figured mats & curious beaded baskets & other curious ornaments' from Fiji. The range of material goods exchanged between Tonga and Fiji are enumerated in Table 21. Most important of the goods sought by the Tongans in Fiji were the large canoes. As Derrick notes:

In Tonga, there was little timber of a size and quality for the construction of these large vessels, and it became the practice for parties of Tongans to sail up on the wind to Lakeba, arrange with the chiefs there for logs and food in exchange for Tongan bark cloth, weapons, or services in war, and then to establish themselves on islands such as Vulanga and Kabara and build, or help to build, the canoes (1946:121; see also Thomson 1908:52).

The construction of a large *kalia*-type canoe could take up to seven years, so that these Tongan footholds in Lau came to be permanent settlements. Hocart (1952:90) reports a class of 'Tongan carpenters' (*matai Tonga*) resident in Thakaundrove. Mariner (Martin 1818, II:263–5) confirms that the large Tongan canoes were 'either purchased or taken by force from the natives of Fiji'. He adds an important point: control of this long-distance exchange was initiated by Tongan chiefs, and maintained by Tongan navigators. 'No native of Fiji, as far as is known, ever ventured to Tonga but in a canoe manned with Tonga people, nor ever ventured back to his own islands, but under the same guidance and protection' (1818, II:264).

Other prestige goods were also obtained in Fiji, including red and green parrot feathers, sandalwood (used for making scented oil), sails, pottery, and other items (Tippett 1968:103–4; Thompson 1940:29–30; Kaeppler 1978). Parrot feathers were symbols of high status and rank in Tonga, where they were sewn onto fine mats, and used in the special *pala tavake* head-dress of the Tu'i Tonga (Kaeppler 1971b). These feathers were also carried by the Tongans to Samoa, where they were prized also for ornamenting fine mats and head-dresses (Buck 1930:281, 619). In exchange for these goods, the Tongans brought to Fiji whale's teeth, fine mats of Samoan origin, ornaments, and barkcloth. Most important, however, were the whale's teeth, as these were the essence of Fijian wealth.

Although traditional relations between Tonga and Samoa appear to be ancient (cf. Br.F. Henry 1980:40–9), exchange of prestige goods was never as developed as that between Tonga and Fiji. The one Samoan item especially prized in Tonga was the fine mat (*kie hingoa*): 'One of the famous Tongan *kie hingoa* or named fine mats from Samoa, of which there are thirty-three original ones extant in Tonga, is "Va ofu mo olosinga", which is said to have been given to a Tu'i Tonga on the occasion of his tatooing in Samoa' (Kaeppler 1978:248). Objects brought from Tonga to Samoa included Fijian parrot feathers, large sleeping mats, and Tongan barkcloth (Table 21).

The material goods brought from Fiji and Samoa to Tonga were not by-and-large utilitarian objects, nor were they necessarily made of materials scarce in Tonga. The large canoes, it is true, were manufactured in Fiji because of a lack of suitable timber in Tonga. Other prestige items, however, such as the red feathers, sandalwood, and fine mats were valued as *koloa*, prestige items vital to Tongan marriage alliances. As Kaeppler observed: 'It appears that the pre-eminent Tongan context for the use of Fijian and Samoan trade goods was, and is, on ceremonial occasions – and especially weddings, funerals, and various kinds of state and religious celebrations (*katoanga*)' (1978:250).

The acquisition of foreign prestige goods by the central polity thus served the important function of binding local chiefs to the political core. Control and redistribution of *koloa* by the paramount lines was one strategy for binding the outer islands to the central polity: the flow of tribute to Tongatapu and Lapaha was balanced by the distribution of prestige goods to the outliers.

This is not to say that there was not some element of material need in the development of long-distance exchange. One of the goals of the Tongan expeditions to Fiji was the acquisition of large sailing vessels, since the smaller, low, Tongan islands had long since been denuded of suitable timber for their construction. Prior to the integration of the Tongan archipelago by the dual paramountship, there would not have been the kind of demand for voyaging canoes that existed later. The maintenance of tributary relations between the outlying islands and Tongatapu required a sizeable fleet, and this too doubtless was a significant impetus to the intensification of Tonga–Fiji exchange.

The Tongan polity as it existed at the point of European contact may now be summarized by a diagram of its topologic structure (Fig. 80). The system was oriented around the central place, Tongatapu and specifically Lapaha, seat of the paramountship. Kinship alliances linked the paramount lines with those of the local ruling chiefs in the core islands and outliers. Such alliances were confirmed by marriage re-lations, for which exotic prestige goods were vital. In turn, the outlying islands affirmed their inferior status and loyalty to the *hau* and Tu'i Tonga through the tribute of the *'inasi*. Thus within the chiefdom there was a circular flow of goods, tribute inwards towards the paramounts, prestige goods outwards to the local chiefs. Monopolization of the sources of prestige goods by the paramounts helped to secure their power over the system as a whole.

To briefly sum up, over the millennia since Tonga was first colonized by Lapita potters, its economic, social, and political systems have undergone major transformations, leading to the maritime chiefdom just described. Gradual population growth clearly played an important role in this process, leading over perhaps 1000–2000 years to a situation of dense settlement under an intensified agricultural regime. Com-petition for arable land resulted in the hegemony of one chiefly line –

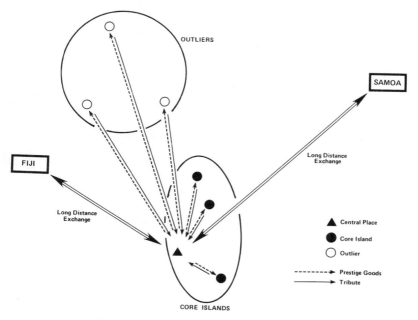

80. The topologic structure of the Tongan maritime chiefdom.

that of the Tuʻi Tonga – in the core islands, and ultimately, conquest and domination over several outlying islands. Fundamental to the political consolidation of this large area were the development of voyaging canoe technology and navigational skills, and control over a system of prestige-good exchange. By the time of European intrusion, Tongan society was marked by such factors as class stratification, a formalized, dual paramountship, and a multi-tiered, decision-making, political apparatus. These transformations are archaeologically best reflected in settlement patterns, such as the development of Lapaha, the chiefdom's central place. The developmental sequence outlined in this chapter depends in many respects, of course, on non-archaeological data, and its further testing remains a challenge for Polynesian prehistorians.

10
Hawai'i

The Hawaiian case differs from Tonga in at least three significant respects. First, whereas Tonga is within relatively easy voyaging contact with the large Fijian and Samoan archipelagos, Hawai'i was truly isolated from the rest of Polynesia. This degree of isolation is evident not only in the distances involved – some 3,862 km from the Marquesas and 4,410 km from Tahiti – but in the difficulties of long-distance voyaging from the southern hemisphere, through the doldrums, into the northern weather patterns (Finney 1977; Levison *et al.* 1973). Second, unlike Tonga, Hawai'i ranks as one of the largest archipelagos, with a total land area second only to New Zealand within the Polynesian Triangle. The eight major Hawaiian islands (Fig. 81) presented vast tracts of fertile land to the Polynesian colonists, not to mention con-

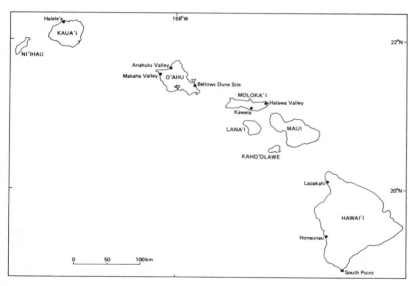

81. The Hawaiian archipelago, showing the location of major sites discussed in the text.

siderable micro-environmental variation. Third, Hawai'i was one of the last areas within Polynesia to be colonized, and its prehistoric cultural sequence is only about 1500 years long, compared with at least three millennia in Tonga. Thus, in Hawai'i we have a relatively late, short time-scale for cultural evolution, but set in the context of a vast, fertile, and isolated archipelago.

The archaeological data base for Hawai'i is well developed, and we are not so dependent upon synchronic, ethnographic materials for an analysis of prehistoric change. Since stratigraphic excavations were first conducted on O'ahu Island by Emory in 1950, more than fifty researchers have accumulated a wealth of data pertaining to several thousand sites on all of the major islands except Ni'ihau (a privately owned island to which no archaeologists have as yet been permitted). Clearly, this chapter can only touch upon a few highlights of thirty years of intensive study (see Kirch, *An Introduction to Hawaiian Archaeology*, University of Hawai'i Press, Honolulu, forthcoming, for a more comprehensive review of Hawaiian archaeology).

Colonization, adaptation, and expansion

Given the statistical uncertainty associated with ^{14}C dating and the short time-span of Hawaiian prehistory, not to mention the tremendous difficulties (in an archipelago as extensive as Hawai'i) of locating the 'earliest' settlement site, pinning down a precise date for Polynesian colonization may be an impossible task. We do have evidence from at least four islands, however, that the chain was settled by AD 300–500, even though sparsely. The evidence includes the early stream-beach settlement site at Bellows Beach, O'ahu (Pearson, Kirch, and Pietrusewsky 1971), evidence of human activity on the slopes surrounding the Kawainui Marsh (then a salt-water bay) about AD 500 (Kelly and Clark 1980), two early dates for burning associated with agriculture in the Hanalei and Lumahai Valleys, Kaua'i (Schilt 1980a; Hoffman 1979), the permanent stream-beach settlement site of Halawa on Moloka'i (Kirch and Kelly 1975) and the Pu'u Ali'i sand dune site on Hawai'i Island.

Excavations at the Bellows site (O18) on O'ahu, and at the Halawa Dune Site (Mo-A1-3) on Moloka'i, provide the basis for reconstructing the nature of early settlement and subsistence in Hawai'i (Pearson, Kirch, and Pietrusewsky 1971; Kirch and Kelly 1975). Both settlements are situated in windward locations, adjacent to permanent streams, with large tracts of fertile alluvial and colluvial farmland available in the immediate vicinity. Permanent residence is in both instances indicated by the presence of dwelling structures, cooking facilities, and a wide range of subsistence as well as domestic activities. At Site O18, permanent residence is further indicated by the presence of burials. In the

Halawa site, stone alignments and postmoulds revealed a pattern of small, round-ended huts; no clear pattern could be reconstructed from the postmoulds and gravel pavements in the Bellows deposits. A diversified subsistence base is clear for both sites, with fishing, shellfish gathering, exploitation of wild birds, animal husbandry, and – by various lines of inference – agriculture. The presence of both domestic pig and dog is significant, not only because these hint at the purposive nature of initial colonization, but because the pig certainly is a clear signal of horticultural practice (cf. Yen 1973a; Kirch 1979c). In the O18 site, a serrated coconut grater (of *Conus* shell) reflects the introduction by Polynesians of the *Cocos* palm, which probably had not achieved natural dispersal to this isolated archipelago (unlike the western Pacific, where the coconut certainly pre-dated man). There is little in either site to indicate social differentiation, but the relatively elaborate grave goods associated with one sub-floor burial in site O18 – a female of about nine years with pendant, pig-tusk anklet, and red coloration possibly indicating dyed barkcloth – do suggest high rank.

The artifact assemblages from Bellows and Halawa, though they share certain elements with early East Polynesian forms, already reflect adaptation to local conditions, the first stage in the differentiation of Hawaiian material culture as distinctive from archaic styles in the southern homeland. Such adaptation is, for instance, evident in the development of two-piece fishhooks of bone, a response to the lack of suitably large pearl shell or *Turbo* shell. As suggested in Chapter 4, the founder effect may have accounted for rapid cultural change, not only in material culture, but in less durable aspects of language and behaviour.

The Hawaiian Islands provide an almost classic validation of the general model of initial colonization in fertile, windward-valley environments, local population growth, and subsequent expansion to more marginal, leeward locales, as argued in Chapter 8 (Fig. 63). By about AD 900–1100, perhaps four to seven centuries following the first colonization of the archipelago, population in the windward regions had increased to such a level that fissioning groups had begun to establish permanent settlements in the more favourable leeward areas. Examples of such settlements are the Kuli'ou'ou area and Makaha Valley, on O'ahu, and at Anaeho'omalu, on Hawai'i Island.

I have already reviewed, in Chapter 5, the evidence for prehistoric population growth in Hawai'i. Within one or two centuries following the establishment of permanent leeward settlements, the population of the archipelago underwent a dramatic, virtually exponential increase. By the AD 1400–1500s, nearly all of the lowlands including even the most marginal regions (such as Waikoloa on Hawai'i) were under some form of occupation, cultivation, or exploitation, and population densities in the more fertile, intensively cultivated areas had reached levels of 250 persons/km² or more. Present evidence suggests that in some areas, population had peaked and was declining by the time of European contact; in other regions, it is likely that growth had not reached a limit.

Local sequences of development

Rather than attempt a summary of the archaeological evidence from the archipelago as a whole, I have chosen two local areas and take their sequences of cultural development as reflective of more general and widespread trends. These two cases represent some of the local or areal variation which makes Hawaiian prehistory especially fascinating. Halawa Valley represents the early-settled, fertile windward localities, whereas Makaha Valley exemplifies a leeward, but not too marginal valley setting. A third area, West Hawaiʻi, has already been examined with respect to its intensive, dryland agricultural field systems (Chapter 7), and its sequence of population growth (Chapter 5).

Halawa Valley (Molokaʻi)

Incised into the 1,170 metre high East Molokaʻi mountains, Halawa is a relatively broad valley, about 3 km deep, with two large waterfalls cascading down its amphitheatre rim, feeding a permanent stream. It was this watercourse (with average flows of about 28 mgd), as well as the many hectares of fertile alluvial floodplain near the valley mouth, that must have made Halawa so attractive to the early Polynesian colonists. The gently sloping colluvial ridges bordering the floodplain offered excellent terrain for the cultivation of non-irrigated crops. In the early historic period, Halawa supported a population of more than 500 persons, and the valley-bottom lands were laid out in a well-engineered reticulate series of irrigated pondfields covering more than 22 hectares (Fig. 55).

Archaeological investigation of the valley, carried out in 1969–70, focussed largely on questions of settlement pattern and human adaptation (Kirch and Kelly 1975). Major projects included excavation of the early stream-beach midden site (Mo-A1-3, described above), an intensive settlement pattern study of one inland valley locale (Kapana), excavation of a series of inland residential sites, and an investigation of the extensive system of irrigated fields and ditches. Based on these studies, a local cultural sequence consisting of three prehistoric phases was proposed, the first such sequence for any region within the Hawaiian chain. This phase sequence is reproduced here as Table 22. Of particular interest is the evidence from Halawa for local changes in settlement pattern, and the development of large-scale irrigation.

Permanent settlement during the Kaawili Phase (AD 650–1350) was evidently restricted to the mouth of the valley, and the excavation at Site

Mo-A1-3 revealed an early form of the small, round-ended hut with internal stone-lined hearths. The Kaio Phase (AD 1350–1650), however, marks a period of considerable change, both in domestic architecture and in settlement pattern. An expansion of permanent residential sites up the valley, to encompass the gently sloping colluvial ridges, apparently mirrors the rapid increase in population witnessed throughout the islands during this era. These residential sites are dispersed throughout the inner parts of the valley, interspersed among dry terraces and other structural modifications for slope agriculture (the settlement of Kapana, Kirch and Kelly 1975, fig. 31, is typical of this pattern). Rectangular dwellings erected on stone-faced terraces replaced the small, ovoid huts of the preceding phase. Separate cookhouses containing earth ovens were situated on adjacent or nearby terraces. Several examples of sub-floor burials in both dwellings and cookhouses were discovered. The pattern of residence established during the Kaio Phase continued largely unchanged into the Mana Phase (AD 1650–1800), although there is a suggestion that dwelling terraces became larger, and more formal, incorporating stone house platforms.

The development of religious or ceremonial architecture in Halawa is as yet only poorly understood. Dispersed throughout the valley are some thirteen stepped terrace sites, identified ethnohistorically as *heiau* or temples, and with areas of about 120–150 m^2. These seem to be closely integrated with the dispersed habitations, and there is some limited evidence that each *'ili*, or named subsection of the valley, had its own terraced temple site. These probably functioned as agricultural temples, and may also have incorporated aspects of the men's house (*mua*). The dispersal of sites throughout the valley is vaguely suggestive of some kind of local corporate organization, though we have no conclusive data on this point. The single stepped terrace that was test-excavated dated to AD 1476–1532. As a class, these sites probably were constructed during the Kaio and Mana Phases.

Two larger stone temples are present in the valley, Mana and Papa *heiau*. Ethnohistoric data (Stokes 1909a) indicate that these were constructed during the Mana Phase, and that they were war temples (*luakini*, dedicated to Ku) built under the aegis of ruling chiefs. These temples cover areas of about 670 m^2 and 1,600 m^2, respectively, and are more complex in construction than their stepped-terrace counterparts. Mana *heiau* is reputed to have been built under the rule of Alapa'inui, a high chief of Hawai'i Island, who conquered Moloka'i sometime around AD 1720.

The earliest direct evidence for agriculture in Halawa Valley comes from a stratified series of colluvial fan deposits (Site Mo-A1-4) at the base of the valley's southern ridge. These deposits reflect extensive forest clearance and burning on the valley walls, for shifting cultivation (Kirch and Kelly 1975:55–64). A basal radiocarbon date of 772 ± 90 BP

Table 22. *The Halawa Valley sequence (from Kirch and Kelly 1975)*

Criteria	Kaawili Phase (AD 650–1350)	Kaio Phase (AD 1350–1650)
Settlement pattern	Coastal village at ecologically focal position	Dispersed habitations, expanding inland, especially on higher taluvial slopes near small watercourses
Domestic architecture	Ovoid houses; pole-and-thatch construction; internal hearths; separate cookhouses	Simple, stone-faced, earth-filled terraces with rectangular houses; hearths; separate cookhouses with earth ovens
Subsistence	Fishing important; dogs and pigs raised and eaten; shifting cultivation and water-control agronomic technologies	Increase in importance of dog and pig; shifting cultivation; water control for pondfield irrigation in side streams (Type II)
Portable artifacts	Untanged or incipiently tanged, reverse-trapezoidal adzes; early-type fishhooks; dog-tooth ornaments; coral and echinoid abraders; basalt and basaltic-glass flakes	Tanged rectangular and reverse-trapezoidal adzes; flakes of basalt and basaltic glass; basalt chisels; grindstones
Burials	No data	Subfloor, flexed in shallow pit
Ceremonial architecture	No data	Small, stepped-terrace sites associated with local social groups, and shrines
Population (estimate)	AD 650: 50 AD 1350: 150	150–350
Type sites	A1-3	A1-1001, -769, -1003, -770, -30

*Added to provide contrast with prehistoric patterns.

indicates that, by the twelfth century, shifting cultivation had begun to initiate environmental degradation and localized erosion. Given the expansion of permanent habitation into the upper valley at the same time, it is likely that much of the original forest cover had been replaced with a mosaic of second growth, grasslands, and garden plots. Excavations by Riley in various parts of the valley almost invariably showed evidence of disturbed, charcoal-flecked subsoils underlying later, permanent pondfields, and these soils have been interpreted as indicative of widespread swidden activity.

The development of Halawa's water-control facilities for the permanent and intensive irrigation of taro was partly elucidated by Riley's

Mana Phase (AD 1650–1800)	Historic Phase* (AD 1800–Present)
Continuation of the Kaio Phase pattern	Settlement concentrated above pond-field system, especially in lower valley; nucleation around church
Addition of stone-filled platforms to the Kaio Phase pattern	Houses surrounded by walled enclosures; wooden structures and thatch structures coexisting until *c.* AD 1900
Animal husbandry important; stabilization of taluvial slopes with crude terracing; construction of major pond-field systems	New domestic animals imported; intensive pondfield cultivation stimulated by commercial prospects
Tripping club; large, rectangular, tanged adzes; octopus lures; very small, rectangular adzes	European goods imported, replaced items of aboriginal material culture; glass, square nails, and flint used early
Same as Kaio Phase	Burial in separate stone cairns or in churchyard
Addition of major ceremonial sites with high-rank associations; continuation of stepped-terrace sites	Christian churches, Protestant and Catholic
350–600	AD 1836: 506 AD 1972: 2
A1-765, -1, -2	A1-736, -1011

work (Riley 1975), although the time-scale remains somewhat speculative. It is probable that some form of wet cultivation of *Colocasia* was practised since initial settlement, and the naturally hydromorphic soils of the alluvial floodplains would have been eminently suited to this purpose. With the expansion of settlement inland during the Kaio Phase, the smaller, side-valley streams were terraced for taro cultivation, and some more formal modification of the lower floodplains began. Not until the Mana Phase, however, do we have evidence that the largest pondfield systems were constructed, incorporating as many as 366 fields (9.5 hectares) in a single hydraulic unit, with main ditches as long as 1.4 km. In the Kapana area, Riley's excavations revealed how

one of the larger, main-stream irrigated pondfield systems was constructed over part of an earlier, side-stream irrigated complex.

Makaha Valley (Oʻahu)

On the south-western, leeward side of the Waiʻanae Mountains, the
Makaha Valley has a permanent stream, but with relatively low discharge and frequent dry periods. In contrast with Halawa only small
areas of permanent pondfield irrigation were developed, in the middle
and upper reaches of the valley. Extensive colluvium and talus on the
lower valley slopes is well suited to dryland agriculture, though the
relatively low annual rainfall (500–1,000 mm annually) restricted the
cropping range, with an emphasis on sweet potatoes, yams, and similar
cultigens. Even then, cultivation was probably organized on a seasonal
basis, since most rain falls during the period from October to
April.

Makaha's archaeological landscape was intensively investigated from
1968–70, under the direction of R.C. Green, and a series of monographs document the results of that project (Green 1969, 1970; Ladd
and Yen 1972; Ladd 1973; Green 1980). My discussion of the valley's
developmental sequence closely follows Green's (1980:71–9) recent
culture–historical synthesis.

Green argues, without direct archaeological confirmation, that initial
occupation in Makaha probably occurred about AD 1100, and was
focussed on the coast near the stream mouth, where a small spring provided a suitable environment for limited wet cultivation. This settlement is viewed as part of the general process of leeward occupation
which resulted from expanding windward populations. The next stage
in Makaha's development, which followed within one or two centuries
(and for which we do have direct archaeological support) was a regular
expansion inland from the coast. This stage is reflected archaeologically
in the modification of the lower valley colluvial slopes for dryfield
agriculture, with various temporary field shelters situated within the
field complex. Several of these C-shaped shelters were excavated, and
date to as early as 730 ± 100 BP. In Green's words,

the first step in Makaha's developing status as an *ahupuaʻa* was one of growth in
the swidden part of the agricultural system through seasonal exploitation of the
dry-land zone of the lower valley. It sustained a growing population, which
exploited a typical Polynesian territorial unit consisting of the sea, the coast,
and the inland area   (1980:74–5).

Green argues that at this period Makaha comprised a territorial unit
(*ahupuaʻa*) which was still organized on an ancestral social model, with a
'localized lineage headed by a chief'.

During the fifteenth to sixteenth centuries, several changes in
subsistence, population density and distribution, and social organization led to a restructuring of the valley's *ahupuaʻa* status. This period

saw the establishment for the first time, of *permanent* settlement in the dry inland and wet upper parts of the valley. Correlated with the shift in settlement pattern was the development of irrigated wet taro systems in the formerly unused wet upper valley. Excavations in one of these irrigation complexes (Yen *et al.* 1972) firmly establishes the beginning of inland taro cultivation by the fifteenth century AD. Subsistence did not shift to a total dependence on irrigation, however, but rather consisted of a mixed cropping system with irrigation on the alluvial flats and shifting cultivation on the valley slopes. This latter environment, once stripped of its natural forest cover, was prone to erosion, leading in at least one case to destruction of an irrigation complex (which was subsequently rebuilt). Thus, 'forest clearance accompanied and introduced an erosional factor into an area that did not possess a great deal of natural stability' (Green 1980:75).

Change in the local socio-political organization during the fifteenth century is marked by initial construction of a major religious temple, Kane'aki *heiau*, at the division between the upper and lower valley (Fig. 82). Green interprets this event as evidence for 'the presence in the valley of a ranking chief able to build his own sizable *lono*-type *heiau* [a temple to the god of agriculture], and the means for achieving a surplus of goods for his own use by intensifying the valley's productive capacity' (1980:75). In short, Green sees the fifteenth-sixteenth centuries as a period when the valley achieved the status of a 'largely self-contained socio-economic unit' (1980:76). He also maintains that this phase saw the 'formation throughout the Hawaiian Group of two separate and endogamous socio-economic classes, one of high-ranking chiefs or *ali'i* and the other of commoners or *maka'ainana*' (1980:75). The latter claim is, of course, only indirectly supported on archaeological evidence from Makaha.

In the final stage of the valley's development, which began about AD 1650, Makaha was integrated into the fabric of the large-scale 'complex rank social systems' which characterized Hawai'i at European contact. Of this phase, Green writes:

There is now evidence both of permanent housing in the form of ordinary rectangular dwellings, and of an increasing number of religious buildings in the form of stepped stone platforms, shrines, and other specialized structures, some of them men's houses. They suggest that the processes of social segmentation and stratification among the elite, known elsewhere in Hawai'i, were underway within the Makaha Valley, and would have continued, had they not been overwhelmed by the consequences of European contact (1980:76–7).

There are two important archaeological signals that mark Makaha's incorporation into a larger complex socio-political system. The first of these was the rebuilding of Kane'aki *heiau* (increasing its size from 400 m^2 to 1,010 m^2), converting it from a Lono-class temple to a *luakini*, or war temple of human sacrifice (Fig. 82). Such an event can only have been directed by a paramount chief. The second important event was the construction of a 'main irrigation ditch down into the dry central part of the lower valley' (1980:77). As Green observed, the significance of this ditch lay in its ability to further increase the productive capacity of the valley, and to provide additional agricultural surplus to the paramount chief and his local representatives.

In general, the developmental sequences of Halawa and Makaha run closely parallel, even though the time-span for Halawa is probably 400 years longer than that of Makaha. The major themes of expanding

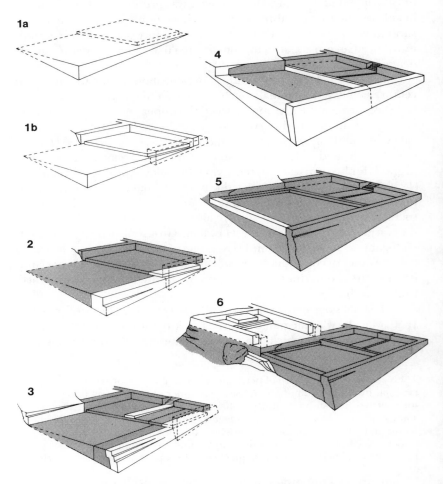

82. Phases in the construction of Kaneʻaki *heiau*, Makaha Valley, Oʻahu Island (adapted from Ladd and Yen 1972). The conversion from Phases 5 to 6 was probably correlated with a change in the temple's function, from an agricultural temple to a war temple (*luakini*).

population, movement into the upper-valley areas, onset of local erosion due to shifting cultivation, intensification of the means of production (especially irrigation), and elaboration of ceremonial architecture reflective of ranking chiefs are remarkably similar. If we further compare the Halawa and Makaha sequences to the model of population growth developed in Chapter 5, and to the evidence for intensification of dryfield cultivation in West Hawai'i outlined in Chapter 7, what emerges is a clear and consistent archaeological framework for the transformation of Hawaiian society from an Ancestral Polynesian base. As indicated in both sequences, the period from about AD 1400 to the advent of European contact is especially critical, for this period saw the major elaborations in irrigation, temple building, and other signals of socio-political development. To gain a fuller understanding of this final period, we may turn to data provided by indigenous oral traditions of political history, and to early post-contact ethnographic accounts.

Traditional accounts of political development

During the late prehistoric period the major islands were divided into several independent chiefdoms, the exact configurations of which varied with the outcomes of territorial conquests and marriage alliances. The larger islands of Kaua'i, O'ahu, Maui, and Hawai'i were each the central focus of an independent political unit; Moloka'i and Lana'i were frequent battlegrounds between the competing paramount lines of O'ahu and Maui. Not until late in the eighteenth century, some years after Cook's voyage, did Kamehameha succeed in subjugating and uniting these independent chiefdoms.

As in Tonga, a rich corpus of indigenous oral traditions recount the genealogies and political events associated with the major ruling lines of chiefs (Fornander 1880, 1916–20; Kamakau 1961; I'i 1959; Beckwith 1932; Malo 1951), and provides a unique body of data for understanding political development in late prehistoric times. Here, I will use simply a small segment of the traditions, those pertaining to the ruling line of Hawai'i Island, and especially the Kona–Kohala chiefs, from whom Kamehameha himself was descended. Hommon (1976) has compiled and synthesized the extensive genealogical and historical material contained in the traditions, and I have drawn upon his work in this discussion.

Figure 83 A presents a condensed version of the genealogy and succession of the Hawai'i Island paramounts, while Figure 83 B shows, on a parallel time-scale, the cycles of conquest, political amalgamation, and fission that accompanied the succession of paramounts. The time period represented in this chart is about 250 years, beginning with the rule of Liloa around AD 1550, and ending with the birth of Kamehameha's heir, Liholiho, in AD 1797. In terms of our archaeological framework, this final quarter-millennium ending with European intrusion was marked by large, dense populations, and was the period during which the leeward dryfield agricultural systems were intensified to their productive limits.

A perusal of Figure 83 reveals several structural patterns of great interest. Not only do we lack the kind of systematized, dual paramountship of Tonga, but the Ancestral Polynesian pattern of patrilineal succession seems hardly in evidence. Rather, we see a complex picture of repeated usurpations by junior collaterals, as in the case of 'Umi-a-Liloa (12) who seized the paramountship from his senior half-sibling Hakau (11) by their father Liloa (10). The story of 'Umi (Kamakau 1961:1–21) is of special interest in several regards, and is virtually paradigmatic. The opposition between 'Umi and Hakau reflects not only the rank differentiation of junior/senior (Hakau was the son of the high chiefess Pinea, whereas 'Umi's mother was a commoner), but an important distinction between a benevolent versus an oppressive chief, a theme that permeates the Hawaiian traditions. The tendency for ruling chiefs 'to eat the powers of the government too much' (Sahlins 1968:92; 1972:144), that is, to become excessively demanding upon the general populace, provided an opportunity for junior collaterals to foment rebellion and seize the reins of power. In 'Umi's case, the strategy was aided by his control of the 'kingdom-snatching' war god, Ku-ka'ili-moku, bequeathed to him by Liloa (a circumstance repeated later by Kamehameha in his usurpation of the paramountship from Kiwala'o). Having defeated Hakau, and offering his body at the altar of Ku (Kamakau 1961:14), 'Umi proceeded to appropriate the high-ranking sister of his opponent (indeed, his own half-sister) as the royal wife, thereby assuring the high rank of his heir.

The political history of the Hawai'i Island line, as of the other major chiefdoms, is complex, and here we can only take note of several dominant themes. Most significant is the cycle of conquest, expansion to encompass neighbouring districts, followed by collapse and retrenchment; more will be said on this point shortly. Also of note is the critical role of high-ranking women, who were more important than their male counterparts in transmitting the sanctity of the chiefly lines. As Valeri (1972) points out, the celebrated sibling (or, more frequently, half-sibling) marriages of Hawaiian chiefs must be understood not so much on the basis of chiefly endogamy as a complex system of alliances between various collateral segments of the ruling 'house'. Such alliances not infrequently extended beyond the borders of single chiefdom, and Kaua'i, O'ahu, and Maui chiefesses figure in the genealogy of the Hawai'i paramounts (Fig. 83).

The power and authority of the Hawai'i Island paramounts, and their ability to mobilize corvée labour, is reflected archaeologically in a series of substantial stone temples (*heiau*) concentrated particularly in

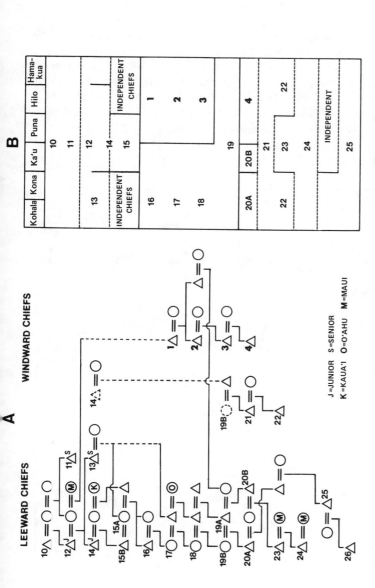

83. A. The genealogical relationships of the paramount chiefs of Hawai'i Island; the numbers indicate the sequence of succession. B. The sequence of amalgamation and fission of political units on Hawai'i Island; numbers refer to the paramount chiefs shown in A. Dashed horizontal lines indicate succession by military conquest; solid horizontal lines indicate peaceful transitions (charts adapted from Hommon 1976).

the Kona district. It was at one of these temple platforms, Hikiau at Kealakekua Bay, that Captain Cook submitted to the ritual of *hanaipu*, the 'feeding of the god' in January 1779 (Beaglehole 1967:506; Sahlins 1981a:21). Perhaps the most sacred, and certainly the most extensive temple complex is that at Honaunau (Emory *et al.* 1957; Ladd 1969a, b, c; Tuohy 1965; Soehren 1962). Here a massive stone wall (3.7 m high, 5.2 m wide; total length 304.8 m; total volume 5,864 m^3) separates a point of land from the surrounding terrain (Fig. 84). The enclosure was a *pu'uhonua*, place of refuge (see Chapter 8), as well as the site of several great temples. Ale'ale'a temple, excavated by Ladd (1969a) was constructed in a series of seven stages, beginning about AD 1475. At the ritual 'core' of the Honaunau complex was the Hale-o-Keawe, a small temple that held the skeletal remains of the deified ancestors of the ruling

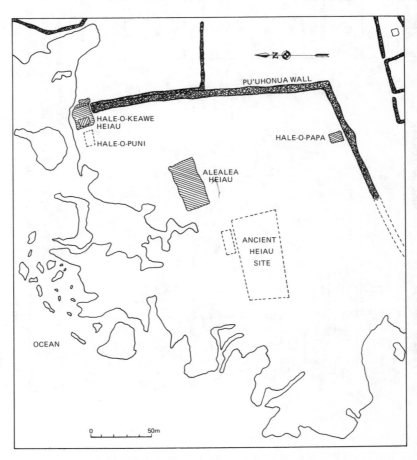

84. Archaeological plan of the ceremonial centre at Honaunau, Kona District, Hawai'i Island.

line. Although, for reasons described below, the Kona paramounts actually resided only intermittently at Honaunau, it served as a ceremonial centre analogous to Lapaha in Tonga. Archaeological work to date suggests that the centre was gradually elaborated throughout the four to five centuries prior to European contact, matching the traditional political history of the increasing power of the Kona-Kohala line.

Late prehistoric Hawaiian society

By the time of European contact, Hawaiian society had undergone two fundamental departures from Ancestral Polynesian Society, which highlight the degree of structural transformation. Both of these changes can be couched in negative terms from the viewpoint of the common people: they lost their genealogies, and they lost direct control of their land. The two, of course, descent and land, went hand-in-hand in Polynesia, and having lost one it is not surprising that they should have given up the other. More precisely, Hawaiian society had come to comprise a conical clan of chiefs superposed over a truncated class of commoners who worked the land and paid tribute to their lords.

The chiefly class, *ali'i*, comprised a kind of very large, segmented and ramified conical clan; membership in this class was determined by one's ability to state or recount genealogical connections to a major chiefly segment. The *ali'i* were divided into a complex series of grades or ranks, most important being the distinction between the paramount, *ali'i-'ai-moku*, and various sub-chiefs (often warriors) who held land sections under the paramount (the *ali'i-'ai-ahupua'a* chiefs). (For indigenous accounts of Hawaiian chiefship and rank, see Malo 1951, Beckwith 1932, Kamakau 1964.) Directly administering these primary land segments (*ahupua'a*) were a group of 'stewards', themselves often chiefs of low rank, called *konohiki*.

Unlike the chiefs, commoners (*noa*, or more commonly, *maka'ainana*) did not lay claim to any genealogical depth, nor were they organized on any kind of corporate descent model. Rather, stress was laid on a network of lateral kin relationships, expressed in the classic bilateral kindred (*'ohana*) described by Handy and Pukui (1958) for Ka'ū District. Among commoners the basic unit of residence, and of production, was the extended household, usually referred to as the group (*ma*) of so-and-so, generally its prominent male leader (e.g., 'Kainiki *ma*'). The term for commoners, *maka'ainana*, is of particular interest, since it is the Hawaiian reflex of Proto-Polynesian **kainanga*, a corporate descent group together with its territorial segment. As the 'people of the land', the term *maka'ainana* retained one aspect of its ancient semantic value, but the implication of corporate descent had disappeared, as had the implication of ownership. Instead, the term had come to represent the *class* of people who worked the land, and who stood in opposition to the class of landowners (*haku'aina*) – the chiefs – to whom the *maka'ainana* owed tribute and labour.

The system of land divisions was itself organized on the typical Polynesian segmentary pattern. The most inclusive unit, the chiefdom (*moku*) – usually an entire island – was subdivided into numerous *ahupua'a*, ideally pie-shaped sections radiating from the island's centre and, again ideally, economically self-sufficient. *Ahupua'a* were subdivided into smaller units, *'ili*, which themselves comprised several *mo'o 'aina*, each of these the unit normally worked by an extended household. (Note that the Hawaiian term *'aina*, 'land', is also a reflex of Proto-Polynesian **kainga*, 'land-holding descent group'.) At the succession of a new paramount, and particularly following a war of conquest, *ahupua'a* were redistributed by the *ali'i-'ai-moku* to the chiefs who supported him, both consanguines and affines (the latter often received a greater share, so as to deny close affinal kin the opportunity to amass a powerful economic base). These *ali'i-ai-ahupua'a*, in turn, designated their own *konohiki* to be responsible for the productive use of their lands, for the mobilization of corvée labour, and for the collection of the annual tribute (*ho'okupu*) to the paramount. Valeri (1972:38) has described the Hawaiian territorial system as 'un squelette qui-n'a pas de correspondances généalogiques à tous ses niveaux', and the divergence from the Ancestral Polynesian pattern can be neatly summarized in a simple diagram (Fig. 85). Hawai'i carried the political, territorially based transformation of Polynesian society to its limits, though as we shall see, it never fully divorced the ancestral bonds of kinship between chiefs and commoners, and thus never fully transcended the 'tribal' level of society (cf. Sahlins 1968, 1972).

The Hawaiian polity can be analysed not only in terms of class stratification and land control, but in terms of its hierarchical, decision-making structure (Fig. 86). Aside from the *ahupua'a* chiefs and their

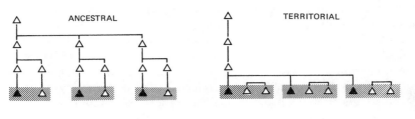

Land Unit   ▲ Chief or Land Manager   △ Commoner

85. Diagrammatic representation of the change from an ancestral Polynesian system of land holding, in which land segments are held by corporate descent groups, to a territorial system like that of protohistoric Hawai'i.

konohiki, there existed a considerable body of councillors, priests, executants, and other retainers who formed a 'court' of the paramount chief. Most important of these officials were the *kalaimoku* and the *kahuna nui*. The *kalaimoku* essentially acted on behalf of the paramount in most secular matters, and his position was in many ways analogous to the Tongan *hau*. Though the position was not hereditary it was, significantly, often accorded to affinal relatives of the paramount. Sahlins (1981a:55–64), through an analysis of the Kamehameha polity, makes the reason for this clear: by handing the secular affairs over to the *kalaimoku* the paramount not only preserved his tabu status, but he kept the power out of the hands of close consanguineal relatives, who were always to be suspected as potential usurpers. Also vital to the operation of government, the *kahuna nui*, or high priest of the order of Ku, god of war, assisted the paramount in vital rituals, especially those pertaining to war and conquest.

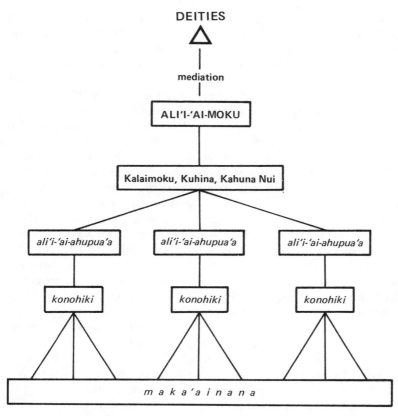

86. Hierarchical organization of the protohistoric Hawaiian chiefdom.

The system of tribute (*ho'okupu*) upon which the polity depended for its economic support was bound up with another great cult, that of Lono, god of fertility and agriculture. Collection of tribute (in the form of barkcloth, cordage, feathers, dogs, and so on) took place in conjunction with the *makahiki*, an annual four-month-long season devoted to the god Lono, and during which the temples of Ku were dismantled and warfare forbidden. As Handy and Handy (1972:351) pointed out, the *makahiki* had its origins in the first-fruits rites that were certainly a part of Ancestral Polynesian ritual; its evolution as a ritualized form of taxation arose later in conjunction with 'the sociopolitical institutions of the late Hawaiian feudal system'. (Firth [1967:1] has noted the similarities between the *makahiki* and the annual cycle of harvest rituals in Tikopia, while the Tongan '*inasi* is also clearly derived from the same ancestral concept of first-fruits ritual.)

In light of the emphasis that has frequently been placed on the concept of redistribution in chiefdom societies (Sahlins 1958; Flannery and Coe 1968; Service 1967), it is important to point out that in Hawai'i, redistribution of the *ho'okupu* was essentially limited to the chiefly class. Malo makes this perfectly clear when he states that 'the king distributed it among the chiefs and the companies of soldiery throughout the land ... No share of this property, however, was given to the people' (1951:143). Thus the *makahiki* served as a political vehicle for the paramount to reward his supporters within the chiefly class (see also Earle 1977). Oliver, incidentally, makes the same point for ancient Tahitian society, that 'goods that were left over from consumption by those at the top of the hierarchy were either appropriated by those *near* the top, or were further redistributed in only token amounts' (1974:1071–2). Despite such political ends, it is important to stress the ritual character of the *makahiki*. In the eyes of the commoners, indeed in the general conception of tribute, it was as Kepelino said, *na lo'ina ho'okupu ali'i*, 'the royal pattern of growth-causing' (Beckwith 1932:148; Handy and Handy 1972:351). The *ali'i-'ai-moku*, as mediator between the fertility-causing gods and men (and as a god on earth himself), accepts the tribute so that the land shall yield again. That he also used the tribute to advance his own aims and ambitions shows the extent to which ritual, economy, and political strategy were intimately bound up in indigenous Hawaiian society.

We should not be misled, however, to believe that the bonds of reciprocity between chief and people were totally severed, that the Hawaiian chiefs had relinquished all obligations to support their followers. Chiefs were, indeed, expected to take care of the people, not only through their ritual mediation with the gods, but more tangibly in providing the means of subsistence when shortage occurred. David Malo, famous custodian of Hawaiian tradition, put it metaphorically: 'As the rat will not desert the pantry where he thinks food is, so the people will not desert the king while they think there is food in his store-house' (1951:195).

The annual *makahiki ho'okupu*, while a significant strategy of the ruling polity for securing and utilizing surplus production, was insufficient for the day-to-day support of the chiefly establishment, which – with its advisers, executants, sub-chiefs, warriors, and so forth – amounted to a sizeable population to be continually fed, clothed, and otherwise sustained. Since tropical Oceanic crops are not readily transformed into storable, easily transported surplus (as in the case with seed crops), the chiefly establishment was required to come to the loci of production, thus creating the uniquely *peripatetic* nature of Hawaiian chiefs. (Among the means used to procure the subsistence requirements of the chiefly establishment were corvée labour, particularly the cultivation of *ko'ele* fields, worked by the commoners for the chiefs.) Moving from place to place within the chiefdom, the *ali'i* spread the burden of support more evenly; the pattern of movement also kept the paramount in direct communication with different regions within the whole territory.

The ingenious strategy was not entirely successful, and the burden upon the *maka'ainana* for support of 'a bloated political establishment' (Sahlins 1972:145) became, at times, oppressive.

Conscious, it seems, of the logistic burdens they were obliged to impose, the Hawaiian chiefs conceived several means to relieve the pressure, notably including a career of conquest with a view toward enlarging the tributary base. In the successful event, however, with the realm now stretched over distant and lately subdued hinterlands, the bureaucratic costs of rule apparently rose higher than the increases in revenue, so that the victorious chief merely succeeded in adding enemies abroad to a worse unrest at home (Sahlins 1972:145).

We thus begin to comprehend the motive force behind the *maka'ainana* revolts, fomented and led by junior collaterals of the ruling faction, mentioned earlier (see also Valeri 1972:32). As Malo put it: 'Many kings have been put to death by the people because of their oppression of the *maka'ainana*' (1951:195). Thus the political history of Hawai'i, at least within the last few centuries of the prehistoric era, was characterized by a cycle of expansion and contraction of political units (diagrammed in Figure 83). As Sahlins so elegantly demonstrated, the Hawaiian political cycle, and its economic base, reveal an essential truth concerning the most highly developed of the Polynesian chiefdoms. Though the ruling elite had managed to greatly distance themselves from the commoner populace, and though they exercised a majority (but *not* a monopoly) of force, they never managed to completely sever the *kinship* bond between chiefs and people which Hawaiian society inherited from Ancestral Polynesian Society. 'They had not broken structurally with the people at large, so they might dishonor the kinship morality only on pain of a mass disaffection' (Sahlins 1972:148). Thus, Hawaiian society pushed the evolution of the chiefdom polity to its structural limits, a threshold which was the 'boundary of primitive society itself' (1972:148).

Hawai'i and Tonga: a comparative note

Hawai'i and Tonga are two of the most elaborated Polynesian chiefdoms, and convergences in their respective evolutionary pathways are of particular interest, since (given the great isolation between the two societies) these must have arisen from the commonly inherited structural base, and from similar evolutionary conditions and constraints.

On a superficial level of analysis, the political organizations of the two societies appear quite different, especially the formal dualism of the Tongan system, and the fluctuating usurpation characteristic of Hawai'i. When we look more closely at the underlying structural patterns, however, these apparent differences lose their initial significance. Friedman and Rowlands have opined that 'the Tongan type structure evolved from a previous structure which was closer in form to that found in Hawaii' (1978:231). To the prehistorian, knowing that Tonga had perhaps two thousand years longer for its society to develop than did Hawai'i, the idea is provocative. In Hawai'i, as we have seen, matrilineal relations had acquired great importance for the inheritance of rank, a system which ultimately might have led to the kind of highly structured bilaterality in rank determination witnessed in Tonga.

There are significant parallels as well in the separation of sacred and secular aspects of the chieftainship. In Tonga, this separation was inherent in the dual chieftainship of Tu'i Tonga and *hau* (Fig. 87). In Hawai'i, the separation is not quite so formal, but operationally we have virtually the same separation of powers between the *ali'i-'ai'moku*

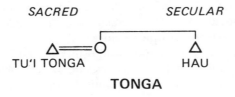

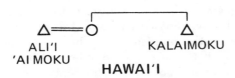

87. The structural relationships between sacred and secular chiefs in Tonga and Hawai'i.

and his *kalaimoku*. When we further realize that the office of *kalaimoku* (as well as those of the *kuhina*) was generally given over to affines (typically, brothers of the high-ranking wife), the structural similarities between Hawai'i and Tonga become all the more apparent. Furthermore, the administrative, decision-making hierarchies of both societies were remarkably parallel as is evident in a comparison of Figures 75 and 86.

Another area of fruitful comparison is in the ritualized, annual tribute paid to the ruling factions in both societies. The Tongan *'inasi* and the Hawaiian *makahiki* had much in common, in their annual timing, in the ritualized nature of the tribute, in the ideological conception of the tribute as offerings to the gods of fertility through the mediation of the sacred chief, and in the institutionalized games and competitions that accompanied both sets of ceremonials. Clearly, both the *'inasi* and the *makahiki* are elaborations of an Ancestral form of first-fruits offering to the tribal deities and the *ariki* (see Chapters 2, 3). In both, an increasingly powerful class of chiefs used its control over ritual to legitimize their control of production and appropriation of surplus.

For the archaeologist, a comparison between the ceremonial centres of Lapaha and Honaunau is also intriguing. The essence of both localities lies in highly sacred sepulchres for deified ancestors of the ruling chiefs. In Tonga, the removal of the Tu'i Tonga from active status as a secular ruler had turned Lapaha into a permanent residence as well, whereas Honaunau was used only periodically as the actual residence of the peripatetic *ali'i-'ai-moku*.

One cannot avoid the urge to speculate on what Hawaiian society would have looked like had Cook and his European successors not burst through the barriers of 'Kahiki' in the late eighteenth century, and if the indigenous course of evolution had been allowed to proceed in isolation for another thousand years. Would a formalized, dualistic chieftainship like that of Tonga have emerged; or, given the far greater resources of the Hawaiian archipelago, would Hawaiian society have evolved even more complex forms of political organization? The answers will always be speculative, but they are part of what makes the study of Polynesia endlessly fascinating.

11
Easter Island

In Tonga, and certainly in Hawai'i, the intrusion of Europeans disrupted internal processes of cultural evolution that had not yet reached endpoints of indigenous development. Easter Island, our third case study, contrasts with the previous two in this regard, for despite certain truly remarkable evolutionary achievements, Easter Island society had – by the time of Roggeveen's discovery in 1722 – already begun a downward spiral of cultural regression. By the end of the nineteenth century, internal strife and conflict, exacerbated by foreign diseases and slave raids, had reduced the island's society to a mere 111 persons, who retained only an impoverished memory of their former state. A brilliant job of salvage ethnography by Métraux (1940) and others, as well as a series of intensive archaeological investigations have fortunately provided a surprisingly detailed picture of the rise and fall of Easter Island society. The fascination of Easter Island lies, not in the purported 'mystery' of its stone statues or *rongorongo* tablets, but rather in its evolutionary record of cultural achievements within a most isolated Polynesian outpost, achievements which were inevitably to crumple under pressures of over-population and environmental degradation. Easter Island is the story of a society which – temporarily but brilliantly surpassing its limits – crashed devastatingly.

Situated 3,703 km west of South America, and 1,819 km east of Pitcairn Island, Easter is among the loneliest, most isolated islands on earth. The islanders' own name for their land, *Te Pito o te Henua*, reflects this, for it is probably best translated 'land's end' (Churchill 1912:2–3). Several geological, oceanographic, and climatic conditions render Easter relatively marginal when compared with most other tropical or subtropical Polynesian islands. Formed by the coalescing flows of three main volcanoes (Fig. 88), the island has a land surface of about 160 km². The land is undulating, with rolling hills and higher volcanic cones; there are no permanent streams, and most rainfall sinks directly into the porous volcanic soil. Several crater lakes provide water, but these are far from the main settlement areas. Rainfall, which averages between about 1,250–1,500 mm per year, is adequate for several

Polynesian crops (sweet potato, yams, bananas, sugar cane), although drought years are not uncommon. Lacking permanent watercourses, irrigation was not technologically possible. Lying just outside the tropics, and swept by cold-water currents from the Antarctic region, the island has no fringing reef (although some limited coral growth is present), and most of the coastline consists of sea cliffs. Consequently, fishing cannot provide the same range and quantity of protein as on other Polynesian islands. All of these environmental constraints were to play a role in the eventual regression of Easter Island society.

As I have noted, the ethnographic and archaeological literature on Easter Island is relatively richer than that for many other Polynesian islands. Archaeological work began as early as 1886, with a short reconnaissance survey (McCoy 1979). Major strides forward in both ethnographic and archaeological knowledge were made by Routledge (1919; 1920), who spent seventeen months on the island in 1914–15. In 1934–5, the Franco-Belgian expedition resulted in Lavachery's monumental study of petroglyphs and pictographs (1939), and in Métraux's classic *Ethnology of Easter Island* (1940), which synthesized all available

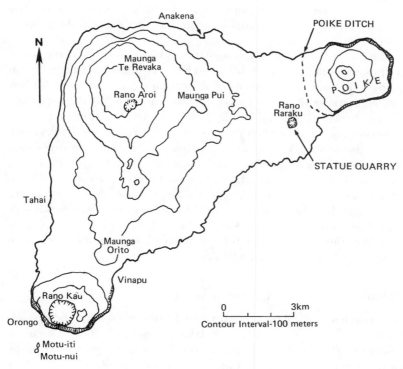

88. Map of Easter Island, showing the principal localities discussed in the text.

data on the island's culture. The famous Capuchin priest, Father Sebastian Englert (1948, 1970), spent many years adding to our knowledge of oral traditions and archaeology. Barthel (1971, 1978) has also contributed greatly to the analysis of oral tradition, and conducted detailed studies of the *rongorongo* script. Heyerdahl (1975) contributed an exhaustive survey of Easter Island art.

Modern investigations of the island's prehistory began with the Norwegian Expedition in 1955–56, organized by Thor Heyerdahl. The four archaeologists of this expedition (Ferdon, Smith, Mulloy, Skjolsvold) introduced techniques of stratigraphic excavation, and applied radiocarbon and obsidian dating to produce the first cultural sequence for Easter Island (Heyerdahl and Ferdon 1965). Although their emphasis on the monumental *ahu*, and certain of their interpretations, have been justly criticized (Golson 1965), their work nevertheless stands as a milestone in Polynesian prehistory. Gaps in their pioneering work have fortunately been rectified by subsequent studies of additional *ahu* by Mulloy (1975), Mulloy and Figueroa (1978), and Ayres (1973), by McCoy's detailed settlement pattern analysis (1976) and excavation of a rectangular house (1973), and by Ayres's excavations at a series of caves and open site dwellings (1975). A recent overview by McCoy (1979) provides a concise summary of the state-of-the-art of Easter Island prehistory.

The Norwegian Expedition archaeologists proposed a three-phase cultural sequence (Early, Middle, and Late Periods) based largely upon changes in religious architecture and statuary. More recently, Mulloy and Figueroa (1978:131–8) have shown that many of the supposed changes between Early and Middle Period architecture are not supported on additional evidence. Ayres's revision of the original sequence (1973, 1975), based on a reconsideration of architectural data, and incorporating other criteria as well, appears to be the best overall schema for organizing the time-frame for Easter Island cultural development, and has been largely adopted here. Fortunately, a series of more than thirty radiocarbon age determinations on some fifteen sites provides a reasonably firm chronological yardstick. Most of these ^{11}C ages are shown in Figure 89, where they are depicted as corrected age ranges at the 95 per cent confidence level (following Klein *et al.* 1982).

Colonization and early developments

Direct archaeological evidence for initial colonization and the first few centuries of settlement in Easter Island is sadly lacking. Linguistic evidence, such as the retention of the Proto-Polynesian velar nasal, clearly indicates that the group which colonized Easter must have departed central East Polynesia early, prior to the development there of numerous innovations (Elbert 1953; Green 1966). On these grounds, a date in the first few centuries AD would be entirely reasonable. The earliest ^{14}C date from Easter (AD 235–615), on charcoal buried on an original land surface beneath spoil from the Poike Ditch, is not in direct association with any evidence for human activity. It is conceivable that it does represent early forest clearance through burning. A further tan-

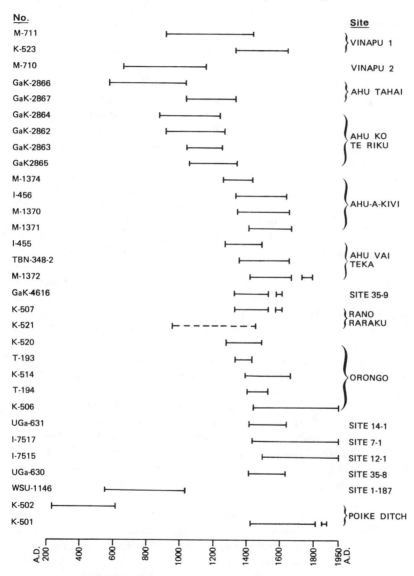

89. Radiocarbon age determinations for Easter Island archaeological sites, plotted as 95 per cent confidence intervals based on Klein *et al.* (1982).

talizing clue suggestive of early settlement lies in the stone vessels which appear to be replicas of late Polynesian Plain Ware ceramics. If so, the idea of pottery must have been carried to Easter Island prior to the cessation of ceramic use in the Marquesas (or elsewhere in central East Polynesia).

Either during the course of the initial colonization voyage to Easter, or in the process of initial reassortment and adaptation to local conditions, the Polynesian crop and domestic animal roster was significantly reduced. Among the plants not successfully transferred from the tropical East Polynesian homeland were coconut, breadfruit, and various fruit trees (e.g., *Inocarpus, Spondias*). Of the domestic animals, only chickens were successfully carried to Easter (along with the inadvertently transported rat, which was to become an item of the later diet). This reduction in the variety of domestic carbohydrate and protein sources is particularly significant in light of the island's restricted natural food resources.

Palynological investigations of the peat deposits in Easter Island's crater lakes, by Flenley (1979, 1981), have demonstrated that prior to Polynesian colonization the island supported a more extensive forest cover, quite different from the treeless landscape seen by the early European voyagers. Thus, in the initial stages of human occupation, one may suppose that an adequate supply of wood for fuel and industrial purposes existed, although larger trees suitable for canoe construction may have been sparse or lacking. (A significant discovery was the presence of the *totora* reed, *Scirpus* sp., in the bog deposits dating older than 30,000 BP. This evidence clearly shows that the *totora* is indigenous to Easter, not the product of human transport from South America as argued by Thor Heyerdahl.)

Among the earliest archaeological materials on Easter Island are the first construction phases of two of the larger religious sites, Ahu Tahai and Vinapu 2 (see Fig. 89), both dating to about the ninth century AD. As Ayres (1973) thoroughly documents, the Easter Island *ahu* is a variant of the East Polynesian *marae* complex, with its essential elements of enclosed court and raised altar at one end (the term *ahu* refers to this altar in other East Polynesian societies, e.g., Tahiti, Emory 1933). The *ahu* concept was undoubtedly brought to Easter by the initial colonists, where it was locally elaborated and developed. The Ahu Tahai and Ahu Vinapu 2 constructions, dated to several centuries after colonization, already reflect local developments, the most notable being 'dressed and fitted rectangular basalt slabs chamfered on their inner superior edges' (Mulloy and Figueroa 1978:128). Earlier stages of *ahu* development have yet to be discovered, though future work will doubtless reveal them. (It is possible that an early, prototypical *ahu* was in fact partially exposed at Vinapu 2, although it has not been recognized as such by the excavator [Mulloy 1965:116]. I refer to an edged pavement of basalt slabs buried under the 'Middle Period' ramp, only partly excavated, and visible in Plate 11a of the excavation report.)

The Ahu Moai Phase (AD 1000–1500)

By the beginning of the second millennium AD, the construction of *ahu* in various areas around the island's coast was in full swing (ultimately some 245 *ahu* were to be built), and Ayres (1973) has termed the ensuing period the Ahu Moai Phase, after its characteristic statues (*moai*) bearing *ahu*. (Ayres dates the phase from AD 1000–1680; McCoy [1976] suggested a major cultural change at AD 1550. Based on a consideration of the radiocarbon evidence, Figure 89, I believe AD 1500 to be a better date.) Although the large *ahu* vary in detail and size, all follow the same basic architectural plan (Fig. 90). Essential to the *ahu* is the raised, elongate platform, often well-faced on the seaward side, and generally oriented parallel to the shore (some *ahu* may have significant solar orientations). These flat-topped platforms (up to 60 metres long and 7 metres high) served as the base upon which the giant statues of Rano Raraku tuff were raised. To landward, a gently sloping ramp descends from the *ahu* platform to a large rectangular plaza, usually artificially levelled. These ramps are frequently paved with carefully positioned rows of water-rolled beach boulders.

The highly stylized statues which are virtually a symbol of Easter Island were carved from the relatively soft tuff of Rano Raraku, and transported (probably by means of fork-sledges and bipods, Mulloy 1970) to the *ahu*. About 324 statues were actually raised on *ahu*, or in the process of being transported, and another 200 in various stages of completion have been recorded in the quarries (Englert 1970:121–3). There has been some debate concerning the development of these statues, and it is possible that a number of variant forms (often carved in softer reddish tuff) may represent an earlier phase of image-making, prior to the development of the highly stylized Rano Raraku type.

From their careful analysis of eleven excavated and radiocarbon-dated *ahu*, Mulloy and Figueroa (1978:122–41) concluded that 'all were products of a single coherent, though evolving, cultural tradition'. The original distinction between 'Early' and 'Middle' Periods of Easter Island culture history drawn by the Norwegian Expedition based on *ahu* excavation no longer holds up on the evidence of the increased sample of dated *ahu*. Nor can the suggestion that changes in *ahu* architecture reflect the immigration of a second culture be supported, since it is now clear that the Easter Island *ahu* sequence reflects an 'unbroken chronological progression such as might be expected from the architectural reflection of the activities of a single continuously developing society' (Mulloy and Figueroa 1978:137). The Easter Island *ahu* complex represents a remarkably elaborate and sophisticated development of the East Polynesian *marae* concept.

Virtually all ethnographic and archaeological authorities agree that the *ahu* were conceived, constructed, and used by local descent groups, and do not reflect some kind of highly centralized, island-wide political authority. Association of various *ahu* with local segmentary descent groups or lineages (*ure*) is clear in oral traditions, and is in keeping with the *ahu* as part of an East Polynesian *marae* complex. The Rano Raraku quarry site, with its large number of unfinished projects, suggests 'the activities of many independently working crews, probably sent

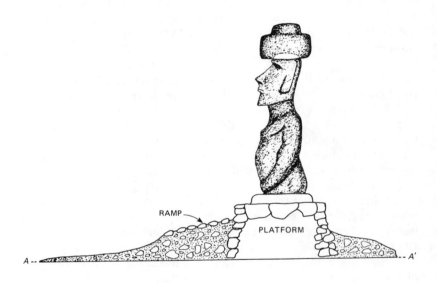

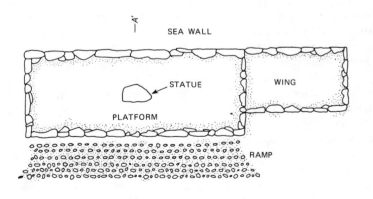

90. Plan and elevation of a typical Easter Island *ahu* or temple.

periodically by their kin groups, rather than the activities of a single work force under centralized direction' (Mulloy and Figueroa (1978:134). The distribution of the *ahu*, and their integration with other components of the total settlement pattern (to be discussed below), further reflect a typical Polynesian segmentary pattern, with each *ahu* representing the religious focus of an ancestor-based kin group. The statues themselves probably commemorated 'illustrious ancestors of the various kin-groups, whose mana was thought to bring benefit to the communities' (Englert 1970:108).

Sahlins (1955) proposed an hypothesis regarding the 'esoteric efflorescence' represented by the image-*ahu*, which also supports the interpretation of these structures as products of individual ramages or lineages. He argued that due to the rather severe ecological constraints of Easter Island, the communal labour and specialized production typical of a ramage organization could not be directed into major technological improvements in subsistence production. Rather, 'these efforts were channeled into an esoteric domain of culture', the carving, transport, and erection of massive stone images (1955:1051).

Despite the fact that the several hundred *ahu* and statues were built over a period of about 700 years, a sizeable population and a well-organized production system are both indicated. Various authors have suggested a maximum population of about 7,000 persons (a density of about $49/km^2$) though this may be an underestimate. Given the local environmental constraints, subsistence was based upon intensive dryfield cultivation, particularly of sweet potatoes, yams, taro, and bananas. The accounts of early European explorers hint at the intensive nature of cultivation practices, though the ethnographic record on agriculture is, in general, rather poor. Curiously, there appear to be few stone or earthen bank field boundaries such as those described earlier for West Hawai'i, or for the Auckland area of New Zealand (Chapter 7). McCoy (1976:26–9, 78–86), however, does describe a range of other sites that bespeak local adaptation of agronomic technique. These include a series of soil-retaining terraces on the steep slopes of Rano Kau, artificial depressions for taro planting, and numerous stone-walled planting enclosures called *manavai*. These latter, associated with other household features (ovens, houses, chicken houses), were an adaptation to the open terrain and windy conditions on Easter, serving to retain moisture and protect the crops from wind damage. The *manavai* may have become particularly important later on in the Easter Island sequence, when increasing environmental degradation worsened local growing conditions.

With fowl as the only domestic protein resource, fishing (and to an extent seabird and bird-egg hunting) played an important role, though environmental constraints were a serious factor. Ayres (1979) has reviewed the evidence for Easter Island fishing, which utilized the techniques of angling, netting, trapping, spearing, and hand collecting. Although exploitation of the near-shore zone was similar around most of the island's coast, exploitation of the deeper offshore waters was largely a monopoly of the occupants of the western and northern areas, particularly the high-ranking Miru clan. In part, this specialization reflects the better offshore fishing localities (*hakanononga*) to leeward (Ayres 1979, fig. 1), though it must be recognized that control of prestigious fish resources (generally the larger, pelagic, carnivorous species) by high-ranking lines is a common phenomenon in Polynesia. Métraux (1940:173) records that during the winter months (July–September) a *tapu* on fish, particularly tuna (*kahi*), was in effect, and 'only the royal canoe (*vaka vaero*) could be used'; *kahi* taken during this period were given to the paramount chief and older, high-ranking men (*tangata-honui*). Ayres (1979) points out the association of fishhooks with the *ahu* (several caches have been found in *ahu* crematoria), evidence, perhaps, of the ritual legitimation of the unequal social distribution of fish.

We have already noted the coastal distribution of the image-*ahu*, each apparently marking the territory of a segmentary ramage; the rest of the settlement pattern was oriented around these major lineage 'seats', as illustrated in Figure 91. The radial division of land characteristic of most Polynesian societies also pertained to Easter, and the term *kainga* designated one of these ramage territories (and may originally have designated the social *group* as well). Inland of the *ahu*, with their landward-gazing statues, were a cluster of well-constructed, boat-shaped houses (*hare paenga*), usually with beautifully dressed and fitted stone foundation alignments. The *hare paenga* were occupied by high-ranking ramage members and probably also by the priests (*ivi-atua*) who officiated at the *ahu*. A particularly large boat-shaped structure, the *hare nui*, was evidently a kind of secular community house. The majority of the lineage members resided further inland, in dispersed residences of various kinds (rectangular, oval, round houses, and habitation caves have all been recorded), each household being marked by a spatially aggregated cluster of dwelling, oven house, *manavai*, and/or *hare moa* (McCoy 1976).

During the Ahu Moai Phase, Easter Island political organization seems to have been dominated by a developed form of the Ancestral Polynesian segmentary ramage system, manifested so elegantly in the image-*ahu* themselves. One maximal ramage, the Miru – direct descendants of the colonizing chief Hotu-Matu'a – was recognized as of necessarily higher rank and provided a paramount chief, the *ariki-mau*. This individual may have exercised more ritual than secular power, however. Other important social categories included the priests, *ivi-atua* ('bones of the gods'), and the warriors, *matatoa*. As we shall see, the succeeding phase of Easter Island prehistory was to witness a reversal of this political system, with the rise of the *matatoa* to frightening power and social control.

One final aspect of Easter Island's unique esoteric efflorescence deserves comment: the *rongorongo* script about which so much has been made. Exactly when the script developed is not clear, though it likely was an indigenous concept and quite probably dates to sometime in the Ahu Moai Phase. The script, with its anthropomorphic and zoomorphic glyphs, and curious reversed boustrophedon pattern, appears to be a mnemonic device 'to aid in the presentation of oral traditions and royal genealogies' (McCoy 1979:158). It is significant that the term *rongorongo* has close cognates elsewhere in East Polynesia. In Mangareva, the *rongorongo* were a class of high-ranking experts charged with memory and recitation of sacred *marae* chants (Buck 1938:304–5). Likewise, in the Marquesas the ceremonial priest was called *tuhuna oʻono* (=Proto

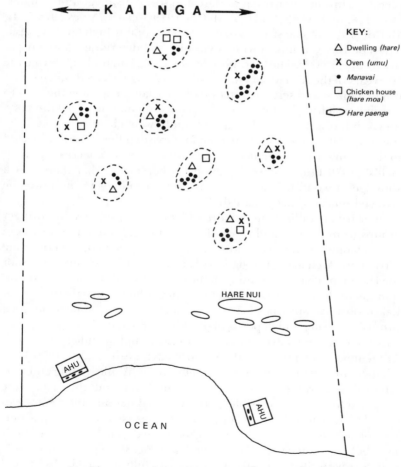

KEY:

△ Dwelling *(hare)*

X Oven *(umu)*

● Manavai

□ Chicken house *(hare moa)*

⬭ Hare paenga

K A I N G A

HARE NUI

AHU

AHU

OCEAN

91. Diagrammatic representation of Easter Island settlement patterns, with *ahu* and residences of high-ranking households near the coast, dispersed commoner households inland.

East-Polynesian *rongorongo*), and was responsible for sacred chants, including genealogies (Handy 1923:228). Clearly, the concept of *rongorongo* is of some antiquity in East Polynesia, and was carried to Easter Island with the initial settlement party. The unique addition on Easter Island was the development of script-carrying tablets as mnemonic devices (curiously, this is paralleled in the Marquesas by the invention of knotted cords for the same purpose, cf. Handy 1923, fig. 30).

Decadent (Huri Ahu) Phase (AD 1500–1722)

By all archaeological indications and in the view of most authorities, by the close of the Ahu Moai Phase Easter Island had reached a state of over-population, which was the proximate cause leading to the ensuing phase of chronic inter-tribal warfare and social disintegration (Englert 1970:138; McCoy 1976:141–7; McCoy 1979:159–61; Ayres 1975:104). McCoy (1976:145–6) stresses that this unacceptably high level of population density was linked with environmental deterioration in a negative feedback cycle. The large population which had built up during the 500 years of the Ahu Moai Phase had increasingly cleared much of the original forest and scrub vegetation of the island, exposing the land to erosion, 'resulting in the loss of a precious soil mantle . . . At the same time soil moisture was reduced, soils underwent chemical change, the soil evaporation rate was increased, and existing fields were subjected to the strong winds. The net effect must have been a decrease in crop yields' (1976:146). Forest depletion further meant that there was a shortage of wood for canoe construction, 'resulting in the probable reduced intake of deep sea fish'.

Inter-tribal conflict, the seizure of lands and property by stronger groups from weaker, and the enslavement of conquered groups were the outcome of this situation of an over-populated, deteriorating ecosystem. Archaeological signals of chronic warfare are numerous for the Decadent Phase, beginning in the sixteenth century. The most ubiquitous of these is the invention of a new implement, the *mata'a*, or flaked obsidian spearhead (Fig. 92), which suddenly appears in great profusion in sites and deposits of this Phase. Englert remarks that 'they used to be scattered over the surface of the island in endless numbers. Tremendous quantities of them must have been made' (1970:139). Changes in settlement pattern also reflect the chronic raiding and warfare; volcanic lava tubes and caves present throughout the island were modified for use as defensible, permanent habitations, their entrances sealed off with fortification walls, only a single, narrow passageway permitting single-file entry. Several of these caves (Sites 7-1, 12-1, 14-1) have been ^{11}C dated to the Decadent Phase (Fig. 89). Significantly, some of these cave walls are constructed of the carefully dressed kerbstones of the old *hare paenga* houses, ripped out of their old foundations. Yet another manifestation of warfare is the Poike Ditch, a large earthwork fortification isolating the Poike Peninsula from the rest of the island (described in Chapter 8). A radiocarbon date from charcoal in the ditch, AD 1420–1810, helps to fix the time period of the Decadent Phase.

Most striking and symbolic of the state of Easter Island society during the sixteenth to nineteenth centuries was the cessation of new image-*ahu* construction, and the deliberate destruction of the existing *ahu* and tipping over of the statues. Ayres (1973:132) notes that 'almost all the statues were tipped over forward toward the court and large blocks of stone were often placed on the ground in a position to decapitate the statue when it fell on it'. The beautifully dressed and fitted stones forming

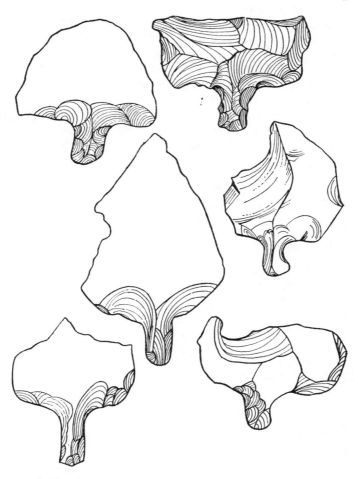

92. Obsidian spearheads (*mata'a*) from Easter Island (from Métraux 1940).

the *ahu* platforms were violently ripped apart and hurled aside. Englert plausibly speculates that this rampant destruction, which undid the toil of countless ancestors of the various lineages, was the work of enemy groups seeking to obliterate the *mana* of their opponents and weakening their ability to resist by destroying the physical symbols of the ancestors (1970:142). Then again, 'the cause may have been only an unfocussed desire to destroy the valued property of an enemy'. Equally plausible is the possibility of a class revolt by the commoners against the excessive demands by an oppressive chiefly class, particularly as the ability to provide an agricultural surplus became increasingly difficult. The destruction took place over a period of several centuries, and from historical accounts it is clear that the last statues were pulled down between 1838–64 (Métraux 1940:86).

During the Decadent or Huri Moai ('statue-toppling') Phase the use of *ahu* also changed fundamentally. Toppled statues were partially covered with rude stone platforms, and burial crypts were fitted among the stone heads (Fig. 93). A new *ahu* form, the 'semi-pyramidal' *ahu*, was constructed atop the ruined platforms. Thus the *ahu* became essentially sepulchres of the deceased descendants of those who originally conceived the remarkable concept of raising multi-ton monuments to the gods. In their sequences of construction and destruction, *ahu* such as those of Vinapu encapsulate the whole cycle of Easter Island society.

The rise of endemic warfare led to a restructuring of the island's

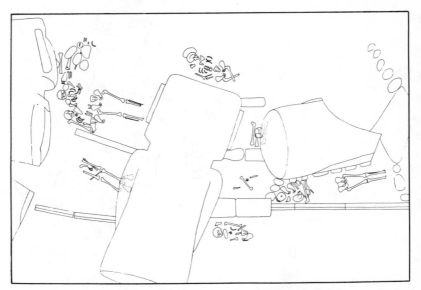

93. A portion of *ahu* Vinapu, showing the use of the temple for burials after the overthrow of the stone statues (from Heyerdahl and Ferdon 1961, *courtesy of T. Heyerdahl*).

political organization. The warring tribes and ramages organized themselves into a loose dual coalition, Tu'u in the west and Hotu-Iti in the east, the two groups constantly opposing each other. The former secular power of the *ariki-mau* declined to the point where he became solely a religious figure, a necessary link between the gods and the declining fertility of the land. In his place, secular power was seized by the *matatoa*, members of the warrior class. Englert writes:

> The most characteristic theme of the traditions of this period, as I have heard them, is that of the ascendancy to power of the matatoa . . . In these troubled times the fear they inspired and the prestige they gained enabled them to acquire ever greater control over the ariki and the priesthoods, who formerly provided through their mana the sources of social control (1970:137–8).

The ruthlessness of the *matatoa*, referred to as the *tangata rima toto*, 'men with bloodied hands', is well documented in oral tradition. It was in this phase, also, that cannibalism developed, evidenced in such archaeological sites as the Ana Kai Tangata ('Cave of the Man Eaters'). Victorious *matatoa* and their groups virtually enslaved those they conquered, creating the *kio* class of persons 'obliged to serve their conquerors or to pay tribute to them with the produce of their lands' (Métraux 1940:139). As Englert summarizes the deteriorating social situation, 'the various communities scattered over the island became more and more like predatory bands, and much of the older, more ordered way of life gradually vanished' (1970:138).

Possibly the most intriguing of all of the changes precipitated by the intense conflict of Easter's final few centuries prior to European contact was the rise of the *manutara* cult, a radical shift in the island's religion. The *manutara* or 'bird-man' cult revolved around the ceremonial centre of Orongo (Routledge 1920; Ferdon 1965; Mulloy 1975), and the offshore islets of Motu-Nui and Motu-Iti (McCoy 1978). Every year, beginning in September, an island-wide competition was held between the most powerful ruling factions of *matatoa*, to see who could find the first egg of the sooty tern (*Sterna fuscata*), the *manutara*, which was laid on the islets and return with it to Orongo. The winner or his warrior-chief was declared the bird man, *tangata manu*, and became the sacred cult-leader for the ensuing year, his group taking *de facto* control over the island. The cult was under the tutelage of a great deity, the god Makemake, who apparently came to replace the ancestral deities as the primary source of *mana*. McCall eloquently describes the fundamental changes represented by this shift in religious practice:

> it is not surprising that the Rapanui, faced with an ecological crisis that threatened their entire social order, if not their very lives, should take the initiative to fashion a new religion more suited to their precarious times. Instead of a king for life, they opted for one elected by ordeal. Instead of many ancestors who descended from many ancestors, they propounded a single god [Makemake], whose image they carved in deserted rocks, on the bases of feud-toppled figures, and even around water-holes (1980:38–9).

Yet, as McCall notes, the social order bestowed annually by the selection of the bird man at Orongo was 'as fragile as the shells of the eggs that were the focus of the annual quest' (1980:38).

Such was the war-torn, debilitated society found by the Dutch explorer Roggeveen on Easter Day, 1722. The ensuing relations between Europeans and the descendants of Hotu-matu'a is a particularly sad and shameful chapter in Pacific history, culminating in the Peruvian slave raid of 1862, which resulted in the extermination of virtually all of the knowledgeable elders and leaders of the society. Thus, through a combination of internal conflict and degeneration, exacerbated by foreign predation, the culture of Easter Island went full circle – from a small band of Polynesian colonists on the shores of a new land, through remarkable heights of cultural brilliance, to a once again small and pitiful band striving to surmount yet another challenge to their island lifeways.

94. Birdman petroglyphs at the ceremonial centre of Orongo, Easter Island (*photo by Métraux, courtesy of Bishop Museum*).

12
Epilogue

In the preceding chapters, we examined three independent pathways of technological, social, and political evolution which led in each instance to a divergent transformation of Ancestral Polynesian Society. Yet, despite the differences between the contact-period societies of Tonga, Hawai'i, and Easter Island, one may recognize in each the imprint of ancestral patterns as well as the results of similar processes (population increase, agricultural intensification, competition, and so forth). That these three societies diverged in their evolutionary pathways can be attributed to significant differences in the local hierarchies of ecological constraint, and to the creativity of individual historical actors. That these societies remained in many respects similar, or followed parallel sequences of development, may be attributed to the common structural base of Ancestral Polynesian Society, and to the influence of the same major dynamics.

As we noted at the outset of this study, one of Polynesia's great advantages for comparative analysis is its diverse canvas of ecological settings. The significant role of environment in the evolution of the Polynesian chiefdoms was the hierarchy of constraints posed in each local area. Of our three case studies, Hawai'i clearly offered the greatest range of environmental opportunities, despite significant differences between particular islands. The Hawaiian Islands are large, well watered, with fertile soils, and while some human-induced degradation occurred, this was frequently offset by the potential for agricultural and aquacultural intensification. Yet, in seizing certain ecological opportunities of the Hawaiian environment, the Polynesian settlers locked themselves into other forms of constraint. Taking advantage of the rich alluvial floodplains to develop taro irrigation to its Polynesian apogee, the Hawaiians simultaneously chose not to develop a magazine economy, a course that led to the uniquely peripatetic nature of the Hawaiian chieftainship. The Tongan archipelago offered ecological opportunities of a different sort, and the local hierarchy of constraints ruled out irrigation as a possible avenue of intensification. Rather, an intensive form of dryfield cropping (focussed on yams) developed with

279

a secondary emphasis on arboriculture. In this case storage was quite feasible and the political system came to rely upon a magazine economy, and indeed, expended considerable effort in maintaining links with the dispersed individual units of production. In contrast with Hawai'i and Tonga, isolated Easter Island posed far greater and more severe ecological constraints. Due to voyaging distance and climatic constraints, a significant percentage of the Ancestral Polynesian crop and domestic animal roster never was successfully transferred to the island. This limitation, combined with an impoverished marine environment, lack of streams, and relatively low rainfall, dictated that production would always be a difficult task, and furthermore, effectively barred most avenues of agricultural intensification. Yet the pressures to produce were no less than elsewhere, both from population increase and from the demands inherent in the ancestral social and political system. Thus in Easter Island the tension between ecological constraint and economic activity was acute, contributing ultimately to late prehistoric social and political disintegration.

While local ecological settings imposed highly significant constraints on economic activity and on human numbers, an ecological paradigm alone comes nowhere near explaining the dynamics of evolution among the Polynesian chiefdoms. For this we must turn to other factors and other analytical paradigms, one of which is demographic. In each of the three cases under consideration, relatively high levels of population density had been achieved by the time of European contact, although in no case had any absolute carrying capacity necessarily been reached. Although the data are presently skimpy, an early phase of rapid population increase and expansion in Tonga probably contributed to the intensity of inter-group competition and unification of the archipelago under a central polity. At contact, Tonga's population appears to have been relatively stable, though the cultural mechanisms of population regulation are not fully understood. Hawai'i presents a contrastive situation, for it is evident that the Hawaiian population had not reached any limits to production, and that substantially larger populations could have been supported in many areas. When we examine the Hawaiian demographic situation *on the local level*, however, we find an uneven geographic distribution of population, a reflection of the local hierarchy of ecological constraints. Thus the West Hawai'i region, in which irrigation was not feasible, appears to have reached .certain limits of agricultural development, which may account for a plateau seen in the local population growth curve. Indeed, *local* population imbalances may have been a significant dynamic factor in the political actions of the ruling chiefs, including the strategy of inter-district and island conquest. Nevertheless, while we can reasonably argue the importance of population increases in spurring on the process of political and social transformation, we must avoid the deterministic trap of mechanical population 'pressure'. While the West Hawai'i field systems may have reached limits of agricultural intensification, they could still have supported much larger populations *if*, for example, pigs had been removed from the production system. Pigs, however, were culturally defined as a vital component of the larger political economy, an essential element in the rituals that validated the paramount's claims to divine chiefship. In short, it is not that demographic pressure did not exist in Hawai'i or elsewhere in Polynesia, but that the local demographic situation was never independent, and was as much a product of social and political systems as of ecological constraints.

In Easter Island, population increase had its most dramatic consequences as we have seen. And yet, even for this ecologically marginal island with its limits to agricultural intensification, we have to seriously question whether it might not have been feasible, under less competitive, alternative systems of social integration, to support a population substantially larger than that actually achieved by the Rapanui Polynesians.

Population increase was surely one dynamic factor in Polynesia, but it too is not sufficient as an explanatory mechanism, and we must widen our scope to encompass other variables and other analytical paradigms in our search of an understanding of particular transformations. An important avenue is that of political economy, and here we are led back to some of the fundamental structures of Ancestral Polynesian Society. Neither the Tongans, Hawaiians, nor Easter Islanders invented the position of *ariki* or its related concepts of *mana* and *tapu*. Ancestral Polynesian Society was already hierarchically structured, and the demand for surplus was an integral part of the political economy. We simply cannot attribute the existence of hierarchical political systems in Polynesia to such functional explanations as the need for chiefs as redistributors of geographically dispersed resources (cf. Sahlins 1958), or as managers of irrigation networks which in turn resulted from 'population pressure'. Rather, the argument must run, in part at least, the other way around. Colonizing Polynesians in every case carried with them concepts of pyramidal social structure, of first fruits and tribute as obligatory to the chiefs, of chiefs as earthly representatives of ancestral deities. The principles of differential access to resources, of domination by the chiefs over labour and the means of production, were present in all Polynesian societies from the beginning.

Politically motivated demands for surplus production to finance the greater public economy, coupled with population increases, were the main factors which gave the spur to the intensification of agriculture and other components of production throughout Polynesia. The particular forms of intensification were constrained by local environmental circumstance, but also reflect such factors as symbolic and ritual systems. This is apparent, for example, in the emphasis placed on the production of ritually valued pigs in Tonga and Hawai'i, or of fowl in Easter Island, even though such production had obvious demographic costs. Likewise, the energy and effort expended in the collection or production of prestige goods – whether fine mats in Tonga or feather cloaks and helmets in Hawai'i – cannot be accounted for in simple ecological or demographic terms. Ultimately, however, the degree to which the political elite could (whether through ritual mystification or by outright coercion) direct the intensification of production to ever higher levels depended on the hierarchy of local ecological constraints, and on the critical balance between human populations and land. Thus it is not surprising that in Hawai'i, where the opportunities for intensification were virtually unsurpassed within the Polynesian region, we should find not only the most impressive technological development of production (irrigation, fishponds), but a scheme of consumption that was correspondingly differentiated on a hierarchical basis. To the extent that chiefs were successful in developing and intensifying production, they simultaneously enhanced their own status and power. In Easter Island, the political motivations of the chiefs ran up against the ecological reality of a too marginal environment, but not before a growing population had been induced to raise multi-ton monuments to the glory of ancestral gods.

The transformation of the Polynesian chiefdoms resulted from a more complex set of processes than just the demands of increasing populations, and of status-conscious chiefs, operating within the constraints of local environments. There is as well the matter of competition and warfare, a most significant dynamic factor in all of the societies we have considered. While competition can certainly be analysed in its ecological and demographic context, and while population increases and the political design of chiefs for aggrandizement of line and hegemony of power were real incentives to conquest, we must recognize that such functionalist explanations cannot fully account for the nature and importance of competition in Polynesia. We are again confronted with the persistence and transformation of ancient structural patterns, for as the linguistic evidence reveals, the concept of *toa*-ship existed before the settlement of most of Polynesia, and certainly before the invention of local patterns of fortification or combat. The structural opposition between *ariki* and *toa* is fundamental and ancient in Polynesia. On the other hand, the particular ways in which this opposition would be worked out depended a great deal on particular environmental and historical circumstances. That the concept of warrior existed in Easter Island is something owed to the ancestral Polynesian heritage, but that *matatoa* should rise to such a position of local political prominence does have a great deal to do with the particular historical interplay of population and production in a marginal, constrained environment.

Finally, along with the ecological, demographic, social, political, and economic paradigms which we have to apply in order to understand Polynesian sequences of evolution and transformation, we must add the symbolic, a recognition of the creativity of the human mind. For archaeologists, a symbolic paradigm is often regarded with, at best, reluctance, or worse, outright rejection as irrelevant, given the material nature of most archaeological data. Yet even if a symbolic or structuralist paradigm is often impossible to implement in archaeology, we cannot afford to lose sight of the dynamic role of individual creativity in cultural evolution. With a knowledge of Ancestral Polynesian social structure, an understanding of the local hierarchy of ecological constraints, an analysis of demographic process, and a comprehension of the technical aspects of production, one might predict that some form of inter-group competition was inevitable in Easter Island. But could one on such bases, possibly explain why these people should have turned their gazes to a sheer volcanic cliff, and imagined in its matrix giant stone images, and furthermore proceeded to the immense task of carving, transporting, and erecting these monoliths as their unique expression of competition? The power of over-arching symbolic systems, themselves the products of human creativity, to lend particular expression and organization to the material world is something that cannot be overlooked in our efforts to explain the human past.

In short, if we are to understand and explain the evolution of the Polynesian chiefdoms (or, indeed, other societies and cultures), it will not be on the basis of a single anthropological or archaeological paradigm. A major aim of this book has been to show the varied roles played by a variety of factors – structural, ecological, political, demographic, technological, and social – but also how each of these contributes only a *partial* understanding. We require *synthetic* explanations that integrate the several paradigms identified above, and yet the sociology of contemporary archaeology is such that most paradigms are constructed as alternative and competitive, rather than suppletive and reinforcing. Keesing (1982) recently addressed this problem in another explanatory context, and rightly observed that 'when we commit ourselves to a paradigm, perhaps powerful but inevitably sharply limited in scope, we try to pretend that it is global, even total' (1982:32). Surely here is a challenge for prehistory, and not only within the geographic confines of Oceania.

I am under no illusion that the attempt in this book to dissect and identify the main processes of evolution in the Polynesian chiefdoms is anything more than one stage in a continuing endeavour. The analyses and explanations presented here reflect very much the present state of our data base, as well as the current theoretical and methodological development of archaeology and anthropology. I close, therefore, with a few comments on where we might consider heading, on the kinds of data and approaches that are necessary if we are to advance our understanding of the prehistory of Polynesian societies.

As this book and other recent volumes demonstrate, the past three decades in Polynesian archaeology have seen great advances in our knowledge of the sequence of island colonization and of basic chronology, of sequences of prehistoric material culture, agricultural systems and fishing strategies, faunal sequences and diet, and prehistoric settlement patterns especially as these relate to local ecology (Kirch 1982c). Most of our efforts have been directed at the definition of culture-historical sequences for individual island groups and on the analysis of patterns of settlement, subsistence, and ecological adaptation. Although numerous problems in these areas remain to be worked out (such as the chronology for initial East Polynesian settlement), we already possess an extensive and valuable data base relevant to issues of chronology, material culture, subsistence, and settlement. It is time now to build on this base while expanding our vision of the kinds of data and approaches which will permit us to move boldly beyond ecological and economic interpretations of Polynesian society.

It is clear that we need more direct archaeological information concerning Ancestral Polynesian Society, that is, on the Lapitoid Period in West Polynesia and even extending into eastern Melanesia. The patterns of social and political organization which were crystallized in Ancestral Polynesian Society influenced the courses of cultural evolution throughout Polynesia, and we must develop a clearer picture of this ancestral baseline. Not only do we need to increase our sample of excavated Lapitoid sites, we must consider ways to improve our strategies of excavation, data recovery, and sampling on the regional level. While modern excavation sampling techniques have now been applied to a handful of Lapitoid sites, there has yet to be a single extensive areal excavation of a Lapitoid community. What insights might we gain to Ancestral Polynesian Society if we had at hand information on the structural layout of a community, including the intra-site distribution of faunal remains and artifacts? We might perhaps be able to make more informed statements on the nature and composition of ancestral household units, and on the degree of status differential. On a regional level, we must also address the issue of interrelations between individual Lapitoid communities; what sorts of exchange relations bound communities together? Did Ancestral Polynesian Society exhibit more highly developed lateral networks of integration than hierarchical integration? These are profound and difficult questions without facile answers, yet they cry out for attention.

Moving to the problem of cultural evolution within individual islands and archipelagos, we need a concerted effort to develop more extensive and precise reconstructions of prehistoric population growth. The Hawaiian data reported in Chapter 5 are only a preliminary attempt in this direction, and suffer from a number of methodological problems. Nonetheless, the Hawaiian data do indicate the potential for reconstructing the population dynamics of past societies. In my view, establishing prehistoric growth curves and rates of demographic change are more immediately significant problems than obtaining precise estimates of actual population sizes, although these too are desirable. The nature of most Polynesian structural sites and of settlement landscapes is such that a census-taking approach in archaeology is feasible. The task, however, will be a laborious one, for large samples must be obtained, and the problem of local and regional distribution of population must be dealt with.

Also worthy of investigation is the matter of the intensification of production systems, and the relationships between sequences of intensification and concomitant or simultaneous developments in demography and socio-political organization. We have made substantial advances in identifying, dating, and obtaining diachronic data from a variety of agricultural and other components of prehistoric production systems. Much of this work, however, is oriented toward functional reconstructions of the operation of systems at single points in time, rather than elucidating the temporal dimension of intensification.

Competition between social groups was a significant dynamic factor in the trend toward rendering Polynesian societies increasingly political and hierarchical, and the direct archaeological evidence of warfare, especially fortifications, can certainly be exploited to greater advantage. While single forts have been excavated in a number of localities, the temporal problem of the development and frequency of use of fortifications has not yet been seriously tackled, although the New Zealand data are becoming increasingly relevant. One may ponder the analytical possibilities for treating the political evolution of Rapan society, for example, if we knew – not just the structure and layout of Moronga Uta – but the constructional sequences and time frames for all of the major Rapan hill forts. Again, the task is almost forbiddingly massive, since the excavation of even a single fortress is often a major undertaking, and we must again be concerned with sampling on a truly regional scale.

Finally, we must explore new methods for exploiting our archaeological data for evidence of former patterns of social grouping, status differentiation, and political organization. The potential for mortuary analysis has hardly been explored in Polynesia, and our settlement pattern studies have tended to stress ecological and economic analyses and interpretations over the spatial evidence for social grouping and hierarchical organization. As in other parts of the world, ceremonial or temple architecture when dissected for sequences of construction and elaboration may reveal clues regarding major political events or realignments of power. In Hawai'i, where there are several thousand *heiau* or temple sites which were intimately linked with the ruling elite of chiefs and priests, we still have but a handful of excavated sites. These few (such as Alealea at Honaunau and Kane'aki in Makaha) have demonstrated the potential of temple architecture to pinpoint major periods or phases of political development or integration. However, anything like a comprehensive study of the temple architecture of even a single Hawaiian island has yet to be seriously conceived. Nor are mortuary or settlement pattern data our only sources for working out the time frame for social and political transformation in Polynesia. Artifacts of various sorts, most of them sitting unused in large museum collections, have the potential to reveal regional patterns of social and economic integration. Some work along these lines is beginning to be formulated in Hawai'i, where McCoy and his colleagues are concerned with the distribution of fine-grained basalt adzes from a limited number of large quarry sites.

Polynesia has finally passed through its stage of 'cowboy archaeology' (Jones 1980). The day is gone when a lone archaeologist can step ashore on archaeological terra incognita and, by excavating a few critically placed sites, lay bare the outlines of an entire island sequence, at the same time resolving age-old questions of cultural origins and time depth. This state of affairs is not so unromantic as it may seem, for the ground work has simply been laid for more significant investigations yet to come. We now have established a firm basis of culture history on which to address more fundamental questions. The origins and migrations of the Polynesians were problems that befuddled scholars for more than two centuries, but which have now been largely resolved. Although we shall probably argue over the minutiae for decades to come, Polynesia has far more important questions and issues to address, issues that extend to the very core of anthropology and prehistory. It could not be a better time to open doorways to the unexpected.

GLOSSARY OF POLYNESIAN TERMS

Terms not attributed to a specific island group are of widespread usage.

ahu (Easter Is.). A temple or place of worship, based on the Polynesian *marae* concept.

ahupua'a (Hawai'i). A radial land division, under the control of a chief, and sometimes considered to be an economically self-sufficient unit.

ali'i-'ai-moku (Hawai'i). Paramount chief.

ariki (variants: *aliki, ari'i, ali'i, 'eiki*). Widespread Polynesian term for chief, head of a descent group.

ariki-mau (Easter Is.). Paramount chief, usually from the Miru clan.

fahu (Tonga). A man's sister's child (especially male child), who has certain rights to appropriate the property of his mother's brother.

fa'itoka (Tonga). A burial mound, generally of sand or earth and sometimes stone-faced, used for multiple interments.

fono. An assembly of people (usually adult males); a decision-making body in some Polynesian societies.

hare moa (Easter Is.). A stone house or coop for keeping chickens (lit. 'house chicken').

hare paenga (Easter Is.). A boat-shaped house with cut-and-dressed foundation kerbstones, used by high-ranking persons.

hau (Tonga). The secular paramount, a position held at European contact by the Tu'i Kanokupolu.

heiau (Hawai'i). A temple, shrine, or similar place of worship; the Hawaiian term for the East Polynesian concept of *marae*.

ho'okupu (Hawai'i). The tribute presented to a chief by the *maka'ainana*, particularly during the annual *makahiki* festival (lit. 'to cause growth').

'ili (Hawai'i). A land division smaller than an *ahupua'a* in size. *Ahupua'a* were generally subdivided into a series of *'ili*.

'inasi (Tonga). An annual presentation of first fruits and other tribute to the sacred paramount, the Tu'i Tonga. Usually held at Mu'a.

ivi-atua (Easter Is.). The class of priests.

kahuna-nui (Hawai'i). Chief priest of the Ku cult and principal officiant at ceremonies involving the paramount chief.

kai. General Polynesian term for food.

kainga (variants: *'ainga, kainanga, mata'einana*). A land-holding, cognatic descent group; term often applies also to the land held by such a group.

kalaimoku (Hawai'i). Councillor and principal executant of the paramount chief.

kalia (Tonga). A large, double-hulled canoe used for inter-island voyaging.

kama'aina (Hawai'i). A native of a particular locality, frequently with usufruct land rights (lit. 'child of the land').

287

kanawai (Hawai'i). Law, code, rule (lit. 'pertaining to water').

kapu (Hawai'i). The Hawaiian reflex of the general Polynesian term *tapu*, sacred, prohibited.

kava (variant: *'awa*). A non-alcoholic, narcotic infusion made from the plant (*Piper methysticum*) of the same name; also a ceremony involving the use of this beverage.

kio (Easter Is.). Commoners; defeated persons obliged to work for and pay tribute to their conquerors, especially *matatoa*.

ko'ele (Hawai'i). A small unit of land (often a set of irrigated fields) worked by commoners for the *konohiki* or chief.

kolo (Tonga). A fortress or fortified village.

koloa (Tonga). Valued property, such as mats and barkcloth, traditionally used as items of exchange.

konohiki (Hawai'i). The steward of a chief, responsible for the administration of his lands, for the mobilization of corvée labour, and for the collection of tribute.

Ku (Hawai'i). The god of war (see *luakini*).

kuaiwi (Hawai'i). A low alignment of stone or earth, dividing garden plots in dryfield cultivation systems (lit. 'back bone').

kuhina nui (Hawai'i). Powerful official during the early monarchy, generally translated as 'premier' or 'prime minister'.

kumara (variant: *'uala*). The sweet potato (*Ipomoea batatas*), an American cultigen introduced prehistorically to East Polynesia, and an important crop in New Zealand, Easter Island, and Hawai'i.

kutunga (Futuna). A maximal, cognatic descent group.

langi (Tonga). Burial mounds of the sacred paramount (Tu'i Tonga) and his immediate family.

Lono (Hawai'i). The god of agriculture and fertility, and of the *makahiki* harvest festival.

luakini (Hawai'i). A class of temple (*heiau*) dedicated to Ku, god of war, at which human sacrifices were offered by the paramount chief.

ma (variants: *masi, mahi*). Fermented, pit-ensiled, starch pastes, particularly of breadfruit, which will store for a number of years.

maka'ainana (Hawai'i). The class of commoners (a reflex of the older Polynesian term **kainanga*).

makahiki (Hawai'i). Annual harvest festival, dedicated to the god Lono; generally beginning about mid October and lasting four months.

makatea. Upraised coral reef.

mana. Supernatural power or efficacy, transferred from the deities to the chief by virtue of his descent.

manahune (Society Is.). Commoners; members of the lowest marriage class.

manavai (Easter Is.). A stone-walled, sometimes sunken, garden enclosure, used for cultivating taro, bananas, and other crops.

manutara (Easter Is.). The sooty tern, and a cult of the same name, based on an annual contest to recover the first tern's egg.

marae (variants: *malae, mala'e*). Throughout Polynesia, a ceremonial precinct; elaborated in East Polynesia as a formal temple.

mata'a (Easter Is.). Flaked spearhead of obsidian.

matapule (Tonga). A chief's attendant and spokesman; generally an inherited position.

matatoa (Easter Is.). The class of warriors (see *toa*).

moa (New Zealand). A class of large, flightless, struthious birds, endemic to New Zealand, and now extinct.

moku (Hawai'i). The territory occupied by an independent chiefdom, usually an entire island (from Proto-Polynesian **motu*, 'island').

mo'o 'aina (Hawai'i). A land division smaller in size than an *'ili*; usually cultivated by a household unit.

mua (Hawai'i). Men's eating house; also the scene of various male ceremonies and incorporating a kind of shrine (*heiau*); (lit. 'front').

muakai (Tikopia). First fruits offered to a chief (lit. 'foremost foods').

'oloa (Hawai'i). Fine white tapa, placed or draped over an image during temple ceremonies.

onge (variant: *honge*). Famine, particularly that resulting from a natural disaster.

'Oro (Society Is.). A principal deity and most powerful god of war, to whom human sacrifices were offered.

pa (New Zealand). A fortified settlement, usually situated on a hill or headland, and with defensive ditches and pallisades.

pare (Rapa). A hilltop fortification or fortified village site.

patu (New Zealand). A hand club (similar clubs have been excavated in the Society Islands).

pi'o, ni'aupi'o (Hawai'i). Offspring of a brother–sister, or half-brother and half-sister union.

po'alima (Hawai'i). Work done on a chief's plantations, on a weekly basis (lit. 'fifth day').

pu'uhonua (Hawai'i). Place of refuge or asylum; usually also a temple.

rahui (variants: *ahui, ra'ui*). A chiefly interdiction or prohibition on the use of particular resources, frequently agricultural.

rauti (Society Is.). Exhorters or orators of battle, who urged on the warriors.

renga (variants: *lena, 'olena*). Turmeric plant (*Cucurma domestica*) and the orange dye produced from its tuber, used ritually.

rongorongo (Easter Is.). Wooden tablets bearing a script in reversed boustrophedon.

tangata manu (Easter Is.). Winner of the annual contest at Orongo to capture the first tern's egg (lit. 'bird man').

tapere (Rarotonga). A radial land segment, the basic territorial divisions of the island.

tapu. Sacred, prohibited.

tautai. Expert navigator, seaman, or fisherman.

tehina (Tonga). Younger sibling of the same sex.

toa (variants: *matatoa, koa*). Warrior.

toafa (Futuna, 'Uvea). Anthropogenic, degraded land, usually laterized, supporting a terminal climax vegetation dominated by a fern (*Dicranopteris linearis*).

tufunga (variant: *kahuna*). Expert, particularly with regard to a special skill or craft (in Hawai'i, *kahuna* were priests).

tu'i (Tonga). A paramount chief; lord of a place (e.g., Tu'i Tonga, Tu'i Ha'a Takalaua).

waiwai (Hawai'i). Property, wealth, valued goods (reduplication of *wai,* 'water').

REFERENCES

Acsadi, G. and J. Nemeskeri. 1970. *History of Human Life Span and Mortality.* Budapest: Akademiai Kiado

Adamson, A.M. 1932. Myriopoda of the Marquesas Islands. *Bernice P. Bishop Museum Bulletin* 98:225–32

    1936. Marquesan insects: environment. *Bernice P. Bishop Museum Bulletin* 139

    1939. Review of the fauna of the Marquesas Islands and discussion of its origin. *Bernice P. Bishop Museum Bulletin* 159

Aitken, R.T. 1930. Ethnology of Tubuai. *Bernice P. Bishop Museum Bulletin* 70

Allen, B. 1971. Wet-field taro terraces on Mangaia, Cook Islands. *Journal of the Polynesian Society* 80:371–8

Allen, M.S. 1981. An analysis of the Mauna Kea Adz Quarry archaeo-botanical assemblage. M.A. thesis, University of Hawai'i

Ambrose, W. 1968. The unimportance of the inland plains in South Island prehistory. *Mankind* 6:585–93

Ambrose, W. and R.C. Green. 1972. First millenium BC transport of obsidian from New Britain to the Solomon Islands. *Nature* 237:31

Ammerman, A.J., L.L. Cavalli-Sforza, and D.K. Wagener. 1976. Toward the estimation of population growth in Old World prehistory. In *Demographic Anthropology*, ed. E. Zubrow, pp. 27–61. Albuquerque: University of New Mexico Press

Anderson, A.J. 1979a. Excavations at the Hawksburn moa-hunting site: an interim report. *New Zealand Archaeological Association Newsletter* 22:48–59

    1979b. Prehistoric exploitation of marine resources at Black Rocks point, Palliser Bay. In *Prehistoric Man in Palliser Bay*, ed. B.F. Leach and H. Leach, pp. 49–65. *National Museum of New Zealand Bulletin* 21

    1980a. Towards an explanation of protohistoric social organisation and settlement patterns amongst the southern Ngai Tahu. *New Zealand Journal of Archaeology* 2:3–23

    1980b. The archaeology of Raoul Island (Kermadecs) and its place in the settlement history of Polynesia. *Archaeology and Physical Anthropology in Oceania* 15:131–41

    1981. A model of collecting on the rocky shore. *Journal of Archaeological Science* 8:109–20

    1982a. North and Central Otago. In *The First Thousand Years: Regional Perspectives in New Zealand Archaeology*, ed. N. Prickett, pp. 112–28. Palmerston North: New Zealand Archaeological Association

    1982b. A review of economic patterns during the Archaic Phase in Southern New Zealand. *New Zealand Journal of Archaeology* 4:45–75

    1983. *When all the moa-ovens grew cold.* Otago: Otago Heritage Books

Anderson, E. 1952. *Plants, Man, and Life*. Berkeley: University of California Press

Angel, J.L. 1969. The bases of paleodemography. *American Journal of Physical Anthropology* 30:427–38

Archey, G. 1941. The moa: a study of the Dinornithiformes. *Bulletin of the Auckland Institute and Museum* no. 1

Athens, J.S. 1983. Prehistoric pondfield agriculture in Hawai'i: archaeological investigations at the Hanalei National Wildlife Refuge, Kaua'i. Typescript report in Department of Anthropology, Bernice P. Bishop Museum, Honolulu

Ayres, W. 1973. The cultural context of Easter Island religious structures. Ph.D. dissertation, Tulane University

  1975. Easter Island: investigations in prehistoric cultural dynamics. Mimeographed report prepared for the National Science Foundation

  1979. Easter Island fishing. *Asian Perspectives* 22:61–92

Baker, P.T. and W.T. Sanders. 1972. Demographic studies in anthropology. *Annual Review of Anthropology* 1:151–78

Barrau, J. 1961. Subsistence agriculture in Polynesia and Micronesia. *Bernice P. Bishop Museum Bulletin* 223

  1965a. L'humide et le sec: an essay on ethnobiological adaptation to contrastive environments in the Indo-Pacific area. *Journal of the Polynesian Society* 74:329–46

  1965b. Histoire et préhistoire horticoles de l'Océanie tropicale. *Journal de la Société des Océanistes* 21:55–78

  1965c. Witnesses of the past: notes on some food plants of Oceania. *Ethnology* 4:282–94

Barrau, J. and A. Peeters. 1972. Histoire et préhistoire de la préparation des aliments d'origine végétal: les techniques d'utilisation de ces aliments chez les cueilleurs et les cultivateurs archaïques de l'Australasie. *Journal de la Société des Océanistes* 35:141–52

Barrera, W. Jr. 1971. Anaeho'omalu: a Hawaiian oasis. *Pacific Anthropological Records* 15

Barrera, W. Jr. and P.V. Kirch. 1973. Basaltic glass artefacts from Hawaii: their dating and prehistoric uses. *Journal of the Polynesian Society* 82:176–87

Barrere, D. and M. Kelly. 1980. Background history of the Kona area, Island of Hawai'i. Typescript report (ms. no. 010181) in Department of Anthropology, Bernice P. Bishop Museum, Honolulu

Barthel, T.S. 1971. Pre-contact writing in Oceania. In *Current Trends in Linguistics*, vol. 8, *Linguistics in Oceania*, ed. T.A. Sebeok, pp. 1165–86. The Hague: Mouton

  1978. *The Eighth Land: the Polynesian Discovery and Settlement of Easter Island*. Honolulu: University Press of Hawai'i.

Bates, M. 1956. Man as an agent in the spread of organisms. In *Man's role in changing the face of the earth*, vol. 2, ed. W.L. Thomas, pp. 788–804. University of Chicago Press

Bayard, D.T. 1976. The cultural relationships of the Polynesian outliers. *University of Otago Studies in Prehistoric Anthropology* 9

Bayliss-Smith, T. 1974. Constraints on population growth: the case of the Polynesian outlier atolls in the precontact period. *Human Ecology* 2:259–95

Bayly, W. ms. Journal of William Bayly (astronomer in *Adventure*, J. Cook's second voyage, 1772–5). Wellington: Alexander Turnbull Library

Beaglehole, E. and P. Beaglehole. 1938. Ethnology of Pukapuka. *Bernice P. Bishop Museum Bulletin* 150

292   *References*

Beaglehole, J.C. (ed.). 1967. *The Journals of Captain James Cook on his Voyages of Discovery*. Vol. 3, *The Voyage of the Resolution and Discovery*. Cambridge: Hakluyt Society
  1969. *The Journals of Captain James Cook on his Voyages of Discovery*. Vol. 2, *The Voyage of the Resolution and Adventure, 1772–1775*. Cambridge: Hakluyt Society
Beckwith, M.W. (ed.). 1932. Kepelino's traditions of Hawaii. *Bernice P. Bishop Museum Bulletin* 95
Bell, F.L. 1931. The place of food in the social life of central Polynesia. *Oceania* 2:117–35
Bellwood, P. 1970. Dispersal centers in East Polynesia, with special reference to the Society and Marquesas Islands. In *Studies in Oceanic Culture History*, ed. R. Green and M. Kelly, pp. 93–104. *Pacific Anthropological Records* 11
  1971. Fortifications and economy in prehistoric New Zealand. *Proceedings of the Prehistoric Society* (n.s.) 37:56–95
  1972a. Settlement pattern survey, Hanatekua Valley, Hiva Oa, Marquesas Islands. *Pacific Anthropological Records* 17
  1972b. Excavations at Otakanini Pa, South Kaipara Harbour. *Journal of the Royal Society of New Zealand* 2:259–91
  1976. Indonesia, the Philippines, and Oceanic prehistory. In *La Préhistoire Océanienne*, ed. J. Garanger, pp. 7–26. Nice: Union Internationale des Sciences Préhistoriques et Protohistoriques, IXe Congrès (prétirage)
  1978a. *The Polynesians: Prehistory of an Island People*. London: Thames and Hudson
  1978b. Archaeological research in the Cook Islands. *Pacific Anthropological Records* 27
  1979. *Man's Conquest of the Pacific*. New York: Oxford
Bennett, K.A. 1973. On the estimation of some demographic characteristics of a prehistoric population from the American southwest. *American Journal of Physical Anthropology* 29:223–32
Best, E. 1925. Maori agriculture. *Dominion Museum Bulletin* 9
  1927. The pa Maori. *Dominion Museum Bulletin* 6
Best, S. 1981. Excavations at Site VL 21/5, Naigani Island, Fiji: a preliminary report. Typescript report, Department of Anthropology, University of Auckland
Bevacqua, R.F. (ed.). 1972. Archaeological survey of portions of Waikoloa, South Kohala District, Island of Hawaii. *Department of Anthropology Report* 72–4. Bernice P. Bishop Museum, Honolulu
Biggs, B. 1971. The languages of Polynesia. In *Current Trends in Linguistics*, vol. 8, part 1, ed. T.A. Sebeok, pp. 466–505. The Hague: Mouton
  1980. The position of East 'Uvean and Anutan in the Polynesian language family. *Te Reo* 23:115–34
Biggs, B., D.S. Walsh, and J. Waga. 1970. Proto-Polynesian reconstructions with English to Proto-Polynesian finder list. *Working Papers in Linguistics*, Department of Anthropology, University of Auckland
Birdsell, J.B. 1957. Some population problems involving Pleistocene man. *Cold Spring Harbor Symposia on Quantitative Biology* 22:47–69
Birks, L. 1973. Archaeological excavations at Sigatoka Dune Site, Fiji. *Fiji Museum Bulletin* 1
Black, S. 1979. Polynesian outliers: a study in the survival of small populations. In *Simulation Studies in Archaeology*, ed. Ian Hodder, pp. 63–76. Cambridge University Press
Bloch, M. 1966. *French rural history* (translated by J. Sondheimer). Berkeley: University of California Press

Bonk, W.J. 1969. Lua Nunu o Kamakalepo: a cave of refuge in Ka'u, Hawaii. In *Archaeology on the Island of Hawaii*, ed. R. Pearson, pp. 75–92. *Asian and Pacific Archaeology Series* 3. Social Science Research Institute, University of Hawai'i.

Borrie, W.D., R. Firth, and J. Spillius. 1957. The population of Tikopia, 1929 and 1952. *Population Studies* 10:229–52

Boserup, E. 1965. *The Conditions of Agricultural Growth: the Economics of Agrarian Change under Population Pressure*. London: Allen and Unwin

Bott, E. 1982. Tongan society at the time of Captain Cook's visits: discussions with her Majesty Queen Salote Tupou. *Polynesian Society Memoir* 44. Wellington

Brailsford, B. 1981. *The Tattooed Land: the Southern Frontiers of the Pa Maori*. Wellington: A.H. and A.W. Reed

Brookfield, H.C. 1972. Intensification and disintensification in Pacific agriculture: a theoretical approach. *Pacific Viewpoint* 13:30–48

1976. On the notion of population thresholds. In *Population at Microscale*, ed. L.A. Kosinski and J. Webb, pp. 31–5. New Zealand Geographical Society.

Brown, J.M. 1907. *Maori and Polynesian: their Origin, History and Culture*. London: Hutchinson

Buck, P.H. (Te Rangi Hiroa). 1930. Samoan material culture. *Bernice P. Bishop Museum Bulletin* 75

1932. Ethnology of Tongareva. *Bernice P. Bishop Museum Bulletin* 92

1934. Mangaian society. *Bernice P. Bishop Museum Bulletin* 122

1938a. Ethnology of Mangareva. *Bernice P. Bishop Museum Bulletin* 157

1938b. *Vikings of the Sunrise*. New York: Frederick A. Stockes Co.

1944. Arts and crafts of the Cook Islands. *Bernice P. Bishop Museum Bulletin* 179

1957. Arts and crafts of Hawaii. *Bernice P. Bishop Museum Special Publication* 45

Burrows, E.G. 1936. Ethnology of Futuna. *Bernice P. Bishop Museum Bulletin* 138

1937. Ethnology of Uvea. *Bernice P. Bishop Museum Bulletin* 145

1938. Topography and culture on two Polynesian islands. *The Geographical Review* 28:214–23

1939a. Western Polynesia: a study in cultural differentiation. *Ethnological Studies* 7. Gothenburg

1939b. Breed and border in Polynesia. *American Anthropologist* 41:1–21

Carneiro, R.L. 1972. From autonomous villages to the state, a numerical estimation. In *Population Growth: Anthropological Implications*, ed. B. Spooner, pp. 64–77. Cambridge: MIT Press

Carrington, H. (ed.). 1948. *The Discovery of Tahiti* [Journal of Captain Wallis]. Hakluyt Society Second Series No. XCVIII. London: Cambridge University Press

Cassels, R. 1974. Explanations of change in New Zealand prehistory. Mimeo. Prepared for Blenheim Conference, New Zealand Archaeological Association

1978–9. Extinction and survival of birds through the prehistoric human occupation of the islands of Oceania: a review. *Ethnomed.* 5:493–6

1979. Whatever happened to New Zealand's moas?. *Wildlife* 21:31–3

ms., n.d. Faunal extinction and prehistoric man in New Zealand and the Pacific Islands. Copy in author's possession

Chanel, P. 1960. Ecrits du père Pierre Chanel. *Publications de la Société des Océanistes* 9. Paris

Chang, K.C. 1969. Fengpitou, Tapenkeng, and the prehistory of Taiwan. *Yale*

University Publications in Anthropology 73

Chazine, J.-M. 1977. Prospections archéologiques à Takapoto. *Journal de la Société des Océanistes* 56–7:191–214

Choy, P. 1973. Analysis of an upland agricultural feature in Lapakahi. In Lapakahi, Hawaii: Archaeological Studies, ed. H. Tuggle and P. Griffin, pp. 147–66. *Asian and Pacific Archaeology Series* 5. Social Science Research Institute, University of Hawai'i

Christensen, C.C. 1981. Preliminary analysis of non-marine mollusks from the Fa'ahia archaeological site (ScH1-2), Huahine, Society Islands. Typescript report in Department of Anthropology, Bernice P. Bishop Museum

Christensen, C.C. and P.V. Kirch. 1981a. Non-marine molluscs from archaeological sites on Tikopia, Solomon Islands. *Pacific Science* 35:75–88

1981b. Landsnails and environmental change at Barbers Point, Oahu, Hawaii. *Bulletin American Malacological Union* 1981:31

Christiansen, F. and T. Fenchel. 1977. *Theories of populations in biological communities.* New York: Springer-Verlag

Chubb, L.J. 1930. Geology of the Marquesas Islands. *Bernice P. Bishop Museum Bulletin* 68

Churchill, W. 1912. Easter Island: the Rapanui speech and the peopling of Southeast Polynesia. *Carnegie Institution of Washington, Publication* 174

Clark, J. 1981. Preliminary report on the intensive archaeological survey of the proposed Lalamilo agricultural park, Kohala, Island of Hawai'i. Typescript report in Department of Anthropology, Bernice P. Bishop Museum

Clark, J. and P.V. Kirch (eds.). 1983. Archaeological investigations in the Mudlane–Waimea–Kawaihae Road Corridor, Island of Hawai'i: an interdisciplinary study of an environmental transect. *Department of Anthropology Report* 83–1. Bernice P. Bishop Museum

Clark, J. and J. Terrell. 1978. Archaeology in Oceania. *Annual Review of Anthropology* 7:293–319

Clark, R. 1975. Comment on Polynesian sibling terms. *American Anthropologist* 77:85–8

1979. Language. In *The Prehistory of Polynesia*, ed. J. Jennings, pp. 249–70. Cambridge (Mass.): Harvard University Press

Collocott, E.E.V. 1922. The speech of Niua Fo'ou. *Journal of the Polynesian Society* 31:185–9

Conklin, H.C. 1957. Hanunoo agriculture. *FAO Forestry Development Paper* 12

1980. *Ethnographic atlas of Ifugao.* New Haven: Yale University Press

Connelly, D.M. 1976. A model for political analysis in Oceania. M.A. thesis, Southern Illinois University

Cook, S. 1972. *Prehistoric Demography.* Reading: Addison-Wesley

Cooke, C.M. Jr. 1926. Notes on Pacific land snails. *Proceedings of the Third Pan-Pacific Science Congress*, pp. 2276–84. Tokyo

1935. Report on the Mangarevan expedition. *Bernice P. Bishop Museum Bulletin* 133:36–56

Cooke, C.M. Jr. and Y. Kondo. 1960. Revision of Tornatellinidae and Achatinellidae. *Bernice P. Bishop Museum Bulletin* 221

Cordy, R. 1974a. Cultural adaptation and evolution in Hawaii: a suggested new sequence. *Journal of the Polynesian Society* 83:180–91

1974b. Complex rank cultural systems in the Hawaiian Islands: suggested explanations for their origin. *Archaeology and Physical Anthropology in Oceania* 9:89–109

1981. *A study of prehistoric social change: the development of complex societies in the Hawaiian Islands.* New York: Academic Press

Cordy, R. and M. Kaschko. 1980. Prehistoric archaeology in the Hawaiian Islands: land units associated with social groups. *Journal of Field Archaeology* 7:403–16

Cox, P.A. 1980. Masi and tanu 'eli: ancient Polynesian technologies for the preservation and concealment of food. *Pacific Tropical Botanical Garden Bulletin* 10:81–93

Cracraft, J. 1976. The species of moa (Aves:Dinornithidae). *Smithsonian Contributions to Paleobiology* 27:189–205

Crozier, S.N. 1971. Archaeological excavations at Kamehameha III Road, North Kona, Island of Hawaii, Phase II. *Department of Anthropology Report* 71–11. Bernice P. Bishop Museum

Cumberland, K.B. 1961. Man *in* nature in New Zealand. *New Zealand Geographer* 17:137–54

1962a. Moas and men: New Zealand about AD 1250. *The Geographical Review* 52:151–73

1962b. The future of Polynesia. *Journal of the Polynesian Society* 71:386–96

Currey, B. 1980. Famine in the Pacific. *GeoJournal* 4:447–66

Dalton, G. 1960. A note of clarification on economic surplus. *American Anthropologist* 62:483–90

Daugherty, J.S. 1979. Polynesian warfare and fortifications. M.A. thesis, University of Auckland

Davenport, W. 1959. Non-unilinear descent and descent groups. *American Anthropologist* 61:557–72

Davidson, J. 1969. Archaeological excavations in two burial mounds at 'Atele, Tongatapu. *Records of the Auckland Institute and Museum* 6:251–86

1971. Preliminary report on an archaeological survey of the Vava'u Group, Tonga. *Royal Society of New Zealand Bulletin* 8:29–40

1979. Samoa and Tonga. In *The Prehistory of Polynesia*, ed. J. Jennings, pp. 82–109. Cambridge (Mass.): Harvard University Press

Davis, B. 1978. Human settlement and environmental change at Barbers Point, Oahu. *Proceedings of the Second Conference in Natural Sciences, Hawaii Volcanoes National Park*, pp. 87–97. Honolulu

Dening, G. (ed.). 1974. *The Marquesan Journal of Edward Robarts, 1797–1824.* Honolulu: The University Press of Hawai'i

Derrick, R.A. 1946. *A History of Fiji.* Suva: Government Printer

Diamond, J.M. 1977. Colonization cycles in man and beast. *World Archaeology* 8:249–61

Dickinson, W.R. and R. Shutler, Jr. 1974. Probable Fijian origin of quartzose temper sands in prehistoric pottery from Tonga and the Marquesas. *Science* 185:454–7

Dobzhansky, T. 1963. Biological evolution in island populations. In *Man's Place in the Island Ecosystem*, ed. F.R. Fosberg, pp. 65–74. Honolulu: Bishop Museum Press

Donovan, L.J. 1973. A study of the decorative system of the Lapita potters in Reefs and Santa Cruz Islands. M.A. thesis, University of Auckland

Duff, R. 1956. *The moa hunter period of Maori culture.* (Second edition.) Wellington: Government Printer

1967. The evolution of Maori warfare. *New Zealand Archaeological Association Newsletter* 10:114–29

Dye, T.S. 1980. The linguistic position of Niuafo'ou. *Journal of the Polynesian Society* 89:349–57 in press. Fish and fishing in Niuatoputapu, Tonga. *Oceania*

Dyen, I. 1971. The Austronesian languages and Proto-Austronesian. In *Current Trends in Linguistics*, vol. 8, part 1, ed. T.A. Sebeok, pp. 5–54. The Hague: Mouton

Dyen, I. and D. Aberle. 1974. *Lexical reconstruction: the case of the Proto-Athapaskan kinship system.* London: Cambridge University Press

Earle, T.K. 1977. A reappraisal of redistribution: complex Hawaiian chiefdoms. In *Exchange Systems in Prehistory*, ed. T. Earle, pp. 213–29. New York: Academic Press

    1978. Ecomonic and social organization of a complex chiefdom: the Halelea District, Kaua'i, Hawaii. *University of Michigan Museum of Anthropology Anthropological Papers* 63

    1980. Prehistoric irrigation in the Hawaiian Islands: an evaluation of evolutionary significance. *Archaeology and Physical Anthropology in Oceania* 15:1–28

Elbert, S. 1953. Internal relationships of Polynesian languages and dialects. *Southwestern Journal of Anthropology* 9:147–73

Emory, K.P. 1928. Archaeology of Nihoa and Necker Islands. *Bernice P. Bishop Museum Bulletin* 53

    1933. Stone remains in the Society Islands. *Bernice P. Bishop Museum Bulletin* 116

    1934. Archaeology of the Pacific Equatorial Islands. *Bernice P. Bishop Museum Bulletin* 123

    1939. Archaeology of Mangareva and neighboring atolls. *Bernice P. Bishop Museum Bulletin* 163

    1946. Eastern Polynesia: its cultural relationships. Ph.D. dissertation, Yale University

Emory, K.P., W.J. Bonk, and Y.H. Sinoto. 1959. Hawaiian Archaeology: Fishhooks. *Bernice P. Bishop Museum Special Publication* 47

Emory, K.P. and Y. Sinoto. 1964. Eastern Polynesian burials at Maupiti. *Journal of the Polynesian Society* 73:143–60

    1961. Hawaiian archaeology: Oahu excavations. *Bernice P. Bishop Museum Special Publication* 49

    1969. Age of the sites in the South Point area, Ka'u, Hawaii. *Pacific Anthropological Records* 8

Emory, K.P. *et al.* 1957. The natural and cultural history of Honaunau, Kona, Hawaii. Mimeo. Bernice P. Bishop Museum

Englert, Père S. 1948. *La tierra de Hotu Matu'a.* Padre las Casas

    1970. *Island at the center of the world.* New York: Charles Scribner's Sons

Epling, J.P., J. Kirk, and J.P. Boyd. 1973. Genetic relations of Polynesian sibling terminologies. *American Anthropologist* 75:1596–1625

Ferdon, E.N. Jr. 1961. A summary of the excavated record of Easter Island prehistory. In *Archaeology of Easter Island*, ed. T. Heyerdahl and E.N. Ferdon, Jr, pp. 527–36. Monographs of the School of American Research 24(1)

    1965. A summary of Rapa Iti fortified villages. In *Reports of the Norwegian Archaeological Expedition to Easter Island and the East Pacific*, ed. T. Heyerdahl and E.N. Ferdon, Jr, vol. 2, pp. 69–76. Monographs of the School of American Research 24(2)

Finney, B. 1966. Resource distribution and social structure in Tahiti. *Ethnology* 5:80–6

    1977. Voyaging canoes and the settlement of Polynesia. *Science* 196:1277–85

Firth, R. 1936. *We, the Tikopia.* London: George Allen and Unwin

1939. *Primitive Polynesian Economy.* London: George Routledge and Sons
1957. A note on descent groups in Polynesia. *Man* 57:4–8
1959. *Social Change in Tikopia.* New York: MacMillan Co.
1961. History and traditions of Tikopia. *Polynesian Society Memoir* 33
1967. *The Work of the Gods in Tikopia.* New York: Humanities Press
Flannery, K.V. and M. Coe. 1968. Social and economic systems in formative Mesoamerica. In *New Perspectives in Archaeology,* ed. S. and L. Binford, pp. 267–84. Chicago: Aldine
Fleming, C.A. 1962. The extinction of moas and other animals during the Holocene period. *Notornis* 10:113–17
Flenley, J.P. 1979. Stratigraphic evidence of environmental change on Easter Island. *Asian Perspectives* 22:33–40
1981. The late quaternary palyno-flora of Easter Island. Paper presented at the XIII International Botanical Congress, Sydney
Fornander, A. 1880. *An Account of the Polynesian Race.* London: Trubner
1916–20. Fornander collection of Hawaiian antiquities and folk-lore, ed. T. Thrum. *Bernice P. Bishop Museum Memoirs* 4–6
Fosberg, F.R. 1963a. The island ecosystem. In *Man's Place in the Island Ecosystem,* ed. F.R. Fosberg, pp. 1–6. Honolulu: Bishop Museum Press
1963b. Disturbance in island ecosystems. In *Pacific Basin Biogeography,* ed. J. Gressitt, pp. 557–61. Honolulu: Bishop Museum Press
Fox, A. 1974. The pa at Pawhetau Point, Kawakawa Bay, Clevedon. *Records of the Auckland Institute and Museum* 11
1976. *Prehistoric Maori fortifications.* Auckland: Longman Paul
1978. Tiromoana Pa, Te Awanga, Hawke's Bay: excavations 1974–5. *New Zealand Archaeological Association Monograph* 8
Fox, A. and R.C. Green. 1982. Excavations at Maioro, N51/5, South Auckland, 1965–66. *Records of the Auckland Institute and Museum* 19:53–80
Fox, R.B. 1970. The Tabon Caves: archaeological explorations and excavations on Palawan Island, Philippines. *Monograph of the National Museum* 1, Manilla
Freeman, J.D. 1961. Review of Sahlins 1958. *Man* 61:146–8
1964. Some observations on kinship and political authority in Samoa. *American Anthropologist* 66:553–68
Freeman, O.W. (ed.). 1951. *Geography of the Pacific.* New York: John Wiley and Sons
Fried, M. 1967. *The evolution of political society.* New York: Random House
Friedman, J. 1979. System, structure, and contradiction in the evolution of 'Asiatic' social formations. National Museum of Denmark, *Social Studies in Oceania and South East Asia* 2
1981. Notes on structure and history in Oceania. *Folk* 23:275–95
1982. Catastrophe and continuity in social evolution. In *Theory and Explanation in Archeology,* ed. C. Renfrew, M. Rowlands, and B. Seagraves, pp. 175–96. New York: Academic Press
Friedman, J. and M. Rowlands. 1978. Notes toward an epigenetic model of the evolution of 'civilisation'. In *The Evolution of Social Systems,* ed. J. Friedman and M. Rowlands, pp. 201–76. University of Pittsburgh Press
Frost, E. 1979. Fiji. In *The Prehistory of Polynesia,* ed. J. Jennings, pp. 61–81. Cambridge (Mass.): Harvard University Press
Gathercole, P. 1964. Preliminary report on archaeological fieldwork on Pitcairn Island, January–March 1964. Mimeo. Cambridge University
Giddens, A. 1981. *A Contemporary Critique of Historical Materialism.* Berkeley: University of California Press

Gifford, E.W. 1924. Tongan myths and tales. *Bernice P. Bishop Museum Bulletin* 8

1929. Tongan society. *Bernice P. Bishop Museum Bulletin* 61

1951. Archaeological excavations in Fiji. *University of California Anthropological Records* 13:189–288

Gifford, E.W. and R. Shutler, Jr. 1956. Archaeological excavations in New Caledonia. *University of California Anthropological Records* 18:1–148

Glassow, M. 1978. The concept of carrying capacity in the study of culture process. *Advances in Archaeological Method and Theory* 1:31–48

Glover, I.C. 1977. The Late Stone Age in eastern Indonesia. *World Archaeology* 9:42–61

Goldman, I. 1955. Status rivalry and cultural evolution in Polynesia. *American Anthropologist* 57:680–97

1970. *Ancient Polynesian society.* University of Chicago Press

Golson, J. 1957a. Field archaeology in New Zealand. *Journal of the Polynesian Society* 66:64–109

1957b. Report to Tri-Institutional Pacific Program on archaeological field work in Tonga and Samoa. Mimeo. University of Auckland

1962. (ed.). Polynesian navigation: a symposium. *Polynesian Society Memoir* 34

1965. Thor Heyerdahl and the prehistory of Easter Island. *Oceania* 36:38–83

1971. Lapita ware and its transformations. In *Studies in Oceanic Culture History*, ed. R. Green and M. Kelly, pp. 67–76. *Pacific Anthropological Records* 12

1972a. The Pacific Islands and their prehistoric inhabitants. In *Man in the Pacific Islands*, ed. R. Ward, pp. 5–33. Oxford University Press

1972b. Both sides of the Wallace Line: New Guinea, Australia, Island Melanesia, and Asian prehistory. In *Early Chinese Art and its Possible Influence in the Pacific Basin*, ed. N. Barnard, pp. 533–95. New York: Intercultural Arts Press

Goodenough, W. 1955. A problem in Malayo-Polynesian social organization. *American Anthropologist* 57:71–83

1957. Oceania and the problem of controls in the study of cultural and human evolution. *Journal of the Polynesian Society* 66:146–55

Gorbey, K. 1967. Climatic change in New Zealand archaeology. *New Zealand Archaeological Association Newsletter* 10:176–82

Gorman, C. 1971. The Hoabinhian and after: subsistence patterns in Southeast Asia during the late Holocene and early Recent periods. *World Archaeology* 2:300–20

Green, R.C. 1963. A review of the prehistoric sequence of the Auckland Province. *New Zealand Archaeological Association Monograph* 2

1966. Linguistic subgrouping within Polynesia: the implications for prehistoric settlement. *Journal of the Polynesian Society* 75:6–38

1967. Fortifications in other parts of tropical Polynesia. *New Zealand Archaeological Association Newsletter* 10:96–113

1968. West Polynesian prehistory. In *Prehistoric Culture in Oceania*, ed. I. Yawata and Y. Sinoto, pp. 99–109. Honolulu: Bishop Museum Press

1969. (ed.) Makaha Valley Historical Project: interim report no. 1. *Pacific Anthropological Records* 4

1970. (ed.) Makaha Valley Historical Project: interim report no. 2. *Pacific Anthropological Records* 10

1971. Evidence for the development of the early Polynesian adz kit. *New Zealand Archaeological Association Newsletter* 14:12–44

1972. Aspects of the Neolithic in Oceania: Polynesia. In *Early Chinese Art and its Possible Influence in the Pacific Basin*, ed. N. Barnard, pp. 655–691. New York: Intercultural Arts Press

1973. Tonga's prehistoric population. *Pacific Viewpoint* 14:61–74

1974a. Adaptation and change in Maori culture. In *Ecology and Biogeography in New Zealand*, ed. G. Kuschel, pp. 1–44. The Hague: W. Junk

1974b. Excavation of the prehistoric occupations of SU-SA-3. *Auckland Institute and Museum Bulletin* 7:108–54

1974c. A review of portable artifacts from Western Samoa. *Auckland Institute and Museum Bulletin* 7:245–75

1976a. New sites with Lapita pottery and their implications for an understanding of the settlement of the Western Pacific. In *La Préhistoire Océanienne*, ed. J. Garanger, pp. 55–87. Nice: Union Internationale des Sciences Préhistoriques et Protohistoriques, IXe Congrès (prétirage)

1976b. Lapita sites in the Santa Cruz group. *Royal Society of New Zealand Bulletin* 11:245–65

1978. New sites with Lapita pottery and their implications for an understanding of the settlement of the Western Pacific. *Working Papers in Anthropology* 51. University of Auckland

1979a. Lapita. In *The Prehistory of Polynesia*, ed. J. Jennings, pp. 27–60. Cambridge (Mass.): Harvard University Press

1979b. Early Lapita art from Polynesia and Island Melanesia: continuities in ceramic, barkcloth, and tattoo decorations. In *Exploring the Visual Art of Oceania*, ed. S. Mead, pp. 13–31. Honolulu: The University Press of Hawai'i

1980. Makaha before 1880 AD. *Pacific Anthropological Records* 31

1981. Location of the Polynesian homeland: a continuing problem. In *Studies in Pacific Languages and Cultures in Honor of Bruce Biggs*, ed. J. Hollyman and A. Pawley, pp. 133–58. Auckland: Linguistic Society of New Zealand

Green, R.C. and J. Davidson. 1969a. Archaeology in Western Samoa, vol. 1. *Auckland Institute and Museum Bulletin* 6

1969b. Description and classification of Samoan adzes. *Auckland Institute and Museum Bulletin* 6:21–32

1974. Archaeology in Western Samoa, vol. 2. *Auckland Institute and Museum Bulletin* 7

Green, R.C., K. Green, R. Rappaport, A. Rappaport, and J. Davidson. 1967. Archaeology on the Island of Mo'orea, French Polynesia. *Anthropological Papers of the American Museum of Natural History* 51(2)

Gregory, H.E. 1921. Report of the Director for 1920. *Bernice P. Bishop Museum Occasional Papers* 8:1–28

Groube, L. 1965. Settlement patterns in New Zealand. *University of Otago Occasional Papers in Archaeology* 1

1970. The origin and development of earthwork fortification in the Pacific. In *Studies in Oceanic Culture History*, ed. R. Green and M. Kelly, pp. 133–64. *Pacific Anthropological Records* 11

1971. Tonga, Lapita pottery, and Polynesian origins. *Journal of the Polynesian Society* 80:278–316

Guiart, J. 1963. Un état palatial océanien: l'empire maritime des Tui Tonga. Appendix to: Structure de la chefferie en Mélanésie du Sud. *Travaux et Mémoires de l'Institut d'Ethnologie* LXVI. Paris

Hamel, J. 1982. South Otago. In *The First Thousand Years: Regional Perspectives in New Zealand Archaeology*, ed. N. Prickett, pp. 129–40. Palmerston North: New Zealand Archaeological Association

Hammatt, H. and W. Folk. 1980. Archaeological excavations with the proposed Keahole agricultural park, Kalaoa Oʻoma, Kona, Hawaii Island. Typescript report, Archaeological Research Center Hawaiʻi, Lawai

Hammond, N. 1977. Ex oriente lux: a view from Belize. In *The Origins of Maya Civilization*, ed. R. Adams, pp. 45–76. Albuquerque: University of New Mexico Press

1978. The myth of the milpa: agricultural expansion in the Maya lowlands. In *Pre-Hispanic Maya Agriculture*, ed. P. Harrison and B. Turner, pp. 23–34. Albuquerque: University of New Mexico Press

Handy, E.S.C. 1923. The native culture of the Marquesas. *Bernice P. Bishop Museum Bulletin* 9

1927. Polynesian religion. *Bernice P. Bishop Museum Bulletin* 34

1930a. The problem of Polynesian origins. *Bernice P. Bishop Museum Occasional Papers* 9:1—27

1930b. History and culture in the Society Islands. *Bernice P. Bishop Museum Bulletin* 79

1930c. Marquesan legends. *Bernice P. Bishop Museum Bulletin* 69

1940. The Hawaiian planter, vol. 1. *Bernice P. Bishop Museum Bulletin* 161.

Handy, E.S.C. and E.G. Handy. 1972. Native planters in old Hawaii: their life, lore, and environment. *Bernice P. Bishop Museum Bulletin* 233

Handy, E.S.C. and M. Pukui. 1958. *The Polynesian family system in Kaʻu, Hawaii.* Wellington: The Polynesian Society

Hanson, F.A. 1970. *Rapan Lifeways: Society and History on a Polynesian Island.* Boston: Little, Brown and Co.

Harris, M. 1959. The economy has no surplus? *American Anthropologist* 61:185–99

Harsant, W. 1981. Excavations at Oue Pa, N43/35, South Auckland. *Records of the Auckland Institute and Museum* 18:63–93

Hassan, F. 1981. *Demographic Archaeology.* New York: Academic Press

Hawthorne, H. and C. Belshaw. 1957. Cultural evolution or cultural change? – the case of Polynesia. *Journal of the Polynesian Society* 66:18–35

Henquel, Le R.P. n.d. Talanoa ki Uvea. Traditional history of ʻUvea. Manuscript in Lano Seminary, ʻUvea Island

Henry, Br.F. 1980. *Samoa: an Early History.* Pago Pago: American Samoan Department of Education

Henry, T. 1928. Ancient Tahiti. *Bernice P. Bishop Museum Bulletin* 48

Heyerdahl, T. 1975. *The Art of Easter Island.* New York: Doubleday

Heyerdahl, T. and E.N. Ferdon, Jr. (eds.). 1961. *Archaeology of Easter Island.* Monographs of the School of American Research 24(1)

1965. *Reports of the Norwegian Archaeological Expedition to Easter Island and the East Pacific*, vol. 2, miscellaneous papers. Monographs of the School of American Research 24(2)

Hjarnø, J. 1979–80. Social reproduction: towards an understanding of aboriginal Samoa. *Folk* 21–22:73–123

Hocart, A.M. 1929. Lau Islands, Fiji. *Bernice P. Bishop Museum Bulletin* 62

1952. The northern states of Fiji. *Royal Anthropological Institute Occasional Publication* 11

Hoffman, E. 1979. Archaeological survey and limited test excavations in Waipa and Lumahai Valleys, Island of Kauaʻi. Typescript report in Department of Anthropology, Bernice P. Bishop Museum

Holloway, J.T. 1954. Forests and climates in the South Island of New Zealand. *Transactions of the Royal Society of New Zealand* 82:329–410

1964. The forests of South Island: the status of the climatic change hypothesis. *New Zealand Geographer* 20:1–9

Hommon, R.J. 1976. The formation of primitive states in pre-contact Hawaii. Ph.D. dissertation, University of Arizona
1980. Multiple resources nomination form for Kahoʻolawe archaeological sites. National Register of Historic Places, Washington, DC
Hooper, A. 1981. Why the Tikopia have four clans. *Royal Anthropological Institute Occasional Paper* 38
Houghton, P. 1980. *The First New Zealanders*. Auckland: Hodder and Stoughton
Howard, A. 1967. Polynesian origins and migrations. In *Polynesian Culture History*, ed. G. Highland, pp. 45–101. Honolulu: Bishop Museum Press
1972. Polynesian social stratification revisited: reflections on castles built of sand (and a few bits of coral). *American Anthropologist* 74:811–23
Hughes, P., G. Hope, M. Latham, and M. Brookfield. 1979. Prehistoric man-induced degradation of the Lakeba landscape: evidence from two inland swamps. In *Lakeba: Environmental Change, Population Dynamics, and Resource Use*, ed. H. Brookfield, pp. 93–110. Paris: UNESCO
Hunt, T. 1980. Toward Fiji's past: archaeological research on south-western Viti Levu. M.A. thesis, University of Auckland
Hutchinson, G.E. 1978. *An Introduction to Population Biology*. New Haven: Yale University Press
Iʻi, J.P. 1959. *Fragments of Hawaiian history*. Honolulu: Bishop Museum Press
Irwin, G. 1980. The prehistory of Oceania: colonization and cultural change. In *The Cambridge Encyclopedia of Archaeology*, ed. A. Sherratt, pp. 324–32. Cambridge University Press
1981. How Lapita lost its pots: the question of continuity in the colonisation of Polynesia. *Journal of the Polynesian Society* 90:481–94
Ishizuki, K. 1974. Excavation of Site Su-Fo-1 at Folasa-a-lalo. *Auckland Institute and Museum Bulletin* 7:36–57
Jennings, J. (ed.). 1979. *The Prehistory of Polynesia*. Cambridge (Mass.): Harvard University Press
Jennings, J., and R. Holmer. 1980. Archaeological excavations in Western Samoa. *Pacific Anthropological Records* 32
Jennings, J., R. Holmer, J. Janetski, and H. Smith. 1976. Excavations on Upolu, Western Samoa. *Pacific Anthropological Records* 25
Jones, R. 1975. The Neolithic, Palaeolithic, and the hunting gardeners: man and land in the antipodes. In *Quarternary Studies*, ed. R. Suggate and M. Cresswell, pp. 21–34. Wellington: The Royal Society of New Zealand
1980. Different strokes for different folks: sites, scale, and strategy. In *Holier Than Thou*, ed. I. Johnson, pp. 151–71. Canberra: Australian National University
Kaeppler, A.L. 1971a. Rank in Tonga. *Ethnology* 10:174–93
1971b. Eighteenth century Tonga: new interpretations of Tongan society and material culture at the time of Captain Cook. *Man* 6:204–20
1978. Exchange patterns in goods and spouses: Fiji, Tonga, and Samoa. *Mankind* 11:246–52
Kamakau, S. 1961. *Ruling chiefs of Hawaii*. Honolulu: Kamehameha Schools
1964. *Ka Poʻe Kahiko: the People of Old*. Honolulu: Bishop Museum Press
Keesing, R.M. 1982. Introduction. In *Rituals of Manhood: Male Initiation in Papua New Guinea*, ed. G. Herdt, pp. 1–43. Berkeley: University of California Press
Kellum-Ottino, M. 1971. Archéologie d'une vallée des îles Marquises. *Publications de la Société des Océanistes* 26. Paris
Kelly, M. and J. Clark. 1980. Kawainui Marsh, Oʻahu: historical and archaeological studies. *Department of Anthropology Report* 80–3. Bernice P.

Bishop Museum, Honolulu

Kelly, R.C. 1968. Demographic pressure and descent group structure in the New Guinea highlands. *Oceania* 39:36–93

Kern, R.A. 1948. The vocabularies of Jacob le Maire. *Acta Orientalia* 20:216–37

Kikuchi, W.K. 1976. Prehistoric Hawaiian fishponds. *Science* 193:295–9

Kirch, P.V. 1973. Prehistoric subsistence patterns in the northern Marquesas Islands, French Polynesia. *Archaeology and Physical Anthropology in Oceania* 8:24–40

1974. The chronology of early Hawaiian settlement. *Archaeology and Physical Anthropology in Oceania* 9:110–19

1975. Cultural adaptation and ecology in Western Polynesia: an ethno-archaeological study. Ph.D. dissertation, Yale University

1976. Ethno-archaeological investigations in Futuna and Uvea (Western Polynesia): a preliminary report. *Journal of the Polynesian Society* 85:27–69

1977a. Valley agricultural systems in prehistoric Hawaii: an archaeological consideration. *Asian Perspectives* 20:246–80

1977b. Ethno-archaeological investigations on Niuatoputapu, Tonga (Western Polynesia): a preliminary report. Mimeo. Bernice P. Bishop Museum (submitted to National Science Foundation)

1978a. The Lapitoid period in West Polynesia: excavations and survey in Niuatoputapu, Tonga. *Journal of Field Archaeology* 5:1–13

1978b. Indigenous agriculture on Uvea (Western Polynesia). *Economic Botany* 32:157–81

1979a. Marine exploitation in prehistoric Hawaii: archaeological excavations at Kalahuipuaa, Hawaii Island. *Pacific Anthropological Records* 29

1979b. Late prehistoric and early historic settlement-subsistence systems in the Anahulu Valley, O'ahu. *Department of Anthropology Report* 79–2. Bernice P. Bishop Museum

1979c. Subsistence and ecology. In *The Prehistory of Polynesia*, ed. J. Jennings, pp. 286–307. Cambridge (Mass.): Harvard University Press

1980a. Polynesian prehistory: cultural adaptation in island ecosystems. *American Scientist* 68:39–48

1980b. The archaeological study of adaptation: theoretical and methodological issues. *Advances in Archaeological Method and Theory* 3:101–56. New York: Academic Press

1980c. Burial structures and societal ranking in Vava'u, Tonga. *Journal of the Polynesian Society* 89:291–308

1981a. Lapitoid settlements of Futuna and Alofi, Western Polynesia. *Archaeology in Oceania* 16:127–43

1981b. Agricultural intensification in Polynesia: the leeward Hawaiian field systems. Paper presented at Conference on Prehistoric Intensive Agriculture, Australian National University

1982a. The impact of the prehistoric Polynesians on the Hawaiian ecosystem. *Pacific Science* 36:1–14

1982b. Ecology and the adaptation of Polynesian agricultural systems. *Archaeology in Oceania* 17:1–6

1982c. Advances in Polynesian prehistory: three decades in review. *Advances in World Archaeology* 1:51–97. New York: Academic Press

1983a. Archaeology and the evolution of social complexity: the Hawaiian case. [Review of Cordy 1981] *Reviews in Anthropology* (in press)

1983b. Man's role in modifying tropical and subtropical Polynesian ecosystems. *Archaeology in Oceania* 18:26–31

Kirch, P.V. and C.C. Christensen. 1980. Non-marine mollusks and paleo-ecology at Barbers Point, O'ahu. Typescript report in Department of Anthropology, Bernice P. Bishop Museum, Honolulu

Kirch, P.V. and T.S. Dye. 1979. Ethnoarchaeology and the development of Polynesian fishing strategies. *Journal of the Polynesian Society* 88:53–76

Kirch, P.V. and M. Kelly (eds.). 1975. Prehistory and human ecology in a windward Hawaiian valley: Halawa Valley, Moloka'i. *Pacific Anthropological Records* 24

Kirch, P.V. and P. Rosendahl. 1973. Archaeological investigation of Anuta. *Pacific Anthropological Records* 21:25–108

1976. Early Anutan settlement and the position of Anuta in the prehistory of the southwest Pacific. *Royal Society of New Zealand Bulletin* 11:223–44

Kirch, P.V. and M. Sahlins. In preparation. Anahulu Valley and the early history of the Sandwich Islands Kingdom

Kirch, P.V. and D. Yen. 1982. Tikopia: the prehistory and ecology of a Polynesian outlier. *Bernice P. Bishop Museum Bulletin* 238

Kirchhoff, P. 1955. The principles of clanship in human society. *Davidson Journal of Anthropology* 1:1–10

Kirk, J. and P. Epling. 1972. The dispersal of the Polynesian peoples: explorations in phylogenetic inference from the analysis of taxonomy. *Working Papers in Methodology* 6, University of North Carolina

Klein, J., J. Lerman, P. Damon, and E. Ralph. 1982. Calibration of radiocarbon dates. *Radiocarbon* 24:103–50

Korn, S.R. Decktor. 1974. Tongan kin groups: the noble and the common view. *Journal of the Polynesian Society* 83:5–13

1978. Hunting the ramage: kinship and the organization of political authority in aboriginal Tonga. *Journal of Pacific History* 13:107–13

Koskinen, A. 1960. Ariki the first born: an analysis of a Polynesian chieftain title. *FF Communications* 181. Helsinki: Suomalainen Tiedeakatemia

Ladd, E.J. 1969a. Hale-o-Keawe temple site, Honaunau. In Archaeology on the Island of Hawaii, ed. R. Pearson, pp. 163–89. *Asian and Pacific Archaeology Series* 3. Social Science Research Institute, University of Hawai'i

1969b. Alealea temple site, Honaunau: salvage report. In Archaeology on the Island of Hawaii, ed. R. Pearson, pp. 95–130. *Asian and Pacific Archaeology Series* 3. Social Science Research Institute, University of Hawai'i

1969c. The great wall stabilization: salvage report. In Archaeology on the Island of Hawaii, ed. R. Pearson, pp. 133–160. *Asian and Pacific Archaeology Series* 3. Social Science Research Institute, University of Hawai'i

1973 (ed.). Makaha Valley Historical Project: interim report no. 4. *Pacific Anthropological Records* 19

Ladd, E. and D. Yen (eds.). 1972. Makaha Valley Historical Project: interim report no. 3. *Pacific Anthropological Records* 18

Lavachery, H. 1939. *Les pétroglyphes de l'île de Pâques*. Anvers: De Sikkel

Law, R. and R. Green. 1972. An economic interpretation of Taniwha Pa, Lower Waikato, New Zealand (N52/1). *Mankind* 8:255–69

Lawlor, I. 1980. Puhinui excavations: an interim report. *New Zealand Archaeological Association Newsletter* 23:11–23

1981a. Puhinui excavation report. Department of Anthropology, University of Auckland

1981b. Radiocarbon dates from Puhinui (N42/17), South Auckland. *New Zealand Archaeological Association Newsletter* 24:160–63

Leach, B.F. and H. Leach (eds.). 1979a. Prehistoric man in Palliser Bay. *National Museum of New Zealand Bulletin* 21

1979b. Environmental change in Palliser Bay. *National Museum of New Zealand Bulletin* 21:229–40

Leach, E.R. 1962. Review of History and traditions of Tikopia (by R. Firth). *Journal of the Polynesian Society* 71:273–6

Leach, H. 1979. Evidence of prehistoric gardens in Eastern Palliser Bay. *National Museum of New Zealand Bulletin* 21:137–61

1980. Incompatible land use patterns in Maori food production. *New Zealand Archaeological Association Newsletter* 23:135–47

Levison, M., R. Ward, and J. Webb. 1973. *The Settlement of Polynesia: a Computer Simulation*. Minneapolis: University of Minnesota Press

Linton, R. 1925. Archaeology of the Marquesas Islands. *Bernice P. Bishop Museum Bulletin* 23

Loeb, E.M. 1926. History and traditions of Niue. *Bernice P. Bishop Museum Bulletin* 32

Luomala, K. 1949. Maui-of-a-thousand-tricks: his Oceanic and European biographers. *Bernice P. Bishop Museum Bulletin* 198

1955. *Voices on the Wind: Polynesian Myths and Chants*. Honolulu: Bishop Museum Press

McAllister, J.G. 1933. Archaeology of Oahu. *Bernice P. Bishop Museum Bulletin* 104

McArthur, N., I. Saunders, and R. Tweedie. 1976. Small population isolates: a micro-simulation study. *Journal of the Polynesian Society* 85:307–26

MacArthur, R. and E. Wilson. 1967. The theory of island biogeography. *Monographs in Population Biology* 1. Princeton

McCall, G. 1980. *Rapanui: Tradition and Survival on Easter Island*. Honolulu: The University Press of Hawai'i

McCoy, P.C. 1973. Excavation of a rectangular house on the east rim of Rano Kau Volcano, Easter Island. *Archaeology and Physical Anthropology in Oceania* 8:51–67

1976. Easter Island settlement patterns in the late prehistoric and proto-historic periods. International Fund for Monuments, Easter Island Committee, *Bulletin* 5

1978. The place of near-shore islets in Easter Island prehistory. *Journal of the Polynesian Society* 87:193–214

1979. Easter Island. In *The Prehistory of Polynesia*, ed. J. Jennings, pp. 135–66. Cambridge (Mass.): Harvard University Press

McGlone, M. 1983. The Polynesian deforestation of New Zealand: a preliminary synthesis. *Archaeology in Oceania* 18:11–25

McKern, W. 1929. Archaeology of Tonga. *Bernice P. Bishop Museum Bulletin* 60

Malo, D. 1951. *Hawaiian Antiquities*. Honolulu: Bishop Museum Press

Margalef, R. 1968. *Perspectives in Ecological Theory*. University of Chicago Press

Marshall, P. 1930. Geology of Rarotonga and Atiu. *Bernice P. Bishop Museum Bulletin* 72

Martin, J. 1818. *An Account of the Natives of the Tonga Islands . . . Arranged from the Extensive Communications of Mr. William Mariner*. 2 vols. London: John Murray

Mayr, E. 1942. *Systematics and the Origin of Species*. New York: Columbia University Press

1945. *Birds of the southwest Pacific*. New York: MacMillan

1961. Cause and effect in biology. *Science* 134:1501–6

Mead, S., L. Birks, H. Birks, and E. Shaw. 1973. The Lapita style of Fiji and its associations. *Polynesian Society Memoir* 38

Menzies, A. 1920. *Hawaii Nei 128 Years Ago*. Honolulu: W. Wilson

Merrill, E.D. 1939. Man's influence on the vegetation of Polynesia, with special reference to introduced species. *Proceedings of the 6th Pacific Science Congress*, vol. 9:629–39

Métraux, A. 1940. Ethnology of Easter Island. *Bernice P. Bishop Museum Bulletin* 160

Molloy, B.P. 1967. Changes in vegetation. In *The Waimakariri Catchment*, ed. J. Hayward. Tussock Grasslands and Mountain Lands Institute Special Publication 5. New Zealand: Lincoln College

1969. Recent history of the vegetation. In *The Natural History of Canterbury*, ed. G. Knox, pp. 340–60. Wellington: A. and A. Reed

Molloy, B.P., C. Burrows, J. Cox, J. Johnston, and P. Wardle. 1963. Distribution of subfossil forest remains, Eastern South Island, New Zealand. *New Zealand Journal of Botany* 1:68–77

Moore, J., A. Swedlund, and G. Armelagos. 1975. The use of life tables in paleodemography. *American Antiquity Memoir* 30:57–70

Morgenstein, M. and P. Rosendahl. 1976. Basaltic glass hydration dating in Hawaiian archaeology. In *Advances in Obsidian Glass Studies*, ed. R. Taylor, pp. 141–64. New Jersey: Noyes Press

Mulloy, W. 1965. The fortified village of Morongo Uta. In *Reports of the Norwegian Archaeological Expedition to Easter Island and the East Pacific*, vol. 2, ed. T. Heyerdahl and E.N. Ferdon, Jr, pp. 26–68. Monographs of the School of American Research 24(2)

1970. A speculative reconstruction of techniques of carving, transporting, and erecting Easter Island statues. *Archaeology and Physical Anthropology in Oceania* 5:1–23

1975. A solstice oriented *ahu* on Easter Island. *Archaeology and Physical Anthropology in Oceania* 10:1–39

Mulloy, W. and G. Figueroa. 1978. The A Kivi-Vai Teka Complex and its relationship to Easter Island architectural prehistory. *Asian and Pacific Archaeology Series* 8. Social Science Research Institute, University of Hawai'i

Murdock, G.P. 1963. Human influences on the ecosystems of high islands of the tropical Pacific. In *Man's Place in the Island Ecosystem*, ed. F.R. Fosberg, pp. 145–54. Honolulu: Bishop Museum Press

Newman, T.S. n.d. *Hawaiian Fishing and Farming on the Island of Hawaii in AD 1778*. Honolulu: Department of Land and Natural Resources

Nye, P. and D. Greenland. 1960. The soil under shifting cultivation. *Commonwealth Agricultural Bureaux Technical Communication* 51

Odum, E. 1969. The strategy of ecosystem development. *Science* 164:262–70

Oliver, D. 1974. *Ancient Tahitian Society*. Honolulu: The University of Hawai'i Press

Olson, L. 1983. Hawaiian volcanic glass applied 'dating' and 'sourcing'. In *Department of Anthropology Report* 83–1. Bernice P. Bishop Museum

Olson, S. and H. James. 1982. Prodromus of the fossil avifauna of the Hawaiian Islands. *Smithsonian Contributions to Zoology* 365

Olson, S. and A. Wetmore. 1976. Preliminary diagnoses of two extraordinary new genera of birds from Pleistocene deposits in the Hawaiian Islands. *Proceedings of the Biological Society of Washington* 89:247–58

Orans, M. 1966. Surplus. *Human Organization* 25:24–32

Panoff, M. 1970. *La terre et l'organization sociale en Polynésie*. Paris: Payot

Papy, H. 1954–5. Tahiti et les îles Voisines: la végétation des îles de la Société et de Makatea. *Travaux du Laboratoire Forestier de Toulouse* V(1:III)

Pawley, A. 1966. Polynesian languages: a subgrouping based on shared innovations in morphology. *Journal of the Polynesian Society* 75:39–64

1979. Proto-Oceanic terms for people: a problem in semantic reconstruction. Typescript report in Department of Anthropology, University of Auckland

1981. Rubbish-man, commoner, big-man, chief? Linguistic evidence for hereditary chieftainship in Proto-Oceanic society. Typescript report in Department of Anthropology, University of Auckland

Pawley, A. and K. Green. 1971. Lexical evidence for the Proto-Polynesian homeland. *Te Reo* 14:1–36

Pawley, A. and R. Green. 1975. Dating the dispersal of the Oceanic languages. *Oceanic Linguistics* 12:1–67

Pearson, H. 1957. The economy has no surplus: critique of a theory of development. In *Trade and Market in the Early Empires*, ed. K. Polanyi, C. Arensberg, and H. Pearson, pp. 320–41. Chicago: Henry Regnery Co.

Pearson, R. (ed.). 1968. Excavations at Lapakahi: selected papers. *State Archaeological Journal* 69—2. State of Hawai'i, Department of Land and Natural Resources

1969. Archaeology on the Island of Hawaii. *Asian and Pacific Archaeology Series* 3. Social Science Research Institute: University of Hawai'i

Pearson, R., P.V. Kirch, and M. Pietrusewsky. 1971. An early prehistoric site at Bellows Beach, Waimanalo, Oahu, Hawaiian Islands. *Archaeology and Physical Anthropology in Oceania* 6:204–34

Peebles, C. and S. Kus. 1977. Some archaeological correlates of ranked societies. *American Antiquity* 42:421–48

Peters, K.M. 1971. Excavations at Lake Mangakaware, Site 1 N65/28. *New Zealand Archaeological Association Newsletter* 14:127–40

Pianka, E. 1974. *Evolutionary Ecology*. New York: Harper and Row

Piddington, R. (ed.). 1939. *Essays in Polynesian ethnology*. By R.W. Williamson (Part II by Piddington). Cambridge University Press

Pielou, E. 1977. *Mathematical Ecology*. New York: Wiley Interscience

Pietrusewsky, M. 1969. An osteological study of cranial and infracranial remains from Tonga. *Records of the Auckland Institute and Museum* 6:287–402

1976. Prehistoric human skeletal remains from Papua New Guinea and the Marquesas. *Asian and Pacific Archaeology Series* 7. Social Science Research Institute, University of Hawai'i

Pilsbry, H.A. 1916–18. *Manual of Conchology*, vol. 24, *Pupillidae*. Philadelphia: Academy of Natural Sciences

Porter, S. 1975. Late Quaternary glaciation and tephrochronology of Mauna Kea, Hawaii. In *Quaternary Studies: Selected Papers from the IXth INQUA Congress*, ed. R. Suggate and M. Cresswell, pp. 247–51. Wellington: The Royal Society of New Zealand

Poulsen, J. 1967. A contribution to the prehistory of the Tongan Islands. Ph.D. dissertation, Australian National University

1968. Archaeological excavations on Tongatapu. In *Prehistoric Culture in Oceania*, ed. I. Yawata and Y. Sinoto, pp. 85–92. Honolulu: Bishop Museum Press

1972. Outlier archaeology: Bellona. A preliminary report on field work and radiocarbon dates. *Archaeology and Physical Anthropology in Oceania* 7:184–205

1976. The chronology of early Tongan prehistory and the Lapita ware. In *La Préhistoire Océanienne*, ed. J. Garanger, pp. 223–250. Nice: Union Internationale des Sciences Préhistoriques et Protohistoriques, IXe Congrès (prétirage)

1977. Archaeology and prehistory. In *Friendly Islands: A history of Tonga*. ed. N. Rutherford, pp. 4–26. Melbourne: Oxford University Press

Purseglove, J. 1968. *Tropical crops: dicotyledons*. New York: John Wiley

Raeside, J. 1948. Some post-glacial climatic changes in Canterbury and their effect on soil formation. *Transactions of the Royal Society of New Zealand* 77:153–71

Ravault, F. 1980. Papeari: l'organisation de l'espace dans un district de la côte sud de Tahiti. *Travaux et Documents de l'ORSTOM* 126. Paris

Reeve, R. 1983. Archaeological investigations in Section 3. In *Department of Anthropology Report* 83—1. Bernice P. Bishop Museum

Renfrew, C. 1973. Monuments, mobilization, and social organization in Neolithic Wessex. In *The Explanation of Culture Change: Models in Prehistory*, ed. C. Renfrew, pp. 539–58. Pittsburgh: University of Pittsburgh Press

Richter-Dyn, N. and N. Goel. 1972. On the extinction of a colonizing species. *Theoretical Population Biology* 3:406–33

Riley, T. 1975. Survey and excavations of the aboriginal agricultural system. *Pacific Anthropological Records* 24:79–115

Rosendahl, P. 1972a. Aboriginal agriculture and residence patterns in upland Lapakahi, Island of Hawaii. Ph.D. dissertation, University of Hawai'i

1972b. Archaeological salvage of the Hapuna–Anachoomalu section of the Kailua–Kawaihae road, Island of Hawaii. *Department of Anthropology Report* 72—5. Bernice P. Bishop Museum

1973. Archaeological salvage of the Ke-ahole to Anaehoomalu section of the Kailua–Kawaihae road, Island of Hawaii. *Department of Anthropology Report* 73—3. Bernice P. Bishop Museum

Rosendahl, P. and D. Yen. 1971. Fossil sweet potato remains from Hawaii. *Journal of the Polynesian Society* 80:379–85

Routledge, S. 1919. *The Mystery of Easter Island*. London: Sifton, Praed and Co.

1920. Survey of the village and carved rocks of Orongo, Easter Island, by the Mana Expedition. *Journal of the Royal Anthropological Institute* 50:425–51

Sachs, I. 1966. La notion de surplus et son application aux économies primitives. *L'homme* 6:5–18

Sahlins, M. 1955. Esoteric efflorescence in Easter Island. *American Anthropologist* 57:1045–52

1957. Differentiation by adaptation in Polynesian societies. *Journal of the Polynesian Society* 66:291–300

1958. *Social Stratification in Polynesia*. Seattle: American Ethnological Society

1963. Poor man, rich, man, big-man, chief: political types in Melanesia and Polynesia. *Comparative Studes in Society and History* 5:285–303

1968. *Tribesmen*. New Jersey: Prentice-Hall

1972. *Stone Age Economics*. Chicago: Aldine-Atherton

1976. *Culture and Practical Reason*. University of Chicago Press

1981a. *Historical Metaphors and Mythical Realities: Structure in the Early History of the Sandwich Islands Kingdom*. Ann Arbor: University of Michigan Press

1981b. The stranger king. *Journal of Pacific History* 16:107–32

Salvat, B. 1970. Etudes quantitatives (comptages et biomasses) sur les mollusques récifaux de l'atoll de Fangataufa (Tuamotu, Polynésie). *Cahiers du Pacifique* 14:1–58

1972. La faune benthique du lagon de l'atoll de Reao (Tuamotu, Polynésie). *Cahiers du Pacifique* 16:31–110

Sanders, W. and B. Price. 1968. *Mesoamerica: the evolution of a civilization*. New York: Random House

Schilt, A. 1980a. Archaeological investigations in specified areas of the Hanalei

Wildlife Refuge, Hanalei Valley, Kaua'i. Typescript report in Department of Anthropology, Bernice P. Bishop Museum

1980b. Interim report on the archaeological survey and limited testing of the Kuakini Highway realignment, North Kona, Hawaii. Typescript report in Department of Anthropology, Bernice P. Bishop Museum

Schwartz, T. 1963. Systems of areal integration: some considerations based on the Admiralty Island of northern Melanesia. *Anthropological Forum* 1:56–97

Service, E. 1967. *Primitive Social Organization: an Evolutionary Perspective*. New York: Random House

1975. *Origins of the State and Civilization*. New York: W.W. Norton

Sharp, A. 1956. *Ancient Voyagers in the Pacific*. Wellington: The Polynesian Society

Shawcross, K. 1967. Fern-root, and the total scheme of eighteenth-century Maori food production in agricultural areas. *Journal of the Polynesian Society* 76:330–52

Shawcross, W. 1970. Ethnographic economics and the study of population in prehistoric New Zealand: viewed through archaeology. *Mankind* 7:279–91

Shutler, R. Jr. and J. Marck. 1975. On the dispersal of the Austronesian horticulturalists. *Archaeology and Physical Anthropology in Oceania* 10:81–113

Sinoto, A. 1973. Fanning Island: preliminary archaeological investigations of sites near the Cable Station. In *Fanning Island Expedition, 1972*, ed. K. Chave and E. Kay, Hawai'i Institute of Geophysics Report 73—13

1978. Archaeological and paleontological salvage at Barbers Point, O'ahu. Typescript report in Department of Anthropology, Bernice P. Bishop Museum

Sinoto, Y. 1966. A tentative prehistoric cultural sequence in the northern Marquesas Islands, French Polynesia. *Journal of the Polynesian Society* 75:287–303

1970. An archaeologically based assessment of the Marquesas Islands as a dispersal center in East Polynesia. *Pacific Anthropological Records* 11:105–32

1979a. The Marquesas. In *The Prehistory of Polynesia*, ed. J. Jennings, pp. 110–34. Cambridge (Mass.): Harvard University Press

1979b. Excavations on Huahine, French Polynesia. *Pacific Studies* 3:1–40

ms. Polynesian migrations based on archaeological assessments. Paper presented at IX Congress, International Union of Prehistoric and Protohistoric Sciences, Nice

Sinoto, Y. and P.C. McCoy. 1975. Report on the preliminary excavation of an early habitation site on Huahine, Society Islands. *Journal de la Société des Océanistes* 47:143–86

Skottsberg, C. 1956. Composition, distribution, and relationships of the flora. *The natural history of Juan Fernandez and Easter Island*, vol. 1(3). Uppsala

Smith, K. and A. Schilt. 1973. North Kohala: agricultural field systems and geographic variables. In Lapakahi, Hawaii: Archaeological Studies, ed. H. Tuggle and P. Griffin, pp. 309–20. *Asian and Pacific Archaeology Series* 5. Social Science Research Institute, University of Hawai'i

Snow, C. 1974. *Early Hawaiians: an Initial Study of Skeletal Remains from Mokapu, Oahu*. University of Kentucky Press

Soehren, L. 1962. Archaeological excavations at City of Refuge National Historical Park, Honaunau, Kona, Hawaii. Typescript report in Department of Anthropology, Bernice P. Bishop Museum

Soehren, L. and T.S. Newman. 1968. The archaeology of Kealakekua. Special publication, Anthropology Departments, University of Hawai'i and Bernice P. Bishop Museum, Honolulu

Solem, A. 1959. Systematics and zoogeography of the land and fresh-water mollusca of the New Hebrides. *Fieldiana: Zoology* 43

— 1978. Land snails from Mothe, Lakemba, and Karoni Islands, Lau archipelago, Fiji. *Pacific Science* 32:39–45

Solheim, W.G. II. 1969. Reworking Southeast Asian prehistory. *Paideuma* 15:125–39

Spencer, J. 1966. Shifting cultivation in southeastern Asia. *University of California Publications in Geography* 19

Spoehr, A. 1957. Marianas prehistory. *Fieldiana: Anthropology* 48

Spriggs, M. 1981. Vegetable kingdoms: taro irrigation and Pacific prehistory. Ph.D. dissertation, Australian National University

— 1982. Taro cropping systems in the Southeast Asian–Pacific region: archaeological evidence. *Archaeology in Oceania* 17:7–15

Stejneger, L. 1899. The land reptiles of the Hawaiian Islands. *Proceedings of the U.S. National Museum* 21:783–813

Stokes, J.F.G. 1909a. Heiau of Molokai. Manuscript, Bernice P. Bishop Museum Library, Honolulu

— 1909b. Walled fish traps of Pearl Harbor. *Occasional Papers of the Bernice P. Bishop Museum* 4:199–212

— ms. [1930]. Ethnology of Rapa. 5 vols. Manuscript, Bernice P. Bishop Museum Library, Honolulu

Suggs, R.C. 1960a. *The island civilizations of Polynesia.* New York: Mentor

— 1960b. Historical traditions and archaeology in Polynesia. *American Anthropologist* 62:764–73

— 1961. Archaeology of Nuku Hiva, Marquesas Islands, French Polynesia. *Anthropological Papers of the American Museum of Natural History* 49(1)

Sugiyama, C. 1973. Analysis of agricultural features in upland Lapakahi. In Lapakahi, Hawaii: Archaeological Studies, ed. H. Tuggle and P. Griffin, pp. 259–93. *Asian and Pacific Archaeology Series* 5. Social Science Research Institute, University of Hawai'i

Sullivan, A. 1972. Stone walled complexes of Central Auckland. *New Zealand Archaeological Association Newsletter* 15:148–60

— 1981. Socio-economic aspects of volcanic zone gardening in Tamaki, Northern New Zealand. Paper presented at Prehistoric Intensive Agriculture Symposium, Australian National University

Summers, C. 1964. Hawaiian archaeology: fishponds. *Bernice P. Bishop Museum Special Publication* 52

Sutton, D. 1980. A culture history of the Chatham Islands. *Journal of the Polynesian Society* 89:67–93

Swadling, P. 1976. Changes induced by human exploitation in prehistoric shellfish populations. *Mankind* 10:156–62

— ms. Analysis of midden molluscs excavated from Lapita sites at Santa Cruz and the Reef Islands. Manuscript on file, Department of Anthropology, University of Auckland

Tate, G. 1951. The rodents of Australia and New Guinea. *American Museum of Natural History Bulletin* 97:189–430

Thomas, W.L. 1963. The variety of physical environments among Pacific Islands. In *Man's Place in the Island Ecosystem*, ed. F.R. Fosberg, pp. 7–38. Honolulu: Bishop Museum Press

Thompson, L. 1940. Southern Lau: an ethnography. *Bernice P. Bishop Museum Bulletin* 162

Thomson, B. 1894. *The Diversions of a Prime Minister.* London: Dawsons

1908. *The Fijians: a Study of the Decay of Custom*. London: Heinemann

Tippett, A. 1968. Fijian material culture. *Bernice P. Bishop Museum Bulletin* 232

Titcomb, M. 1952. Native use of fish in Hawaii. *Polynesian Society Memoir* 29

Tuggle, H. and P. Griffin (eds.). 1973. Lapakahi, Hawaii: Archaeological Studies. *Asian and Pacific Archaeology Series* 5. Social Science Research Institute, University of Hawai'i

Tuggle, H. and M. Tomonari-Tuggle. 1980. Prehistoric agriculture in Kohala, Hawaii. *Journal of Field Archaeology* 7:297–312

Tuohy, D. 1965. Salvage excavations at City of Refuge National Historical Park, Honaunau, Kona, Hawaii. Typescript report in Department of Anthropology, Bernice P. Bishop Museum

Umebayashi, C. 1973. The relationship between water resources and archaeological features in North Kohala. In Lapakahi, Hawaii: Archaeological Studies, ed. H. Tuggle and P. Griffin, pp. 321–5. *Asian and Pacific Archaeology Series* 5. Social Science Research Institute, University of Hawai'i

Underwood, J. 1969. Human skeletal remains from Sand Dune Site (H1), South Point, Hawaii. *Pacific Anthropological Records* 9

Urbanowicz, C. 1973. Tongan culture: the methodology of an ethnographic reconstruction. Ph.D. dissertation, University of Oregon

Valeri, V. 1972. Le fonctionnement du système des rangs à Hawaii. *L'Homme* 12:29–66

Vancouver, G. 1798. Vol. I. *A Voyage of Discovery to the North Pacific Ocean and Around the World*. London

Vansina, J. 1965. *Oral Tradition: a Study in Historical Methodology*. Chicago: Aldine

Vayda, A. 1960. Maori warfare. *Polynesian Society Maori Monograph* 2

1961. Expansion and warfare among swidden agriculturalists. *American Anthropologist* 63:346–58

1976. *War in Ecological Perspective*. New York: Plenum Press

Vayda, A. and McCay, B. 1975. New directions in ecology and ecological anthropology. *Annual Review of Anthropology* 4:293–306

Vayda, A. and R. Rappaport. 1963. Island cultures. In *Man's Place in the Island Ecosystem*, ed. F.R. Fosberg, pp. 133–42. Honolulu: Bishop Museum Press

Vérin, P. 1969. L'ancienne civilisation de Rurutu. *Mémoires ORSTOM* 33. Paris

Villiers, J.A.J. de (trans.). 1906. *The east and west Indian mirror, being an account of . . . the Australian navigations of Jacob le Maire*. Hakluyt Society, Series II, No. XVIII. London: Cambridge University Press

Visher, S. 1925. Tropical cyclones of the Pacific. *Bernice P. Bishop Museum Bulletin* 20

Walsh, D. and B. Biggs. 1966. *Proto-Polynesian word list I*. Auckland: Linguistic Society of New Zealand

Wardle, P. 1973. Variations of the glaciers of Westland National Park and the Hooker Range, New Zealand. *New Zealand Journal of Botany* 11:349–88

Weisler, M. and P. Kirch. 1982. The archaeological resources of Kawela, Molokai. Typescript report in Department of Anthropology, Bernice P. Bishop Museum

Weiss, K. 1973. Demographic models for anthropology. *Society for American Archaeology Memoir* 27

West, T. 1865. *Ten years in south-central Polynesia*. London

White, J.P. 1979. Melanesia. In *The Prehistory of Polynesia*, ed. J. Jennings, pp. 352–77. Cambridge (Mass.): Harvard University Press

Wiens, H. 1962. *Atoll Environment and Ecology*. New Haven: Yale University Press

Williamson, R.W. 1924. *The Social and Political Systems of Central Polynesia*. Cambridge University Press

1937. *Religion and Social Organization in Central Polynesia*. Ralph Piddington (ed.). Cambridge University Press

Wilson, E.W. and W. Bossert. 1971. *A Primer of Population Biology*

Wittfogel, K. 1957. *Oriental Despotism*. New Haven: Yale University Press

Yen, D.E. 1961. The adaptation of kumara by the New Zealand Maori. *Journal of the Polynesian Society* 70:338–48

1973a. The origins of Oceanic agriculture. *Archaeology and Physical Anthropology in Oceania* 8:68–85

1973b. Agriculture in Anutan subsistence. *Pacific Anthropological Records* 21:112–49

1974a. The sweet potato and Oceania. *Bernice P. Bishop Museum Bulletin* 236

1974b. Arboriculture in the subsistence of Santa Cruz, Solomon Islands. *Economic Botany* 28:247–84

1975. Indigenous food processing in Oceania. In *Gastronomy: the Anthropology of Food and Food Habits*, ed. M. Arnott, pp. 147–68. Chicago: Aldine

1977. Hoabinhian horticulture: the evidence and the questions from northwest Thailand. In *Sunda and Sahul: Prehistoric Studies in Southeast Asia, Melanesia, and Australia*, ed. J. Allen, J. Golson, and R. Jones, pp. 567–99. London: Academic Press

Yen, D.E. and J. Gordon (eds.). 1973. Anuta: a Polynesian outlier in the Solomon Islands. *Pacific Anthropological Records* 21

Yen, D.E., P.V. Kirch, P. Rosendahl, and T. Riley. 1972. Prehistoric agriculture in the upper valley of Makaha, Oahu. *Pacific Anthropological Records* 18:59–94

Zimmerman, E.C. 1948. *Insects of Hawaii*, vol. 1, Introduction. Honolulu: The University of Hawai'i Press

INDEX